Alex Miller

SYDNEY STUDIES IN AUSTRALIAN LITERATURE

Robert Dixon, Series Editor

Shirley Hazzard: New Critical Essays
Ed. Brigitta Olubas

Alex Miller

The Ruin of Time

Robert Dixon

SYDNEY UNIVERSITY PRESS

First published by Sydney University Press
© Robert Dixon 2014
© Sydney University Press 2014

Reproduction and Communication for other purposes
Except as permitted under the Act, no part of this edition may be reproduced, stored in a retrieval system, or communicated in any form or by any means without prior written permission. All requests for reproduction or communication should be made to Sydney University Press at the address below:

Sydney University Press
Fisher Library F03
University of Sydney NSW 2006
AUSTRALIA
sup.info@sydney.edu.au
sydney.edu.au/sup

National Library of Australia Cataloguing-in-Publication Data

Author:	Robert Dixon, 1954–
Title:	Alex Miller: The Ruin of Time
ISBN:	9781743324073 (paperback)
	9781743324080 (ebook: epub)
	9781743324097 (ebook: mobipocket)
Notes:	Includes bibliographical references and index
Subjects:	Miller, Alex, 1936--Criticism and interpretation.
	Miller, Alex, 1936--Ruin of time.
	Authors, Australian--20th century--History and criticism.
	Australian fiction--20th century--History and criticism.
Dewey Number:	A823.3

Cover image: photograph by John Tsiavis, *Portrait of Alex Miller*, 2013
Cover design by Miguel Yamin

Contents

Acknowledgements	vii
Introduction	ix
1 Unravelling the Change: *The Tivington Nott* and *Watching the Climbers on the Mountain*	1
2 Multiple Modernities: *The Ancestor Game*	23
3 Black Mirror: *The Sitters*	53
4 The Iron World: *Conditions of Faith*	75
5 The Central Queensland Novels: *Journey to the Stone Country*	95
6 The Third Hand: *Prochownik's Dream*	117
7 The Central Queensland Novels: *Landscape of Farewell*	137
8 The Economy of the Gift: *Lovesong*	155
9 Eye of the Storm: *Autumn Laing*	169
10 Reading Lessons: *Coal Creek*	195
Afterword	211
Works Cited	215
Index	224

Acknowledgements

My first thanks are to Alex and Stephanie Miller for their generous and tactful engagement in this project. Alex and I first met at the 2004 Brisbane Writers' Festival, where we were "in conversation", and we have remained in conversation ever since. On 13–14 May 2011, I hosted a symposium on "The Novels of Alex Miller" at the University of Sydney, which resulted in the edited collection, *The Novels of Alex Miller: An Introduction*, published by Allen & Unwin in 2012. I am grateful to colleagues contributing to that collection, all of whom retain an ongoing interest in Miller's work: David Brooks, Frank Budby, Adrian Caesar, Raimond Gaita, Elizabeth Hatte, Anita Heiss, Col McLennan, Elizabeth McMahon, Brigitta Olubas, Peter Pierce, Brigid Rooney, Ronald A. Sharp, Ingeborg van Teeseling, Brenda Walker, Shirley Walker, Elizabeth Webby, Geordie Williamson and Liliana Zavaglia. For their detailed and insightful comments on drafts of *Alex Miller: The Ruin of Time*, I am grateful to Nicholas Birns, Bernadette Brennan, Melpomene Dixon, Brigitta Olubas, Brigid Rooney (to whom I also owe the title), Ronald A. Sharp, Susan Sheridan and Liliana Zavaglia. Research and administrative assistance were provided by Roger Osborne and Liliana Zavaglia. Finally, thanks to Susan Murray-Smith, Agata Mrva-Montoya, and Bronwyn O'Reilly at Sydney University Press. *The Ruin of Time* is published in SUP's Sydney Studies in Australian Literature series, which includes sole-authored studies of contemporary Australian writers and edited collections of essays on important issues in the study of Australian literature. My work on this project was supported by an Australian Research Council DORA (2013–2016): DP130101706, *Scenes of Reading: Australian Literature and the World Republic of Letters*. This book is dedicated to my granddaughters, Eila and Elena Brescia.

Robert Dixon
The University of Sydney
April 2014

Introduction

Alex Miller: The Ruin of Time is the first sole-authored critical survey of Miller's novels as a complete body of work. In the absence, as yet, of a definitive biography or autobiography, my approach has been to devote a chapter to each of the novels in turn, placing them briefly in their relevant biographical and historical contexts, describing the people, circumstances and sources that inspired them, and offering interpretations that are intended to be thorough and well informed though not in any sense definitive: a reliable and stimulating point of reference, it is hoped, for future critical conversations. I have attempted to illustrate the wide scope and complexity of Miller's subject matter, and his abiding aesthetic and ethical preoccupations in each of the novels while also attending to the rich network of connections, both formal and thematic, that exists between them. Readers who require a more detailed account of Miller's life can turn to my earlier edited volume, *The Novels of Alex Miller: An Introduction*, which includes a chronology, an introductory essay placing Miller's novels in the context of his life and describing their major themes, and an autobiographical memoir, "The Mask of Fiction".[1]

In thinking about my approach and responsibilities in writing this book, I was aware that Miller has had a good deal to say about the relationships between art, literary fiction and criticism, both in the novels and in his published essays. In *The Ancestor Game*, for example, the Melbourne writer Steven Muir is introduced to the artist Gertrude Spiess, who is soon to hold an exhibition of her work at the Falls Gallery in Richmond. She shows Steven an "extended essay in biography and criticism" that has just appeared in a fashionable Melbourne art magazine:

> The article posed as scholarly, but possessed none of the enthusiasm and generosity one hopes to find in a work of scholarship. It was disappointing. It lacked an ardent desire to share understanding, to bring lucidly before the reader certain precious results of a search for knowledge. It was, in fact, little more than a promotion for a one-woman exhibition of Gertrude's drawings, which was to be mounted later in the year at a Richmond gallery. There was, however, another, more concealed, meaning to the text, evident in certain passages: "The merging of different motif areas in her drawings and the transformation of spatial relationships into flat correspondences gathers towards a distortion of depicted

---

[1] Robert Dixon, ed., *The Novels of Alex Miller: An Introduction* (Sydney: Allen & Unwin, 2012).

reality and the dissolution of its phenomenal form". I didn't try to reach the sense of this. I understood the point of it was to transpose the locus of authority from the works to the discussion of the works. The writer had assumed the role of validating authority for the images he discussed. In order to do this he had been required to transform what he saw with his eyes into ideologies that he could "see" with his intellect.[2]

"Enthusiasm", "generosity", an "ardent desire to share understanding"; to bring "lucidly" before the reader the results of one's research; to avoid the temptation of transferring the focus from "the works to the discussion of the works": these are worthy and challenging goals for an academic critic setting out to write an "extended essay in biography and criticism". In the light of Miller's own frequent comparisons between writing and art, I am drawn to the idea of curatorship as a way to think about the responsibility literary critics have toward creative writers. My aim in this book has been to convey what my colleague Pat Buckridge would call an informed *appreciation* of Miller's novels,[3] and while my readings are certainly informed by critical and cultural theory, even to the point of setting out to demonstrate how richly the novels answer to the interests of contemporary theory, I have tried to avoid their being theoretically overdetermined.

Central to Miller's work is the importance of friendship, hospitality and gift exchange, both as themes in the novels themselves, and as part of Miller's understanding of the conditions of their creative production. The American critic Ronald A. Sharp, who has himself written a book about friendship in contemporary fiction, argues that his understanding of the gift is "Miller's central trope . . . for . . . defining act[s] of friendship and . . . artistic creation".[4] Miller has told the story many times of how he came to write his first published work of fiction: it has acquired the status of an originary event in his career. Miller has said that while he had been a storyteller from early childhood, it took many years before he found his "authentic material". A key to this was the wise counsel of his friend, Max Blatt, whom Miller recalls as "a central European intellectual of the kind J.P. Stern and W.G. Sebald write about with such beautiful nostalgic elegance". Max interpreted European literature and philosophy to him in a way that he had not encountered at university in Melbourne in the 1960s, and helped him to find his vocation as a writer. At his farm in the Araluen Valley near Goulburn, where he lived between 1968 and 1974, Miller wrote three manuscripts, which he describes as his "pre-novels". Max would come up to visit by train from Melbourne, staying for a week at a time.

On one of Max's visits, Miller presented him with a 400-page novel in manuscript, which he read through the day and into the early evening. Miller recalls: "I was woken by the thump of the 400 pages landing beside my head. I sprang up. Max was lighting a cigarette. With a mixture of disappointment, frustration and regret, he said, 'Why don't you write about something you *love*?' " And then an exchange took place between the two men that resonates throughout Miller's novels. That night, Max told Miller the story of his own escape from an anti-Semitic attack in Poland at the beginning of the war. Miller did not sleep, but wrote his own, fictional version of the story, which he gave to Max to read the next morning: "When he finished reading it, he said with feeling, 'You could have been

---

2 Alex Miller, *The Ancestor Game* (Ringwood, Vic.: Penguin, 1992), 18–19.
3 Patrick Buckridge, "The Age of Appreciation: Reading and Teaching Classic Literature in Australia in the Early Twentieth Century", *Australian Literary Studies* 22, no. 3 (2006): 342–56.
4 Ronald A. Sharp, "More Than Just Mates", *Australian Literary Review* 4, no. 6 (July 2009): 19; and *Friendship and Literature: Spirit and Form* (Durham: Duke University Press, 1986).

there', and embraced me".⁵ The result was the short story, "Comrade Pawel", which is set on the outskirts of Warsaw on the eve of the Nazi invasion in 1939.⁶

This sharing of a personal story foreshadows the way Steven Muir reworks Gertrude Spiess' translation of her father's diaries in *The Ancestor Game*; it foreshadows the way the portrait painter's creativity is revived by his encounter with Jessica Keal in *The Sitters*, and again when Toni Powlett first speaks of his father's death to Marina Golding during their picnic on Bream Island in *Prochownik's Dream*; it prefigures Max Otto's writing up of Dougald Gnapun's oral account of his ancestor's military leadership in *Landscape of Farewell*; and it is echoed nearly forty years later in the novelist's appropriation of John Patterner's story in *Lovesong*. Friendship, hospitality and literary hospitality, or intertextuality, are fundamental to Miller's thinking about the art of fiction. Other friendships, other artistic collaborations that are important to understanding his work, and to which I will return in this book, include his friendships with the Melbourne artists Rick Amor, Lyndell Brown, Charles Green, Allan O'Hoy and Patrick Pound; the poet and *Overland* editor Barrett Reid; and Miller's circle of Indigenous friends and collaborators, including the Jangga elder Col McLennan and his partner, Liz Hatte, the Barada elder Frank Budby, and the writer Anita Heiss.

It is one of the laws of friendship, as Jacques Derrida has shown, that one friend will always be left to mourn the death of the other, and that friendship is a form of *a priori* mourning. In their introduction to Derrida's eulogies for his own friends who have died, beginning with the death of Roland Barthes in 1980, Pascale-Anne Brault and Michael Naas suggest how the *oeuvre* of a writer becomes, with the passing of time, a memorial to friendship and an ongoing work of mourning:

> By gathering these works of mourning – by incorporating them – into a single volume, we hope to make even more apparent the ways in which the *oeuvre* or corpus of Derrida has, to cite Proust ... come to resemble "a huge cemetery in which on the majority of tombs the names are effaced and can no longer be read," a cemetery where some of the names are nonetheless still legible because of these acts of mourning and friendship, even if these names mask or refer to others that have long been obscured. We will ultimately be asking, therefore, about the encryption of names and friends in an *oeuvre*, about the way in which an *oeuvre* does not simply grow larger, but thickens with time, ages, comes to have time written across it, becomes wrinkled, furrowed, or folded, its volume worked over like a landscape, or indeed, like a cemetery.⁷

In one of his most recent public addresses, The Gifford Memorial Lecture, given at Vassar College in 2013, Miller has spoken about this "thickening" of his work over time, and the work of mourning for friends and family who have died. Three names, in particular, are singled out for memorialisation: Max Blatt, Allan O'Hoy and Barrett Reid. Miller's first published work of fiction, the short story "Comrade Pawel", was literally a gift of friendship – and a citation – from the life of his friend Max Blatt. His first written, though second published novel, *The Tivington Nott*, is dedicated "in loving memory of my father". The An-

---

5   Alex Miller, "Waxing Wiser than Oneself", *The Australian*, 7 October 2009, 24–5.
6   Alex Miller, "Comrade Pawel", *Meanjin Quarterly* 34, no. 1 (1975): 74–85.
7   Pascale-Anne Brault and Michael Naas, "Editor's Introduction", Jacques Derrida, *The Work of Mourning* (Chicago and London: University of Chicago Press, 2001), 4.

cestor Game is again dedicated "for Ruth & Max Blatt", and was written as a memorial to the life of Miller's friend, the painter Allan O'Hoy, who committed suicide in 1982: "Writing people back into the record is something I have often found myself doing." The initial inspiration for *Conditions of Faith* was Miller's reading of his mother's diary for 1923, written before her marriage at a time when she was living in France, and sent to him in Melbourne by his brother Ross after Winifred's death in 1994: she appears in the novel as Marie, the young niece of George and Emily Elder's landlady, Madame Barbier. *Autumn Laing* begins with a quotation from W.B. Yeats: "*New Year's Day 1991.* They are all dead and I am old and skeleton gaunt." Autumn's voice, Miller explains, came from his love for another dead friend, the poet Barrett Reid, whom he met at Heide in 1990, who appears in the novel as Barnaby Green. Miller has said that "the voice of Autumn Laing ... is really in the spirit of Barrett Reid, not biographically, but in the spirit of his energies and determinations ... his passion for getting the truth out and for his generosity". "My life is full of dead friends", Miller writes: "At my age that is not unusual."[8]

During the late 1990s and early 2000s, the relationship between the writing and publication of Miller's novels, and their biographical sources and contexts, became quite complicated. After travelling to China in 1987–88 and the critical breakthrough with *The Ancestor Game* in 1992, *The Sitters* in 1995 reflects Miller's increasing engagement with Melbourne's art scene, especially his friendship with Rick Amor. To that extent it forms part of a sequence of novels that constitutes one of the most sustained and insightful examples of *ekphrasis*, or writing about art, in all of Australian literature. They are *The Ancestor Game* (1992), *The Sitters* (1995), *Prochownik's Dream* (2005) and *Autumn Laing* (2011). The writing and publishing histories of this sequence, however, were interrupted by another, the Central Queensland novels: *Watching the Climbers on the Mountain* (1988), *Journey to the Stone Country* (2002), *Landscape of Farewell* (2007) and *Coal Creek* (2013). In 1997 Miller visited Liz Hatte and met Col McLennan in Townsville, and in 2000 he travelled with them to the Central Highlands, where he met Frank Budby: these friends were the inspiration for Annabelle Beck, Bo Rennie and Dougald Gnapun in *Journey to the Stone Country* and *Landscape of Farewell*. These two major sequences, which reflect what Miller himself has described as the two apparently separate hemispheres of his Australian life, the one rural and regional, the other urban and cosmopolitan, were in turn interrupted by *Conditions of Faith* (2000) and *Lovesong* (2009), which are themselves connected in having women protagonists and by their sources in Miller's experiences in Paris and Tunisia.

Miller has said that when he first began to draw upon his memories as the source of fiction while writing *The Tivington Nott*, he felt like an archaeologist beginning to excavate "a buried city of great complexity".[9] The architectural metaphor indicates the extraordinary complexity with which some of his individual novels are designed, especially *The Ancestor Game* and *Autumn Laing*, but also the many intricate connections between the novels, which require that his readers come to see them, cumulatively and progressively, as a coherent body of work. Wherever possible in this book I have sought to capture not only the

---

8 Alex Miller, "You Could Have Been There (Unmasking the Fictional Voice)", The William Gifford Memorial Lecture, Vassar College, 5 November 2013. *Antipodes* 28, no.1 (June 2014): 216, 222.
9 Alex Miller, "This Is How It's Going to Be Then", *Australian Book Review*, no. 127 (1990): 30. In "Constructions in Analysis" (1937), Freud suggests that the work of the analyst "resembles ... an archaeologist's excavation of some dwelling-place that has been destroyed or buried or of some ancient edifice". Quoted in Vilashini Cooppan, *Worlds Within: National Narratives and Global Connections in Postcolonial Writing* (Stanford: Stanford University Press, 2009), 295.

intricate internal design of Miller's individual novels but also this architecture that links them together as a body of work, an *oeuvre*, a coherent intellectual and aesthetic project – a life's work. Often the relationships between the novels are chiastic or mirror images, as in the relations between *Conditions of Faith* and *Lovesong*. Emily Elder travels from Paris to Tunisia in quest of her professional identity, which is interrupted when she becomes pregnant to a priest, while Sabiha travels from Tunisia to Paris, where she feels incomplete until she becomes pregnant to Bruno Fiorentino, while her eventual journey to her husband's home in Australia completes the mirror image of Emily's journey from Melbourne to Paris and Tunisia.

Names, dates and snippets of conversation recur throughout Miller's novels, not only joining one with the others, but also connecting the body of fiction to its sources in Miller's life. Max Otto and Alex Miller, for example, were both born in 1936, while Max Blatt and Miller's father, "Jock" Millar,[10] were both born in 1907. Autumn Laing casts aside Edith Black's beautiful impressionist painting in 1937, the same year that Lang Tzu destroys his grandfather's mirror and book of the ancestors: the near-identity of their names is surely intentional. *The Ancestor Game* and Victoria Feng's fictional book, *The Winter Visitor*, both have 302 pages. The name of Miller's mother, Winifred Croft, is given to the young English stockman, Robert Crofts, in *Watching the Climbers on the Mountain*, and to Max Otto's dead wife, Winifred Otto in *Landscape of Farewell*, while Marie, Emily's daughter in *Conditions of Faith*, is the name of the dead wife of the novelist, Ken, in *Lovesong*. Max Blatt's statement to Miller after reading "Comrade Pawel" ("You could have been there") is repeated by Lang Tzu after reading Steven's account of his birth in Hangzhou in *The Chronicle of the Fengs*, and by Dougald Gnapun in response to Max Otto's account of his great grandfather's armed resistance to the settlers in *Landscape of Farewell*. Poignantly, the dying words of Sabiha's father, "It will be alright when Sabiha gets here", echo Miller's mother's words before her death in England in 1994, "It will be alright when Alex gets here."[11] The topography of personal relationships and of creativity established in the relationships between Ward Rankin's enclosed study, Ida's bedroom, and the men's quarters in the early novel *Watching the Climbers on the Mountain*, is echoed in the layout of the cabins aboard the *Kairos* in *Conditions of Faith*, the gazebo in the garden at Coppin Grove where Victoria writes her book, *The Winter Visitor*, in *The Ancestor Game*, and the location of Toni Powlett's studio across the courtyard from his wife Teresa's kitchen in *Prochownik's Dream*. Enclosed spaces like Ward Rankin's study, Captain Anderson's map room, and the valleys of the Barle and the Exe in *The Tivington Nott*, and of Ranna Creek in *Journey to the Stone Country*, all places of containment, exhaustion and failure, contrast with the horizons and open vistas seen elsewhere in the landscape, or with the routes of the characters' journeys, their "voyages out" to new, more productive relationships and new worlds. These are just some of the signs of Miller's "buried city of great complexity", which readers of his novels will continue to discover as they begin their own excavations. These tiny but deliberate repetitions in the *oeuvre*, like the warp and weft of a fabric, are the clues to its larger design and patterns.

---

10 The inconsistent spelling was a consequence of clerical error.
11 Alex Miller, "In the End It Was Teaching Writing", *Australian Literary Review* 3, no. 2 (2008): 17.

My title, *The Ruin of Time*, is meant to capture Miller's pervasive awareness of historical change, of the human experience of being-in-time.[12] Its most conspicuous manifestation is the disappearance of established worlds and the people who live in them, including the wartime London of his boyhood, the traditional rural society of Somerset that had survived into the postwar years, the apparently failed project of settler colonialism in Australia, with its projection of vast pastoral enterprises into Aboriginal lands, and the remnants of the Qing Dynasty, which survived the European presence in Shanghai and Hangzhou until the second Japanese invasion of 1937. The most visible emblem of being-in-time is the unconserved ruin: Huang's dilapidated traditional house in Hangzhou and his grandson Lang Tzu's equally dilapidated boom-era mansion in Coppin Grove, Hawthorn; the termite-eaten remains of Ranna Station; the stone playgrounds of the Jangga at Mount Bulgonunna; the ruins of Verbena Station; and the burial cave of Gnapun at the summit of the Expedition Range. The presence there of his skeleton, his mortal remains, is a poignant reminder that the human body is also one of the ruins of time, as evidenced by Steven Muir's sense of the vulnerability of his friend Lang's damaged face, the ulcerous skin of the dying Theo Schwartz in *Prochownik's Dream*, and the aged body of the once beautiful debutante, Autumn Laing.

Miller's powerful and memorable images of the ruin of time include the dribbling hour-glass of debris suspended over the dining table at Ranna and the debris stuffed into a hole in the floorboards of Panya's cottage at Mount Coolon, but also the cold air that blows across the ruined body of Theo Schwartz after his stroke, and the "powerful wind" into which the figure of her father bends in Nada Powlett's sketch of the running man. Miller calls this "the rush of time", while W.G. Sebald describes it as "the Rings of Saturn", the gravitational field that catches up the debris of cosmic catastrophes.[13] Walter Benjamin called it the storm of progress:

> A Klee painting named "Angelus Novus" shows an angel looking as though he is about to move away from something he is fixedly contemplating. His eyes are staring, his mouth is open, his wings are spread. This is how one pictures the angel of history. His face is turned toward the past. Where we perceive a chain of events, he sees one single catastrophe which keeps piling wreckage and hurls it in front of his feet. The angel would like to stay, awaken the dead, and make whole what has been smashed. But a storm is blowing from Paradise; it has got caught in his wings with such violence that the angel can no longer close them. The storm irresistibly propels him into the future to which his back is turned, while the pile of debris before him grows skyward. This storm is what we call progress.[14]

As with Benjamin's angel of history, the characters in Miller's novels can only look backwards, not forwards in time. At the beginning of *The Ancestor Game*, *Journey to the Stone Country* and *Landscape of Farewell*, Steven Muir, Annabelle Beck and Max Otto each see their past self-reflected back at them in the mirror as if they are looking back from the future self they are already in the process of becoming; but the Becks and the Bigges cannot

---

12 I am indebted to Brigid Rooney, "The Ruin of Time and the Temporality of Belonging", in *The Novels of Alex Miller*, 201–16.
13 W.G. Sebald, *The Rings of Saturn* (1995; London: Harvill, 1998).
14 Walter Benjamin, "On the Concept of History", in *Illuminations: Essays and Reflections* (1968; New York: Schocken, 2007), 257.

Introduction

see from Ranna Station in the mid-nineteenth century into the future that Annabelle Beck inhabits: her modern Australia – *our* Australia – is their future, but not one that they could have imagined or would have wanted for themselves.

While Miller has received high praise for the technical mastery of his storytelling, and the transparent and often lyrical ease of his writing, one of the central arguments of this book is that we are only now beginning to see the complexity and self-reflexiveness that lies just beneath that apparently realistic surface. This is nowhere more obvious than in the novels' rich intertextuality, which enhances both the drama of character and the drama of ideas. Miller has been read too quickly, too transparently as a realist. His characters exist in and come to life through a rich fabric of metafictional devices, and historical and intertextual allusions: indeed, they often communicate with each other *through* intertextuality. Here is an example from *Autumn Laing*. It takes place in the library at Old Farm, where Miller's characters are surrounded by the books and paintings that are an integral part of their conversations. Autumn has been reading to Pat Donlon from Oscar Wilde's *The Critic as Artist*. The book lay "face down in her lap", as if the reader were required to notice its title and to ponder its significance.[15] Wilde's *The Critic as Artist* is a dramatic dialogue that takes place in the library of a house in Piccadilly, overlooking London's Green Park. Gilbert and Ernest represent different aspects of the relationship – we might say, using one of Miller's own terms, the *collaboration* – between the critical and creative faculties, as do Autumn and Pat in Miller's novel. When Ernest speaks appreciatively of the current vogue for memoirs and biographies, Gilbert cuttingly remarks that "every great man nowadays has his disciples, and it is always Judas who writes the biography". "Cheap editions of great books may be delightful", Gilbert declares, "but cheap editions of great men are absolutely detestable". When Ernest asks, "to whom do you allude?", Gilbert replies:

> Oh! To all our second-rate litterateurs. We are overrun by a set of people who, when poet or painter passes away, arrive at the house along with the undertaker . . . They are the mere body-snatchers of literature. The dust is given to one, and the ashes to another, and the soul is out of their reach.[16]

We are reminded here of Adeli Heartstone's arrival at Old Farm on 1 January 1991:

> She . . . parked her car by the front door then walked around the side, coming through the rhododendrons to the back door as if she was one of our old group . . .
> "Who are you?" I asked . . . She has the ruthlessness of a scavenger . . . I know them, the scavengers. They feed off our flesh before we're dead . . .
> "I'm the one who's writing your biography", she said . . . Breathless with self-esteem.[17]

Adeli is one of Wilde's literary "body-snatchers". But so, we must conclude, is the novelist Alex Miller, for despite the transparent fiction of his "Editor's note" and the invention of Professor Heartstone, it is *he* who is writing a fictionalised biography of Sunday Reed and

---

15 Alex Miller, *Autumn Laing* (Sydney: Allen & Unwin, 2011), 317.
16 Oscar Wilde, *The Critic as Artist: With Some Remarks Upon the Importance of Doing Nothing*, in *Intentions* (London: Methuen, 1913), 98–9.
17 Miller, *Autumn Laing*, 4–5.

Sidney Nolan, the great painter for whom he has had a life-long admiration. As I hope to demonstrate in subsequent chapters, Miller's readers must also be alert to the implications of his allusions to Carson McCullers' *Reflections in a Golden Eye* in *Watching the Climbers on the Mountain*; to Edward, Duke of York's *The Master of Game* in *The Tivington Nott*; to Henry Adams' *Chartres* and Samuel Smiles' *The Lives of the Engineers* in *Conditions of Faith*; to his references to works by Rembrandt, Salvador Dali, Pierre Bonnard and Walter Sickert in *The Sitters* and *Prochownik's Dream*; to Arthur Rimbaud's poem, "Un Saison en Enfer", and Guy de Maupassant's novel *Une vie* in *Autumn Laing*; and to Rolfe Boldrewood's *Robbery Under Arms* and Herman Melville's *Billy Budd, Sailor* in *Coal Creek*.

The largest of Miller's novels – the largest, that is, not just in their length and scope, but also in the complexity of their biographical and historical source material – are historical novels in the classic sense of that term described by one of Miller's benchmark critics, Georg Lukács.[18] That is to say, they use a fictional protagonist to provide a window on to the larger canvas in the history or culture of a period. As Geordie Williamson has rightly said, Miller's novels are at their most engaging when they expose "the clasp between reality and invention".[19] Although Miller has been widely recognised for his subtle creation of character and his intimate exploration of the ethics of cross-cultural relationships, he has not been as well recognised for the substantial intellectual achievement of his most ambitious novels, which offer formidably original historical interpretations of global modernity in the late nineteenth and twentieth centuries in its various vectors of migration, war, colonialism and global commerce. In some of the novels, including *Conditions of Faith* and *Autumn Laing*, this is combined with the classic forms of the *bildungsroman* and the *kunstlerroman*, in which the individual character undergoes a maturity or development in their personal or professional life. As Elizabeth McMahon argues in a passage I will have need to cite more than once in this book, Miller's achievement is that his novels move so effortlessly from the abstract to the concrete, from the historical or the philosophical to the fictional: they negotiate "the leap from the abstraction of metaphor into the grounded realities of history and culture – and back again".[20]

In Miller's novels, the relations between individual characters and their historical circumstances are rarely static, but often involve them in journeys across space, time, culture, or social class – or all of these categories at once. His characters are all engaged in quests and journeys, but as McMahon again points out, these quests typically involve not just a journey from one place or state of being to another, but a *double* displacement, a pattern of migration or journeying to one destination or state of mind that has then to be disrupted again or doubled by a further journey, often into the homeland or the heartland of the other.[21] In this way, Lang travels from Hangzhou to Shanghai and then on to Melbourne, while Steven migrates from England to Melbourne and then, through his imaginative engagement with Lang's history, to Shanghai; August Spiess travels from Hamburg to Shanghai, and then to Melbourne; Emily Stanton marries and moves to Paris, but then travels to Tunisia; Annabelle Beck returns from Melbourne to Townsville, but then

---

18 Georg Lukács, *The Historical Novel*, trans. Hannah and Stanley Mitchell (1962; Harmondsworth: Penguin, 1981).
19 Geordie Williamson, "Autumn's Fading Words Are Pure and Living Art", review of Alex Miller, *Autumn Laing*, *The Weekend Australian*, 1–2 October 2011, 20.
20 Elizabeth McMahon, "Continental Heartlands and Alex Miller's Geosophical Imaginary", in *The Novels of Alex Miller*, 125–6.
21 McMahon, "Continental Heartlands", 129.

goes on to Central Queensland with Bo Rennie, while Max Otto travels from Hamburg to Mount Nebo, but then goes on a final journey with Dougald to the Expedition Range; Sabiha travels from Tunisia to Paris, and eventually to her husband's home in Australia.

In exploring the links between individual characters and wider social forces, Miller also has a recurring philosophical interest in the relation between human agency and social determination, between the individual and what he has called the "vast impersonal forces of culture and history".[22] Miller is well read not only in history but also in philosophy. In the first edition of *The Ancestor Game*, the problem of the relation between individual agency and external forces in modernity was captured by the epigraphs he selected from Søren Kierkegaard's *Either/Or* and Judith Wright's *The Generations of Men*. In the quotation from *Either/Or*, Kierkegaard suggests that the modern individual is a self-creator, free from those "substantive determinants" of family, race and nation that control the fate of individuals in classical literature, especially Greek epic and tragic drama. The Judith Wright quote, however, suggests the continuing importance of those determinants, of the individual experiencing their rootedness to family and place and culture. Miller was disappointed that reviewers had not grasped the tension in the novel between these opposing forces, and as a consequence the epigraphs were omitted from the American edition. In an interview with Simon Caterson, Miller explained, "there is a tension between these two positions which the book explores", and he went on to object that "this was a bit too subtle for the reviewers, who ignored the Wright and concentrated on whether the Kierkegaard is borne out nor not".[23]

It has perhaps been too easy for critics to think of Miller as championing the "extraterritoriality" of art in George Steiner's sense of that word: "A great writer driven from language to language by social upheaval and war is an apt symbol for the age of the refugee".[24] August Spiess and Lang Tzu, and Autumn Laing and Pat Donlon all appear, in their different ways, to be examples of modern extraterritoriality or cosmopolitanism. And yet, as we will come to see, Miller has an uncanny ability to dramatise different points of view without necessarily investing in them personally, and the opinions and passions of his characters are often undercut by narrative irony or brought into juxtaposition with opposing points of view. It is always a mistake to think that the opinions of Miller's characters are his own. This is the case with Spiess' diaries, for example, in which his modernist espousal of the artist as exile or émigré is carefully grounded in a particular time and place – Germany in the late nineteenth century – and then subjected to a forensic interrogation by his Chinese friends that has shocking consequences. Another example of Miller's disinterested handling of ideas is his use of Henry Adams' medievalism in *Conditions of Faith* as a counter to the heroic materialism of the novel's modern engineers, though without himself investing in Adams' idealisation of Catholicism and pre-modern cultures. The apparent cross-cultural equivalences among his various figures of the artist as migrant or émigré – including Steven Muir, August Spiess, Lang Tzu and the autobiographical figure of Alex Miller himself – with Aboriginal loss of country and dislocation in figures like Dougald Gnapun, whose fibro-cement house is near Mackay in *Journey to the*

---

22 Quoted in Shirley Walker, "The Frontier Wars: History and Fiction in *Journey to the Stone Country* and *Landscape of Farewell*", in *The Novels of Alex Miller*, 156.
23 Alex Miller, "Playing the Ancestor Game: Alex Miller Interviewed by Simon Caterson", *Journal of Commonwealth Literature* 29, no. 5 (1994): 10.
24 George Steiner, *Extraterritorial: Papers on Literature and the Language of Revolution* (New York: Macmillan, 1971), 11.

Stone Country and at Mt Nebo in *Landscape of Farewell*, also raises difficult questions of cross-cultural comparison. These questions even threaten to ground Miller's central preoccupation with hospitality and the gift in the profoundly unequal opportunities available to white and Indigenous Australians within the Australian postcolony. As August Spiess puts it after witnessing the damage he has caused by his colonial presence in China, "For twenty blissful years I had lived as if the condition of extraterritoriality were a kind of literary conceit."[25]

While Miller's novels are immediately accessible to the general reading public, they are manifestly works of high literary seriousness – substantial, technically masterly and assured, intricately interconnected, and of great imaginative, intellectual and ethical weight. Among his many prizes and awards, Miller has twice won the Miles Franklin Literary Award, for *The Ancestor Game* in 1993, and *Journey to the Stone Country* in 2003; the Commonwealth Writers' prize, also for *The Ancestor Game* in 1993; and the New South Wales Premier's Literary Awards Christina Stead Prize, for *Conditions of Faith* in 2001 and *Lovesong* in 2011. He received a Centenary Medal in 2001 and the Melbourne Prize for Literature in 2012. In 2011 he was elected a Fellow of the Australian Academy of the Humanities. Having published his eleventh novel, *Coal Creek*, in 2013 – which won the Victorian Premier's Fiction Award in 2014 – Miller is currently writing an autobiographical memoir with the working title "Horizons".

---

25   Miller, *The Ancestor Game*, 268–9.

1
Unravelling the Change: *The Tivington Nott* and *Watching the Climbers on the Mountain*

Alex Miller's first two published novels, *Watching the Climbers on the Mountain* (1988) and *The Tivington Nott* (1989), were originally conceived as a single work drawing on his experience as a farmhand on Exmoor, his emigration to Australia in 1952, and his years in Central Queensland and the Gulf of Carpentaria. It was to be called "Jimmy Diamond", in tribute to an Aboriginal friend with whom he had worked as a ringer in the Gulf Country in the mid-1950s. In its original conception, however, the project proved to be too large and unwieldy, and when he reached the end of the Exmoor section, he realised that the first novel had emerged whole and complete. Because it was about English rural life, Miller was unable to find a publisher for it in Australia, and so the second novel to be written, *Watching the Climbers on the Mountain*, which is set in Central Queensland, was published first, by Pan Macmillan, in Sydney in 1988. The Exmoor novel, *The Tivington Nott*, was published the following year by Robert Hale, an independent publisher in London's Clerkenwell. In the end, Miller recalls, "I found an English publisher... through a contact with a west country bookseller from whom I had bought a collection of books on stag hunting on Exmoor, which were useful to me in researching the detail of the novel."[1]

In this chapter I discuss Miller's early novels in the order of their composition rather than their publication, under the title "Unravelling the Change". It is a term from the ancient ritual of stag hunting for a potential turning point in the hunt when the stag may either escape its pursuers or go on to be trapped and killed. I find it suggestive both for Miller's negotiation of the move from England to Australia, which was also for him a ritual coming of age, and for his later negotiation of the equally difficult transition to becoming a professional writer. As he explains in "The Mask of Fiction: A Memoir", "[Jimmy Diamond] was going to bridge the two lives, the two worlds, and their apparently unconnected realities."[2] While *The Tivington Nott* is a powerful and compelling novel that speaks to the concerns of contemporary criticism, *Watching the Climbers on the Mountain* is in some ways an anomaly in Miller's *oeuvre*, for reasons that I will explain later in this chapter. Both of them can be understood as early works that precede and in certain respects anticipate

---

1 Alex Miller to Robert Dixon, 29 May 2013.
2 Alex Miller, "The Mask of Fiction: A Memoir", in *The Novels of Alex Miller: An Introduction*, ed. Robert Dixon (Sydney: Allen & Unwin, 2012), 31–2.

the spectacular arrival of his first major novel in 1992, the Miles Franklin Literary Award winning *The Ancestor Game*.

The Tivington Nott

The Tivington Nott derives from Miller's experience as a young farmhand in Somerset in the early 1950s. In 1951, at the age of fifteen, he had left school and was working in a factory in South London when he was given the chance to join a program offering work experience to young Londoners wishing to learn farming. Handycross was a small tenant farm near the village of Lydeard St Lawrence (or St Lawrence Lydiard), eleven kilometres north west of Taunton in Somerset. The tenant farmer, Bill ("the Tiger") Warren, was a bullying, even violent man, with a dangerous obsession for hunting the wild red deer. Yet Miller spent almost two years there working happily, for the most part, under the supervision of Morris Aplin, a skilled farmhand. Above all, he was given responsibility for the care of the farm's horses, and rode Warren's second horse in the historic Devon and Somerset Staghounds. The hunt began further west in the long, narrow village of Winsford in the valley of the River Exe, where the country rises to the high uplands of Exmoor. In 1954, shortly after Miller left for Australia, this region was gazetted as the Exmoor National Park.

Critics have seen *The Tivington Nott* as a novel about the outsider in a closed rural community. Brenda Walker suggests that it "is centrally concerned with the situation of the outsider"; it is "a meditation on issues of territory and intrusion";[3] Peter Pierce says of *Watching the Climbers on the Mountain*, we are "a hemisphere away, but we are again with a closed rural community, as in *The Tivington Nott*, one that is about to be disrupted by an outsider".[4] Miller himself describes it as "a parable of the stranger".[5] Certainly, in the novel's early scenes, Miller's unnamed boy is marked as an outsider in the village. Other farmhands from nearby Taunton persecute him for being "an alien" and "a foreigner", and he fears that they will send him back to London "in a box".[6] His boss, Tiger Westall, subjects him to a regime of vicious bullying, aided and abetted by "yokels" from the village, while Mrs Westall makes it clear that "boys from London cannot be trusted" (2). Instinctively, the boy aligns himself with the other outsiders: his supervisor, Morris, who is a native of Wiltshire; Alsop, the retired Australian army officer who wants to sell Westall his prized Irish stallion, Kabara; Kabara himself, who is "not an Exmoor hunter" (18); and the two stags hunted by the Devon and Somerset Staghounds, the Haddon stag and the elusive Tivington nott. The Westalls, on the other hand, have been in Somerset for generations, and although he is a struggling tenant farmer, the Tiger is fanatically devoted to stag hunting as a sign of his family's connection to the district and its traditions:

> He likes to turn out just right on hunting days . . . Hunting is his reward in life for all the skimping and grinding. Hunting the wild red deer. They've been doing it here since the

---

3 Brenda Walker, "Alex Miller and Leo Tolstoy: Australian Storytelling in a European Tradition", in *The Novels of Alex Miller*, 48–9.
4 Peter Pierce, "My Memory Has a Mind of Its Own: *Watching the Climbers on the Mountain* and *The Tivington Nott*", in *The Novels of Alex Miller*, 59–60.
5 Alex Miller, "My First Love", *The Age*, Sunday Extra, 18 March 1995, 3.
6 Alex Miller, *The Tivington Nott* (1989; Ringwood, Vic.: Penguin, 1993), 27–8. All subsequent references are to this edition and appear in parentheses in the text.

Anglo-Saxon kings were around. It's not something they just decided on yesterday. It's in their blood. And the Westalls have been here forever, so when it comes to his hunters the Tiger watches me every inch of the way. Criticizing mostly. Offering abuse. Sarcasm. Looking for perfection where it isn't to be found. (12)

While he describes *The Tivington Nott* as "a parable of the stranger", Miller immediately goes on to say that it is also "a meditation on the power the stranger has to negotiate a way into a settled community and to change the community forever. And the powerlessness of the community . . . to resist the changes the stranger brings".[7] Central to this negotiation of change in the novel is the ritual – if that is the right word – of the stag hunt. Miller recalls his Exmoor years with great affection and speaks of the hunt not as a closed, aristocratic ritual, but as a more encompassing event in which, as an outsider, he was able to mix and excel regardless of his social class. While fox hunting in the Home Counties retained its socially exclusive nature until it was banned in 2004, Miller recalls that "stag hunting in the West . . . was always open to anyone with a horse and the courage to join the chase – the fairest hunting was how it was still known in the fifties". Some in the Devon and Somerset Staghounds were perhaps more closed to outsiders than others: Miller recalls the harbourer, in particular, as "a deeply ritualised being of the antique forest ways". Yet he also recalls, "the amazing part of it that liberated me was [that] social class did not come into it, only courage and decency of behaviour. I hope that something of this love that [was] aroused in me by the whole thing comes through in *The Tivington Nott*".[8]

The Hunt as Social Ritual

The hunt in Miller's novel has a complex, even ambivalent, status as a social ritual. To some, like the Tiger, it is an index of social hierarchy and exclusion; to others, like the boy, it is potentially a vehicle for freedom from persecution and even a means of social mobility. This ambiguity is reflected in debates about the meaning of the hunt in contemporary scholarship, especially as it is described in the great medieval hunting manuals. The books in Miller's own "West Country hunting collection" include a modern English translation of *The Master of Game*, written around 1410 by Edward of Norwich;[9] *Memories of a Stag Harbourer* (1931) by Fred Goss;[10] and H.P. Hewett's *The Fairest Game: Hunting and Watching Exmoor Deer*, published by J.A. Allen in 1963.[11] Goss had been harbourer for the Devon and Somerset Staghounds for twenty-eight years between 1894 and 1921, and his *Memories* are a practical, down-to earth account of the hunt from the harbourer's perspective: it is the source of many of the novel's descriptive details. Goss lived and worked in the Had-

---

7   Miller, "My First Love", 3.
8   Alex Miller to Robert Dixon, 30 May 2013.
9   *The Master of Game by Edward, Second Duke of York*, eds W.A. and F. Baillie-Grohman (London: Chatto and Windus, 1909).
10 Fred Goss, *Memories of a Stag Harbourer: A Record of Twenty-Eight Years with the Devon and Somerset Stag Hounds 1894–1921* (London: Witherby, 1931).
11 H.P. Hewett, *The Fairest Hunting: Hunting and Watching Exmoor Deer* (London: J.A. Allen, 1963). At this time, Miller's publisher, Robert Hale, was consolidating its reputation as a publisher of equestrian books, and acquired J.A. Allen and Co., which had been Britain's leading publisher of equestrian and hunting titles since 1926, http://www.halebooks.com/.

don district, and he refers to many locations that also appear in the novel, including the valleys of the Barle and the Exe, Haddon Hill, the Quantocks, Dunkery, Exford, Winsford and Taunton. The title of Hewett's book, *The Fairest Game*, is itself an allusion to *The Master of Game*, in which Edward of Norwich describes the *chasse par force des chiens* (chase by strength of hounds) for the hart, the male red deer (*Cervus elaphus*), as "the fairest hunting that any man may hunt after". By 1963, when *The Fairest Game* was published, Miller was already an undergraduate student at the University of Melbourne, but it deals with the 1950s, when he lived on Exmoor. On its cover is a photograph of the Devon and Somerset Staghounds led by the then huntsman, Sidney Bazley, who broke his neck, Miller recalls, "while hunting hinds in the winter and recovered from the injury shortly after I left Somerset".[12]

The stag hunt as Miller experienced it in the early 1950s was introduced into England by the Anglo-Normans between 1066 and 1250, and had remained almost unchanged, at least in its outward forms, across the intervening centuries. One of the most important of the many hunting manuals that were written from the thirteenth century on, *The Master of Game* was translated and adapted by Edward of Norwich, second Duke of York, from an earlier French manual, Gaston Phoebus Count of Foix's *Livre de Chasse* (1389). Miller's own copy is a modern English translation, published in London in 1909. He places it in the hands of his young protagonist, the unnamed boy, who reads it at night on the farm in Somerset:

> It is lying here on the bed now in front of me. It is *The Master of Game* and was written by King Edward III's grandson in 1406. My copy was printed in 1909 and what's left of the cover is grey-green cloth with a gold medieval design. It is inscribed on the front endpaper: "Peter Staines, on his twenty-first birthday, With best wishes from Sir Guy & Lady Fentner; June 1923" . . . It is a book that I can open at any page and begin reading with pleasure. (46–7)

The subject and original purpose of the book, its well-worn condition, the medieval design, and the inscription are all significant, indicating the continuity of the hunt as a social ritual from medieval to modern times, even beyond the supposed watershed of the Great War; its connection with the aristocratic classes – "Sir Guy & Lady Fentner" – which may now be fading; and the association of both the manual and the hunt itself with ideals of chivalry, manliness, and coming of age: it was given to Peter Staines on his twenty-first birthday, and is now read by Miller's boy on the eve of his own coming of age.

Edward describes the *chasse par force des chiens* for the hart as the most noble of sports. The *par-force* hunt began before dawn, when huntsmen took the lymers or scent-hounds out to harbour a hart in the "gray dawnyng", a phrase that recurs in Miller's novel. While the huntsmen were tracking the hart, the lord and his company would breakfast beside a stream in a clearing of the woods. After locating one or more harts, the huntsmen would bring back the fewmets or droppings for examination so that the most robust, the most challenging and worthy hart, usually at least six years old, might be chosen for pursuit. The chase itself was prosecuted by packs of hounds handled by men on foot and followed by the hunting party on horseback, the various groups communicating with horns. A seasoned and wily hart might give chase for many hours, crossing streams, dou-

---

12   Alex Miller to Robert Dixon, 29 May 2013.

bling back on his tracks, and even crossing the paths of other deer to conceal his scent, until he was surrounded by the dogs, exhausted and at bay. In the medieval hunt, the lord and his mounted company would then arrive, and a huntsman was chosen to break or butcher the deer, cutting it up according to ceremony for division among the entire party as a confirmation of the reciprocal obligations that bound feudal society together.[13]

Modern scholars characterise the hunt variously as a ritual, a sport and a game. Susan Crane describes it as a ritual, a pervasive, even coercive, allegorical rite signifying aristocratic domination.[14] Following influential models in ethnography and social anthropology, including Clifford Geertz's account of Balinese cockfighting and James Howe's study of modern fox hunting, Crane offers a closed reading in which she assumes that the ideological effects of the ritual can be inferred directly from the major texts, including *The Master of Game*. She argues that "the hunt *a force* is a mimetic ritual designed to celebrate and perpetuate aristocratic authority"; it is "less a manifestation of a prior consensus than a means by which people are persuaded to consent to the social hierarchy, or if they cannot be entirely persuaded, a means by which they can be induced to give conventional signs of assent".[15] That Miller thinks of the hunt as to some extent a ritual in this sense is suggested by the epigraph he has chosen for the novel, from the French playwright Paul Claudel: "Everything is either symbol or parable." While the hunt was clearly associated with forms of social authority, Crane's reading of the relation between the hunting manuals, the practice of the hunt, and the maintenance of aristocratic authority seems too instrumental to be persuasive. Miller's hunt in *The Tivington Nott* is a less predictable, less manageable affair altogether.

Ryan R. Judkins offers a more nuanced account, proposing that the hunt is best understood as a "game" rather than a ritual, which corresponds more closely to medieval usage, the word "game" being frequently used in *The Master of Game* in the sense of "entertainment", "play", "risk", "sport", and "pleasure".[16] The element of risk, willingly engaged by the hunters, should caution us against more closed readings of the hunt as coercive ritual. The risks include those of physical danger, the potential instabilities arising from disparate classes of people and animals working together, and the uncertainty of capturing the deer, upon which the entire outcome of the hunt depends: "if the hunt were successful, then this ritual took place and the hunt and breaking expressed this communal, feudal vision"; if it were not successful, "then the absence of that meaning implicitly endangered that view".[17]

Judkins' understanding of the hunt as an open contest over social status is closer to Miller's novel than is Crane's coercive ritual. The hunt, after all, was a risky game or sport whose social meanings could be contested. Judkins' insights into the changing social meanings of the hunt during the fourteenth century, when aristocratic privilege came under increasing challenge from below, might also be extended into the first half of the twentieth century, when Miller lived on Exmoor. There was by then strong opposition to

---

13 This account is derived from Ryan R. Judkins, "The Game of the Courtly Hunt: Chasing and Breaking Deer in Late Medieval English Literature", *Journal of English and Germanic Philology* 112, no. 1 (January 2013): 72–3.
14 Susan Crane, "Ritual Aspects of the Hunt *a Force*", in *Engaging with Nature: Essays on the Natural World in Medieval and Early Modern Europe*, ed. Barbara A. Hanawalt and Lisa J. Kiser (Notre Dame, Indiana: University of Notre Dame Press, 2008), 63–84.
15 Crane, "Ritual Aspects of the Hunt", 68, 71.
16 Judkins, "The Game of the Courtly Hunt", 74–5.
17 Judkins, "The Game of the Courtly Hunt", 84.

stag hunting by landholders because of the damage caused by hounds and hunters to sheep, crops and farm infrastructure. Meetings of the Devon and Somerset Staghounds were regularly disrupted by representatives of the newly established League for the Prohibition of Cruel Sports, which objected to the hunt's cruelty to dogs and horses, as well as to the stag.[18] While Miller's reading of the hunt manuals made him aware of its ritual-like aspects, his fictional account of it, derived from first-hand experience in the socially turbulent postwar years, registers its ambiguities, tensions and complexities, as the ritual was put to the test by a variety of participants coming from different social classes, each with different skills, and under unpredictable circumstances.

At the commencement of the hunt, Miller's young farm labourer speculates on what meanings it might hold for the various groups and individuals who assemble in "the gray dawnyng" in the yard of the Royal Oak in the village of Winsford:

> It's a long, thin village, jammed tight up its narrow valley, overlooked by the steep, thickly wooded slopes of the moor, the River Exe down one side of the main street and houses down the other. It's only just after ten o'clock but already there's quite a crowd; cars parked each side of the road, and riders and people on foot wandering around in the middle. The locals out in force. A few tourists, labourers, housewives, kids, and, of course, those who've come here specially for the hunting season. (74)

The hunt's patron is the elderly and aristocratic Mrs Allen: "Perry and Tolland, the Tiger and the rest of them salute her as we go by, doffing their hats." The boy has heard that "she nurtures religiously the old ways of hunting", and he wonders, "Do they mean the ways... that are spoken of in *The Master of Game*? Ways as old as that?" (75). Miller, of course, is writing fiction: he is not writing as a social anthropologist or a scholar of medieval ritual. Yet the questions addressed by contemporary scholars to the medieval hunting manuals resonate with his young outsider's speculations, and they provide one way of approaching the role the hunt plays in organising his fictional account of westcountry society in the mid-1950s. Is the Devon and Somerset Staghounds a coercive ritual, more or less successfully reinforcing a class-based society, as Crane's approach would suggest? Is Judkins' model of communal effort and reciprocal obligation in the face of mutual risk closer to the mark, so that "a chase is only successful if all of its disparate parts... work together"? Setting aside the abstract ideals of the hunting manuals, upon which both these theories are based, is "the actual practice of the hunt and the breaking... [even] murkier"?[19] Miller's version of the hunt is consistent with a postwar rural society whose once rigid ways are being broken down by decades of complaint about damage to farmlands and cruelty to animals, and by social mobility and the presence of outsiders. In *Memories of a Stag Harbourer*, written between the wars, Goss is adamant that the hunt worked toward social inclusion rather than class distinction:

> Among townspeople there seems to be a general idea that stag-hunting [is]... only for the "idle rich". This certainly does not apply to the West Country... Far from emphasising class distinction, stag-hunting produces a sense of good fellowship that most other

---

18 "The Persecution of Red Deer on and Around Exmoor and the Quantocks: A Review of the Literature", http://www.acigawis.org.uk/bloodsports/staghunting/a-review-of-staghunting-literature.
19 Judkins, "The Game of the Courtly Hunt", 78, 84, 86.

sports would find hard to beat. Those who can afford to ride horses form only part of the total numbers to whom stag-hunting gives some of the greatest pleasure in their lives.

Of the motors that attend the meets many are hired by local enthusiasts with money saved especially for the occasion. Next come the cyclists, and after them the crowds that enjoy themselves on "shanks" ponies.[20]

The fraternity of the hunt is apparent from the moment that Tiger and the boy arrive at the Royal Oak. The Tiger's friend Harry Cheyne, the chairman of the Hunt Damages Committee, forces his horse boldly through the assembled riders to stand alongside him, addressing him by his name, which is used here for the first time: "A fair morning, Bill" (76). The boy notices initially that they are both big men, "packed into their clothes. Bursting at the seams" (77), but he also notes that Cheyne's grey gelding is a much finer and more expensive mount that the Tiger's Finisher. This leads him to reflect on the class differences between the two of them, and the friendship and respect they show for each other across that class boundary by virtue of the camaraderie of the hunt:

> The thing with Cheyne is, he's not a tenant farmer like the Tiger. He owns a freehold estate of over twelve hundred acres ... Really he's in another class altogether to the Tiger, an enviable position somewhere between the responsibilities of the old gentry and the dependence of people like Tiger himself, but he doesn't let that get in the way of his friendship for him. Cheyne's a squire. And in some ways Tiger's probably about the only man he really respects. As an equal, or near-equal. Of course that's not down there in the valley crutching sheep and feeding pigs ... It's a respect that only operates up here. On the hunting field. (78)

Before the hunt begins, there are hints of dissent against the old ways. The master, Mrs Allen, the huntsman or lymerer, Jack Perry, and the leading riders, Harry Cheyne, Tiger Westall and Mrs Grant, all wait for the harbourer, John Grabbe, to return from the woods with news of a warrantable stag. Grabbe is the character based on Miller's harbourer, versed in the ancient ways of the forest. His first duty is to report signs of the quarry to the master of the hunt, but the others are impatient:

> If they could get away with it, Perry and his hounds would chase almost any huntable stag they could rouse from the covers ... They want to get out there and get on with it. But she will insist that the stag to be hunted today is ... the oldest stag harboured in the area. And as far as she's concerned they can spend the whole day looking for that one rather than settle for something less. (84)

Although Tiger Westall is a demanding, capricious and even cruel employer, insisting that the boy call him "Master" – which he declines to do, acceding only to "boss" – his strategy for the hunt requires the boy's cooperation. A keen hunter, Westall wants to buy the magnificent stallion Kabara from his wealthy neighbour, Alsop, an expatriate Australian who has been injured in a motor accident and can no longer ride the spirited entire. Westall cannot normally afford to ride with a second horse, but on this occasion he has the boy ride Kabara, not as a second but as a hunter among the others, his plan being to tire Kabara

---

20   Goss, *Memories*, 206.

out, so reducing his apparent value. But to achieve this he needs the boy's cooperation. Just before the hunt begins, the Tiger turns to him and orders, " 'Hunt with him, boy! Hunt with him!' . . . Making doubly certain that I don't dawdle around all day, second-horsing and saving his champion's wind for a late run" (97). The boy knows that Westall's desire for the horse and his plan to buy it advantageously places him in a position of power over his "boss":

> I wonder if he thinks he's bought me off? . . . when he's home this evening and he's telling her all about his day in the hunting field, I bet he doesn't mention . . . that he paid his second-horseman to go hunting . . . For, in permitting it, it must surely seem to her, the Tiger was doing our bidding. (99)

The boy is prepared to ride "companionably" beside Tiger (134), holding back the impatient Kabara to keep pace with Tiger's exhausted mount, until Tiger deliberately fails to warn him of a dangerous jump, which the boy successfully covers. From that moment on he leaves Tiger behind and is in at the kill with the best of the hunters, who include Lord Harbringdon and Perry, the master of hounds. William H. Forsyth's account of the final stages of the medieval hunt, derived from *The Master of Game*, indicates how closely Miller's account corresponds to its ideal form:

> As the hunt proceeds the hart may resort to various ruses to throw the hounds off his track. He may "change" with another stag . . . [he] may double in his tracks, called "foiling", or he may take to the river and swim upstream, called "beating up the river", or swim downstream, called "foiling down". Whenever the main pack are confused by such ruses, the lymerer and his scent hound are brought up to "unravel the change" and to start the pack off on the right track again . . .
> The winded stag, if he has not been able to escape by these ruses, stands at bay surrounded by the hounds, and the horn is sounded for the capture. The master of the hunt then rides up and dispatches him . . . no easy task when the desperate animal uses a large pair of antlers in self-defence. The dead stag is "undone", or cut up. The huntsmen sound the mort, and the hounds are rewarded with prized titbits.[21]

The breaking of the hart is the climax of the medieval ritual, in which the lord ceremonially distributes portions of the animal to members of the hunt as a sign of their courage and virtue, cementing feudalism's reciprocal obligations. In *The Tivington Nott*, the boy is the only hunter to sight the stag at the moment of unravelling the change but he declines to sound the alarm, and he is there at the end when Lord Harbringdon and Perry, who performs the breaking, acknowledge the boy's courageous ride on Kabara by blooding him in front of the other seasoned male riders. Again, Miller's description follows the conventions of the medieval hunt closely. It begins with the encorning, when the hunter turns the hart upside down to rest on its antlers, its breast exposed ready for disembowelling and dismemberment:

---

21 William H. Forsyth, "The Medieval Stag Hunt", *Bulletin of The Metropolitan Museum of Art*, http://www.metmuseum.org/pubs/bulletins/1/pdf/3258066.pdf.bannered.pdf.

> Perry is standing holding the knife, dangling in his hand, his other hand holding the top point of the stag's antlers, waiting to go on with his work. He and Tolland exchange a look and Tolland reaches into the cavity of the stag's carcass. He comes up with a handful of blood, holding his dripping palm away from his body in front of him. We watch him. Waiting to see what he will do. He takes two quick strides towards me and splashes the blood in my face.
>
> They all look at me and say nothing as I recoil and try to wipe the wretched stuff off. I see Harry Cheyne's hard features, his gaze focused on me, and Lord Harbringdon's pale grey eyes, remote and slightly hooded, turned for this instant in my direction, including me in the group. And in front of me Tolland, his open and generous features for this occasion unsmiling.
>
> "Fair hunt, boy", he says, and Perry and the other two voice their ready agreement.
>
> Perry bends to his task and severs the stag's head. (152)

It is a deeply ritualistic moment, acknowledging the boy's coming of age through a centuries-old ritual performed exactly as prescribed, and acknowledged by Tolland's "generous" allusion to *The Master of Game*: "Fair hunt, boy." In his study of the manuals, Judkins describes the breaking as a "traditional and meticulous process" that is the symbolic climax of the hunt: "the meaning of the ritual is most present at this time, because the hunt and, especially the breaking, transform a disparate and disjointed set of different social groups, genders, and species (aristocrats and peasants, men and women, human and companion animals) into one communal whole".[22] Although his perspective is decidedly practical rather than aristocratic, in his *Memories of a Stag Harbourer*, Goss also recalls that during his time with the Devon and Somerset Staghounds, "prized trophies" such as the slots (the feet) were formally presented by the Master, after the kill, "to the lucky few, among whom youngsters in at the death of their first stag often find themselves favourably regarded".[23]

But Miller's breaking is not a ritual of quite such "generosity" and "inclusion". Specifically, Mrs Grant, the only woman still among the leaders near the end, fails to be there at the kill, arriving just after the breaking, her expensive riding breeches soiled, and "leading her beaten horse" (153). The Tiger also fails to be in at the kill. He is excluded not exactly on class terms, for his friendship with Cheyne transcends that, as we have seen, but from a failure of manly courage. The boy realises that what has always kept Tiger from the kill is not his social class or the want of a good horse, but an "ambivalence in the heart": "His passion for the hunt is not complete enough for him to risk everything as Tolland and the others do" (153). In Lord Harbringdon's offer to buy Kabara from Alsop at a price that "Tiger will not be able to match" (153–4), there is, though, an element of class exclusion, albeit one that is aligned with the critique of his masculinity.

The breaking in *The Tivington Nott* is an ethically ambivalent moment, for it is preceded by the boy's earlier failure to call the hunters to the stag during the unravelling of the change. The novel has in effect two climaxes: the first, in which the boy sees the stag in its final moments and does not warn the hunters, and his triumphant ride which allows him to be in at the kill with the most seasoned hunters. These two conflicting episodes make

---

22 Judkins, "The Game of the Courtly Hunt", 80, 84.
23 Goss, *Memories*, 40.

the conclusion to the novel ambivalent in terms of the contemporary concerns of ecocriticism, to which I now turn.

The Ecological Sublime

The idea of wilderness is central to Miller's narrative of the young labourer's accession to manhood, which takes place in what is now the Exmoor National Park, and he used topographical maps to plot the route accurately. Yet, in current debates in the field of ecocriticism, narratives that utilise the idea of wilderness seem inevitably to reinforce either the triumph of the human (Western male) subject over nature, or the fundamental separation of the human from nature. The hunters pursue the Haddon Stag through the deeply wooded valley of the Exe on to the uplands of Exmoor before finally pursuing it down again into the uninhabited valleys of what is now the national park. They begin their climb where the land becomes too steep for the plough (100), and the point that marks the boy's final liberation from the Tiger corresponds with his arrival on the summit of Exmoor, from which he has a commanding view across the Bristol Channel to Wales and the Atlantic:

> Out on the open upland, the landscape dropping away from us in gentle undulations, falling, then rising and falling again as far as the eye can see . . . Way past the high distant cairn on Dunkery Beacon, even beyond the moor and across the Bristol Channel, I can make out the coast of Wales. And beyond that, a final backdrop, the remote dark shapes of the Black Mountains of Glamorgan, grey shadows through this summer haze, mysterious and foreign. (127–8)

To pursue the stag, the elite hunters now drop down into the uninhabited valleys: "Anything could be hidden there . . . There are no signs of cultivation . . . Steep-sided, here, narrow, rough sheep country, never broken by the plough" (130). Finally, at the kill, the last of the leading hunters drop down into a narrow valley into which pour cataracts from the recent storm: "We dive full-throttle into this steep, shaded tunnel; the slope drops away abruptly on my left as we go in, a practically vertical wall falling hundreds of feet through the scrub and loose rocks to the white water of the torrent far below us in the bed of the dark combe" (139). These landscapes offer the boy the classic experience of sublimity: the overwhelming sense of terror that comes either in the "dynamic" form of corporeal fear or the "mathematical" form of the imagination's failure to comprehend infinitude.

Edmund Burke, in *A Philosophical Enquiry into the Origin of Our Ideas of the Sublime and Beautiful*, describes the sublime in terms of natural imagery: "it comes upon us in the gloomy forest, in the howling wilderness, in the form of the lion, the tiger, the panther, or rhinoceros".[24] At such moments, according to Kant in *The Critique of Judgement*, we "measure ourselves against the apparent almightiness of nature":

> Bold overhanging, and, as it were, threatening rocks, thunderclouds piled up the vault of heaven, borne along with flashes and peals, volcanoes in all their violence of destruction,

---

24   Edmund Burke, *A Philosophical Enquiry into the Origin of Our Ideas of the Sublime and Beautiful* (1795), quoted in Christopher Hitt, "Toward an Ecological Sublime", *New Literary History* 30, no. 3 Ecocriticism (Summer, 1999): 605.

hurricanes leaving desolation in their track, the boundless ocean rising with rebellious force, the high waterfall of some mighty river, and the like, make our power of resistance of trifling moment in comparison with their might.[25]

In many aspects of recent humanities research, the aesthetics of the sublime has been at the centre of critiques of asymmetrical power relations: between human and nature, self and other, male and female, conqueror and oppressed. Laura Doyle and Sara Suleri point to the relationship between sublime aesthetics and British imperialism;[26] feminists like Bonnie Mann argue that the sublime has been a site for Euro-masculine self-constitution;[27] while in a recent essay, "The Trouble With Wilderness", William Cronon offers a critique of the contemporary inclination to idealise nature – as expressed in the gazetting of national parks like Exmoor – arguing that the concept of the sublime wilderness reinscribes the idea of nature's otherness, or the separation between the human and the nonhuman realms.[28] *The Tivington Nott* has much to say about all of these issues, which remain important in many of Miller's subsequent novels. Is its male protagonist's coming of age achieved through the kinds of asymmetrical power relations associated with the conventional aesthetics of the sublime?

In his essay, "Toward an Ecological Sublime", Christopher Hitt engages with Cronon's concerns, arguing not only that the sublime is not "*fundamentally* or *intrinsically* maleficent", but that it offers an important opportunity for us to define a more responsible perspective on our relationship with the natural environment. He calls this "the ecological sublime".[29] I want to argue that Miller's writing about nature and animals in *The Tivington Nott*, and especially the relation between his young protagonist and nature and animals, anticipates this movement toward an ecological sublime. This is especially apparent in the *temporalisation* of that relation, which finds its clearest expression in the novel's dual climax: one moment in which the protagonist is ceremonially blooded for his triumphant pursuit of the stag, and another, earlier moment in which, silently and alone with the animal, he declines to participate in its slaughter.

Hitt's starting point is to return to the contradictory nature of the sublime experience as it is described by Burke and Kant: it is both humbling *and* ennobling; it involves both the subjection of the human to nature, *and* the eventual triumph of the human over nature by the apotheosis of reason. Although it appears that Kant, in particular, is describing the *simultaneous* experience of these contradictions, Hitt observes that the sublime is in fact a diachronic experience rather than an instantaneous reaction: it is, for Kant, a "movement of the mind". The rediscovery of this temporal structure allows Hitt to separate those elements of the sublime that might be consistent with a modern ecological perspective, such as the experience of humility, from those that are not, such as the reassertion of human

---

25 Immanuel Kant, *The Critique of Judgement* (1790), quoted in Hitt, "Toward an Ecological Sublime", 605.
26 Laura Doyle, "The Racial Sublime", in *Romanticism, Race and Imperial Culture, 1780–1834*, eds Alan Richardson and Sonia Hofkosh (Bloomington: Indiana University Press, 1996); Sara Suleri, *The Rhetoric of English India* (Chicago: Chicago University Press, 1992).
27 Bonnie Mann, *Women's Liberation and the Sublime: Feminism, Postmodernism, Environment* (Oxford Scholarship Online: Oxford University Press, 2006).
28 William Cronon, "The Trouble with Wilderness; or, Getting Back to the Wrong Nature", in *Uncommon Ground: Rethinking the Human Place in Nature*, ed. William Cronon (New York: Norton, 1995).
29 Hitt, "Toward an Ecological Sublime", 605, 607.

rationality over and above nature. As a temporal sequence, this sublime "movement of the mind" is divided into three phases: first, a normal, pre-sublime stage in which "the mind is in a determinate relation to the object"; second, a "rupture in which a disequilibrium between mind and object" occurs; and a third stage in which equilibrium is restored. This third stage is achieved by "the triumphant emergence of reason, revealing to us, finally, 'our pre-eminence over nature' ". As Hitt puts it, "humility is thus transformed into self-apotheosis, validating the individual's dominion over the nonhuman world". Ideally, then, to begin to understand an "ecological sublime", we would need to attend to this temporal movement of mind, focusing on the second stage of humility before nature and resisting or relinquishing the third stage, in which rationality and human subjectivity are separated from and placed in triumph above nature.[30]

In the final phase of his argument, Hitt turns to the problems of language and representation that have been of central concern to ecocriticism in the United States. He argues that if the second phase of the Kantian sublime constitutes a rupture between the subject and object, a movement that leaves nature "outside the domain of mind" in a way that does not subject it to triumphal recuperation by reason and the *logos*, then we appear to be approaching a category that has been anathema to structuralist and poststructuralist theories of language: that is, "the notion that an unmediated experience might be possible".[31] In some of the most influential works of modern ecocriticism, including Lawrence Buell's *The Environmental Imagination*,[32] Hitt finds a reluctance to confront theoretical problems concerning the linguistic depiction of nature, and even a privileging of "realism", a desire for modes of description that could bring us closer to the "facticity" of the "thing itself". The ecological sublime would involve not avoiding but embracing "critical theories that focus on the instability, indeterminacy, and opacity of language".[33] Such theories provide a better way of understanding the second stage of the Kantian sublime as a confrontation with the "wholly other", with an object world that precedes and continues to stand outside the human, and which resists recuperation by *logos*, or reason. In the ecological sublime, the third phase, in which the subject transcends nature through reason, would be replaced by the subject's transcendence of reason itself. For the literary critic, for the *eco*critic, this would involve not a nostalgia for mimesis, for a correspondence between words and things, but a *transcendence* of the word. At such moments we experience "a 'collapse' of the 'linguistic apparatus' ".[34]

Is there evidence of the ecological sublime in *The Tivington Nott*? In fact, its relinquishment of mastery over nature is anticipated early in the novel when the boy recounts his discovery of the soiling pit of the Tivington nott, a rare, mature male red deer that has failed to grow antlers. In this episode, Miller first establishes his own version of the sublime, which involves a relinquishment of the third phase of the classic three-stage movement of mind: that is to say, the boy experiences the rupture of human subjectivity that is characteristic of the second stage but does not move on to the third stage, physically backing away from the stag, acknowledging his own fear and vulnerability as an entirely appropriate response, and leaving the stag a master of its own domain. Its territory is to the

---

30 Hitt, "Toward an Ecological Sublime", 607–9.
31 Hitt, "Toward an Ecological Sublime", 613–4.
32 Lawrence Buell, *The Environmental Imagination: Thoreau, Nature Writing, and the Formation of American Culture* (Cambridge, Mass.: Harvard University Press, 1995).
33 Hitt, "Toward an Ecological Sublime", 617.
34 Hitt, "Toward an Ecological Sublime", 616.

west of the Tiger's farm at Lydeard St Lawrence, in the remote valleys at the headwaters of the River Barle, a tributary of the Exe (18). It is a holiday for the Bampton Fair, and the boy has gone walking on the moor and in the surrounding woodlands, "making the most of my opportunity for penetrating the wilderness" (21). Forcing his way into a hidden glade under a dark canopy of larches, he is confronted by the nott:

> the nott barks a sudden warning. I stop dead in my tracks. My heart thumping. I don't know what it is and can see nothing at first.
>
> Then, stationary in the dark jumble of shadows, I see him. The wide-set, slanting eyes of a satyr. Wild and aggressive. Staring directly into mine. Neither of us moving. His thick neck-hair shaggy and standing out, knotted and sopping, with black mud cascading from his flanks. Something mad and savage rising from the wallow to confront me.
>
> Staring at him it takes me seconds to work out that I am looking at a red stag and not at something from rumour and fear. (22)

In such passages, Miller succeeds in conveying the boy's absorption in and by the forest, a place that confounds his initial impressions, and which he senses in a pre-linguistic way through sound and smell: "As we step forward, entering the dim glade, there's a whiff of mint hanging in the still air. He has moved out silently ahead of us, crushing the wild herb that grows on the edge of the stream" (19). The boy knows that the stag may kill him and he accepts his fear:

> Who knows what he might do? He looks to me to be capable of anything. A sudden extreme.
>
> I'm not hanging around to find out.
>
> I ease my weight onto my toes and very slowly, taking extreme care to make no sudden movement, I make ready to start backing off. The instant I tense up he barks again. I freeze. It is a sharp, urgent warning. A mad shout in the forest. And a wave of fear goes through me. As if in slow motion I see him gathering himself. Then he leaps away to one side and is gone.
>
> I take hold of a branch, steadying myself, listening . . .
>
> The woods are silent again and still. Only his smell remains. (23–4)

As the boy retreats from the encounter, he hears ahead of him the sounds of the human world, the classic sounds, in fact, of the English pastoral – "the sound of a clocktower bell from a village somewhere" (24) – but behind him, in the woods, there is a warning from the stag, a voice that is not of that human world:

> Striking down the stream at a good pace. And then from behind me there comes the sudden roaring challenge of an old stag assured and firm in his rut. The whole darkening combe around me filling and echoing with his deep bellowing, low, archaic and malicious towards men and hounds and horses, tailing off into a bolking and rattling in his throat. (24–5)

The boy's encounter with the nott has all the hallmarks of the sublime: the dynamic confrontation with a wild animal, a pre-linguistic communication through sight and sound and smell, an experience of life-threatening power and fear. Unlike the hunters, the boy is content to retreat, to relinquish human authority over nature. This is expressed by his decision not to reveal the location of the soiling pit to the locals, who wish to kill the nott out of concern that it may breed, and so produce offspring without the prized antlers: "I'm not about to tell them where he is . . . keeping the whereabouts of the Tivington nott a secret would burn a hole in their brains . . . You couldn't trust them with the information" (20). In this early encounter, then, Miller refuses that compensatory moment of egotistical transcendence, with its movement towards mastery over death. Instead, as Brigid Rooney puts it in her account of the ecological sublime, "relinquishment of self and acceptance of difference enable another kind of transcendence: the transcendence of ego".[35]

In this early encounter with the nott, the boy has been able to determine the temporal structure of his experience of the sublime, literally backing away from the reassertion of ego. In the hunt itself, however, his encounter with nature is embedded in a narrative structure – a social ritual – designed to culminate in that third phase. How does Miller deal with this culmination of the sublime? What kind of apotheosis of the self in relation to nature does the boy experience at his coming of age? As we have seen, medieval manuals like *The Master of Game* recognise a phase of the ritual when, through its ruses such as "foiling", "beating down", and "leaping", the hart may, whether temporarily or permanently, evade the hunters and their dogs. In other words, there is a temporality in the ritual that aligns with the temporality of the sublime. In light of Hitt's definition of the ecological sublime as a moment when the categories of human knowledge "collapse", these ancient terms for the hart's ruses are interesting and suggestive, as if the very language of the hunt acknowledges that its practices may be "foiled" or evaded altogether by a creature whose "ruses" it cannot fathom. And although the boy is present at the death and breaking of the hart, it is during an earlier moment, when the hart has outwitted the hunters, and the lymerer is brought in to "unravel the change", that the boy encounters the animal in its own domain:

> Tolland checks the soft bank for the deer's slot, determining its direction where it entered the water . . . and within minutes it's clear we've lost him . . . A moment of confusion, loss of direction, then Perry comes crashing down the combe through a pathless scrub ahead of us, driving stragglers in front of him and calling the staunch and seasoned hounds to him by name. Back they go, falling over each other as their master rides through them, chased by his voice and his whip, back to the point where the deer entered the water. Perry ignores us, maybe even not seeing us, and almost pushes Tolland off the bank and in to the water as he passes, working his hounds feverishly, as if he knows the stag's ruse and must unravel it within seconds or forfeit the chance forever. (147)

It is the crisis of the unravelling, and what happens next is of the utmost significance. Lord Harbringdon, the most senior figure in the social hierarchy, orders the boy to "stand": "I suppose it's an order, so I pull up. This is my post. Watch and wait. Report enemy movements. All round us a scrubby wilderness, down to the bank and overhanging the rushing water" (148).

At this point, under strict instructions to stand, the boy nonetheless dismounts, loosening Kabara's harness. It is the first time the boy has been out of the saddle in many hours, and he immediately experiences two sensations: a sense of weakness in his own legs and

---

35 Brigid Rooney, "Pathological Geomorphology and the Ecological Sublime: Andrew McGahan's *Wonders of a Godless World*", *Southerly* 72, no. 3 (2012): 72.

Unravelling the Change: *The Tivington Nott* and *Watching the Climbers on the Mountain*

an instinctive knowledge that his mount would like to roll in the sand. It is at this very moment, when the bonds of the boy's own obligations to the social world are at once acknowledged and partially relinquished, that the stag appears in the very act of performing one of its ruses, the foiling down:

> We're making our way along the path when he [Kabara] is alerted to something. He stiffens and snorts a quick breath out of his wide nostrils, gazing fixedly toward a great mat of interwoven willow fronds and rubbish, which is heaving slowly upward out of the water about ten yards in front of us. We stand and watch. Pushing up through this great sodden pad, the festooned antlers of the stag emerge. Slowly and carefully he climbs out of the pool, draped with trailing lines of weed and rubbish, garbed like a circus creature for some special performance, the water cascading from his sleeked coat. There is a blindness of fatigue about him, for he doesn't see us, sees *none* of the usual warning signs of danger, no longer sensitive to the forest about him, but searching single-mindedly for his life out of this day. I call to him softly; "Hey, stag", and he falters but doesn't look round. The wilderness calling his name.
>
> I should alert the hunt, tighten my girth, leap on to Kabara's back and let rip with that cry that will bring Perry and his fierce dogs scorching down here in a hungry pack within seconds.
>
> What then, stag? . . .
>
> I am a hunter on station. Shall I call them?
>
> With infinite care and daintiness he is sneaking through the tangle of scrub, his massive antlers a burden, laid back along his shoulders, his black nose pointing forward up the hill towards the moor. He is silent except for his breathing; which is a series of short, repeated sharp exhalations of breath, distinctly audible above the rushing water. Climbing step by step through the tangle towards the clearer going of the larch plantation, his body dark and hollowed at the flanks – he is going away.
>
> He's giving them the slip. (148–9)

At this moment we can see why Miller has not given his boy a name: he stands outside the social order, or at least at some point on its edge where phenomena take place to which he has become sensitive, but for which there are no words. At first, as in his earlier encounter with the nott, the boy can scarcely believe his eyes as the dynamic experience of the sublime ruptures human understanding. There are several kinds of language and communion in play in this passage. The boy is narrating his account of the event in words, but his horse is also communicating by his snorts and quick breath, and the boy understands him. The stag is literally part of the wilderness, part of the object world, but it is also a sentient creature, practising its "ruses", and perhaps with a language of its own that is different to that of the boy or the horse. The boy speaks to the stag, using human language, "Hey, stag", but the stag does not hear him: it is listening to the wilderness. The boy knows that he should be speaking in another language altogether, the language of the hunt, but instead of calling the lymerer he asks the stag, again using human language, what the consequences of that would be for the stag. The stag does not answer, but the boy knows the answer anyway. The boy is part of the human world of the hunt. He is "on station". He is obligated to "call them", but he declines. He listens instead to the language of the stag, its "repeated sharp exhalations of breath", not understanding fully, but perhaps understanding enough. At least for this moment, outside of language, outside of time, outside the ritual of the hunt, "He's giving them the slip." And the pronoun "he" is of course ambiguous, referring to both the stag and the boy. Although the hunt culminates in the killing of the stag, Miller has opened a space for a different kind of encounter with nature, in which the boy establishes a relation to the stag on his own terms, independently of the ritual of the hunt. As Rooney argues in her discussion of such moments, "In the process perhaps, a space is opened for . . . the decentering of humanity, suggesting that this new transcendence must also entail a return of the human. Humanity is restored to itself through relinquishment."[36]

In so far as *The Tivington Nott* is a parable about coming of age, and in so far as it can be read as a fictionalised autobiography, the space within the ritual of the hunt in which the boy's life touches that of the wild stag is a space of becoming, a space in which he begins to discover his authentic being. Through his triumph in the hunt, the boy, like the stag, has "given the slip" to the closed community of the Exmoor villages. In this autobiographical sense, the boy's view from Dunkery Beacon out to the Bristol Channel and beyond to the distant Atlantic foreshadows Miller's own emigration to Australia, where the novel was written: "We look for a moment longer in to the darkening valley. Across the other side are the Quantock Hills . . . For Kabara's sake I regret nothing, but I wonder what it is that I am making my own way towards" (154).

Northern Gothic: *Watching the Climbers on the Mountain*

In the closing pages of *The Tivington Nott*, when the boy is finally done with the ritual of the hunt and is liberated from the enclosed valleys on to the high country of Exmoor, the unbounded horizon is a harbinger of his future life, an objective correlative of his hopes and aspirations. It is to be a recurring image in Miller's mature novels. It derives from one of John Berger's essays in *About Looking*:

> there is a close parallel between pictorial representations of space and the ways in which stories are told. The novel, as Lukács pointed out in *Theory of the Novel*, was born of a yearning for what now lay beyond the horizon: it was the art form of a sense of homelessness".[37]

While Miller was working in Somerset in the early 1950s, an Australian living at Lydeard St Lawrence – the model for Alsop in *The Tivington Nott* – had shown him a collection of "richly suggestive" black and white photographs of the Australian outback, most likely, as he was to learn many years later, the work of Sidney Nolan.[38] The photograph he remembers most clearly was of stockmen lounging on the veranda of a cattle station: "The stockmen and the veranda are in black silhouette against the luminous sky . . . [They] seem to be watching the horizon, which is an unhindered line. The caption . . . said: 'You can ride for months here and never strike a fence.' "[39] Inspired by Nolan's image of the outback, Miller planned his escape from the austerity of postwar Britain by emigration to a new country that he was coming to see in near-mythical terms. In *The Ancestor Game*,

---

36 Rooney, "Pathological Geomorphology", 74.
37 John Berger, "Seker Ahmet and the Forest", in *About Looking* (1980; London: Vintage, 1991), 83.
38 Miller, "The Mask of Fiction", 38–9.
39 Miller, "My First Love", 3.

the young Lang Tzu, who is establishing the grounds of his own freedom by severing his ties with his ancestors, is advised to "Long for something you can't name ... and call it Australia. A thing will come into being ... A land imagined and dreamed, not an actual place."[40]

Miller arrived in Sydney in 1952 at the age of sixteen aboard the P&O liner *Arcadia*. He was travelling in a group of under-age boys with a supervisor who, it was understood, would help them to find work and remain responsible for them until they turned eighteen, but as soon as he disembarked, Miller hitchhiked north up the Pacific Highway in search of Nolan's outback. For the next six years he would work in a variety of rural jobs, initially on a dairy farm at Gympie in southeast Queensland, then as a stockman at Goathlands Station, south of the Central Highlands town of Springsure. The owner of Goathlands, Reg Wells, was a reader with a good library, and he encouraged Miller to read and discuss books. In 1954, after two years at Goathlands, Miller travelled further north to Rockhampton, then by train to Longreach and on to Cloncurry in the Gulf of Carpentaria, where Wells had found work for him as a ringer on the remote Augustus Downs cattle station.[41] Goathlands Station provided the setting for *Watching the Climbers on the Mountain*.

As we have seen, *The Tivington Nott* and *Watching the Climbers on the Mountain* were originally conceived as a single work that would present a fictional account of his time in Exmoor, his emigration to Australia, and his years in the bush from 1952 until his move to Melbourne in 1958. Despite having received a positive reader's report for the manuscript of *The Tivington Nott*, Hilary McPhee rejected it on the grounds of its non-Australian subject matter, and Miller's agent at the time, Caroline Lurie, agreed, telling him that he would never secure an Australian publisher. In protest, Miller wrote *Watching the Climbers on the Mountain* as a pastiche of the Australian outback romance. It was conceived as a "knock off" with distinctively Australian content in the style of a pastoral romance, hence the odd stylistic register, which makes it unlike any of Miller's other novels. He recalls,

> I wanted to demonstrate that I could write a commercial novel in one hit. In fact *Watching the Climbers on the Mountain* was written quickly in one draft. Penny Hueston, who edited it for Pan Macmillan, found that claim difficult to believe. But it was nevertheless true.

It is for this reason that for many years Miller declined requests from Allen & Unwin to republish it.[42]

To signal his parodic intention, Miller left a series of clues on the opening page of the novel. Each paragraph begins as a thinly disguised copy of the opening page of Carson McCullers' novel, *Reflections in a Golden Eye* (1941):[43]

> A small Queensland cattle station during the height of summer is a place where events that are quite out of the ordinary may sometimes occur. There is, at that time of the year in such places, an enforced dislocation of the regular rhythms of daily life. The sense of

---

40   Alex Miller, *The Ancestor Game* (Ringwood, Vic.: Penguin, 1992), 259.
41   Alex Miller, "Once Upon a Life", *The Observer Magazine*, 26 September 2010, 12–13.
42   Alex Miller to Robert Dixon, 25 November 2013, and 10 March 2014. *Watching the Climbers on the Mountain* was eventually reprinted with a new preface in 2008.
43   McCullers' novel was made into a movie, directed by John Huston and starring Elizabeth Taylor and Marlon Brando, in 1967.

isolation deepens with the coming of the season of storms and the intensification of the heat.[44]

An army post in peacetime is a dull place. Things happen, but then they happen over and over again. The general plan of a fort in itself adds to the monotony . . . all is designed according to a certain rigid pattern. But perhaps the dullness of a post is caused most of all by insularity and by a surfeit of leisure and safety . . . At the same time things do occasionally happen on an army post that are not likely to re-occur.[45]

There is a cattle station in the Central Highlands of Queensland where a few years ago an event took place which shocked the local community and for which there seemed at the time to be no rational explanation. The people involved in this tragedy were a young stockman, the owner/manager of the station and his wife, together with their two children, a boy aged eleven and a girl aged thirteen. (9)

There is a fort in the South where a few years ago a murder was committed. The participants of this tragedy were: two officers, a soldier, two women, a Filipino, and a horse.[46]

Miller's clues went undetected for many years until he received a letter from Marie Davidson, the widow of the novelist Frank Dalby Davidson, pointing out her discovery, and affirming her late husband's belief that "all artists, including himself", were "liars and thieves".[47]

The relationship between *Watching the Climbers on the Mountain* and McCullers' Southern Gothic tale goes some way toward explaining the style and mood of Miller's novel, which one reviewer described as having "the pressure-cooker air of a Louisiana potboiler with Queensland stockmen replacing the southern cotton pickers".[48] Although Miller has said that beyond the first page any other similarities between the two texts would be "coincidental", there are a number of parallels. McCullers' plot is generated by the four-way relationship between Captain Penderton, a repressed homosexual, his lubricious wife, ironically named Leonora, and her two admirers, Major Langdon, who is currently her lover, and Private Ellgee Williams. Williams is Leonora's stalker, creeping into their home at night to crouch beside her bed while she sleeps, but he is also stalked, in turn, by Penderton, who employs him as a gardener and watches him obsessively from afar. In Miller's novel, this four-way relationship is converted into the triangle of the pastoralist Ward Rankin, who is also a repressed homosexual, his young wife Ida, and the "beautiful" young English stockman, Robert Crofts, whose role as Ida's lover and the object of Ward's homosexual desire combines the roles of Major Langdon and Private Williams. The additional tensions in McCullers' novel associated with Major Langdon's wife, Alison, and her homosexual housekeeper, Anacleto, are displaced in Miller's plot on to the incestuous re-

---

44 Alex Miller, *Watching the Climbers on the Mountain* (Sydney: Pan, 1988), 9. All subsequent references are to this edition and appear in parentheses in the text.
45 Carson McCullers, *Reflections in a Golden Eye* (1941; London: Cresset, 1942), 7.
46 McCullers, *Reflections*, 7.
47 Alex Miller to Robert Dixon, 10 March 2014. The letter from Marie Davidson has not survived.
48 Greg Flynn, "Mills and Boon Meets the Colonial Potboiler", review of Alex Miller, *Watching the Climbers on the Mountain*, *The Weekend Australian*, 19–20 November 1988, 9.

lationship between the Rankin children Janet, who tries to seduce Crofts, and her jealous brother Alastair.

The two novels share a number of themes, including repressed homosexuality, voyeurism and incest, though in Miller's climax, Ward Rankin's suicide is substituted for Penderton's murder-suicide, in which he shoots Williams in his wife's bedroom before turning the gun on himself, not out of love for his wife, but out of despair that Williams is attracted to Leonora. Some of the episodes in *Reflections in a Golden Eye* also provide the basis for events in *Watching the Climbers on the Mountain*, including Williams' work around the base while he is watched by Penderton, Penderton's abuse of Leonora's horse, which is rescued by Williams, and Williams' nude sunbathing on a rock in the woods. Both novels are intensely aware of voyeurism or scopophilia as symptoms of repressed desire, and in both the lines of sight are mapped on to the gun culture that is common to both societies: the "watching" in the title of Miller's novel frequently takes place through the telescopic sights of a high-powered rifle.

Ward Rankin's sexual ambiguity is modelled closely on Penderton's. Rankin "had found satisfaction in neither of the two fundamental areas of life – sex and the fulfilment of dreams. And these failures were connected. The most promising relationship of his youth – a deep love for his English master at school . . . had remained unconsummated" (19). Penderton also has "a sad penchant for becoming enamoured of his wife's lovers": "He stood in a somewhat curious relation to the three fundaments of existence – life itself, sex, and death. Sexually the Captain obtained within himself a delicate balance between the male and female elements, with the susceptibilities of both the sexes and the active powers of neither".[49] The complex topographies of Rankin's and Penderton's desires are expressed in similar domestic arrangements, each house having its separate bedrooms, Leonora's and Ida's with windows that open on to the surrounding district, and Rankin and Penderton occupying unhealthily enclosed studies, where they drink to excess. Private Williams' fights with his fellow soldiers, an expression of his frustrated desire for Leonora and his victimisation by Penderton, are echoed in the boxing match at Springtown in *Watching the Climbers on the Mountain*, in which Rankin interacts with Crofts by proxy, with the same mixture of desire and repulsion.

Although *Watching the Climbers on the Mountain* began as a pastiche of McCullers' Southern Gothic novel, and although Miller's rapid composition was clearly driven by the generic considerations of "commercial" fiction, within this form we can recognise his early exploration of many of the themes and situations that would become characteristic of his mature literary fiction, beginning with his third novel, *The Ancestor Game*, in 1992. Despite McCullers' template, *Watching the Climbers on the Mountain* also has obvious structural and thematic similarities with *The Tivington Nott*. If the Exmoor novel shows the capacity of the outsider to transform a closed community, this impact is even greater in the Central Queensland novel, where the effects of the young English stockman on the Rankin family are profound: as the cover blurb has it, "his arrival on the station changes their lives forever".

At the beginning of the novel, the Rankin family is at a point where their internal tensions have become fissile, and Crofts' arrival is a catalyst for their inevitable disintegration. The arrival of the outsider in an enclosed community is a staple of the American western, a genre to which McCullers' Southern Gothic and Miller's Northern Gothic are

---

49   McCullers, *Reflections*, 15, 14.

both indebted. At fifty-six, Rankin is a frustrated and unfulfilled man who inherited the responsibility for the remote cattle station against his wishes. Educated at boarding school and with a taste for European travel, he returned reluctantly to take over the management of the station after the death of his father. Rather than choosing the land, he has become a farmer by default, staying on to look after his aged and semi-invalid mother, and then "putting off his plans one year after another" (11). Shortly before his mother's death he had married the eighteen-year-old Ida Sturgis, a girl from the neighbouring station. In Ida's family background, Miller draws on his own experience at Araluen near Goulburn, where he owned a farm in the early 1970s, and makes the first reference to the Cullin-la-Ringo massacre:

> Her great-grandparents had trekked their belongings, their cattle and their horses almost two thousand kilometres from the Goulburn district of New South Wales to settle on the Nogoa River in 1862, less than a year after the local Aborigines had been exterminated by the settlers in retribution for the massacre of the Wills family at Cullin-la-Ringo. (20)

Undeveloped here in 1988, the issue of frontier violence will return in the Central Queensland novels: 1862 is the year that the Bigges complete their overland journey to the Ranna Valley in *Journey to the Stone Country*, while the Cullin-la-Ringo massacre is the subject of *Landscape of Farewell*.

The brittleness of the Rankins' marriage, established through the clichés of romantic fiction, is the pretext for Ida's affair with Robert Crofts: "Love had never really come into it for either of them . . . At the deepest level of her being Ida Rankin knew that she was not complete" (21, 25). The difference in age between them, and their lack of deep feeling for each other, is exacerbated by Rankin's latent homosexuality. Crofts' arrival, and his attractiveness to both Rankin and Ida, triggers the tensions between them, which are expressed by the different locations with which they are associated, and to which they retreat from each other: Ward to his windowless study in the centre of the house, and Ida to the freedom of the bush, especially the white sandstone peak of Mt Mooloolong, whose summit she once climbed as a girl. Ward's enclosed study and its homosocial companionship anticipate Captain Anderson's cabin and map room, which he shares with Georges Elder in *Conditions of Faith*, while Ida's ascent of Mount Mooloolong with Crofts foreshadows Max Otto and Dougald Gnapun's ascent of the Expedition Range in *Landscape of Farewell*.

While the scenes associated with Rankin come to have an increasingly gothic quality as he descends into alcoholism and paranoia, Miller's account of the developing relationship between Crofts and Ida Rankin follows the conventions of the pastoral romance, and exploits his memorable descriptions of the natural environment. Their relationship is consummated in her bedroom during a violent storm and is compared to the moment in her childhood when she climbed Mt Mooloolong: "It was the summit of Mt Mooloolong all over again . . . There was only one real option and she was going to take it. She smiled tightly to herself as she thought, 'This is my jumping-off point' " (141). In an optical figure that will become much more sophisticated in the subsequent novels, Ida has her bedroom mirror set up so that from inside the room in which she is trapped she can see outside to Mt Mooloolong. Steven Muir in *The Ancestor Game*, Annabelle Beck in *Journey to the Stone Country*, and Max Otto in *Landscape of Farewell* all begin to examine their lives critically when they look at their reflection in a mirror.

Ida's window introduces another motif that will also appear in the later novels, and which Miller shares with his friend, the painter Rick Amor: the various versions of the bridge or portal between different times and places, or different stages of becoming. While Rankin's study is windowless, Ida's bedroom window is a portal to the place that she will share with Crofts in the second phase of their life's journey together. The landscape version of this portal is the vast crevasse that leads, after a difficult climb, to the other world of Mt Mooloolong:

> Only when he caught up with her at the very base of this cliff did he see a cleft no more than a metre wide, worn down through the pure sandstone by the eroding action of water... The hole was at least five metres across at the neck, and below the neck it widened, forming a great hollow bowl fifteen to twenty metres deep in the pure rock. Crofts stood on the edge and looked down into the cool dark interior... When he looked up he saw that Ida was on her hands and knees crawling out into the narrow groin of smooth stone overhanging the hole, the only access to the cleft beyond. He watched her. If she were to slip the rock would offer no hold. (220)

The image of a geological portal anticipates the figure of the *mise-en-abyme* that recurs in Miller's mature novels, from the hole in the wall of the boy's bedroom at Handycross farm in *The Tivington Nott*, to the secret passageway to China at Coppin Grove in *The Ancestor Game*, through which Victoria Feng's father passes between worlds, to the cracks in the earth at Burranbah Coal in *Journey to the Stone Country*, and the ravine on the Nebo River in *Landscape of Farewell*, where Max Otto undergoes his terrible ritual of atonement.

When he was writing the manuscript of "Jimmy Diamond" in Melbourne in the mid-1980s, Miller had hoped that it would capture in fictional form something of his journeying, both culturally and personally, from London to Exmoor, and then from England to Sydney, and on to Central Queensland and the Gulf Country. Although the circumstances of their publication meant that *The Tivington Nott* and *Watching the Climbers on the Mountain* became separate and very different kinds of novels, in 1995 Miller wrote a beautifully structured essay for the Melbourne *Age*, titled "My First Love", in which he gives some sense of this series of momentous cross-cultural journeys. Ironically, although Exmoor had seemed like a long-established and very traditional world when he arrived there in 1951, when he and his wife Stephanie returned in the early 1990s that world as he had known it no longer existed:

> Several years after I'd written the novel I revisited Exmoor for the first time since I was a boy. It was lucky I hadn't gone back before I'd written the novel. There was nothing left. Thirty years of change had erased it all. Where Tiger's farmhouse had been – an old stone building squatting in the groin of a lane – there was a self-service petrol station on a motorway. And they were all dead, the people I'd written about.

The lost world of Exmoor in the 1950s is juxtaposed to the world Miller found in the Gulf of Carpentaria, where he had gone in search of Nolan's outback, which is personified by the Aboriginal stockmen:

> When I reached the cattle station on the Leichhardt River in the Gulf of Carpentaria, I found myself surrounded by Sidney Nolan's uneventful horizon line: the artist's perfect

line that had lured me all the way from Exmoor. The stockmen were all Maigudung clansmen, all 35 of them, all mounted, all with long black hair and beards and all with skin that was shining in the sun as if they had oiled themselves in preparation for my reception. They rode up to me out of a cloud of red dust and stared at me in silence; calm and relaxed and curious and arrogant in their possession of the situation. One of them, who later became my first Australian friend, challenged me to reveal myself.

"If you're really English, where's your English saddle?" But I wasn't really English. It was more complicated than that.

Poignantly, both of these apparently established worlds into which Miller arrived as a young stranger were now vanishing into the realm of lost time:

He told me later, glancing at Nolan's horizon as he did so, that his ancestors had been living on this stretch of country for ever. I'd arrived just as the end of his forever was beginning. Within a couple of years of my arrival, the equal pay judgement had given the lessees the excuse to exile Frank and the rest of the Maigudung from their land. It was the elaboration of one of those negotiated changes that strangers bring among a settled people, and which the settled people have no power to resist . . .

Two years later I left. Everyone left. The thing changed. Frank's forever had come to an end.[50]

It is precisely this sense of being caught up in the process of historical change, the experience of being-in-time whose most visible expression is the disappearance of established worlds and the people who inhabit them, that I will argue is the central preoccupation of Miller's novels: it is what I have called "the ruin of time".

---

50   Quotations from Miller, "My First Love", 3–4.

2
Multiple Modernities: *The Ancestor Game*

Alex Miller's third novel, *The Ancestor Game* (1992), brought him national and international recognition. In 1993, it won the Miles Franklin Literary Award, the Commonwealth Writers' Prize and the Barbara Ramsden Award, and he was feted at literary events in Australia, Canada, the United States and the United Kingdom, where he was granted a private audience with the Queen.[1] He began writing it in the mid-1980s as a way of coming to terms with the suicide of a friend. After moving back to Melbourne from Paris in 1975, he had taught humanities at Brunswick Technical School, where he formed a close friendship with one of the art teachers, Allan O'Hoy, who was also a painter, art collector and dealer. For some years, O'Hoy had been spiralling into alcoholism and depression, and in 1982 Miller received from him a letter announcing, "by the time you read this letter I will be dead". O'Hoy had shot himself. His family had been in Melbourne since 1848 and had long since married into families of Irish and Scots descent, yet Miller believes that one of the factors contributing to his friend's depression and his failure to achieve recognition as an artist was "the inability of Australians generally at that time to view the work of an ethnic Chinese as representative of their culture".[2]

Although Miller began the new book by writing about friendship, it also became a meditation on the condition of migrancy, and a timely recognition of the contribution made by generations of Chinese migrants to Australian culture. As he digested the biographical sources of his friend's life, they became the vehicle for themes that touched upon his own life, and on the wider society: "The novel turns on images of refugees and colonists. It explores the fact that humankind is a migrant species and it offers the alternative view that the displaced are not victims but are the ironic progenitors of the cultural process".[3] This is to see the condition of exile "as opportunity, rather than as cultural deprivation".[4]

By 1987, Miller realised that he would have to go to China to do research and to gather personal impressions. The history of the Chinese diaspora in Australia was only then coming to be widely known. Three influential books soon to appear were Alison Broinowski's

---

1 For a witty and irreverent account of that meeting, see Alex Miller, "Inside Buckingham Palace", *Brick: A Journal of Reviews* 48 (1994): 35–8.
2 Alex Miller, "Impressions of China", *Meridian* 15, no. 1 (1996): 85.
3 Alex Miller, "In Touch with the Displaced", *Sydney Morning Herald*, 20 November 1993, 13.
4 Miller, "Impressions of China", 85.

The Yellow Lady (1992), and Eric Rolls' *Sojourners* (1992) and *Citizens* (1996). Miller read widely over a period of several years in the fields of Chinese history, politics, art and memoir. Michael Sullivan's *A Short History of Chinese Art* (1967) was especially useful, including detailed chapters on architecture and "the combined notion of calligraphy as visual art, the act of writing as the act of making art".[5] Alex and Stephanie Miller and their son Ross went to China for the first time over the Christmas–New Year period in 1987–88, travelling to Shanghai and Hangzhou, where they visited the West Lake and the temple of Ling Yin. An important connection was provided by Ruth Blatt, the wife of Miller's Polish friend, Max Blatt. After fleeing from Nazi Germany, Ruth had lived in Shanghai before coming to Melbourne, and one of her former German students there, Bao Chien-hsing, had gone on to become a professor at the Shanghai Foreign Languages Institute, and had married the traditional painter Yeh Ching. Miller recalls, "Bao and Yeh Ching enabled us to 'be' Chinese while in China . . . [and] with their assistance we were able to bypass the still very strict laws governing foreign visitors".[6] The Australian writer Nicholas Jose, who was then Cultural Counsellor at the Australian Embassy in Beijing, also gave them introductions to people in Shanghai, including Professor Huang Yuanshen, director of the Australian Studies Centre at East China Normal University. At East China Normal, Miller met the writer Ouyang Yu, who emigrated to Melbourne in 1991, and in 1996 published a Chinese translation of *The Ancestor Game*.[7]

Miller has written of what he calls the "honeymoon" period that travellers to new places often experience, which gives them the confidence to take in impressions and to form judgements. In this initial phase, he describes himself as "a detached observer of life, a kind of carefree visiting parasite": "It was in Hangzhou, while walking among the evening crowds on the shores of West Lake, that I began to feel for the first time a confidence in my ability to write of Lang's life and his Chinese family background". This honeymoon period was brought to an abrupt end when Professor Bao warned him that where Miller could see only friendliness and openness, he as a Chinese could see deep underlying hatreds and conflict: " 'China', he said, 'cannot be at peace with herself for long'. That was in January 1988." Speaking at the World Chinese Writers' Association Congress in Singapore in 1995, Miller was alluding to the Tiananmen Square protests of April to June 1989, only months after he and Stephanie were in China, which culminated in the massacre of 4 June: "This man's words entered into my work in *The Ancestor Game*, and gave to it a sense of a more vengeful side of Chinese history than the word honeymoon could ever generate."[8]

When *The Ancestor Game* was published, reviewers recognised it as a major contribution to what Tom Shapcott described as the "flourishing sub-genre" of "Australian fiction on Chinese themes".[9] Citing Brian Castro's *Birds of Passage* (1983) as the first, he includes David Brooks' *The Book of Sei* (1985), Rod Jones' *Julia Paradise* (1986), Nicholas Jose's *Avenue of Eternal Peace* (1989) and Castro's *After China* (1992), which Susan Geason reviewed together with *The Ancestor Game* under the title "Imagining China".[10] Others saw

---

5   Michael Sullivan, *A Short History of Chinese Art* (London: Faber, 1967). Alex Miller to Robert Dixon, 6 March 2014.
6   Alex Miller to Robert Dixon, 18 March 2014.
7   There have been two translations into Chinese: the first by Li Yao, *Lang Zi* (Chongqing: Chongqing chu ban she, 1995), and the second by Ouyang Yu, *Zhu xian you xi* (Taipei: Mai Tian, 1996).
8   Miller, "Impressions of China", 86, 88–9.
9   Tom Shapcott, "There is Another World and It Is Here", review of Alex Miller, *The Ancestor Game*, *Overland* 128 (Spring 1992): 79.

that *The Ancestor Game* represented a qualitative change in Australia's fictional engagement with China, Ouyang Yu hailing it as a "breakthrough" in moving beyond an earlier "stereotyping and orientalizing tradition".[11] For Peter Pierce, *The Ancestor Game* was "a high point in that second wave of Australian fiction that confronts Asia". Christopher Koch in *The Year of Living Dangerously* (1978), Robert Drewe in *A Cry in the Jungle Bar* (1979), Blanche D'Alpuget in *Turtle Beach* (1981), and Ian Moffitt in *The Retreat of Radiance* (1982) had "dramatised . . . by indirection the assuagement of guilt of Australia's role in Vietnam". As part of the "second wave", Miller and Castro, by contrast, "examine . . . the complicated, long-term presence of the Chinese *within* Australian history".[12]

"The *Overland* Crowd"

In 1990, while Miller was re-drafting *The Ancestor Game* after visiting China, *The Tivington Nott* won the Royal Victorian Institute for the Blind's Tilly Aston Braille Book of the Year Award. The judges were poet and *Overland* editor Barrett Reid and historian Paul Carter. At the awards ceremony, Reid invited Miller to Heide, the home of the late John and Sunday Reed, at Bulleen, east of Melbourne, where he was then living, and Miller was introduced to the painter Rick Amor. It was an important meeting that would introduce him to two overlapping networks, both centred at that time on Reid: these were "the *Overland* crowd",[13] and the survivors of what Janine Burke in *The Heart Garden*, her biography of Sunday Reed, calls Heide's second and third circles.[14]

Reid had been editing *Overland* since the death of Stephen Murray-Smith in 1988 and Amor was a regular contributor of illustrations to the journal. The publication of *Overland* 121 (Summer 1990) was an important moment, indeed a turning point, in Miller's career. Its "Stories" section includes an extract from his then work in progress, *The Ancestor Game*, with an illustration by Amor: it is a Chinese statue of a horse, an early version of an image that would reappear in Amor's major oil paintings over the next few years.[15] In *The Ancestor Game* the horse is Tianma, a supernatural creature that travels between worlds. At the same time, Amor made a woodcut portrait of Miller, the second in a projected "Contemporary Authors Series" that includes portraits of Patrick White and Helen Garner.[16] The extract that Reid published in *Overland* immediately displays the accomplished postmodern technique of the new novel, with its complex themes of cross-cultural exchange, intertextuality and diasporic subjectivity. The development in Miller's style and material between *Watching the Climbers on the Mountain*, with its generic links to the outback romance, and the postmodern complexities of *The Ancestor Game*, which is unmistakably a work of high literary fiction, is unmatched elsewhere in Miller's work:

---

10 Susan Geason, "Imagining China", review of Brian Castro, *After China*, and Alex Miller, *The Ancestor Game*, *Sun-Herald*, 6 September 1992, 118.
11 Ouyang Yu, "Out of the Orient", *Modern Times*, September 1992, 30.
12 Peter Pierce, review of Alex Miller, *The Ancestor Game*, *Bulletin*, 15 September 1992, 101. My italics.
13 The phrase is from David Marr, "From: *Patrick White*", *Overland*, no. 121 (Summer 1990): 6.
14 Janine Burke, *The Heart Garden: Sunday Reed and Heide* (2004; Sydney: Vintage, 2005).
15 Gary Catalano, *The Solitary Watcher: Rick Amor and his Art* (Melbourne: Miegunyah Press, 2001), 138.
16 Rick Amor, "Patrick White 1912–1990", *Overland*, no. 121 (Summer 1990): 4; "Portrait of Alex Miller", *Overland*, no. 128 (Spring 1992): 4; and "Portrait of Helen Garner, 1992", *Overland*, no. 129 (Summer 1992): 4.

On the threshold I turned and looked back to see my reflection at the far end of his dark hall stepping into the bright rose-perfumed world of the mirror. Resolutely departing from it, I was entering more deeply into Lang Tzu's domain. Leaving him I was becoming the person inhabiting the landscape within his mirror.[17]

Miller had arrived as a serious contemporary Australian writer. Reviewing the novel for the *Australian* newspaper in August 1992, Gerard Windsor would write, "Miller is not a name in literary Australia, but he should be."[18]

In the late 1980s and 1990s, Rick Amor exhibited regularly at William Nuttall's Niagara Galleries at 245 Punt Road, Richmond. At this time, he had begun painting eerie, often empty inner-city landscapes, including *Celestial Lane (Three Trees)* (1989), *Celestial Lane* (1989) and *The Gate* (1990). After meeting him at Heide, Miller went along to Amor's current exhibition at the Niagara and he wrote to him on the day after the show closed:

> Your pictures at Niagara were superb... The show was like the next volume of your great fictional construction... The chords of a tragic polyphonic study resonate through pictures like *The Gate*, through all your work... It's a perception of the mythologic in present human affairs. It's the hardest thing for an artist (or writer) to do, to penetrate the impermeable face of present reality.[19]

Miller obviously felt that his writing and Amor's art had a number of things in common. In August 1989, Reid had used *Celestial Lane* on the cover of *Overland*. Years later, in an opening speech at an exhibition of Amor's work, Miller recalled, "I was writing my novel *The Ancestor Game* at the time... and the moment I saw that image... I knew the picture possessed exactly the emotional tone for the cover." The solitary figure climbing into the window in the middle distance "could have been the main character at the centre of my book".[20] While he was writing the novel, Miller had a colour reproduction of *Celestial Lane* pinned to a board in his study, and he told the reviewer Helen Elliot that he was struck by the fact that "two Melbourne artists in two different mediums should be contemplating the same themes at the same time".[21] A detail from *Celestial Lane*, using its middle distance and background, appeared with the artist's permission on the cover of the novel when it was published by Penguin in 1992. Amor was there when the novel was launched by Barrett Reid at the Millers' home in Port Melbourne.

What was it about this painting that attracted Miller's interest? Most immediately, of course, is its manifest "Chinese" content, including the statue of a mythological creature, a wall with a sign in a Chinese script, and some vaguely oriental architectural forms. There is also the striking juxtaposition between these signs of the Orient and architecture of European origin, including the Victorian-Italianate building in the background and the colonial terrace house in the middle distance, suggesting both the hybridised architecture of Shanghai and the cultural diversity of inner Melbourne. Yet these features also have the typically invented, stage-like quality of Amor's cityscapes of this period, suggesting that they are as

---

17 Alex Miller, "From: *The Ancestor Game*", *Overland*, no. 121 (Summer 1990): 8.
18 Gerard Windsor, "Fruitful Mating of Cultures", review of Alex Miller, *The Ancestor Game*, *The Weekend Australian*, 15–16 August 1992, 4.
19 Alex Miller to Rick Amor, 28 April 1991, quoted in Catalano, *The Solitary Watcher*, 109.
20 Alex Miller, "Rick Amor's Show at Castlemaine Gallery, 1 June 2003", unpublished speech.
21 Quoted in Catalano, *The Solitary Watcher*, 139.

much anchored in a mysterious or dream-like other realm than they are in reality. Miller has said that when he first began to draw upon his own memories as a source of fiction, he felt like an archaeologist who had only just begun to excavate "a buried city of great complexity".[22] This is echoed, in turn, in his description of Amor's body of work as "your great fictional construction".

Celestial Lane features a number of variants on one of Amor's signature architectural motifs, the bridge or portal: these include the figure climbing up a ladder into a darkened window; the laneway itself, which is a passage from one unidentified place to another; the ramp that drops away into an obscure underground entrance; the darkened windows of the tall building in the background; and the series of empty spaces between the receding screens from which the composition is built. As Gary Catalano argues in his reading of another of Amor's paintings, *The Beach*, the bridge and its variants – ladders, windows, mirrors, doors, passageways – is a portal in Amor's works between the present and the past, between one text and another, between reality and memory, and the self and its others. In so far as they function as devices of citation – linking Amor's paintings to other paintings – the bridge and its variants are also metaphors for intertextuality. *Celestial Lane*'s vertiginous and recursive structure, in which real and constructed spaces are linked together by various kinds of portals – like an Oriental version of snakes and ladders – is analogous to the complex and mysterious topography of *The Ancestor Game*. As Miller writes in his letter to Amor, "It's the hardest thing for an artist (or writer) to do, to penetrate the impermeable face of present reality."[23] This figure of the portal had already appeared in *Watching the Climbers on the Mountain*. It is there in the contrast between Ward Rankin's windowless study and the placing of Ida's bedroom mirror, which allows her to look through the window of the house in which she is entrapped to Mt Mooloolong, the place she associates with her best self, and to which she will later travel, through another geological portal, with Robert Crofts. The co-presence of these motifs in Amor's art and Miller's writing at this time is not a simple matter of the direct influence of one upon the other, but of a more subtle convergence and complementarity of preoccupations between the writer and the painter to which they responded with mutual surprise, sympathy and friendship. In *The Ancestor Game*, these shared motifs are elaborated through Miller's growing engagement with the imagery of Amor's paintings and his own meditation on the techniques of portraiture and self-portraiture.

"Containers Containing Containers": The Labyrinth of *The Ancestor Game*

The Ancestor Game is the story of four generations of a Chinese family, the Fengs, who have had connections with the Port Phillip District since 1848, before the gold, but who have also retained both personal and business links with China well into the twentieth century. It is told from the narrative present of 1976 by Steven Muir, an English-born Melbourne novelist who is writing an account of the family saga to be called *The Chronicle of the Fengs*.

Orphaned during the First Opium War, when the city of Amoy in Fukien province fell to the British in 1841, the first Feng signs on as an indentured labourer with the captain of

---

22   Alex Miller, "This is How It's Going to Be Then", *Australian Book Review*, no. 127 (December 1990 – January 1991): 30.
23   Quoted in Catalano, *The Solitary Watcher*, 109.

the British ship *Nimrod*, landing at Geelong in 1848, just three years before the discovery of gold in 1851. Working initially as a shepherd in the Ballarat district, Feng is befriended by an Aboriginal man, Dorset, and an Irishman, Patrick Nunan, and after Dorset is killed by pastoralists, Feng and Nunan discover gold and make their fortune.[24] Feng travels between Melbourne and Amoy as the head of a labour-recruitment agency, the Society of the Phoenix (the meaning of his name). He marries Nunan's daughter Mary, and in 1876 builds a polychrome brick mansion at Coppin Grove in Hawthorn,[25] but he also maintains a second, Chinese, family in Amoy. The story of Feng's double life, *The Winter Visitor: A Life in Two Hemispheres* (1912), is written by his and Mary's daughter Victoria, who is born at Coppin Grove in 1878. She lives on in the family home after her brothers and sisters marry, eventually becoming its heiress and the family archivist. She dies at Coppin Grove in 1968. The second Feng, Victoria's half-brother from Shanghai, makes only a brief appearance in the novel when he comes to Melbourne to settle his father's affairs at the time of his death on 27 May 1908.

The third Feng, Feng Chien-hsing, has consolidated the family fortune and become an immensely wealthy businessman in Shanghai. He adopts the Europeanised name of C.H. Feng, lives in a modern European-style villa in the International Settlement, dresses and comports himself as a European, and enjoys close relations with foreigners. In 1926, at the time of the first Japanese invasion, Feng has married for the third time to Lien Hua, the daughter of Huang Yu-hua, an elderly scholar and literary painter who lives in a once grand though now dilapidated house in the provincial capital of Hangzhou. When she becomes pregnant, Lien persuades her husband to allow her to give birth at her father's home under the supervision of his own physician, the expatriate German doctor August Spiess. Lang Tzu, the fourth Feng, is born in his grandfather's house in Hangzhou on 19 December 1927. Although he has no time for Chinese traditions, C.H. Feng allows his son to be trained in the art of literary painting by his grandfather. By the time of the second Japanese invasion in 1937, when Lang is ten years old, Huang's China is "a disintegrating world" (290), and Feng sends his son to be brought up in Australia under the guardianship of Dr Spiess, who is now his tutor. Lang is taken to live with distant relatives, the Hallorans, in Ballarat, while Spiess lives in a boarding house at St Kilda. Now in his late sixties, Spiess meets and falls in love with Victoria Feng at Coppin Grove, and their daughter Gertrude is born in 1946.

In the summer of 1976, the year of the narrative present, the writer and English teacher Steven Muir meets the Chinese-Australian Lang Tzu, an artist and art teacher at the same school, and through Lang, his cousin Gertrude, a lecturer in drawing at the Prahran College of Advanced Education, and a successful artist with her first exhibition planned for later in the year. Lang has inherited the house at Coppin Grove and encourages Steven to write an historical novel about his family. Among the sources he makes available to him are the enormous cache of family records held at Coppin Grove, Victoria Feng's published book *The Winter Visitor*, and the diaries of August Spiess, which Gertrude translated during the 1960s. As a young man in the 1950s, Lang had some success as a portrait painter,

---

24 Miller's trio, the Chinaman, the Aborigine and the Irishman, is an allusion to J.C.F. Johnson's painting *A Game of Euchre* (1867), now hanging in the Art Gallery of Ballarat, which was once owned by Allan O'Hoy. Its subject and provenance are discussed in Erika Esau, *Images of the Pacific Rim: Australia and California, 1850–1935* (Sydney: Power Publications, 2011), 70–1.

25 Coppin Grove is a street in the Melbourne suburb of Hawthorn with a number of boom-era mansions, but the Fengs' home is fictional.

but Melbourne society was not at that time prepared to embrace a Chinese-Australian artist, and he is now an alcoholic. The final event recorded in the novel is the exhibition of Gertrude's drawings at the Falls Gallery in Richmond on 10 September 1976.[26] Lang and Steven are meant to leave for the opening together from Coppin Grove, but in the final pages Steven finds that Lang is not at home and drives to the gallery alone, expecting to see him there with Gertrude.

While these events, chronologically arranged, constitute the story of *The Ancestor Game*, its narrative emplotment is a far more complex achievement. The novel is a massive cross-cultural and historical canvas with vertiginous shifts of time and place, its different periods and locations connected by various kinds of portals, both real and symbolic. Puzzled by her father's long absences from Coppin Grove, for example, Victoria Feng imagines that the home must contain "a hidden staircase or passage" that allows him to travel to his "Chinese other-world" (41). This recursive structure led several reviewers to invoke the idea of a hall of mirrors, or *mise-en-abyme*.[27] While some remembered the portals between worlds in the works of Lewis Carroll and C.S. Lewis – "Step through the details, or as C.S. Lewis wrote in his Narnia series, through 'the chinks' in space"[28] – others invoked Borges' labyrinth.[29] Susan Geason compared the structure of Miller's novel to the postmodern design of the hotel built by the Chinese architect in Castro's *After China*: "The book is built around the hotel, which stands as a metaphor for the construction, or rather the deconstruction, of the book".[30] For Miller, there was also a direct relationship between the novel's structure, and the home and art collection of his friend Allan O'Hoy, which was "full of mirrors and locked doors and ways into rooms one hadn't previously seen":

> The whole "oriental" mystique of Allan's house and his life collection and memories that it contained was shaped like *The Ancestor Game*, [which] . . . mirrored that mysterious rooms-within-rooms like structure that was peculiarly Allan's.

Miller recalls "the exhausting struggle I had to find a way of depicting this labyrinth of sense and experience without losing the thread of it".[31]

Of the novel's thirteen chapters, six are set in Melbourne in the narrative present, tracing the growing friendship between Lang, Steven and Gertrude from February to September 1976 as they move between their school, Lindner's Gallery, the house at Coppin Grove, and the Falls Gallery in Richmond, where Steven expects to see Lang and Gertrude together on the night of 10 September. These chapters are interspersed by others set in Shanghai and Hangzhou at the time of Lien's third pregnancy and Lang's birth in 1926–27, and again at the time of Lang's childhood between 1932 and 1937; in Amoy and Ballarat during the period of the first Feng's voyages between 1848 and his death in 1908; and fi-

---

26   The name of the fictional gallery, the Falls, alludes to the Niagara.
27   Peter Davis, "New Book Like Chess Played on Mirrors in Three Dimensions", review of Alex Miller, *The Ancestor Game*, *Canberra Times*, 2 August 1992, 22; Diana Giese, "Two-Way Asian Mirror", review of Alex Miller, *The Ancestor Game*, *The Weekend Australian*, 6–7 November 1993, 7; Thomas Shapcott, "There is Another World and it is Here", *Overland*, no. 128 (Spring 1992): 79–81; Helen Daniel, "Trapped in an Ancestral Mirror", *The Age* 15 August 1992, 9.
28   Sara Sanderson, "Artful Game Twice Played Reflects Yet Another Mirror", review of Alex Miller, *The Ancestor Game*, *Indianapolis News*, 30 July 1994.
29   Shapcott, "There is another world", 80.
30   Brian Castro, quoted in Geason, "Imagining China", 118.
31   Alex Miller to Robert Dixon, 11 August 2013.

nally in Ballarat, St Kilda and Hawthorn in 1937 at the time of Lang's and Spiess' arrival from Shanghai. This recursive series of times and locations is made yet more complex by the fact that within any one of these chapters, whatever its initial setting might be, there are further shifts in time and place brought about through the characters' memories, and by the interpellation of passages from the three fictional texts contained within the narrative itself, *The Winter Visitor*, *The Chronicle of the Fengs*, and the Spiess diaries. Chapter 4, for example, recounts Steven's first visit to the house in Coppin Grove in the summer of 1976, where Lang gives him a copy of Victoria's *The Winter Visitor*, which takes him back to Coppin Grove as it was in the 1870s and 1880s, when her father, the first Feng, might appear unannounced from China. Uncannily, both *The Winter Visitor* and *The Ancestor Game* have 302 pages. Chapter 8 of *The Ancestor Game*, "An Interlude in the Garden", is set at Coppin Grove in the autumn of 1976, but Steven is there given Spiess' diaries to read for the first time, which are then interpellated as chapter 9, "A Memoir of Displacement". This recursive intertextuality is made even more complex when Steven gives Lang drafts to read of "The Lotus and the Phoenix", "No Ordinary Child", and "The Mother". Diegetically, these are chapters from Steven's work in progress, *The Chronicle of the Fengs*, but extradiegetically they are also chapters 3, 5 and 7 of *The Ancestor Game*.

The Ancestor Game's labyrinthine design is the type of structure that Jacques Derrida, in his discussion of Plato's *Timaeus*, terms *khoratic*. Derrida reads the *Timaeus* as a textual *mise-en-abyme* (literally, "a fall into the abyss"): "a vertiginous play of reflections, as when an image is infinitely reflected in a mirror held up against a mirror". The figure of the *mise-en-abyme* both describes the nested structure of the *Timaeus* and performs Derrida's concept of *khora* as "an 'abyss', a void of empty space" that is also host to meanings without limit, a great void that is nonetheless "filled" with signification.[32] Through its association in the Christian tradition with the Virgin and the annunciation, *khora* is also a feminine principle, a principle of welcome that receives the other without prejudice or imposition. For Derrida, it is this paradoxical combination of fullness and emptiness that is a feature of textuality in general:

> Derrida's point . . . is that every text, written or oral, is a bastard or an orphan, its father/author having departed, and that this *structural* feature of discourse, which is always already interwoven and *contained by* other texts, whose roots sink into a dense context which we have only limited success in unravelling. Even a book of genesis is caught up in a genealogy and family history we cannot make out or remember. The text is always a bastard. This system of boxes inside boxes, containers containing containers – this '*khoral*' quality – is a feature of textuality itself.[33]

The Ancestor Game is a *khoratic* receptacle, a vast hall of mirrors that welcomes the other without imposing its own will or identity upon him. We might say that Miller's understanding of geo-social space, of Australia-in-Asia as a disestablished world and as a spatial field of migration and diaspora, is that it is *khoratic*, or potentially *khoratic*, in just this sense of being a space of hospitality, a space that is open to the other.

---

32 John D. Caputo, ed., *Deconstruction in a Nutshell: A Conversation with Jacques Derrida* (New York: Fordham University Press, 1997), 85–7.
33 Caputo, *Deconstruction*, 91.

In citing Derrida on the threshold of my own reading of *The Ancestor Game*, I do not mean to imply that Miller's novels are in any systematic way informed by theoretical or philosophical concepts: on the contrary, as Miller's friend, the philosopher Raimond Gaita, remarks, he is the least didactic of writers.[34] Yet Miller's novels, and especially *The Ancestor Game*, engage deeply with the major issues of Derrida's late work, including questions of friendship, hospitality, the gift and the work of mourning. Derrida is useful here as an interlocutor not because he offers a key to understanding Miller's novels, but because he offers some of the richest and most suggestive formulations of these themes, to which Miller is also drawn as a novelist. In this chapter I will consider, in turn, the role of the image in friendship and mourning, intertextual hospitality and the art of fiction, the extraterritoriality of art, and finally, Miller's understanding in *The Ancestor Game* of the poetics of modernity.

Friendship, the Work of Mourning and the Image of the Other

Miller wrote *The Ancestor Game* in the spirit of both friendship and mourning. As Derrida has established, it is a law of friendship – and thus a law of mourning – that there can be no friendship without the knowledge that one friend will die before the other, and that the surviving friend will be left to commemorate and to mourn.[35] When Pascale-Anne Brault and Michael Naas collected Derrida's orations on the deaths of his friends under the title *The Work of Mourning*, they were mindful of the ways in which his *oeuvre* had become, to cite Proust, "a huge cemetery in which on the majority of the tombs the names are effaced and can no longer be read". In their introduction to *The Work of Mourning*, they speculate about "the encryption of names and friends in an *oeuvre*", about the way in which "an *oeuvre* does not simply grow larger but thickens with time ... its volume worked over like a landscape or, indeed, like a cemetery".[36] In one of his most recent public addresses, Miller reflects on the way in which his own *oeuvre*, his corpus of eleven novels, has come to resemble a cemetery, the ruin of time, in which the names of the dead are made legible through acts of friendship and writing. They include his parents, "Jock" and Winifred Millar; the editor Barrett Reid; his first mentor Max Blatt; and his Chinese-Australian friend Allan O'Hoy. Referring to the description in *The Ancestor Game* of Lang's birth in Hangzhou on 19 December 1927, Miller explains, "the baby that is born that night was based on my friend, the Chinese/Australian artist who had killed himself because he failed in his art. It was he I was struggling to bring back to life."[37]

The Ancestor Game begins with a kind of prelude titled "The Death of the Father", in which Steven Muir briefly returns to England, where he remains estranged from his mother and unreconciled to the memory of his father, who has recently died. He has come

---

34 Raimond Gaita, "Trusting the Words: Reflections on *Landscape of Farewell*", in *The Novels of Alex Miller: An Introduction*, ed. Robert Dixon (Sydney: Allen & Unwin, 2012), 218.
35 Jacques Derrida, *The Politics of Friendship*, trans. George Collins (London and New York: Verso, 1997).
36 Pascale-Anne Brault and Michael Naas, "To Reckon with the Dead: Jacques Derrida's Politics of Mourning", in *The Work of Mourning*, eds Pascale-Anne Brault and Michael Naas (Chicago and London: University of Chicago Press, 2001), 4.
37 Alex Miller, "You Could Have Been There (Unmasking the Fictional Voice)", The William Gifford Memorial Lecture, Vassar College, 5 November 2013. *Antipodes* 28, no.1 (June 2014): 216.

back for the launch of his first book, which is to be published in London by the same firm that published Victoria Feng's memorial to her father, *The Winter Visitor*. It is only by coincidence that Steven's father dies just at this time, and he is not to be remembered in either of Steven's books: "There was to be no lasting memorial. There had been no service. There was no patch of ground to remain sacred to his memory. He probably would have liked there to have been a headstone" (3–4). Like the first Feng – and like Derrida's theory of the text – Steven Muir is therefore an orphan in the world, an exile, a kind of "bastard". The book he is writing now, *The Chronicle of the Fengs*, will not be a memorial to his first family or to his roots in the old world of Europe, but to his lateral, new-world friendships with the novel's other "only children", the Chinese-German Australians Lang Tzu and Gertrude Spiess.

It is a signal fact that in the 302 pages of *The Ancestor Game* we do not see Steven Muir at home. Although he frequently describes himself on the thresholds of the homes of others, he never shows himself inside a home of his own. As he contemplates his return to Australia from his mother's home in England, he asks, "Was I returning to Australia in the morning to continue my exile, or was I going home?" (8). Some reviewers marked this down as a defect in the novel, Susan Geason, objecting that "Steven and his ancestor problems get swallowed up in Lang's story."[38] Others grasped that Miller's opening is deliberately "deceptive", only "seeming" to place Steven himself "at the centre of things".[39] In this prelude to Steven's account of his friendship with Lang Tzu – on the book's threshold – Miller denies his narrator the authority of proprietorship and thereby avoids what Derrida describes as "the violence of the host". In contemporary Australia, with its heightened sensitivity to the presence of "others", this has both ethical and political implications. In welcoming his audience to a seminar in honour of his dead friend in *Adieu to Emmanuel Levinas*, Derrida warns that "to dare to say welcome is perhaps to insinuate that one is at home here, that one knows what it means to be at home, and that at home one receives, invites, or offers hospitality, thus appropriating for oneself a place to *welcome* [*accueillir*] the other".[40] In warning against "the violence of the host", against feeling too much at-home-with-oneself, Derrida reminds us that this also applies to nations:

> The ground or territory has nothing natural about it, nothing of a root, even if it is sacred, nothing of a possession for the national occupant. The earth gives hospitality before all else, a hospitality already offered to the initial occupant, a temporary hospitality granted to the *hôte*, even if he remains the master of the place.[41]

By analogy, we might say that Australia offers even to those of British stock, like Steven Muir, only a temporary protection visa: relatively recent arrivals themselves, they have no right to act like hosts to others, such as the Chinese. Steven describes Australia as "a European civilization that had failed to take root in an environment hostile to its ageless central icons" (7). Hospitality is not in one's gift; it is not under one's authority. If one's home is indeed a place of asylum or refuge – and neither the British nor the Chinese have their

---

38   Geason, "Imagining China", 188.
39   Shapcott, "There is Another World", 80.
40   Jacques Derrida, *Adieu to Emmanuel Levinas*, trans. Pascale-Anne Brault and Michael Nass (Stanford: Stanford University Press, 1999), 15.
41   Derrida, *Adieu*, 93.

"roots" here – then it follows that the inhabitant who dwells here is himself a refugee or an exile, a guest and not a proprietor.[42]

It is this first law of hospitality – that the host has no authority in his own home, that he is always already a hostage to the other – that explains the uncertain relation of so many of Miller's characters to place. Ward Rankin hosts Robert Crofts in his parent's house, while his wife Ida is displaced from her own home and entrapped in Ward's; Steven Muir is an exile from Europe who is made welcome in the Melbourne home of his Chinese-Australian friend, which Lang Tzu inherited in turn from his great aunt, Victoria Feng; in *Journey to the Stone Country*, Dougald Gnapun's fibro-cement house is on the outskirts of Mackay, while in *Landscape of Farewell* he welcomes the visiting German Professor Max Otto to what appears to be the same house, now at Mount Nebo in the Central Highlands, yet neither of these places is his true country of origin.

Back in Melbourne in the summer of 1976, Steven finds himself adrift, unable to ground himself either in his family past or in his present life in Australia. Hungry for friendship, he detects within himself an absence that is open to being colonised by another:

> I'd believed that if I could only reach deeply enough inside myself, one day I'd come upon extensive and complex landscapes rich with meaning and mystery, waiting for me to explore them. I'd believed the purpose of my adult life would lie in the exploration of these places. My confidence in the existence of this internal homeland, however, had eroded over the years. (10)

As his confidence in the existence of this inner "homeland" recedes, Steven meets the novel's other "only children", Gertrude and Lang, who provide him with alternative directions for his journey of friendship.

Friendship is one of the central themes of Miller's novels, as recognised in an important early article by Ronald A. Sharp,[43] whose book about friendship in contemporary fiction, *Friendship and Literature* (1986), Miller has read.[44] Among the classical sources that recur in both philosophical and literary discussions of friendship are Aristotle's *Nichomachean Ethics* and Cicero's *De Amicitia*, or *On Friendship*. According to Elizabeth McMahon, in Aristotle and Cicero we are presented with a paradoxical conflation of the friend as other and the friend as the self. When Aristotle inquires "What is a friend?", he answers, "A single soul dwelling in two bodies." Similarly, for Cicero, "he … who looks into the face of a friend beholds, as it were a copy of himself". This paradox of the friend as both a mirror image of the self and as other is essential to the maintenance of ethical distance, for as McMahon points out, "a relation of pure resemblance, of interchangeability alone, cannot allow for difference or freedom".[45] In Miller's novels, the ethical imperative to recognise and maintain difference, to acknowledge the freedom of the other, is particularly marked in friendships that cross lines of ethnic and cultural difference, as is the case with Steven and Lang in *The Ancestor Game*, and Annabelle Beck and Bo Rennie in *Journey to the Stone Country*.

---

42 Derrida, *Adieu*, 36–7.
43 Ronald A. Sharp, "More Than Just Mates", *Australian Literary Review* 4, no. 6 (July 2009): 18–20.
44 Ronald A. Sharp, *Friendship and Literature: Spirit and Form* (Durham: Duke University Press, 1986).
45 Quotations in Elizabeth McMahon, "Continental Heartlands and Alex Miller's Geosophical Imaginary", in *The Novels of Alex Miller*, 133.

Cicero's optical metaphor of friendship as a mirroring of the self in the other and the other in the self is the starting point for Derrida's thinking about friendship, for when he writes that the dead must be kept alive "in us", he means primarily in the form of the image. In "By Force of Mourning", his eulogy for the French art historian Louis Marin, he refers to Alberti's discussion of portraiture in his treatise *On Painting*. Also alluding to Aristotle, Alberti suggests that "if painting has within itself a force that is absolutely divine (*vim divinam*) it is because it makes the absent present: 'as friendship is said to do' ".[46] Optical and pictorial images are especially important in Steven's account of the growth of his friendship with Lang Tzu, who is himself an artist and art collector. The trajectory of that friendship is depicted across the course of the novel as a tentative mirroring of the self in the other that culminates in the eventual internalisation of the image of the other within the self. In this account, Miller draws on his own deep understanding of the techniques of portraiture in both painting and photography, though in the beauty of his writing he is perhaps closer in spirit to *Camera Lucida*, Roland Barthes' lyrical and profoundly romantic meditation on friendship, death and photographic portraiture, than he is to the writing of Derrida.

Steven's account of his first sight of Lang in the school common room is like an initial note-taking for a portrait of the man's face that focuses on his most distinctive feature, the misalignment resulting from a breech birth: "There was a disturbing and fixed misalignment to his features. It was as if the right side of his face had been given a permanent upward nudge ... I thought of him as having been touched, as having been wounded" (11). This is what Barthes calls the *punctum* of the photographic image, the point at which it strikes us with a profound affective force:

> A Latin word exists to designate this wound, this prick, this mark made by a pointed instrument: the word suits me all the better in that it also refers to the notion of punctuation, and because the photographs I am speaking of are in effect punctuated, sometimes even speckled with these sensitive points ... A photograph's *punctum* is that accident which pricks me (but also bruises me, is poignant to me).[47]

For Steven, this *punctum* in the image of his friend is also a *stigma* that betrays both to him and to the reader, here, right at the moment of friendship's earliest beginnings, an awareness of the friend's mortality. This, as Derrida says, is the law of friendship.

At the end of their first meeting, the potential for these two "only children" to enter into each other's centres of being is yet to be realised. They have not yet fully created that image of the other self "in us", and to that extent they remain for each other like unfinished portraits, preliminary sketches or still-developing photographs. As he parts from Lang, Steven imagines that he sees the face of his friend framed in a window: "As I turned to go I saw someone at an upstairs window. The window was protected from stones by a grill of weldmesh. A pale oval face observed me. It was unmoving and squared off by the steel wire. A preparatory study for a portrait" (23). Like the frames within frames that are typical of Amor's self-portraits, where they constrain the movement of the eye and the interchange of gazes between the subject and the viewer,[48] the grill and window frame the face of the

---

46 Quoted in Derrida, *The Work of Mourning*, 153–4.
47 Roland Barthes, *Camera Lucida: Reflections on Photography*, trans. Richard Howard (New York: Hill and Wang, 1981), 26–7.
48 David Hansen, "Vacant Possession", in *A Single Mind: Rick Amor*, curated by Linda Short (Bulleen, Vic.: Heide, 2008), 95–109.

other, offering it forcefully to Steven's gaze, but that image of the friend in potential is still external to the self and, at this stage, visually unresolved.

This is also Steven's first encounter with Lang as "the face", a central concept in Levinasian ethics, from which Derrida builds his own work on hospitality. Hospitality is "the very name of what opens itself to the face". Commenting on this term (*visage*) in Levinas, Derrida defines it variously as "for the other man, for man as other or stranger, for the other to man, the other *of* man or the other *than* man?"[49] And he punctuates this definition, as he often does, with a question mark, leaving all of these possibilities in play at once. Just as Levinas' term "the face" contains multiple meanings, Derrida uses it in his own writing as part of a "series of metonymies that bespeak hospitality": to welcome, to receive, to recollect, tending to the other, friendship.[50] This can be understood as a state of ethical comportment characterised by one's being-toward-the-other. The alternative is "the closing of the door, inhospitality, war, and allergy" and "the refusal or forgetting of the face".[51]

At the opening of *The Ancestor Game*, at the threshold of its elaborate architectural structure, and at the threshold of his friendship with Lang, Steven avoids the violence of the host, not claiming mastery of either the house or nation, not feeling too much "at-home-with-himself". He "effaces" himself while also being attentive to "the face", being for the other, in friendship. One symbol of openness to the other, which provides the cover image for the paperback edition of *Adieu to Emmanuel Levinas*, is the open door or portal.[52] Derrida writes that "The welcome orients, it *turns* the *topos* of an opening of the door and of the threshold toward the other."[53] In addition to memorialising his own friend, Allan O'Hoy, we might say that in *The Ancestor Game* Miller is also invoking the face as an ethical and political category, as a "concern for the stranger", as "a preoccupation with the other person".[54] And if the welcome "orients", then the Occident's "orient" is China, the place of Lang's birth. Here we return to Elizabeth McMahon's comment that Miller excels at making "the leap from the abstraction of metaphor into the grounded realities of history and culture – and back again".[55] Lang, the character who stands for Miller's lost friend Allan O'Hoy also stands for the politics of the Chinese diaspora in Australia, and yet more generally for the problem of the stranger as an ethical challenge.

The figure of the portal is repeated in *The Ancestor Game*, as it is in the work of Rick Amor: the window of the school through which Steven sees the face, the front door at Coppin Grove. Steven is on the threshold of his relation to Lang. Like the various versions of Amor's bridge motif, the door or window is both the potential frame for a portrait – a portal into another self – or the "hidden passage" to another world. The detail from *Celestial Lane* used for the cover of *The Ancestor Game*, as we have seen, includes the image of a man climbing a ladder and about to pass through the dark portal of a window into the mysterious, private space within. In the novel, this image of the window as a portal not yet entered, or a portrait not yet drawn, signals both the threshold of Steven's entry into the otherness of friendship and the novel's first major re-orientation, its first shift in time and

---

49 Derrida, *Adieu*, 120–21.
50 Derrida, *Adieu*, 20.
51 Derrida, *Adieu*, 48–9.
52 The cover is a detail from the French painter Jean-Daniel Bouvard's *Door-Frame*.
53 Derrida, *Adieu*, 54.
54 Levinas quoted in Derrida, *Adieu*, 123.
55 McMahon, "Continental Heartlands", 125–6.

place to the Orient, the modernising Shanghai of Lang's father, C.H. Feng, which is the subject of the following chapter. Miller locates Steven's perception of the mysterious face at the window in a kind of shudder in the narrative's realistic account of time and space, creating the effect of a puncture in present reality. At one moment, at the end of the chapter, Stephen is looking up at a window from a Melbourne street in 1976; in the next moment, at the beginning of the next chapter, Lang's mother, Madame Feng, is looking out of a window in her husband's villa on to a park in Shanghai in 1926.

Steven's developing engagement with the other, the mutual creation of his friendship with Lang, is enhanced by Miller's interest in the intimacy of looking and his sophisticated use of painterly terms. When they visit Lindner's Gallery together to collect a nineteenth-century portrait of Victoria Feng, Steven watches his friend indirectly by looking at his reflection in the glass that covers a portrait. Like Amor's own portraits, which often explicitly cite other well-known portraits, Miller's image is richly allusive to pictorial traditions that build up the complex economy of the gaze: "I directed my attention to one of the ink drawings that lined the walls on either side of the gallery . . . it was a female nude . . . I realized I could see Lang among the group around the desk reflected in the picture glass" (37). This is an image of friendship as the chiastic incorporation of the other within the self, and of Cicero's view that the friend is "a copy" of the self. Steven observes Lang across the gallery and reflects, "Looking at Lang, I could have been looking at myself. As I once had been. Ages ago. On the bank of a river somewhere, waiting to attempt a crossing" (38). Like Derrida's memories of Barthes and other friends who have died, Lang is incorporated into the self through the memory's creation and storing of images – these images are our way of "attempting a crossing".

After visiting Lindner's Gallery, Lang takes Steven for the first time to his home at Coppin Grove. As Steven leaves the house later that night and closes the front door, he turns for a last glimpse into the hallway and there beholds another portrait, this time a self-portrait caught in the glass of Lang's hall mirror. It is a later version of the passage originally published in *Overland*:

> At the end of his entrance hall, facing the front door, there was positioned a very large movable mirror in an ornate mahogany frame. As I turned to pull the front door I saw my reflection in this mirror, apparently entering a garden hidden within his house. Resolutely departing from it, I witnessed myself penetrating more deeply into Lang's domain. Leaving him, I could not resist the impression that I was becoming the person inhabiting the landscape within his mirror. (39)

Closing Lang's front door on the way to his own home, Steven leaves behind the striking visual trace of a self-portrait framed inside Lang's house, an image of the self progressively incorporated by or relocated inside the territory of the other.

On a later visit to the house at Coppin Grove, Steven has a chance to study the portrait of Victoria Feng that Lang had bought from Lindner's. As his friendship with Lang deepens, their examination of the portrait suggests the erotics of friendship. The portrait of Lang's great aunt was painted in the late 1880s, when Victoria was eleven years old. In it she appears naked, and the two friends intuit from this that she has seduced the young painter commissioned by her mother to make a series of family portraits. As they examine the painting, Steven and Lang become absorbed in an intricate series of interpersonal and intertextual exchanges, delving into Victoria's past through the twin portals of her portrait and her book, but also reflecting on the complex series of exchanges that take place between a painter or writer, their subject, and their reader or viewer. In looking at the portrait of Victoria they are also looking through it at each other. This erotics of portraiture has the same economy as friendship: portraits make the absent present, "as friendship is said to do". Steven experiences the intensity of the exchange between Victoria and the painter: "She was looking directly into the eyes of the artist" (59) – and into his own. Writing as a woman of thirty about herself as a child of eleven, Victoria reflects on how the writer and the artist – or two friends – are like parasites, incorporating the other into the self:

> She writes not with an end in mind but with a desire to make the material of her scrutiny her own, to possess it by means of the location of herself at its centre. She enters it by degrees. She insinuates herself. She is in fear of and is fascinated by her power to entice and to mock the artist. (60)

This process of insinuation also applies to Steven in his relations with the Fengs, including Lang, who as his host at Coppin Grove invites him to partake of intertextual hospitality by making available to him the family archive, including its rich heritage of images. It is located on and around the dining table, the traditional site of hospitality and exchange between host and guest:

> Completely covering the ample surface of the table, to a depth of half a metre or more, was a disordered heap of unstretched oils and watercolours and sketches and books and catalogues and other marginalia relating to Australian art; a collection, a hoard really... Still holding my arm, he turned to me and looked into my face, examining my features as if he were searching for attributable painterly characteristics... his cold right eye observing me, unmoved and disinterested. *Her* stuff's under this... Under my stuff. (66–7)

In this finely etched scene, a mirror image of Steven's earlier scrutiny of Lang's face in the school common room, friendship is actively constituted by Lang and Steven's chiastic creation and introjection of images of each other.

Victoria's prior occupation of the house at Coppin Grove suggests another parallel to Derrida's work on hospitality. To further explain the principle of the host's lack of ownership, of his prior subjection to a higher principle of welcome in his own home, Levinas proposes the abstract figure of "woman" as a "hospitable welcome *par excellence*", as "welcoming in itself".[56] It may be for similar reasons – that is, to displace the principle of authority of ownership from either Steven or Lang, from either the European or the Chinese in Australia – that Lang owes his at-homeness at Coppin Grove to his great-aunt Victoria, who is an absent presence for Steven in his explorations of the house. For Derrida, following Levinas, this *a priori* principle of welcome is "feminine" in the abstract sense of a law or principle of openness to the other, but not in the literal sense that it requires the presence of an actual woman: "The welcome, the anarchic origin of ethics belongs to 'the dimension of femininity' and not to the empirical presence of a human being of the 'feminine sex' ".[57] Derrida's own gloss on this "archaic" principle of welcoming im-

---

56 Levinas, quoted in Derrida, *Adieu*, 38.
57 Derrida, *Adieu*, 44.

plies that it is *khoratic*: "the welcoming *par excellence*, is feminine; it takes place in a place that cannot be appropriated, in an open 'interiority' whose hospitality the master or owner receives before himself then wishing to give it".[58] This *khoratic* quality, the suggestion of a welcoming abyss or receptacle that has no identity of its own but within which others may come into the fullness of being, is again suggested by the emptiness of the mirror as the medium in which Steven sees his image reflected in Lang's hallway and in *The Winter Visitor*, a *khoratic* text into which Victoria, Lang and Steven, in turn, project their own autobiographies.

The Ancestor Game ends abruptly on 10 September 1976. It is the day Mao died and a fierce storm swept over Melbourne. It is a day of deaths, of interruptions, and of elemental disturbances whose latent meanings, like the mighty storms that sweep through Rick Amor's Melbourne landscapes of this period, seem mysteriously to presage mortality. Steven and Lang have arranged to go together to the exhibition of Gertrude's drawings at the Falls Gallery, but when Steven goes to Lang's home to collect him he is not there. He expects to see him at the Falls with Gertrude but the novel ends abruptly and without resolution while Steven is anxiously "attempting a crossing" toward his friend, caught in the traffic *en route* between Coppin Grove and the Falls.

Some reviewers objected to the novel's ending, finding it abrupt and inconclusive.[59] In fact, it is deliberately unresolved. In the relationship between this ending and his public comments on *The Ancestor Game*, Miller has knowingly created an aporia in its interpretation. Within the fictional world, Lang is absent in the final moments of the narrative present on the night of 10 September. There is no reason within the fictional world to assume that he is dead: indeed, in his last phone call to Steven, he even speaks of returning to China, now that Mao is dead. Outside the text, however, Miller has announced that the novel is a memorial for his friend, Allan O'Hoy, who committed suicide. Miller has said, "there is indeed a mysterious residue that hangs over and beyond the book". He has said that "within the book Lang is never literally or really dead and this was always important to me. I was acutely aware that in Australian fiction, whenever there were Chinese characters, they invariably finished up dead." Allan O'Hoy was dead, "but in this book, which is a book of mourning . . . as well as a celebration of his life, I absolutely needed him to survive". While it may have proved a source of dissatisfaction for reviewers, this aporia, this "mysterious residue", is an elegant sign of respect for friendship, for life, and for otherness. As Miller puts it, "the spirit of Allan and I hope of Lang contains something of the Western sense of the opaqueness of Eastern cultures".[60] There is a comparable moment of absence toward the end of *Landscape of Farewell*, when Dougald Gnapun disappears during the night at the summit of the Expedition Range, leaving his friend Max Otto stricken with anxiety. It is through that absence that Miller suggests the presence, in that novel, of the Aboriginal sacred. Lang, too, has vanished. His absence in the narrative at this point might be understood in terms of Levinas' definition of death as "the patience of time", as "without-response", a gap in the (narrative) series.[61]

It is the irony of friendship's creation of the image of the other that the other will eventually come to be represented *in their absence* only by the presence of that image "in us".

---

58 Derrida, *Adieu*, 45.
59 Geason, "Imagining China", 118.
60 Alex Miller to Robert Dixon, 24 March 2014.
61 Derrida, *Adieu*, 131.

As Derrida observes in his commentary on Louis Marin's "What is the Image?", the inevitable replacement of the other by an image is fundamental to the initiation of mourning. The originary scene of this moment in the Christian tradition is the presence of the angel at the tomb on the morning of the Resurrection, which signifies, "he is not here, he is elsewhere".[62] What is introjected of the friend at this moment of their absence is the image: "Ever since psychoanalysis came to mark this discourse, the image commonly used to characterize mourning is that of an interiorization (an idealising incorporation, introjection, consumption of the other, in effect, an experience that would have received one of its essential aspects from the Eucharist)."[63] When we say that the friend "can no longer be but *in us*", we mean specifically in the form of the image:

> *We are speaking of images.* What is only *in us* seems to be reducible to images, which might be memories or monuments, but which are reducible in any case to a memory that consists of *visible* scenes that are no longer anything but *images*, since the other of whom they are the images appears only as the one who has disappeared or passed away, as the one who, having passed away, leaves "in us" only images.[64]

But this internalised image, which we know only exists "in us", appears to be looking at us as if from the outside, as it did in life, and this inversion of the gaze, a trick of the memory, causes a dramatic reorganisation of space. The inside of the self, which welcomes and encrypts the image of the dead, is ruptured by the apparent fact that the image is looking at us from the outside, like the subject of a portrait:

> The image looks at us . . . [and] in the end . . . this inversion of dissymmetry . . . can be interiorized only by exceeding, fracturing, wounding, injuring, traumatizing the interiority that it inhabits or that welcomes it through hospitality, love or friendship . . . Louis Marin is outside and he is looking at me, he himself, and I am an image for him. At this very moment.[65]

Writing in Lang's absence, Steven remembers the last phone call he received from him on the morning of 10 September. He remembers the sound of Lang's voice addressing him on the telephone: "Are you still there Steven?" (296). He remembers that he was to pick Lang up from Coppin Grove in the evening at five to take him to the Falls. And then, in the act of writing in Lang's absence, he imagines an alternative to what really happened, going to the house to find Lang present. Steven is not literally at the house, but imagines himself going to the house to look for Lang, who now only exists in Steven:

> I approached the house and entered the hallway. Having come from his bedroom at this hour, or from the kitchen, he would be facing the front door. In the large mirror at the far end of the hall there would be my reflection, standing as Sickert might have had me stand, against the light, looking in at him. As if I really were emerging from the hidden inner garden. And there would be a reflection of his back. At this hour he would be wear-

---

62 Derrida, *The Work of Mourning*, 150.
63 Derrida, *The Work of Mourning*, 158–9.
64 Derrida, *The Work of Mourning*, 159.
65 Derrida, *The Work of Mourning*, 160.

ing a pair of loose yellowed drawers with button-up flies. Apart from these, which he would have slept in, he would be naked. His body, which I love with a strange, resisting tenderness, is small and hairless and exceedingly pale. (296)

Steven knows that he is now describing an event that did not take place, an imaginary visit to Coppin Grove on 10 September in which Lang is present rather than absent, and so he writes in the conditional past tense: "As if I really *were* emerging from the hidden inner garden." And because Steven is only imagining the event, because Lang really is absent, his presence can only be in the form of an internalised image, like an angel, or like a painted or photographic portrait. Perhaps for this reason his description of the imagined event is increasingly attentive to the idea of portraiture, and to the portraits that he knows hang in the house, even though he could not actually see them from that position – were he to have been there:

> A network of blue veins is visible, rising to the opalescent surface then diving deep into the interior. His musculature is poorly defined. His is an almost adolescent body and not unlike that of his great-aunt's in the portrait of her as a child, which now hangs to the right of the front . . . room where the other portraits hang – and which cannot therefore be viewed by someone standing, as I am, in the doorway itself. He is hunched over the telephone and he is shivering. His tight black hair is standing straight up on his scalp, like the closely shorn mane of a hunter. Its appearance is surprising, giving him the look of someone belonging to an elect caste. It is his most striking feature. (296–7)

This poignant description of Lang's skin, or Steven's memory of Lang's skin, is again the *punctum* of the image, the part of it that "shoots out of it like an arrow, and pierces me".[66] It evokes the conventions of religious painting in genres such as the Crucifixion, the Deposition and the Resurrection, to which Miller will return in the Central Queensland novels, especially in the death of the goat in *Landscape of Farewell*, resonating with Derrida's comparison of introjection to the rite of the Eucharist. But this *mise-en-abyme* of images that seem, like oil painting itself, to capture the depths of real flesh, is an illusionistic "surface", a signal that the absent friend is only present by virtue of the tricks of memory, or what is actually an invented memory, or by the painted or photographic image.

Finally, Steven *sees* the image of Lang: "His tight black hair is standing straight up on his scalp" (297). He describes this in the present tense. But Lang is now an absence, present only through the internalisation of his image by Steven, or by his fictional re-creation in Miller's novel, *The Ancestor Game*. Like the presence of the angel at the tomb, that very image declares, "he is not here, he is elsewhere".

Intertextual Hospitality and the Art of Fiction

In chapter 8 of *The Ancestor Game*, Steven, Lang and Gertrude sit together in the garden at Coppin Grove reading, reciting poetry and drinking wine. Lang is reading the drafts of "The Lotus and the Phoenix", "No Ordinary Child", and "The Mother". These are the titles of chapters 3, 4 and 7 of *The Ancestor Game*, which deal with the meeting of Lang's par-

---

66   Barthes, *Camera Lucida*, 26.

ents, Lien Hua and C.H. Feng, their marriage, and Lang's birth in Hangzhou in 1927. The drafts Lang is reading are from the book Steven is writing, *The Chronicle of the Fengs*. Based partly upon the family records Lang has made available to him, it has also been inspired by Victoria Feng's *The Winter Visitor*, itself an imagined recreation of her father's journeys between Australia and Amoy. A third source is the journal of August Spiess, which Gertrude has just given him to read in her own English translation. It is reproduced as the next chapter of *The Ancestor Game*, "A Memoir of Displacement". When he finishes reading Steven's imagined account of the events in Shanghai and Hangzhou, Lang says, "You could have been there, Steven" (108). These are the very words Max Blatt had used when he finished reading the draft of the short story, "Comrade Pawel".

Placed near the centre of *The Ancestor Game*, chapter 8, "An Interlude in the Garden", is the first and one of the most complex scenes of literary hospitality in Miller's novels. Lang has let Steven into the centre of his life, and into the history of his family and culture. Steven is a guest in Lang's home at Coppin Grove, and the materials he uses for his writing are given to him by his host at the family dining table, the traditional scene of hospitality. *The Chronicle of the Fengs* is not an original text, but one that has come into being through the gifting of other texts; these are acts of friendship and hospitality – and of intertextuality. These structures of ingestion and incorporation, of the self and the text as a series of nested structures inherited from others, are all versions of the host–parasite relation that recurs throughout Miller's thinking about hospitality, the gift, friendship, writing and travel: in his account of his visit to Hangzhou in 1987, Miller had described himself as "a kind of carefree visiting parasite". As the three friends sit reading each other's texts at Coppin Grove, Steven reflects on their relationship:

> Parasites customarily recognize their hosts by means such as passionate intuition. The recognition is instinctive. In burrowing into the substance of their hosts, from which they are to draw their sustenance and proceed to the fulfillment of their life's purpose, they are setting out on a predestined journey, a project about which they are unable to exercise choice. To proceed with it is their only allowable activity. They have no other purpose in existing. If they do not respond to the signal to advance then they and their species perish. One would not speak of motives and aims in such a matter, or of conceptual certainty. The sustaining substance reacts to one's entry into it. It is not what it would have been if one had not entered it. The result, therefore, cannot become a biography of one's subject. Nor a history, either, of one's own progress. The result must be something one has not foreseen. (99–100)

This is a complex passage that offers one of the richest expressions of Miller's aesthetic preoccupations. Miller has said that in Steven's pursuit of Lang, he wanted to capture both the "altruistic" yet also the "selfish" motivations of the novelist: "I followed the idea of the fiction writer being a parasite . . . the novelist, Steven, chews up his friend, Lang Tzu. He chews up his past, he chews up his stories and makes a fiction of them."[67] The parasite's journey into the territory and body of the host, the host's openness to the other, and the host's subsequent transformation by the parasite, refers not only to the creation of art through intertextuality, but equally to friendship, migration, journeying and colonisation.

---

67 Alex Miller, quoted in Louise Carbines, "A Book of Freedom and Belonging", review of Alex Miller, *The Ancestor Game*, *The Age*, 15 August, 1992, 9.

This is what Miller means when he speaks of the condition of the migrant as being not just incidental to a culture in its widest sense, but constitutive of it.

In *Derrida and Hospitality*, Judith Still remarks that "one of the most striking features of discussions of (in)hospitality is their particular intertextual quality – how elements from a range of earlier or otherwise distant theories and practices are introduced and transformed in the new context".[68] In Derrida's major works on friendship, the gift, and hospitality – in *Adieu to Emmanuel Levinas*, *The Gift of Death*, *The Politics of Friendship*, *The Work of Mourning* and *Of Hospitality* – he joins in many conversations, citing, close reading, and incorporating into his own texts the texts of others, including Homer, the Bible, Plato, Aristotle, Cicero, Kierkegaard, Montaigne and Levinas. As two possible models of literary (in)hospitality, Still cites Harold Bloom's Oedipal agon and J. Hillis Miller's classic defence of deconstruction in "The Critic as Host". For Bloom:

> Any poet . . . is in the position of being "after the Event", in terms of literary language. His art is necessarily an *aftering*, and so at best he strives for a selection, through repression, out of the traces of the language of poetry . . . The caveman who traced the outline of an animal upon the rock always retraced a precursor's outline.[69]

For Hillis Miller:

> The poem . . . any poem, is, it is easy to see, parasitical in its turn on earlier poems, or contains earlier poems as enclosed parasites within itself, in another version of the perpetual reversal of parasite and host. If the poem is food and poison for the critics, it must in its turn have eaten. It must have been a cannibal consumer of earlier poems.[70]

At Coppin Grove, where Steven and Gertrude are Lang's guests, the three friends consume together a bottle of wine that has itself been imported into Australia from Germany. As Lang reads the drafts of *The Chronicle of the Fengs* that Steven has written after first consuming *The Winter Visitor* and other texts, Steven reads the diaries of August Spiess, while Gertrude recites a poem for Steven. It is her father's favourite, Heine's "*In der Fremde*" ("In Exile"): "Heine, she said . . . [my father] was only ever at home in exile. Now it's one of my family heirlooms, the poem is, from the old world" (103). Each of these acts of incorporation produces something new – a new text, a new friendship, a new transnational relationship between cultures. This, as we have seen, is the "*khoral*" quality of textuality: "The text is always a bastard. This system of boxes inside boxes, containers containing containers".[71]

These seemingly abstract considerations of intertextuality as a form of hospitality have profound implications for the ethics and politics of contemporary Australia's place in the world, confirming Pierce's original assessment of *The Ancestor Game* as part of that "second wave" of Australian fiction about China that examines "the complicated, long-term presence" of "the Chinese stranger *within* . . . this society".[72] The friendship between Lang

---

68 Judith Still, *Derrida and Hospitality: Theory and Practice* (Edinburgh: Edinburgh University Press, 2010), 83.
69 Harold Bloom, *Poetry and Repression*, quoted in Still, *Derrida and Hospitality*, 85.
70 J. Hillis Miller, "The Critic as Host", *Critical Inquiry* 3, no. 3 (Spring, 1977): 446.
71 Caputo, *Deconstruction*, 91.
72 Pierce, review of *The Ancestor Game*, 101. My italics.

and Steven and Gertrude, their sharing of texts and images and stories, suggests that in contemporary Australia, in the most fruitful ways, the boundaries between inside and outside, self and other, have been wounded and ruptured – and then redrawn. This is to see writing as part of a network of intertextual borrowings without origin. It is to see a culture like modern Australia's not as closed, discrete and finally complete in itself, but porous at the edges, a work in progress that is open to or *oriented* toward the other.

Extraterritoriality and the Artist

In tracing Spiess' aesthetics back to Heine, Miller appears to ground his thinking within romantic and modernist ideas about the artist as solitary and an exile, as one whose natural location is " '*In der Fremde*'. In exile". In his later novels about art, however, we will come to see that Miller is consistently ambivalent about such commonplace ideas, tending instead to juxtapose conflicting theories and positions without clear resolution – as he does, for example, in the conflict between art and industry in *Conditions of Faith*, in the relationship between solitary artistic creativity and collaboration in *Prochownik's Dream* and *Autumn Laing*, and in the conflict between proponents of Australian impressionism and modernism, also in *Autumn Laing*. In part two of *The Ancestor Game*, the motifs of enemy occupation, parasitism, and the ambiguities of hospitality explored in Spiess' presence as an extraterritorial in China are applied to the work of the writer. This looks initially like an argument for the "extraterritoriality" of the artist, in George Steiner's sense – "A great writer driven from language to language by social upheaval and war is an apt symbol for the age of the refugee"[73] – as exemplified by Spiess' exile from Germany, the young Lang Tzu's repudiation of Chinese tradition, and their flight to Australia after the Japanese invasion of China. Yet these ideas may prove to be an illusion engendered by what Miller calls the "honeymoon" period of the traveller abroad, and through Spiess' devotion to Heine he questions the romantic and modernist claims for art's extraterritoriality.

In chapter 10, "The Entrance to the Other-World", Steven approaches the house at Coppin Grove like a thief at the back door, a parasite in the territory of his host. He discovers that this was also Gertrude's way as a writer, making her approach to her family history from her base camp in the summer house, her scene of writing. Like the artist's studio in *Prochownik's Dream*, the summer house signifies the artist's status as exile and romantic outsider, but also their desire to observe and occupy the place of the other:

> The summerhouse ... was in fact the interstitial place from which, with the cunning trigonometry of her fiction, she had surveyed her landscape ... I knew I'd realized something that ought to have been obvious to me for a long time. Something that had been obscured, however, until this last week or two, by the tremulous mask of aspen leaves, the dense thicket of suckers that was at last leafless and no longer able to conceal the secret hidden at its heart. It was a shock to find myself seated there. It seemed I had found my way there ... by the instinctive homing intuitions of a true parasite ... I was delighted by this extension of my metaphor, of myself as a parasite, as "one who eats at the table of another". (153–4)

---

73 George Steiner, *Extraterritorial: Papers on Literature and the Language of Revolution* (New York: Macmillan, 1971), 11.

In Chinese culture, Lang tells Steven, the summer house or gazebo is regarded as "the entrance to the other-world" (158), playing a similar function in Miller's novels to the bridge, the window and the doorway in Amor's paintings. Given the ambivalent economy of friendship, the gift and hospitality, it is also ironic that in Chinese culture "a gazebo was originally a lookout for the enemy" (156).

Steven's discovery of the gazebo is a fable about the artist as an observer and an invader in the homeland of the other that is developed further in chapter 11, "Reflections from the Gazebo". Drawing on Spiess' journal and other sources, it is an account of events in Hangzhou and Shanghai between 1932 and 1937. During this period, Lang is trained by his grandfather in the art of calligraphy, but he also discovers his "dimorphic" nature, the conflict within him between Chinese tradition and Western modernity, and at the time of his grandfather's death he makes a commitment to modernity by destroying his grandfather's book of the ancestors. Lang's dimorphism, which is expressed symbolically in his asymmetrical facial features, is a reflection of the historical forces driving the modernisation of China in the decade before the Second World War: "Lang existed in two distinct forms. In Hangzhou he was a student of the classical arts of China and in Shanghai he was no less than the child of honorary European expatriates in the International Settlement" (166). Spiess, who is Lang's tutor and himself an expatriate, compares him to two-headed Janus, "the Roman god of the doorway" (166) – and of bridges.

The conflict between tradition and modernist innovation is also apparent in the art world of Melbourne during the same period in *Autumn Laing*. Lang's nature is "dimorphic", but like the young Pat Donlon he chooses to break with his roots and commit himself solely to modernity, thereby denying one half of his nature. It is important to remember, however, that Lang's invasion of his grandfather's study, his theft of the book of the ancestors, and his subsequent burning of the book, is the response of a ten-year-old boy to his sense of exclusion when his dying grandfather refuses to take him on his final pilgrimage to the shrine of his ancestors: "His grandfather's refusal . . . and his mother's collusion in this decision, was too large a detail for Lang to measure" (176). Miller shows a similar ambivalence about Pat Donlon's "childish" refusal to take instruction at art school, while Lang's casting away of his grandfather's mirror foreshadows Autumn Laing's casting of Edith Black's beautiful pastoral landscape into the loft at Old Farm. Lang's subsequent actions and his understanding of his own condition are governed by adolescent feelings of rejection and exclusion: "How could the ancestors call to *him*? There was his divine Western dimorphism. The presence of his father in him. There was the *West* in him. His line was broken" (177).

Far from being Miller's own definitive theory about the rootlessness and modernity of the artist, Lang's behaviour in breaking into his grandfather's study can be seen in part as a youthful fantasy that he enacts with two other boys, Shu and Shin, and the decision to renounce his ancestors is justified, in his own mind, by the example of Spiess, whose own sense of "extraterritoriality" has its roots in European modernity:

> To set out, to depart from the old way, was for Lang the inescapable imperative of the moment, not to reconcile the opposing positions of his parents. He did not think of an end to the journey, any more than the migrating bird thinks of the end. His desire was to set out, not to go somewhere in particular. August Spiess alone had offered him a resolution to the dilemma of his dimorphism. Without considering it, without being exactly aware

of what he was doing, it was into this proferred interstice between the way of his mother and the way of his father than Lang at this moment inserted himself. (184)

The young Lang Tzu identifies neither with Hangzhou and tradition nor Shanghai and modernity, but with the condition of travelling between them: "Travelling between Shanghai and Hangzhou . . . he was in the only place he had ever been able to call his own" (193). Ironically, however, this idea of the artist as an exile without roots has its own roots in a specific time and place, in Europe in the late nineteenth century.

The modernist idea that the artist is an "extraterritorial" is illustrated in Spiess' reflections on the imaginary landscapes of the painter Claude Lorraine, who was himself neither German nor French nor Italian. The international settlement at Shanghai is just such a Claudian landscape and Spiess sees himself as one of its "extraterritorials", "beings not from present reality", "inhabitants of a No-land" (93). In such phrases, Miller appears to celebrate extraterritoriality, and he has spoken positively of "the ambiguities bestowed on artists and writers by cultural displacement".[74] This is certainly the fate Lang chooses as a young man. Having violated his grandfather's study, he plays the ancestor game, a process of self-invention in which he is free to make up the rules as he goes along. If art is beyond nation, then Lang has no place in China, and Spiess suggests that he may find a home in Australia: "You are literally un-familiar here. But in Australia, which is I believe a kind of phantom country lying invisibly somewhere between the West and the East, you may find a few of your own displaced and hybrid kind to welcome you" (260). As a place of exile and migration, Spiess' Australia anticipates the condition of postmodernity. Miller might be seen as espousing the ideas of hybridity, diaspora and indeterminacy that were popular in postcolonial and postmodern theory in the late 1980s. Yet these ideas at play in Spiess' diaries are subject to narrative irony, as are the accounts of Pat Donlon's doctrinaire enthusiasms in *Autumn Laing*. The extraterritorial is not, after all, immune from reality, as Spiess discovers when he is attacked by a mob of Chinese workers and then forced to witness their torture and execution in a Shanghai police cell. Spiess' disillusionment about the neutrality of exile and the extraterritoriality of the artist is comparable to that moment in Miller's own visit to China that he described as the end of his "honeymoon" period. It is marked by a turn from the ethics to the *politics* of hospitality.

The Politics of Hospitality or the Violence of the Guest

Miller's use of the terms "parasite" and "colonist" in such apparently different contexts as friendship, art and the transnational movement of people and commodities – such as the British incursion into China during the Opium Wars, or the first Feng's migration to Port Phillip in 1848 – raises questions about the *politics* of hospitality, including the politics of the artist as guest or parasite upon his host. While the domain of inter-personal relations is governed by ethical concerns, the political field governs relations between individuals and the state, or between states. Hospitality, as Judith Still observes, "is always about crossing thresholds", including those between such domains as the public and private, the personal and the social.[75] What does Spiess' presence in the heart of Huang's

---

74 Alex Miller, "Playing the Ancestor Game: Alex Miller Interviewed by Simon Caterson", *Journal of Commonwealth Literature* 29, no. 2 (1994): 5–11.

traditional home in Hangzhou reveal about the politics of hospitality and the politics of art? If Miller is careful to deny his narrator, Steven Muir, any right to feel "at-home-with-oneself" in Australia, thereby avoiding "the violence of the host", this does not mean that the person who avoids putting down roots, like Spiess, the German romantic, is free from political risk. On the contrary, the exile, the émigré, the rootless person, and even the artist as conceived by modernism as an exile from his homeland, may be, from the perspective of others, a colonist. This is the politics of what Mireille Rosello calls "postcolonial hospitality".[76] We might call it "the violence of the guest".

Since coming to Shanghai from Hamburg twenty years earlier, Spiess has enjoyed the status of an "extraterritorial". Until his visit to Hangzhou, a centre of Chinese tradition, he has been spared the burden of self-examination. His experiences while visiting Huang's home in Hangzhou, however, reveal to him forcefully that his is not a neutral presence in China, and that he is seen by the Chinese as a representative of a foreign power, a colonial "occupier". Spiess is treated as an honoured guest in Huang's home and offered lavish feasts at a vast dining table in the "guest hall" (117, 138). This is a formal, ceremonial expression of hospitality, but Spiess is an unruly and troublesome guest who reveals the double meaning of that word as one who is potentially an enemy, "hostile" to the interests of the host. Even as he accepts Huang's hospitality, Spiess recognises the ambiguity of his position. Like any gift, hospitality is in part an expression of the host's own virtue, to which the guest must submit. For the purposes of this ceremony, Spiess is dressed in a grey fox fur cape given to him by the head of Huang's household, Yu Hung-meng, which makes him look like the larvae of the region's famous silk worms. Reflecting on the etymology of that word, Spiess uncovers its link with the words "mask" and "spectre", which Steven associates with the writer: "Here, then, was the word *larva* in its original usage! For in Latin it signifies a mask or spectre whose true form is hidden, a form yet to be revealed" (119). As a foreigner in China, Spiess may well feel that he is travelling with a kind of neutrality or invisibility: this is the "honeymoon" period. But in accepting Chinese hospitality, in becoming Huang's guest, Spiess enters into a political relation with the other in which his identity can no longer be masked or determined solely by himself. Even the extraterritorial is subject to the gaze of the other.

The occasion of this unmasking is Spiess' decision, contrary to his host's wishes, to leave the security of Huang's house and walk alone through the surrounding farmlands to the ruins of a pottery on Fenghuang Hill where the famous celadon porcelain was made during the Sung Dynasty. Knowing how hated foreigners are in Hangzhou, Madame Feng does not wish Spiess to leave the house, though out of courtesy to her guest she has not told him why. He resolves to undertake the excursion without informing her: "Fearing she might not approve and would find the means to prevent me from proceeding with it . . . I said nothing to Madame Feng" (126). In the countryside, surrounded by hostile peasants and young communist students, Spiess cannot comprehend that they see him as a foreign invader until he is stoned and beaten with sticks and has to be rescued by Madame Feng. The foreign visitor has made a breach with protocol, not only endangering his own life, but inadvertently sacrificing the lives of those who have attacked him, who will now be executed by the police. Madame Feng reproaches him angrily:

---

75 Still, *Derrida and Hospitality*, 7.
76 Mireille Rosello, *Postcolonial Hospitality: The Immigrant as Guest* (Standford: Stanford University Press, 2001).

There is no end to the harm you have done! ... Will you attend the executions of these wretched people? ... Will you let them know you hate them as implacably as they hate you? Will you grant them this assurance, that they are dying for a reason and have been defeated by a real enemy? Will their deaths dignify you, Doctor Spiess? In some way? In a European way I have not understood? If that is the case, explain it to me and I shall be satisfied. Extraterritoriality? What does it mean to you? Why invent such an idea for the occupation of a country? (135–6)

The "guest" is an enemy and an invader after all, hated, not honoured, in the foreign culture whose protocols he has misunderstood.

The politics of hospitality and the violence of the guest, explored here indirectly through the "mask" of Miller's setting in Hangzhou in the 1920s and 1930s, had profound significance for Australian readers of *The Ancestor Game* in 1992. At that time, Australians were struggling with reconciliation, with the realisation that settler Australia was itself a "guest" in that place, and that it was guilty of the violence of the guest toward Indigenous Australians. These are questions to which Miller would return more directly in the Central Queensland novels, *Journey to the Stone Country* and *Landscape of Farewell*. Spiess' blundering into the countryside is echoed there in Annabelle Beck's unwitting offence to Dougald Gnapun when she presents him with a stone artefact whose ceremonial meanings his people have forgotten, or later at Mount Coolon when Panya, "the last stone woman", throws back in her face the aims of the Council for Aboriginal Reconciliation.[77] Like Max Otto, who is compelled to return to the scene of the death of Dougald's goat in *Landscape of Farewell*, Spiess is required to witness the execution of the young Chinese peasants into whose territory he has blundered.

Spiess may be the novel's exemplary "extraterritorial" but his thinking is formed by European modernity – by the illusory idea that the artist is one who lives "*in der fremde*". As we will see again and again in Miller's novels, he is able to dramatise such ideas without committing himself to particular points of view. It is a mistake to take the opinions of his characters for Miller's own. "Art", Spiess tells Lang, "belongs to no nation. Art is the displaced" (260). But as a result of his experience at Hangzhou, Spiess realises that he cannot stand apart from history and locality: that he is not an extraterritorial but a colonist, like the others. This is the lesson he learned on Fenghuang Hill. In 1937, on the eve of their departure for Australia, he recounts to Lang the effect of witnessing the executions: "For twenty blissful years I had lived as if the condition of extraterritoriality were a kind of literary conceit ... After Fenghuang Hill and Laozha Police Station I saw that we were a part of the tragic history of China. And I could stand apart from it no longer" (268–9).

Multiple Modernities

I want finally to consider *The Ancestor Game* from the perspective of what is known as "the new modernist studies".[78] The recursive structure of *The Ancestor Game*, with its abrupt shifts in time and place, allows Miller to explore a new conceptual geography that arises

---

77 Alex Miller, *Journey to the Stone Country* (Sydney: Allen & Unwin, 2002), 344.
78 Douglas Mao and Rebecca L. Walkowitz, "The New Modernist Studies", *PMLA (Publications of the Modern Language Association of America)* 123, no. 3 (2008): 737–48.

from thinking of Australia and Asia not as separate though proximate entities, but as a set of relations. Through its many portals, or "chinks in time and space", linking together Australia-in-Asia as a massive canvas in space and time, Miller evokes what Susan Stanford Friedman calls the new conceptual geography of "multiple modernities".[79] Ironically, while Stanford Friedman's theoretical model provides a compelling framework for reading Miller's novel, *The Ancestor Game* pre-dates her ideas by more than a decade. This is a measure of Miller's achievement not only as a novelist, but as an historical novelist seriously concerned with the drama of ideas.

Friedman argues convincingly that we should set aside the old "diffusionist" model of modernism and modernity, in which innovation takes places exclusively in Euro-America during a finite period – roughly between 1875 and the 1930s – and then spreads, unevenly and belatedly, to the peripheries, in favour of the idea of "multiple modernities". This is the error to which Spiess clings through his outdated devotion to Heine. The new thinking requires re-spatialising and re-periodising the origin and global poetics of modernism:

> Recognizing modernisms on a planetary landscape involves identification of intensified and proliferating contact zones that set in motion often radical juxtapositions of difference and consequent intermixing of cultural forms that can be alternately embraced, violently imposed, or imperceptibly evolved. Traveling and intermixing cultures are not unidirectional, but multidirectional; not linear influences, but reciprocal ones.[80]

The complex relations between Miller's London, Melbourne, Shanghai, Hamburg, Tokyo and Hangzhou are examples of such multiple sites and vectors of modernity: they maintain their traditional relations of exchange with Europe, but superimposed on those older imperial axes is a series of portals or contact zones between the peripheries of China, Japan and Australia. This is a new "poetics of relation" that abolishes notions of centre-periphery in favour of multiple centres and flows of cultural exchange and innovation. And this new geography, concerned with the simultaneous engagement with modernity in multiple locations, brings with it a new periodisation: "Instead of looking for the *single* period of modernism, with its (always debatable) beginning and end points, we need to locate the *plural* periods of modernisms".[81]

Friedman describes three principles at work within this new relational economy which she terms "friction", "indigenisation", and "rupture". The concept of friction is meant to capture both the positive and negative aspects of the cross-cultural exchanges that produce multiple modernities: "*Friction* carries with it the connotations of conflict and serves as an apt metaphor for interculturality in colonial and postcolonial contexts".[82] Cross-cultural exchange involves both movement and resistance in a spatial field characterised by gross inequalities of power, and the vectors of contact are often facilitated by violent, disruptive and invasive circumstances, including war: "modernity is often associated with the intensification of intercultural contact zones, whether produced through conquest, vast migrations of people (voluntary or forced), or relatively peaceful commercial traffic and technological or cultural exchange".[83]

---

79   Susan Stanford Friedman, "Periodizing Modernism: Postcolonial Modernities and the Space/Time Borders of Modernist Studies", *Modernism/modernity* 13, no. 3 (September 2006): 427.
80   Friedman, "Periodizing Modernism", 430.
81   Friedman, "Periodizing Modernism", 432.
82   Friedman, "Periodizing Modernism", 431.

The second principle associated with modernity's movement across cultural boundaries is that of mutual transformation, for which Friedman uses the metaphors of ingestion and cannibalisation:

> The terms *indigenization* and *nativization* additionally suggest a kind of cultural cannibalism, if you will, an ingestion of the other which transforms both the cannibal and the cannibalized. This association of modernity with indigenization, nativization, and cannibalism appears to fly in the face of the conventional association of these terms with the traditional and primitive… Indigenization reminds us that modernity involves a forgetting of origins, a claiming of cultural practices from elsewhere as so much one's own that the history of their travels is often lost.[84]

As we have seen, Miller uses remarkably similar metaphors to describe cross-cultural exchange in *The Ancestor Game*: the military and parasite metaphors in the novel testify to the paradoxically creative and conflictual nature of the cross-cultural exchanges between Australia and China in the nineteenth and twentieth centuries, and the mutual transformations to which they give rise, both generally in Anglo-Chinese culture and specifically in the texts this exchange produces, including the Spiess diaries and *The Chronicle of the Fengs*.

Friedman's third principle is that of "rupture", a defining feature of multiple modernities, which are experienced as a violent break from the past, from "tradition". Friedman puts these elements together to form a complete account of her concept of multiple modernities, which assumes "divergent articulations of modernity in various geohistorical locations":

> modernity involves a powerful vortex of historical conditions that coalesce to produce sharp ruptures from the past that range widely across various sectors of a given society. The velocity, acceleration, and dynamism of shattering change across a wide spectrum of societal institutions are key components of modernity as I see it – change that interweaves the cultural, economic, political, religious, familial, sexual, aesthetic, technological, and so forth, and can move in both utopic and dystopic directions. Across the vast reaches of civilizational history, eruptions of different modernities often occur in the context of empires and conquest.[85]

In the massive and complicated topography of *The Ancestor Game*, these ruptures of modernity and its breaks with tradition take place simultaneously in both China and Australia, mapped not only in space in the contrast between traditional Hangzhou and modern Shanghai, but also across the generations and the genders in the Feng family. That is to say, Australia and China are not in themselves representative of modernity and tradition, but are co-equal and inter-connected sites in modernity's rupture with tradition. The aftermath of the First Opium War in 1848, when the first Feng flees a disintegrating Fukien province, is one such moment and place of rupture:

---

83 Friedman, "Periodizing Modernism", 433.
84 Friedman, "Periodizing Modernism", 431.
85 Friedman, "Periodizing Modernism", 433.

> Just as a corpse left unburied for a few days seethes with a mighty colony of maggots, so the Middle Kingdom seethed with war and banditry and opportunism in the aftermath of the first opium war, and in the West it was the year of revolution. The World had forgotten peace and the victims of war were to be seen everywhere. (214)

Miller is quick to point to the relations of equivalence between China and the West rather than their hierarchical relation: the social disruptions in Fukien province are not only caused by its engagement with Europe, but are mirrored in Europe's own revolutions at that time.

A second point of rupture is Shanghai during the second Japanese invasion in 1937, when Lang Tzu, the fourth Feng, leaves for Australia:

> Although it was only just after three in the afternoon, there was a kind of twilight outside. Heavy smoke from the ironworks and from the steamers and from the naval guns was bellying against a dark overcast of rain clouds. The river and waterfront were illuminated in a coppery light, as if a great Bessemer converter were discharging its load of molten steel nearby. The solid structures of the buildings along the waterfront and the ships on the river, and the river itself, were rendered in a variety of soft, metallic hues which made them look like lurid shadows cast up against the more solid, the darker sky. They had lost their detail, they had become a painter's idea of a city under siege... There was a peculiar and sinister calmness over everything, in which small events continued to unfold. A British cruiser had begun maneuvering to a new station in the middle of the river... He watched her making a pale bow wave as she turned against the thrust of the current. Less than two kilometres downstream, out of sight, the Japanese battleships continued at regular intervals to fire over the Settlement into the Chinese city... Each time the ships fired a salvo of shells from their big guns the window pane in front of Lang rattled and the floor trembled. An earthquake. (258–9)

Subject to the vectors of international capital and military invasion, Shanghai is the very essence of modernity as Marx defined it in his famous phrase, "all that is solid melts into air".[86] Traditional China, Huang's China, is "a disintegrating world" (290), but it is also a modernising world.

Miller therefore resists seeing Australia or Europe as more "modern" than China: the disruption caused by the Opium Wars in 1848 is echoed in Europe's year of revolution while Japan's invasion of China anticipates Hitler's annexation of Austria and invasion of Poland by only two years. Both Europe and Asia are "disestablished worlds", and there is an "intercultural contact zone", a portal between them. Because these ruptures are both positive and negative in their effects, producing both utopic and dystopic circumstances, the affective dimension of modernity is similarly contradictory: "modernity has a self-reflexive, experiential dimension that includes a gamut of sensations from displacement, despair, and nostalgia to exhilaration, hope, and embrace of the new".[87]

---

86 Marshall Berman, *All That is Solid Melts into Air: The Experience of Modernity* (London: Verso, 1983).
87 Friedman, "Periodizing Modernity", 433–4.

Multiple Modernities: *The Ancestor Game*

The interior of Feng's villa is neither authentically Chinese nor authentically European. Like (the Irish) Mrs Muir's home in Dorset or Lang Tzu's English-styled mansion in Melbourne, it is a proof of the cannibalising power of colonial modernity:

> The room was "European" in the sense that a room in Sydney or London might be said to be "Chinese". That is it reflected the desire of its owner for a certain effect. To a genuine European there might have seemed to be something incongruous about the furnishings, something possibly to cause amusement, especially among the English who often found themselves amused by the Chinese. *They* might have detected an element of burlesque, of unintentional parody, in the resolute elaboration of the "European" theme which was set forth in the furnishing of the room. For there was no object in this room, nor indeed in the entire house, that was Chinese. Not even one or two of the chinoiseries one might confidently expect to find in a real European room... C.H. Feng, to whose design the furnishing of this room and of all the other rooms in the house conformed, was accustomed to express his commitment to internationalism with a degree of purity that was considered, by those who knew him, to be eccentric. (28–9)

In moving between her husband's city of Shanghai and her father's city of Hangzhou, Madame Feng, moves between the two poles of tradition and modernity that constitute the fluid state of China in the 1920s and 1930s. Her father, Huang, is a literary painter who lives in a traditional Chinese house in the "provincial capital" of Hangzhou (46), though it is now dilapidated. Haung's traditional house in Hangzhou is mirrored in Lang's equally dilapidated 1870s house in Coppin Grove, forestalling any assumption that Australia is more modern that China: "It was a polychrome brick mansion and was in a state of serious dilapidation" (39). By contrast with both of these "traditional" houses, C.H. Feng's villa in Shanghai does not look inward to tradition and the past, but outward to the "ochreous tides" of the Whangpu River (91), a portal of exchange between China and other centres of modernity. When Spiess looks out from Lien's bedroom window at the "mighty Whangpu River", he reflects on "the vast tonnage and diversity of cargo that was disposed of through the port of Shanghai each day" (91). When asked by friends why he does not return to Hamburg, he points out that "Hamburg and Shanghai have in common a regular exchange of goods and merchant tonnage" (89).

Miller's understanding of the complexity of multiple modernisms and a decentred modernity is conveyed in his selection of epigraphs for *The Ancestor Game*. These also have a direct bearing on my argument earlier in this chapter that he is ambivalent about the extraterritoriality of the artist rather than a champion of the romantic and modernist doctrine of exile. The first epigraph is from Søren Kierkegaard's *Either/Or*: "Our age has lost all the substantial categories of family, state and race. It must leave the individual entirely to himself, so that in a stricter sense he becomes his own creator." While some reviewers seized on the apparent relation between creativity, modernity and exile, others recognised the novel's essentially dialectical structure, which involves both deracination and rootedness; both the youthful compulsion to leave one's family and the past, and the equally strong compulsion to seek a homeland. As Sophie Masson wrote in her review, "We no longer believe that the individual can actually 'create himself'; we are as much shaped by our past, by our ancestors, as by our own actions."[88] For Louise Carbines, *The Ancestor Game* is about freedom but it is also about belonging, or the delicate balance between them. She cites Miller: "To gain one is to lose the other. To gain absolute freedom is to cease to belong anywhere. To belong totally somewhere is to lose one's freedom."[89]

This contrary impulse to belong, to seek a homeland, is captured in the novel's second epigraph, from Judith Wright's *The Generations of Men*: "Indeed there was about their story something of the atmosphere of the Book of Genesis, and some aura, too, of supernatural descent clung to them." Together, these two epigraphs constitute a dialogue between the ruptures of modernity and the lure of tradition. Like Friedman, Miller sees them as relational rather than exclusionary: the Judith Wright quote suggests the continuing importance of those substantive determinants, of the individual experiencing their rootedness to family and place and culture. It is just this need that brings the novel's three "only children", Steven, Lang and Gertrude, together in the opening chapters as they seek to fill the absence each experiences at their centre of being.

As I have noted, Miller was disappointed that reviewers had not grasped these tensions between solitariness and collaboration, tradition and modernity, rootedness and deracination. When they repeatedly cited the epigraph from Kierkegaard and ignored the implications of the Wright quotation, he decided that neither would appear in the American edition of the novel.[90]

---

88 Sophie Masson, "Where Are You From Really?" review of Alex Miller, *The Ancestor Game*, *Australian Book Review*, no. 143 (August 1992): 4.
89 Alex Miller quoted in Carbines, "A Book of Freedom and Belonging", 9.
90 Alex Miller, "Playing the Ancestor Game", 10.

3
Black Mirror: *The Sitters*

The Sitters (1995) is the second in a series of Alex Miller's novels, beginning with *The Ancestor Game* and including *Prochownik's Dream* and *Autumn Laing*, that constitutes one of the most sustained examples of *ekphrasis* (or writing about art) in Australian literature. While Miller's father, his first wife Anne Neil, and his friend Allan O'Hoy were all accomplished painters, his descriptions of the art galleries and studios in these novels are also informed by Miller's knowledge of Rick Amor's studio practice and regular exhibitions at the Niagara Galleries in Richmond. Curator David Hansen has written an insightful account of Amor's studio practice for the exhibition catalogue, *A Single Mind*, which accompanied a major retrospective of Amor's work at Heide in 2008,[1] to which Miller contributed an essay on Amor's self-portraits.[2] Hansen argues that Amor is one of the few painters working in Melbourne today who retains a commitment to the traditional craft values, which he calls Amor's "Old Master" approach: "there is aesthetic resistance, in the artist's determined maintenance of figuration against the late twentieth century's various conceptualisms and abstractionisms".[3] As a writer, Miller maintains a similar commitment to the craft of narrative fiction.

Amor had made a woodcut portrait of Miller for his "Contemporary Authors Series" in *Overland* in 1992, and during the winter of 1994 Miller sat for him again for a portrait in oils.[4] After one of the sittings, as they stood together looking at the work in progress, Miller realised that his friend had given him the idea for a new novel based on a portrait painter coming to terms, through his art, with the deaths of people with whom he has been intimate, including his sister and a former lover: "It was the artist in his studio and he was painting a portrait of his lost sister . . . [she] was not in front of him, as I had been in front of my artist friend . . . for she was dead long ago, but she was there in his mind's eye." Such are the mysterious displacements of memory, however, that the painting the artist produces is not of his sister, nor of the lover, but of her empty bedroom:

---

1 David Hansen, "Vacant Possession", in *A Single Mind: Rick Amor*, curated by Linda Short (Bulleen, Vic.: Heide, 2008), 95–109.
2 Alex Miller, "The Artist to Himself: The Self Portraits of Rick Amor", in *A Single Mind*, 131–4.
3 Hansen, "Vacant Possession", 98.
4 Rick Amor, *Portrait of Alex Miller* (1995), oil on canvas, 100 x 74 cm, collection of Alex and Stephanie Miller. Alex Miller, "Rick Amor's Show at Castlemaine Gallery, 1 June 2003", unpublished speech.

It contained no likeness of his lover, but only her bed, the door to her room open, the light from the window driving shadows and presences from the room until it seemed her figure had only that moment departed. It was a portrait of absence and longing, and there was no likeness in it but the one he recollected each time he looked on that scene of lost intimacy.[5]

The Sitters is about the process or, more accurately, the *experience* of a process that is at the centre of Miller's art, "the ruin of time": it is concerned with being-in-time, with longing, absence and silence, and with the intimate connections between art, memory and death. In recalling its formative moment in Amor's studio, Miller used the image of a black mirror to describe that dark and mysterious space where the artist must wait patiently, like a hunter, for the substance of his art to appear. Significantly, he refers almost without distinction to both "the black mirror of his art" and "the black mirror of his memory".[6]

Miller's essay, "Writer's Choice: The Black Mirror", suggests something of the multiple biographical and even epistemological complexities of his meditation on portraiture in the novel. In an illuminating essay on *The Sitters*, Brigitta Olubas observes that Miller "imagines the space of the portrait as comprised of multiple images and planes, as a point of meeting, observation and entanglement". A portrait is "the point where two stories, or the stories of two lives, grow together" through the work of both memory and forgetting.[7] This is borne out in the complex accounts of looking at art in *The Ancestor Game*, such as Steven's inspection of his friend, Lang Tzu, reflected in the glass covering a nude hung in Lindner's Gallery, or their examination together of the portrait of Lang's great aunt, Victoria Feng. In each of these instances, the structures of looking are chiastic, as the self and the other engage in what Veronica Brady describes as "a ceremonious introspection". Portraiture in *The Sitters* is "at once profoundly intimate and yet paradoxically impersonal, as the artist pursues [his subject] . . . in himself and himself in her through the labyrinthine ways of memory".[8] The novel's subject matter is complex and refractive in just this way, so that not even Miller found it easy to give a straightforward account of its contents. In a difficult series of locutions in his biographical essay, "The Mask of Fiction", he has said, "*I thought* . . . I was writing about a working-class Australian woman who had gone from Australia to England and become a professor." He saw this as "a kind of reverse version of my own history – a mirror-image of my own portrait". But he goes on to add, "*I now acknowledge The Sitters* to have been a meditation on my relationship with my father and my lost sister [Kathy]."[9] The novel's achievement is that it is not simply about a friendship conducted through the business of portrait painting, but that it uses the theory and practice of portraiture to conduct an aesthetically and philosophically rich exploration of Miller's signature themes: the nature of friendship, the relation between art, friendship and death, and the craft of fiction. As Ronald A. Sharp observes, "this is a novel that foregrounds the connections between literary and visual art, between a novelist creating a character and a painter creating a portrait".[10]

---

5   Alex Miller, "Writer's Choice: The Black Mirror", *Art & Australia* 43, no. 3 (2006): 446.
6   Miller, "Writer's Choice", 446. Gail Jones had earlier used this phrase in the title of her novel about art, *Black Mirror* (Sydney: Picador, 2002).
7   Brigitta Olubas, "Like/Unlike: Portraiture, Similitude and the Craft of Words in *The Sitters*", in *The Novels of Alex Miller: An Introduction*, ed. Robert Dixon (Sydney: Allen & Unwin, 2012), 93, 95.
8   Veronica Brady, "A Portrait of Absence and Silence", *Australian Book Review*, no. 170 (May 1995): 43.
9   Alex Miller, "The Mask of Fiction: A Memoir", in *The Novels of Alex Miller*, 34. My italics.

Like *The Ancestor Game*, *The Sitters* derives a great deal of its subtlety from the transformation of its story into a complex narrative that is refracted through associative memory. The story concerns the friendship between an unnamed portrait painter and an Australian-born professor, Jessica Keal. Jessica has grown up on a farm in the Araluen Valley near Canberra, but left there for London on a scholarship at the age of eighteen, and has lived and worked for the past thirty years in England, where she is now an eminent historian. Her story of migration is a mirror image of the portrait painter's: "It's a kind of reverse of my own story."[11] The painter was born into a working class family in England, but migrated as a young man to Australia, where he married, had a family, and became a successful portrait painter. He and Jessica meet at an event to welcome her as a visiting scholar at the Australian National University in Canberra, where he also has an honorary affiliation. The painter, who has been experiencing a creative blockage, accepts a commission to make a series of engravings of ten eminent Australian women only because it gives him a reason to meet her again, and after an initial session at his studio they agree that he will go on to make a portrait in oils. As their friendship develops, Jessica takes him to meet her mother at the family farm, which she expects to inherit. He there makes a preparatory sketch for her portrait, in which she sits for him in her childhood bedroom, although she is surprised to find that he has left her out of it entirely, merely painting the empty room. Just as their friendship seems to be deepening into love, Jessica returns to England, where she becomes ill and dies. The painter goes on to complete his portrait of her posthumously, and eventually buys the farm that she was to have inherited.

The narrative begins with the painter's recollection of their meeting in Canberra and his account of the development of their friendship, interspersed with memories of his own childhood, which his relationship with Jessica encourages him to revisit and reconsider. There is no overt sign that the central character of the book has died, although there are many references to her death that are obvious on a second reading. The tone of the narrative might therefore be described as one of proleptic mourning.[12] At the point of the apparent blossoming of the friendship and Jessica's return to England, the narrative shifts suddenly back to the present, and the painter's account of his completion of the portrait after her death. The portrait is his imagined version of her last illness, and is set in her bedroom or hospital room in England, which he has not seen.

The Sitters has its origin in the interruption of death, in "absence and longing" for the other. It is this foundational moment of interruption that gives the novel its severely fragmented quality, which it shares with Derrida's eulogies, collected in *The Work of Mourning*. Apologising for the fact that his thoughts on the death of Roland Barthes are so fragmentary, Derrida says that he values them "for their pronounced incompleteness", for their "punctuated yet open interruption": "These little stones, thoughtfully placed, only one each time, on the edge of a name as the promise of return."[13] The elegy is inherently fragmentary because it is generated by the interruption of death, which is also an interruption of the self by its interiorisation of the other, who is now present only "in me", "in us". The

---

10 Ronald A. Sharp, "The Presence of Absence in *The Sitters*", in *The Novels of Alex Miller*, 78.
11 Alex Miller, *The Sitters* (Melbourne: Viking, 1995), 43. All subsequent references are to this edition and appear in parentheses in the text.
12 The phrase is used in Tanya Dalziell, "An Ethics of Mourning: Gail Jones' *Black Mirror*", *JASAL: Journal of the Association for the Study of Australian Literature* 4 (2005): 49–61.
13 Jacques Derrida, *The Work of Mourning*, eds Pascale-Anne Brault and Michael Naas (Chicago and London: University of Chicago Press, 2001), 35.

"interruption" of death sets in train an alteration of the self, in which one's own memories and personal narratives are re-opened and altered (literally, made other to themselves). Speaking of the remembered image of Barthes, Derrida writes, "it is within us but it is not ours . . . Roland Barthes looks at us (inside each of us) . . . and we do not do as we please with this look".[14] In his eulogy for the art historian, Louis Marin, Derrida explains that this introjection of the other, which is a kind of wound, causes a reorganisation of the spatial boundaries between the inside and the outside.[15] While the death of the friend is an interruption – of time, of narrative series – it is also an interruption of the self by the introjection of the image of the other, which requires adjustment, accommodation and alteration.

The Sitters is a chronically "interrupted" work in just this sense. Miller's portrait painter begins with his internalisation of the image of his dead friend, Jessica Keal, but also with the way the memory of her "alters" his sense of himself, the interruption turning what has been a "paralysis of the self" into a productive, generative state of incompleteness: "And that is what she gave me, Jessica Keal, the subject of this altered memory, a memory entangled with certain family likenesses and forgotten moments of my childhood; her roots and mine mysteriously grown together" (1). *The Sitters* is fragmented and incomplete not only because it springs from the interruption of friendship by death, but also the interruption of the self by the other, and the alteration of the self this sets in train, in which the painter's memories of his own life are interrupted and altered by those of his sitters. Jessica's childhood reminds him of symptomatic moments in his own childhood. The portrait of Jessica merges with memories or portraits of his sister; the scene of Jessica's death in England, which he does not witness, is imagined by cannibalising his earlier memories of a former lover, abandoned in his youth; the portrait of his friend Henry, another "bedroom" or deathbed portrait, is conflated with his (imagined) deathbed portrait of Jessica. This altering and intertwining of the roots of memory is the source of art. It is what Derrida describes as the "eucharistic paradigm" of friendship and mourning.[16] Once we open the self to the other, once we take "a piece [*morceau*]" of the dead inside us, the self is punctuated, fragmented, made incomplete by absence and longing. This begins from the first moments of friendship, which means that friendship is an anticipatory "*a priori* mourning".[17]

Like Steven and Lang's friendship in *The Ancestor Game*, the painter's friendship with Jessica Keal is charted by their mutual creation and interiorisation of images, both the images of memory and those made through representation – through writing, photography, drawing and painting. As Alberti puts it in *On Painting*, portraiture "makes the absent present: 'as friendship is said to do' ".[18] In each novel, this process of interiorisation culminates in the absence of one of the friends – Lang and Jessica respectively – and their survival "in us", in the other, in the form of images. In *The Sitters*, this culminates in the painter's posthumous portrait of Jessica on her deathbed, which he describes in the final pages of the novel.

As readers of *The Sitters*, we come to understand the development of the painter's friendship with Jessica as an economy of the image. It begins as an external gaze, but as the friendship develops they increasingly internalise images of each other, and images that

---

14 Derrida, *The Work of Mourning*, 44.
15 Derrida, *The Work of Mourning*, 160.
16 Derrida, *The Work of Mourning*, 169.
17 Derrida, *The Work of Mourning*, 49–50.
18 Quoted in Derrida, *The Work of Mourning*, 154.

were initially withheld are increasingly exchanged freely as gifts. In his recollected account, the painter is acutely aware of the *politics* of the image: of issues of intrusion, violation and consent, and of the fact that looking and being looked at are dialectical, not singular activities. In *The Sitters*, this results in an ambivalence about the artist's possession of the image, an erotics and ethics of the image. Here Miller develops a series of metaphors already explored in *The Ancestor Game* of the artist as a hunter, a parasite, a colonist or invader in the territory of the other. As we will see, these ideas are captured by his references, relatively late in the novel, to two utterly different painters whose work he admires: Pierre Bonnard and Walter Sickert. The painter's exchanges with Jessica involve both the domestic lyricism and romanticism of Bonnard, and the forensic realism and ethical ambiguity of Sickert. The painter is enraptured by his subject both in the sense of being taken out of himself by Jessica, but also in the sense that he is himself a raptor: Jessica is the painter's muse and she is also his prey.

Hester

The painter's first memory of Jessica is of seeing her across the room at a function to welcome her as a visiting scholar at the Canberra university with which he also has an affiliation: "In my memory of her that day Jessica has dark hair that gleams with an auburn light and falls in a soft line at the nape of her neck. There are purplish shadows of fatigue and uncertainty beneath her eyes" (2). This first memory, which already contains the signs of proleptic mourning in the painter's registration of the fragility of Jessica's skin, is suggestive of the cover of the first edition of *The Sitters*. Like *The Ancestor Game*, *The Sitters* was published with a carefully chosen cover image that reflects Miller's profound knowledge and understanding of contemporary art: it is an untitled pen and ink drawing made by Joy Hester in 1955. Miller bought the painting as a gift for his first wife, Anne Neil, who left it to him after her death in 2004, and it is now on permanent loan to the National Portrait Gallery. It was Barrett Reid who first identified the untitled work as a double portrait of John and Sunday Reed.[19] Between 1938 and 1947, Hester was part of the circle of artists, including Sidney Nolan, Arthur Boyd, John Perceval and Albert Tucker, who met regularly at Heide, the home of the art patrons John and Sunday Reed. Born in Melbourne in 1920, Hester married Tucker in 1941, but left him in 1948 to live with Gray Smith, whom she married in 1959. Her work is dominated by portraits, especially of her family and friends, executed in her favoured medium of brush and ink on paper. Like Miller, she has said that she was strongly affected by the newsreels shown in 1945 of Nazi concentration camps,[20] whose monochrome images of the dead haunt her own ink drawings of the living, including her portrait of the Reeds.

Hester's portrait has complex resonances for Miller. It is another early sign – almost a secret confession, given that it is untitled – of his lifelong interest in Nolan, Sunday Reed, and Heide's second circle. Through the figure of Sunday Reed it also announces the motif of the artist and his muse. While this theme was left as an absence in *The Ancestor Game*, where the potential relationship between Steven and Gertrude Spiess is not ex-

---

19 Alex Miller to Robert Dixon, 27 September 2013.
20 Janine Burke, "Hester, Joy St Clair (1920–1960)", *Australian Dictionary of Biography*, Australian National University, http://adb.anu.edu.au/biography/hester-joy-st-clair-10493.

plored, it is central to *The Sitters*, *Prochownik's Dream* and *Autumn Laing*. It speaks to *The Sitters'* central theme of portrait painting and, via the biographies of both Sunday Reed and Joy Hester, it evokes the relationship between portraiture, friendship and death. Hester's poignant registration of the marks beneath her friend Sunday Reed's eyes is echoed in the novel, in the portrait painter's memory of his first sight of Jessica Keal, the "purplish shadows of fatigue and uncertainty beneath her eyes" (2). Like the "wound" that Steven first sees in Lang's damaged face, this is the *punctum* of the image, the part of it that "shoots out of it like an arrow, and pierces me".[21] In 1947, Hester was diagnosed with Hodgkin's lymphoma, and she died on 4 December 1960 after a protracted illness and long periods in hospital. In 1983, more than twenty years after her death, Tucker painted a moving portrait of Hester in which a breaking wave behind her signifies the presence of death in the world. These associations are suggested by the art historian Richard Haese in his commentary on Tucker's portrait:

> The tragic dimension of Joy Hester's life, especially the long and terrible fight against cancer from which she died in 1960, is present in the anguished turn of the head and the dark wall of breaking waves behind her. The sea refers not only to the beachside world of her youth but also, as Tucker has revealed, to a passage "the long joyful sea hateth me" from Sidney Nolan's collection of poems on the period entitled *Paradise Garden*. As Tucker states, "power and menace. Something coming to overwhelm her, as it did".[22]

Alongside the names Bonnard and Sickert, the proper name "Joy Hester" is therefore a potent signifier of Miller's preoccupations in *The Sitters*, including the relationship between portraiture, memory, friendship, mourning and death. Like Jessica Keal in Miller's novel, "Joy Hester" in Tucker's portrait stands for what the French writer and critic Maurice Blanchot calls "death in the process of becoming".[23]

We might think here in terms of both Levinas' image of hospitality to the other as the "vulnerability of a skin explored, in wounds",[24] and Barthes' *punctum* as a wound or bruise.[25] At this early stage, however, the painter is aware of Jessica's separateness, even her sense of being preyed upon: "She's withholding herself. She is wary" (3). When he looks at her too often and for too long, she responds like a creature that is aware it is being hunted: "She must have been aware of my scrutiny, and eventually she turned and looked directly at me. Her gaze was filled with enquiry and challenge, and even with a certain enmity" (3–4). His gaze is actively challenged and returned: "Well, what is it you want from me? Her look demanded ... A strong look from across the room letting me know of her annoyance. Then she looked away" (4). As Olubas notes, this is a struggle for possession of the image, the index to one's own self-identity, which is heavily invested in the visual: "This visuality comes almost immediately to stand in for her, for her known or imagined self-

---

21   Roland Barthes, *Camera Lucida: Reflections on Photography* trans. Richard Howard (New York: Hill and Wang, 1981), 26.
22   Richard Haese, introduction to Albert Tucker, *Faces I Have Met* (Melbourne: Hutchinson, 1986), 6.
23   Maurice Blanchot, "Literature and the Right to Death", in *The Station Hill Blanchot Reader*, ed. George Quasha, trans. Lydia Davis, Paul Auster, and Robert Lamberton (New York: Station Hill, 1999), 392.
24   Levinas, quoted in Jacques Derrida, *Adieu to Emmanuel Levinas*, trans. Pascale-Anne Brault and Michael Naas (Stanford: Stanford University Press, 1999), 141.
25   Barthes, *Camera Lucida*, 26.

hood."[26] This is why, in both *The Ancestor Game* and *The Sitters*, the friend whose image is "taken" by the other, by the writer or the painter, is less than fully pleased, sensing that this brings with it an unsettling "distortion" or, as Derrida would say (himself incorporating the text of Levinas), an "interruption" of the self by the other. When he reads *The Chronicle of the Fengs*, Lang is troubled by Steven's "Australian fiction of China", and Jessica bristles at the artist's refusal to let her see his first sketches for her portrait: "She's angry with me . . . The likenesses are hers, that's what she thinks. She'd be confused, she might even feel misrepresented, if she saw what I've done" (21–2). The artist acknowledges that the image is "something that belongs to her", but at the same time he wants to impose his own interpretation upon her: "Observing her you might imagine there's something Mediterranean in her ancestry, perhaps even Spanish. This, and her air of detachment, remind me of [a] woman . . . in my youth" (3). The comparison, one of the painter's earliest references to his former lover in England, is a reminder of the ethically compromised role of the artist as a serial predator.

This is what Derrida, in *The Politics of Friendship*, calls "reckoning" with friendship: the apparent obscenity of serially comparing the memory of different friendships, each of which deserves to be treated as a singularity.[27] Prior to his meeting with Jessica, as he is later to confess, the painter has already "taken" the image of a young English woman, whose integrity he feels that he has violated. In a complex and indirect way, this also violates Jessica's memory not just by comparing her to a former lover, but by the fact that in both instances – and this is what causes him to recall the earlier instance – he finds the violation of the women's privacy sexually arousing: "it made her deeply attractive to me, the person I was imagining. Her detachment a kind of grandeur . . . I saw her turn towards me, her bare arms, the straps of her dress pressing into her shoulders . . . And I saw her turn away again" (6). As the painter preys upon Jessica's image, the hunter in him is both aware of, and excited by, the wounded appearance of her skin, by her vulnerability, just as he was excited by the abjection of the English woman: "Her dark eyes with the soft purplish shadows beneath them . . . and their aggressive question to me still hanging in the air unanswered, *What do you want from me?*" (7). As we will see, the painter whose name stands for this darker, more predatory side of the artist is not Hester but Walter Sickert.

Bonnard

When the painter is offered a commission to make a series of etchings of ten eminent Australian women by the editor of a scholarly journal, he sees Professor Keal's name on the list. Although he does not want to do the engravings and at first declines the invitation, he later accepts because it will allow him to invite her to his studio. His motives are neither transparent nor ethical, and as she sits for him while he sketches, he is aware of the "delicate physics of desire" (20). Again, Miller uses the image of the artist as a predator, a raptor seeking to catch his prey and carry it off: "In portraiture it's the shy beast you're after not the mask . . . You've got to entice the beast out of hiding into the open . . . You have to gain its trust" (38–9).

---

26 Olubas, "Like/Unlike", 92.
27 Jacques Derrida, *The Politics of Friendship* (London: Verso, 1997).

As Jessica and the painter work more closely together in preparation for the portrait, exchanging images and memories from their past lives, their memories begin to intertwine. Moved by Jessica's return to her family and the scenes of her childhood after thirty years abroad, the painter recalls his own estrangement from his sister and her death from breast cancer. (Is this how Jessica herself is to die?) At her family home at Araluen, the painter sketches Jessica in the intimate space of her childhood bedroom. His memories flow unconstrained and at times ambiguously between the doorway of his sister's bedroom in England and Jessica's at Araluen, where he paints the portrait of her absence:

> I set up my easel and the rest of my gear in the open passage outside her bedroom door and that's where I began to paint my first study... But she wasn't in it. That first study was of her absence. That's what it turned out to be. The room through the door seen from the passage. Vertical, enclosed, dark. The door frame an additional frame within the simple composition. Cramping the perspective. Forcing the viewer to look more searchingly, into the narrow vertical enclosure. The bed a short section of horizontality, stopped, blocked at either end, pushed up and curtailed tightly. I kept her right out of it. (107–8)

This use of multiple frames within a single compositional space is a characteristic of Amor's self-portraits, whose grid-like structures he derives ultimately from Nicolas Poussin. In *Portrait of the Artist* (1650), Poussin sits before a series of framed canvases of various sizes leaning against a wall, so that his eyes are exactly positioned between the top edges of two of these frames. David Hansen observes that many of Amor's portraits and self-portraits work in a similar way, "framing the image of the sitter within a treble structure":

> the face is... fixed in place within the canvas by the rigid geometry of design... and then the whole apparatus is further contained by the edges of the frame... The self-conscious framing of the artist's face makes the reference to the fundamental idea of easel painting as a window or mirror, while the quotation of one of the world's earliest naturalistic paintings [Poussin's *Portrait of the Artist*] makes further play with history and representation. Indeed the whole painting is something of a game, a ludic meditation on perception and illusion... Most if not all of Amor's figures and their implicit narratives are caught within such tight geometric structures.[28]

A Gary Catalano puts it, "the channels of space within the paintings ruthlessly determine the manner and direction in which the eye can move".[29] Yet in the image made by Miller's painter, this elaborate framing structure encloses nothing: there is no face; the room is empty.

In his book about the art of Rick Amor, *The Solitary Watcher*, Catalano compares this passage from *The Sitters* with one of Amor's paintings, made while Miller was working on the novel. A month after Amor and his second wife, Meg Williams, moved into their new house at Alphington in 1994, he painted their bedroom. In *The Room (Memory)* (1994), the bedroom is empty except for a huge wardrobe in one corner and a white towelling

---

28   David Hansen, "Vacant Possession", 95–6.
29   Gary Catalano, *The Solitary Watcher: Rick Amor and his Art* (Melbourne: Miegunyah Press, 2011), 152.

bathrobe hanging from a hook behind its half-opened door. Catalano's analysis of the painting is revealing of Amor's and Miller's mutual interest in recording the shared intimacies of domestic life, and the powerful relation between absence and longing. The name that stands for these intimacies is "Bonnard":

> The bathrobe (which Amor on one level associates with Bonnard, having seen just such a robe in a photograph of his bathroom) is beautifully modelled and evokes a sense of bodily presence, while the subdued light leaking into the room around the lowered blind bounces off the mirrored door in the cupboard and catches the edge of the door handle, and in doing so subtly reminds us that those two doors are partly opened.
>
> Given this poetic charge, we hardly need to be told that the work once contained a human figure in order to sense that it is dealing with two people and the intimacies between them. Like that in the painting Miller describes in *The Sitters*, Amor's empty room is filled with the sense of human presence. We can probably be more specific about it. In its oblique and suggestive way, *The Room (Memory)* appears to be dwelling on the trust and vulnerability that are necessary in any relationship. Both doors are open, yet we can see through neither. Just as the darkened interior of the cupboard forbids exploration, so the door is opened in such a way that it hides the doorway itself. The painting is thus a metaphor for the private life.[30]

Other critics have also noted the importance of absence in Amor's paintings, which tend to imply a narrative while leaving the precise details of the story and its motivation mysterious. As Peter Corrigan suggests, "we sense presences lurking just around the corner or deep within the shadows".[31]

While Catalano's comparison of Amor's and Miller's treatment of domestic intimacy is insightful, he underestimates the extent to which the passage from the novel and the painting are both rendered more poignant by the way absence speaks of the imminence of death. In the novel, the passage describing Jessica's bedroom at Araluen has emerged directly out of the painter's memories of his sister's bedroom as a child in London, and of her death from breast cancer at a time when they lived in different countries. This conflation of his sister with Jessica, and of three different bedrooms – his sister's childhood bedroom in London, Jessica's childhood bedroom at Araluen, and the bedroom or hospital room in London where she dies – is most immediately motivated not just by his growing intimacy with Jessica, but also by his grief for his sister and his proleptic mourning for Jessica. In attempting to explain her absence in the painting, he reflects:

> We paint portraits from our alienation from people. It's nostalgia for company we don't have and can't have. Absence and loss. People we've lost. We're haunted by our memories of them, of ourselves with them. We're always dealing with these things. How to deal with them, that's always the problem. How to visualize them in their absence. (110)

In another parallel between their work, Amor has recently returned to the subject of *The Room (Memory)*. In the self-portrait, *The Window* (2011), he revisits this scene from his own past, and as an older man he now struggles to look in through the bedroom window

---

30 Catalano, *The Solitary Watcher*, 146–7.
31 Peter Corrigan, "A Civil Society", in *A Single Mind*, 127.

from outside the house.³² The open door of the wardrobe inside the empty room again discloses an interior darkness. This is perhaps an image of Bonnard's domestic intimacy, but it is an intimacy rendered "vulnerable", as Miller puts it, to time and death – not least the imminence of the artist's own death. The temporal structure of the 2011 painting, with the artist now looking back on a scene from the past, parallels the structure of Miller's narrative. In his catalogue essay for the 2013 retrospective of Amor's work at the Niagara Galleries, Miller writes, "Our own hopes and fears, the nameless anxieties of our brief existence here, seem to inhabit Amor's paintings."³³ And on the relation between art, intimacy and death, Amor has said, "Most art is about death and the inevitability of decay . . . that's the only thing worth painting about."³⁴ This is the ruin of time.

In an insightful discussion of this haunting passage from *The Sitters*, Bernadette Brennan uses the work of Maurice Blanchot and Martin Heidegger to discuss the significance of absence and silence in the novel, arguing that "death is represented through the unsaid, the absent".³⁵ Having faced the moment of his own death as a young resistance fighter captured by the Nazis during the war, Blanchot was driven to reflect in both his fictional and theoretical writings on the role that death, or being-toward-death, might play in consciousness and everyday life. In "Literature and the Right to Death", he writes that "Death works with us in the world; it is a power that humanizes nature, that raises existence to being, and it is within each one of us as our most human quality."³⁶ Since no one can really know what it is to die, it is the role of art to represent the incomprehensibility of death:

> the only relation that the living can maintain with death is through representation, an image, a picture of death, whether visual or verbal . . . [But] the representation of death is not the representation of a presence, an object of perception or intuition – we cannot draw a likeness of death, a portrait, a still life, or whatever. Thus, representations of death are *misrepresentations*, or rather they are representations of an absence.³⁷

The paradox at the heart of representations of death is best conveyed by the figure of prosopopoeia: "that is, the rhetorical trope by which an absent . . . person is presented as speaking or acting". Etymologically, prosopopoeia means to make a face: "in this sense we might think of a death mask . . . a form which indicates the failure of a presence".³⁸

In *The Sitters*, Brennan argues, art is "not about capturing likenesses; it is about finding a way to articulate loss and absence".³⁹ This is why, when Miller's portrait painter first attempts to paint Jessica, he paints her absence: "But she wasn't in it. The first study was of her absence . . . I kept her right out of it" (107–8). This first study for the portrait, however,

---

32   Rick Amor, *The Window* (2011), in *Rick Amor Recent Paintings 30 July – 7 September 2013: 30 Years with Niagara* (Richmond, Melbourne: Niagara Galleries, 2013), plate 13.
33   Alex Miller, "Rick Amor: The Poetry of What Is Seen", catalogue essay, *Rick Amor Recent Paintings*, n.p.
34   Rick Amor, quoted in Trent Walker, "Rick Amor: Artist Profile", *Australian Art Review*, 5 July 2012, http://artreview.com.au/contents/8518968-rick-amor.
35   Bernadette Brennan, "Literature and the Intimate Space of Death", *Antipodes* 22, no. 2 (December 2008): 103.
36   Blanchot, "Literature and the Right to Death", 392.
37   Simon Critchley, "*Il y a* – Holding Levinas' Hand to Blanchot's Fire", in *Maurice Blanchot: The Demand of Writing*, ed. Carolyn Bailey Gill (London: Routledge, 1996), 108.
38   Critchley, "*Il y a*", 108.
39   Brennan, "Literature and the Intimate Space of Death", 103.

was not made after Jessica's death, but before the painter was even aware that she is ill. Although his *recollection* of making the study at Araluen post-dates her death in England, the making of the study itself takes place in her presence. The absence that is registered here is more aptly described as the artist's *a priori* mourning of his friend – the sense of anticipatory absence that, according to Derrida, always attends the growth of friendship.

Conjuring Death

The relationship between art, friendship and death is explored in another of the painter's portraits in *The Sitters*, which he compares with his work-in-progress, the portrait of Jessica. It is another "bedroom" painting, a portrait of his friend Dr Henry Guston on his deathbed. *Henry* hangs in the painter's own bedroom: it is there before him as he is talking to Jessica Keal by telephone in her hospital bed in London. He explains, "My portrait of Henry wasn't like Rembrandt's *Anatomy Lesson*. I mean I didn't begin it expecting to do a corpse" (58). Presumably this means that Henry died during the composition of the painting, as Jessica does during the painting of hers, and that it finally became, at least in some sense, the painting of a corpse. He later submits it to the Archibald Prize for portraiture: "*Henry*, as I called it, created a controversy with the Archibald committee. They couldn't decide whether a corpse was a proper subject for portraiture" (58).

We can approach the fascinating issue of why *Henry* is *not* like Rembrandt's *Anatomy Lesson* through Sarah Kofman's last essay (left unfinished at her own death), "Conjuring Death: Remarks on *The Anatomy Lesson of Doctor Nicolas Tulp* (1632)". Published posthumously after her suicide in 1994, it plays a central role in Derrida's untitled eulogy for Kofman, later published in *The Work of Mourning*, in which he describes the "eucharistic paradigm" of friendship and mourning. Kofman begins by setting the scene:

> A professor – recognizable right away, as he is the only one wearing a hat (this is Doctor Nicholas Tulp, Amsterdam's top surgeon . . .) – is situated at the far right of a group of seven doctors, his audience, arranged in a pyramid. At the base of the pyramid, and in contrast with this group, there is stretched out horizontally a cadaver.[40]

Kofman's attention is caught not by the dramatic figure of the cadaver, but by the way these men of science are so absorbed in Doctor Tulp's lesson that they appear no longer to see the lifeless body laid out before them. As Pleshette DeArmitt puts it, "It is precisely this forgetting, this not seeing, . . . this conjuring away of the corpse to which Kofman wants to draw our attention and about which she will offer a lesson."[41] Kofman writes: "They do not seem to identify with the cadaver stretched out there (*là*). They do not see in it the image of what they themselves are in the process of becoming."[42] Their gazes have moved away from the cadaver toward the book that is wide open at the foot of the dead man, who might now be nothing more than a lectern to support the book. It is as if the book and not the body

---

40   Sarah Kofman, "Conjuring Death: Remarks on *The Anatomy Lesson of Doctor Nicolas Tulp* (1632)", in *Selected Writings*, eds Thomas Albrecht, Georgia Albert and Elizabeth Rottenberg, trans. Pascale-Anne Brault (Stanford: Stanford University Press, 2007), 239.
41   Pleshette DeArmitt, "Conjuring Bodies: Kofman's Lesson on Death", *parallax* 17, no. 1 (2011): 4.
42   DeArmitt, "Conjuring Bodies", 238.

were the subject or source of the "lesson". Derrida describes this substitution of the body for the book:

> This book stands up to, and stands in for, the body: a corpse replaced by a corpus, a corpse yielding its place to a bookish thing, the doctors having eyes only for the book facing them as if, by reading, by observing the signs on the drawn sheet of paper, they were trying to forget, repress, deny, or conjure away death.[43]

Rembrandt's modern men of science conjur away death and, by implication, religious illusion, but Kofman's point is that they conjur up another illusion, the idealisation of scientific knowledge as a replacement for the older "magical" religion, and a belief in science's capacity to preserve, perhaps even to restore, life: "a sleight of hand has taken place as the wisdom of man has replaced the word of God and an 'anonymous' cadaver, a common criminal, stands in for the body of Christ".[44]

Rembrandt's painting conjures death by diverting the gaze from the corpse to the book and all that it represents: the faith in modern science. *The Sitters* conjures away death by diverting the gaze from the corpse of Jessica Keal to her portrait, or at least the painter's memoir of his meeting with her and how he came to paint her portrait (that is, the death-bed painting after Sickert described at the end). While the presence of the book in Rembrandt's painting is an effect of the artistic medium – of oil painting – so the presence of the portrait in Miller's novel is an effect of *that* artistic medium: the first person narrative and Miller's brilliant ekphrastic description. But what is Miller's view of the relation between art and death? Does *The Sitters* finally perform an occultation, drawing the veil of art over the corpse? Or does it work to reveal what we are all "in the process of becoming?" Does portrait painting in the novel enter into the conspiracy of art and science to conjur death? Or does the image of presence merely remind us, as Derrida says of the body of Christ after the Crucifixion, that "he is not here; he is elsewhere"? Miller's portrait painter understands the relation between presence and absence in his art. He understands that the portrait is merely a "likeness", not the presence of the person, who is indeed absent. He does not believe he is successfully conjuring death. The submission of *Henry* for the Archibald is a test case. Can a painting of a corpse be a portrait? He seems to say openly that it is a portrait of a corpse, *sans* veil, and he hangs it together with his portrait of Jessica.

While the portrait painter in Miller's novel is careful not to conjur death, for his father, who is now dead, the figure of the book once played a similar role to the book in Rembrandt's *Anatomy Lesson*, conjuring death, or at least conjuring the absence of creativity and the presence of a negative attitude to life. The painter's father, who before the war was a talented and enthusiastic amateur watercolourist, has been traumatised and defeated by his experience of war. The symptomatic expression of this crisis is his hobby of restoring damaged books, whose broken spines give them an anatomical quality. In recalling this time of despair in his father's life, the painter echoes the novel's opening line, which is an account of a similar period in his own life:

> When he was old and had given up painting he started picking up second-hand books in the markets and spending his evenings at the dining table repairing their bindings . . . he's

---

43   Derrida, "Introduction", Kofman, *Selected Writings*, 9.
44   DeArmitt, "Conjuring Bodies", 12.

bent over the table dabbing oil or glue or something on the spine of a book . . . I'm looking into his secret, and it's empty, and he doesn't know how to defend its emptiness from the destruction of my gaze. (14, 30, 31)

The old, broken-backed books are meant to distract the family's gaze from a series of absences or impending absences – the father's failure, the presence of his trauma, the absence of his former love of painting, his own impending death – "My father's gone of course" (28) – but in their resemblance to human corpses, they signify the very absences they are meant to conjure away. As symbols of the absences in his father's life and of the absence of his father through death, they echo the paralysis of will the artist himself experiences prior to meeting Jessica Keal, whose own death he conjures by painting her portrait.

Ellipsis

As the painter's relationship with Jessica Keal deepens, their exchange of looks and images becomes freer, and their memories more entwined. On the banks of the Araluen Creek, among the scenes of her childhood, Jessica freely gives the painter images of herself: "She stands straight, making a picture of herself . . . embracing her childhood playground. She knows I'm watching. She's proud of the way she looks" (75). In her absence, while she goes downstream alone to swim in a waterhole, the painter captures the image she has given him: "While I wait I get out my little notebook and do some small sketches of her standing up on the bank" (75). When she returns, she asks again whether she can see the notebook, expecting a rebuff, but he hands it to her without hesitation. She touches the drawings with the tips of her fingers, questioning the image he has made of her, testing it against her own self-understanding.

The proximity of love and death is foreshadowed here by the fact that Jessica and the painter experience the beginning of their love at the very place where her ancestors are buried: "There are the grave mounds of her grandmother and her great-grandmother. The Keal women" (117). The force of that "there" is telling: there are the graves, *there*. It is this series, the series of the Keal women, that Jessica's return to London and her death there will interrupt. But it is also a moment when Jessica agrees to take the artist to the swimming hole where she has recently swum naked, provoking an image of herself in his mind that she has not wanted to share with him until now. At this moment, they are "self-conscious and alert and clumsy with each other" (118). It is a moment of rapture, of being carried out of oneself by the other: "There's a shimmering in the light now, with the wine and the air . . . We walk down the hill together, the last of the sun in our eyes dazzling us, and there's the click and scrape of her mother's hoe" (117–8). The impaction of love and death is striking: the autumnal "*last* of the sun", and the ambiguous, potentially funereal scrape of the hoe.

The painter's memories of this radiant moment in the past are interrupted by his need to speak now of Jessica's return to London and her death: "She's gone" (118). It is an echo of an earlier ellipsis, when his memory of the death of his parents interrupts his account of the beginning of his friendship with Jessica: "My father's gone of course. Long ago. My mother too now. There's no one left" (28). At each of these points of interruption, these breaks in the narrative series, the transformation of the painter's life begins again: "This was really the first inkling I had that she was going to change things for me" (28).

On page 118 of *The Sitters*, an ellipsis in the text marks the central point of its silence and absence: "She's gone." In The *Work of Mourning*, Derrida uses an ellipsis – (. . .) – in lieu of a title for his eulogy for Sarah Kofman, the ellipsis performing the interruption and unspeakability of her death. Miller's ellipsis in *The Sitters* is literally an empty space between the first and second paragraphs. It is here that the narrator turns back from his recollections about the past to the narrative present, now going forward in time to recall the events of Jessica's return to England, her death, and his completion of the portrait. It is the moment when his account of his friendship with Jessica must finally be interrupted by speaking about her death, his posthumous completion of her portrait, and the working of his altered memories of his own family and childhood, "that cold legacy of silence and absence" (2). It is a moment in the narrative when the painter makes a wrenching leap in time, from the rapturous annunciation of their feelings for each other that day on the Araluen Creek, to the time after her death when he is living alone on her farm. This gap in narrative time is literally a place of silence and absence, but it is also a hinge in time, the turning point at which the painter's transformative experiences of love and death propel him to make this great leap of faith away from his creative paralysis and back into the present, back toward life and his own creative future: "I don't believe I'll ever suffer such a paralysis of my will again. Now I'll go on painting until the end" (1).

We can approach this ellipsis in *The Sitters* by looking at Derrida's eulogy for Emmanuel Levinas, "Adieu". Derrida says that he wants Levinas' death to be an occasion to resist the commonplace idea of death as "nothingness". Derrida is working to displace nineteenth-century philosophy's classic opposition between being and nothingness, which can only conceive of death as emptiness, as annihilation. That, he suggests, would be a kind of murder, for "It is [only] the murderer who would like to identify death with nothingness." The ellipsis on page 118 is the interruption of death, but must it also be a space of nothingness and annihilation? Death, Derrida insists, is "not, first of all, annihilation, non-being, or nothingness, but a certain experience for the survivor".[45] Our responsibility to the other means that there is an "interdiction" against their annihilation: "The face of the Other forbids me to kill." Derrida is thinking here of the "eucharistic paradigm" of mourning, where the dead survive "in us" as images. He notes that Levinas frequently uses the words "ravish" and "rapture" to speak not only of what it is that attracts one to the face of the other, but also of death itself.[46] These words have rich and varied resonances in Miller's body of work. Rapt means to be lifted up, as by a supernatural force, or else to be transported by love, into a state of trance, ecstasy or rapture. It comes from the Latin *raptus*, meaning to plunder, to live on prey. Rapture is the act or power of transporting, carrying forcibly away; a state of being rapt, or carried out of oneself. As a transitive verb, rapt means to draw a person forcibly into some condition or action; to remove a person from earth, especially to heaven; also to transport a person in spirit. Ravish, from the Latin *rapere*, which is also the root for rape, is to seize or carry off by an act of violence.[47]

We might say that the central theme of *The Sitters* is the close relation between the experiences of love and death, and the ability of both to transform the self by its responsiveness to, its interruption by, the other. It follows from this that the death of the other may well be a space of silence and absence, but it is not *necessarily* a space of nothingness

---

45 Derrida, *Adieu*, 6.
46 Derrida, *Adieu*, 8.
47 *OED* Online.

and annihilation. It is a space of interruption, of non-response, but it is the responsibility of the "survivor" to understand that this is also a space of potential rapture, where the other is kept alive "in us" as a monitory image, and that this has the potential to transform the self.

The ellipsis in *The Sitters* is a space of silence and absence where the painter contemplates his responsibility to the other, despite – or perhaps because of – her non-response. This means that it is not a space of annihilation and nothingness. From this moment in time, and at this space of interruption and absence, the painter experiences a proliferation of images of Jessica, though they are all marked by the *punctum* of death:

> I was surrounded by Jessica's images. My studio was covered in them. Drawings, etching, linocuts, watercolours, oil studies, gouaches, those little black and white snapshots she gave me. A picture of her grandmother and herself standing by the gate to the garden ready to catch the school bus to Braidwood . . . There's something wistful and beautiful about her in this one. She's got her hair in plaits. Vulnerability, that's what it is, to time. The quick leap of time. It gives me a tight feeling in my stomach to look into this little picture of her. (118–9)

This cache of images, like Lang's family archive on the dining table at Coppin Grove, is Jessica's gift to the painter, the material that he will carry off, like a predator, and into which he will insinuate himself.

In the ellipsis, the narrator makes a great leap in time from the past to the present, and within that space of absence comes the presence of his portrait of Jessica; within that space of silence he narrates his memoir of their relationship, which begins in this moment of return to the narrative present: "She's gone . . . " Into this moment of interruption erupts the rapturous force of death that produces the language and imagery of *The Sitters*. And this is a "gift", the gift of death. The phrase is repeated throughout the novel: "those little black and white snapshots she gave me"; "And that is what she gave me, Jessica Keal, the subject of this altered memory" (1). It is just this turn toward the death in the present, now embraced for its creative potential, that Miller had excluded from the final pages of *The Ancestor Game*, in which Lang is left mysteriously absent.

Sickert

After the ellipsis of death, in the final pages of *The Sitters*, now in the novel's narrative present, the portrait painter is living at Jessica Keal's family property and has put down roots – or rather, he has adopted her roots, living at the farm that she was to inherit from her mother, where the other women in her family are buried beneath an ancient walnut tree. It is there that he imagines the scene of her death in England, and from this imagined scene he makes a series of paintings, several of which he destroys.

In imagining the scene of a naked women on an iron bed receiving a visit from death, the portrait painter draws partly on his own guilty memories of the lover he abandoned in England as a young man before coming to Australia, and partly on Walter Sickert's paintings of the infamous Camden Town Murder. This is one of numerous intertextual references in the novel to paintings that in one way or another deal with the relationship between art, death and mourning:

> She woke herself with a great shuddering snore, lying on her back on the iron bed as if she'd been felled by a blow, her mouth agape, her throat dry and roasting, one naked leg unslung loosely over the side of the bed . . . Light . . . was seeping into the room at a low, sneaky angle. Sidling in and washing about the little room. Searching for something. Seductive fingers of light seeking out the form of the woman on the bed, modelling her . . .
>
> Now that the day is withdrawing the room has ceased to resist and is warm, and she has become all softly crumpled shadows and a sense of disarray. Her face is turned away from the viewer. She might be the victim of a brutal murder. A crime of passion. A momentary rage. A bedroom portrait. One of Sickert's sinisterly anecdotal fables, *The Sunday Visitor*. A violent death. You can still smell her visitor in the stuffy air, and smell their passion. (129–30)

Miller is alluding here to the German-born British painter Walter Sickert, whose suite of paintings and works on paper associated with the Camden Town Murder of 1907 are a regarded as a seminal condensation of the style and themes of British art and popular culture in the late nineteenth and twentieth centuries: they stand mid-way between Sigmund Freud and Jack the Ripper in the 1880s, and Lucian Freud, Francis Bacon, Brett Whiteley and the Christie Murders in the 1950s. Above all, as art historian Lisa Tickner observes, they established the banality of death as the quintessential subject of modern British painting.[48] As we will see in chapter 6, it is this modern history of the nude with which Toni Powlett struggles when he returns to figurative painting in *Prochownik's Dream*. Miller has said, "I was made aware of Sickert's darker side through the person who introduced me to his art, Allan O'Hoy . . . I had also read widely commentaries on Sickert's own writings, particularly Osbert Sitwell's *A Free House* and Marjorie Lilly's *The Painter and his Circle*."[49]

On his return to Britain from Dieppe in 1905, Sickert settled in the London suburb of Camden Town. It was then in the process of de-gentrification, its large, middle-class houses being split up into slum tenements for the Irish labourers and their families who were recruited as construction workers on King's Cross, St Pancras and Euston stations. Prostitution was widespread in the district, often as a means of supplementing family incomes, giving rise to the popular music-hall line, "And what shall we do for the rent?" Sickert took lodgings at 6 Mornington Crescent, and using local prostitutes as his models he began a series of works with the signature theme of naked women on narrow iron beds in small, shabby rooms, often juxtaposed with the menacing presence of clothed men.[50] Marjorie Lilly, who accompanied Sickert on one of his searches for locations, recalls, "All I saw was a forlorn hole, cold, cheerless . . . All he saw was the *contre-jour* lighting that he loved, stealing in through a small single window, clothing the poor place with light and shadow, losing and finding itself again on the crazy bed and floor . . . these four walls spoke only of the silent shades of the past, watching us in the quiet dusk."[51]

---

48   Lisa Tickner, "Walter Sickert: *The Camden Town Murder* and Tabloid Crime", in *The Camden Town Group in Context*, eds Helena Bonett, Ysanne Holt and Jennifer Mundy, May 2012, http://www.tate.org.uk/art/research-publications/camden-town-group/lisa-tickner-walter-sickert-the-camden-town-murder-and-tabloid-crime-r1104355.
49   Alex Miller to Robert Dixon, 18 March 2014.
50   Antoine Capet, "Walter Sickert: The Camden Town Nudes", Courtauld Gallery exhibition, 25 October to 20 January 2008, http://www.thearttribune.com/Walter-Sickert-The-Camden-Town.html.
51   Marjorie Lilly, *Sickert: The Painter and his Circle* (London: Elek, 1971), 42–3.

In the early hours of 12 September 1907, Emily Dimmock, a young, part-time prostitute living at 29 St Paul's Road, Camden Town, was murdered in her bed. With its echoes of the Ripper Murders in Whitechapel twenty years earlier, the crime was sensationally reported in the popular illustrated press and became a *cause célèbre*. Dimmock's funeral at St Pancras Cemetry attracted thousands of spectators, while the ensuing trial of the suspected murderer, Robert Wood, at the Old Bailey, brought the traffic in central London to a standstill. Wood was acquitted, leaving the case legally unresolved, like the Ripper murders before it. The Camden Town Murder was a remarkable condensation of many of the themes that defined modern urban life and its media of representation: prostitution, sex-murders, sexology, criminal investigation, detective stories, and illustrated journalism. As the *Southern Guardian* put it, "We are face to face with some mysterious and awful product of modern civilization."[52] Already obsessed by the Ripper legend – indeed, he was later accused of *being* Jack the Ripper[53] – Sickert came to see the sex-crime as the defining subject of modern art. Re-titling a number of the nudes he had already painted between 1905 and 1907, and immediately beginning new works on related themes, in 1911 and again in 1912, he held two successive exhibitions of works linked to the Camden Town Murder at the Carfax Gallery in the fashionable St James' district of central London.

Given his cavalier attitude to the titling of his works, the catalogue of Sickert's Camden Town pictures remains uncertain, but there are three main oil paintings together with a number of preparatory studies: *Summer Afternoon or What Shall We Do for the Rent?* (c. 1907–09), *The Camden Town Murder or What Shall We Do About the Rent?* (c. 1908), *L'Affaire de Camden Town* (1909), *La Hollandaise* (c. 1906), and *The Poet and His Muse*, also titled *Collaboration* (c. 1906–07).[54] Sickert's signature themes are perhaps best captured in *L'Affaire de Camden Town*. It depicts a fully clothed man gazing down at the body of a naked woman slumped on an iron bed. The point of view is from the foot of the bed, which fully exposes the woman's body to the spectator. Her face is only partially visible, but her open thighs display her genitals, which align with a chamber pot beneath the bed in the foreground.

Why has Miller invoked Sickert's Camden Town Murder pictures in his account of the portrait painter's imagining of the death of his own muse and prey, Jessica Keal? One reason is perhaps that these images of a notorious, unsolved sex crime allow him to personify the figure of death as a mysterious and unidentified "visitor" to Jessica's bedroom. Sickert's paintings are about the paradox that death and sexual violence are at once mysterious and ubiquitous – that is to say, that in the modern world, death has become banal. Miller's suggestion of an unidentified "visitor" at the scene of Jessica's death is taken up again in the painter's conflation of her bedroom in London, which he has not seen but imagines via Sickert, with her childhood bedroom in the farmhouse at Araluen, which he has painted himself, and where he now imagines the unexplained presence of a car on the road at dusk:

> There's only one road through the Araluen Valley. The surface of this road is gravel. It scrambles past the Keal place a hundred metres or so up the hill... Jessica sits on her

---

52 Quoted in Tickner, "Walter Sickert", 8.
53 See Stephen Knight, *Jack The Ripper: The Final Solution* (London: Collins, 1977) and Patricia Cornwell, *Portrait of a Killer: Jack the Ripper – Case Closed* (London: Little Brown, 2002). For a refutation of these claims, see Wendy Baron and Richard Shone, eds, *Sickert: Paintings*, exhibition catalogue (London: Royal Academy, 1992), 213.
54 These pictures are reproduced in Tickner, "Walter Sickert".

bed massaging her chest and listening to the sound of the vehicle as it comes and goes, hollowing a space into the silence of the afternoon, then withdrawing out of earshot into a timbered gully, before returning again, louder than before, the illusion that it is getting closer, as if the driver has changed his mind and is coming back. (131)

Just as Sickert's paintings exploit the imagery of the era's most popular genres, the detective story and illustrated journalism, Miller's language echoes the idiom of detective fiction, suggesting that a crime is about to be committed. But who is the mysterious driver? Why is he waiting in the gully? Is he coming back? What is his purpose? These are in fact the final lines of *The Sitters*, and they make its ending as inconclusive and mysterious as that of *The Ancestor Game*.

Sickert's Camden Town series was a conscious attempt to re-think the classical genre of the nude from the perspective of modern urban life. It is this that makes him such an important precursor to Bacon: *La Hollandaise*, for example, is an obvious source for Bacon's photographs and paintings of Henrietta Moraes on her bed.[55] The critic R.H. Wilenski, who defended Sickert from the charge of gratuitously "sordid" subject matter, explained in 1943 that *The Camden Town Murder* was "a technical experiment by Sickert who thought it would be fun to take Manet's *Olympia* and paint it the other way round".[56] Despite its flippant tone, this is an incisive observation. Sickert reorients the spectator's position from standing beside the bed at a distance to standing immediately at its foot in a confined, intimate space; he modifies the classic disposition of the nude by opening the thighs, exposing the genitalia at the centre of the visual field; and he abandons the idealised, youthful form for what Wendy Baron and Richard Shone call "the leg o'mutton corpse".[57] This, as Tickner argues, is the *modern* nude, "the nude turned corruptible flesh"; it is "the underside, the abject ... the body with orifices, the body that leaks and dies". By his unrelenting realism, Sickert "displaces the nude as an allegorical or idealizing category with the particularity of flesh, pain, weight, muscle-tone and vulnerability".[58] This is a vision of the human body as the ruin of time.

By mapping the nude so explicitly on to the figure of the prostitute, Sickert also challenges another tradition that is best represented by Bonnard's many paintings of his naked wife. Bonnard (1867–1947) and Sickert (1860–1942) were almost exact contemporaries, yet their nudes epitomise two utterly irreconcilable visions, the one a lyrical celebration and the other a forensic critique of bourgeois life and domestic intimacy: "If the bourgeois interior is a space of seclusion from the public world, [then Sickert's] bruised, stained bodies on dishevelled beds are commodities in their place of work."[59] Miller's portrait painter is an admirer of Bonnard, and Brassaï's famous portrait is a personal touchstone: "That's Bonnard. He was strong ... You only have to look at Brassaï's photograph of him. Pierre Bonnard, the Frenchman. There's a portrait ... " (99). But it is in the spirit of "registering the ordinariness and the ultimate *unknowability* of the modern world",[60] and perhaps also of farewelling Bonnard's bourgeois domestic idyll, that Miller's painter comes finally, sadly,

---

55 Anthony Bond, ed., *Francis Bacon: Five Decades* (Sydney: Art Gallery of New South Wales, 2012).
56 From Lilian Browse, ed., *Sickert*, "with an essay on his art by R.H. Wilenski" (London: Faber, 1943), 25–6, quoted in Tickner, "Walter Sickert", 11.
57 Baron and Shone, eds, *Sickert*, 208, quoted in Tickner, "Walter Sickert", 13.
58 Tickner, "Walter Sickert", 14.
59 Tickner, "Walter Sickert", 18.
60 Tickner, "Water Sickert", 15.

perhaps even regretfully, to visualise Jessica Keal *not* as a Bonnard but as a Sickert, her death-ravaged body slumped, *contre-jour*, on an iron bed: "she has become all softly crumpled shadows and a sense of disarray. Her face is turned away from the viewer. She might be the victim of a brutal murder" (130).

Miller's invocation of Sickert (and perhaps even of Bacon, who returns in *Prochownik's Dream*) also allows him further to develop the theme, already explored in *The Ancestor Game*, of the artist as a vivisector or parasite, preying upon his "sitters". As we have seen, this theme is implicit in the early pages of *The Sitters*: that is, prior to the ellipsis of Jessica's departure and death. In Sickert's work, there is a challenging conflation of the artist with the murderer, and then of both with the spectator. This is another aspect of his re-interpretation of the academic nude from the vantage point of modernity. As Antoine Capet points out, Sickert "deliberately turns the spectator into a voyeur".[61] What lies at the core of Sickert's understanding of modernity is the conjunction of art, sex, death and the commodity. This is expressed in the series of relations between the artist, the murderer and the spectator, and the muse/model and the prostitute/murder victim. The psychological drama of Sickert's murder paintings is identical with, and in fact emerges from, the cognate relation between the artist and his model.[62] This can be seen in the parallels between *The Studio: The Painting of a Nude* (1906) and *Camden Town Murder* (c. 1909). What these paintings present is a disturbing series of substitutions between the spectator, the artist and the murderer, and the muse and victim, that constitute what can be called, literally, the consumer economy of modern life and modern art.

This visual economy of control, exploitation, desire and guilt corresponds with the portrait painter's deepest understanding of himself and his art in *The Sitters*. Is Miller's portrait painter, then, no better than a voyeur? Is he the thief of Jessica Keal's image and identity? Is he her stalker, her murderer, the mysterious "Sunday visitor"? In the final pages of *The Sitters*, the painter describes intimately to the reader his painting of Jessica's death. It is already overlaid with suggestions of eroticism, a sense of voyeuristic intrusion and violation, which is achieved by his imagining of the time and place of her death as one of Sickert's "bedroom scenes". He also confesses, with apparent indifference, that he has "destroyed" several earlier versions of the final painting, and then goes on to describe its subject and composition. This is the painter's "keyhole" device, which turns him – and the spectator – into a voyeur:

> I destroyed several of these but three versions have survived. The last one, the one in which she's sitting up with her hand pressed to her chest and the room is almost in darkness, is once again a narrow, vertical painting, tightly enclosing the scene. Her pale arm and her pale thigh. Viewed at a diagonal through an exceedingly tall doorway. A big painting. One of my biggest. But just a glimpse of something, a concentration on this little moment that is driven inward by the tight framing of the doorway. (131)

In this passage Miller's painter again uses language appropriate to the description of a modern nude, or to the erotically charged scene of a sex crime, to describe his painting of Jessica's death.

---

61 Capet, "Walter Sickert", 2.
62 Tickner, "Walter Sickert", 16–17.

The painter's "guilt", his inherently predatory relation to his subject matter, is further illustrated by another remarkable conflation of scenes. Not only does the painter imagine Jessica's death as if it were one of Sickert's Camden Town murders, he also conflates her bedroom with another: his memory of the bedroom of the young woman with whom he had sex and then callously abandoned as a young man in England before emigrating to Australia. His account of the affair is deeply informed by an artist's awareness of the politics of vision, but it begins as if it might be the formal confession of a stalker, a voyeur, a peeing Tom, or perhaps a serial killer:

> That's how I met her. I'd started going in to Taunton on a Saturday afternoon to look for a bit of relief. I'd go to the pictures then hang around the Blue Dolphin watching the loving couples . . . Except for one or two stragglers like me the bus station was deserted at that time of night. There was just this van where you could get a ham sandwich and a cup of tea. I sat out in the dark in one of the shelters and watched her. It was a little drama. A private theatre. She and her mother in the lighted van serving the stragglers, framed by the enormous dark allotment of the deserted bus station. I'd go to the bus station early just to watch her. Her fresh white apron over her blouse and her bare arms. (32)

It comes as something of a shock to recognise the visual and verbal echoes that, in the painter's memory, connect this moment to his chronologically later (narratively earlier) account of his first sight of Jessica: "I saw her turn towards me, her bare arms, . . . and I saw her turn away again" (6).

The scene of his sexual encounter with the English girl, the bedroom scene, is again like one of Sickert's small tenement rooms, and the painter is a predator, we might now say a *serial* predator, "murdering" the young woman's innocence and reputation:

> I'm excited by her tears. Her nakedness. The way she lies on the bed with her back to me, curled away from me, curled into herself and into her despair, her bare thighs glistening in the blue light from the street and the rain . . . I can't wait to be gone and to have her complete, as my memory. Light and safe . . . Her humiliation is so compelling I almost decide to stay.
>
> I get dressed and go out the door and down the stairs and I leave the house where she has her room. (35)

The link between art, sexual predation and death is pointedly made by the painter's confession that what he most wanted was to get out with the image of the girl's body safely captured in his memory. Not yet a professional painter, he is nonetheless already rehearsing his later "crimes" through his desire for the girl's image, the image of her thighs and turned-away face, which are the hallmark of the modern nude. Finally, he confesses that in summoning up the image even now, after all the years that have passed, even after Jessica Keal's death, he still feels a combination of guilt and sexual desire when he remembers that other, earlier bedroom scene: "I remember only her nakedness, cool and pale and glowing on the bed . . . She's still with me. There's the guilt, the secret joyful guilt, and there's this faint arousal" (36–7). And then, as if the young woman were one of Sickert's victims, perhaps the woman leaning forward on her elbow in *Mornington Crescent Nude, Contre-Jour*, she follows him to the door to curse him: "Damn you! Damn you! Damn you! Three times to make it stick. And we deserve it" (36).

It is the *seriality* of these conflated bedroom scenes and images of lovers that raises what Derrida thinks of as the scandalous *infidelity* of memory: "each time we mourn ... we add another name to the series of singular mournings and so commit what may be called a sort of 'posthumous infidelity' with regard to the others".[63] This is the paradox that Derrida refers to as the "politics of friendship", which requires that we quantify singularities; the paradox that we must be concerned with the relationship between singularity – of death, of friendship, of love – and its banality, its inevitable repetition: "Since it is a question of singularities, this is an inevitable consequence: one must prefer *certain* friends. The choice of this preference reintroduces number and calculation into the multiplicity of incalculable singularities, where it would have been preferable not to reckon with friends as one counts and reckons with things."[64]

The deathbed scene that I have been examining here is in fact the portrait painter's second reference to the paintings of Walter Sickert. The earlier one occurs during his recollections of his first visit to the Jessica's farm at a time when their friendship is still beginning. Jessica has wandered off along the creek on her own and returned, after an interval, to where the portrait painter sits sketching an image of her that she has left with him in his visual memory just before her departure. When she tells him that she has been swimming at a pool further downstream, he is aroused by the idea of her swimming naked and she reacts defensively and modestly, as if he had stalked her and stolen a glance. Her awareness that he has imagined her naked causes almost the same response as if he had seen her naked. In response to the information that she has been swimming, the portrait painter recalls one of Sickert's nudes. It is his way of imagining her naked in the *absence* of her actual presence, just as the later reference is his way of imagining her death in her absence:

> I can feel her thinking. I'm remembering a painting which my wife brought for me in London more than twenty years ago. It's a Sickert. A Mornington Crescent nude, *contre jour*. It hangs in my bedroom in my house in Canberra opposite Henry, arrested in his sideways plunge. In the Sickert the dark form of the naked woman shimmers against the light. The blaze of light along the edge of the naked female body, that was Sickert's contribution. The woman's body is heavy and flowing and is in the splendid assurance of middle-age. She is raised on her elbow, anticipating the attention of the viewer. (86)

While there is no actual Sickert painting titled *The Sunday Visitor*, there is a painting titled *Mornington Crescent Nude, Contre-Jour* (1907). Its subject is just as Miller's painter describes it. A naked woman in middle age is lit from behind by the light from her bedroom window: the French term *contre-jour* means lit from behind, so that the effect of a silhouette is produced. She leans forward on one elbow as if in response to the entry of another person into the room. Like all of Sickert's Camden Town pictures, the viewer is invited actively to engage with the subject. Who is it that has just entered the bedroom, and towards whom she leans in anticipation? Is it the woman's husband or a lover? If she is a prostitute, is it a client or a more menacing "visitor", perhaps the Camden Town murderer himself?

---

63 Pascale-Anne Brault and Michael Naas, "To Reckon with the Dead: Jacques Derrida's Politics of Mourning", in Derrida, *The Work of Mourning*, 16.
64 Jacques Derrida, *The Politics of Friendship*, trans. George Collins (London: Verso, 1997), 19–20.

Or is she leaning toward the viewer, thereby implicating him again in the ethical conundrum of the genre?

Just as Sickert's nude rises on her elbow in response to an intrusion, and just as there remain ethical doubts about our spectatorship of that painting, so Jessica Keal responds ambivalently to the painter's inquiry about her swimming:

> I look at her and wait for her to notice that I'm looking at her with all this in my mind. I say, "I could smell the water on you when you got back, Jessica."
>
> She shuffles at the stones with her bare toes. Maybe she's shy about the image in my mind of herself naked, swimming in the private bath as a young girl with her grandmother, or on her own in the autumn sunlight today, no longer a young girl. Maybe that's it. Maybe it's not an image she wants me to have. (85)

There can be no question here that the painter understands the ethical complexities of the image, that he *knows* that even his imagined image of her is a potential violation. Lest there be any doubt, his surprisingly carnal reference to the smell of the water "on her" ties this episode as it recurs in his memory to that other, later reference to Sickert: "Her face is turned away from the viewer . . . You can still smell her visitor in the stuffy air, and smell their passion" (130).

Walter Sickert's crime was to have taken the figure of Manet's *Olympia*, which had been at the centre of the nineteenth-century's cult of beauty and the erotic, and to have turned it into the ruin of time. Her secret visitor, of course, is death, and his accomplice in crime is the modern figurative painter. In 2005, Miller would return to these issues in his seventh novel, *Prochownik's Dream*, the next in his series of novels about art.

4
The Iron World: *Conditions of Faith*

The immediate inspiration for Alex Miller's fifth novel, *Conditions of Faith* (2000), was his reading of his mother's diary for 1923, written at a time when she was still "a free-spirited young woman dreaming of her own future".[1] Born in Leeds, Winifred Croft had been removed from the care of her Irish parents and brought up in a teaching convent in Chantilly in France. She later worked as a maid and governess in Paris before returning to London at the age of eighteen, where she met and married Miller's father. But for Miller, a portrait is always a space of encounter between the artist and his sitter. He had lived in Paris for much of 1974, and in the weeks and months after reading Winifred's diary, he found himself picturing her as a young woman occupying the sixth-floor apartment he had rented on the Rue Saint-Dominique: "I saw in my mother's youthful longings the same longings to escape that had preoccupied my own youth, and which had fired my decision to get away from the grey landscape of a council estate in post-war London".[2] The circumstances of Winifred's childhood are most immediately recognisable in the novel in those of the Elders' young maid, Sophie, the niece of their concierge, Madame Barbier, though the spaces of encounter between Miller and his mother, and Miller and his own youthful self, are also refracted in complex ways in the central figure of Emily Stanton.

In *Conditions of Faith*, as in *The Ancestor Game*, Miller recreates the vast landscape of globalising modernity, and it is in relation to these powerful impersonal forces that his individual characters must chart the course of their lives – like swimmers or ships at sea. The focus, however, has shifted from Australia's connections with East Asia to those with Europe, the Mediterranean and the transatlantic world. The novel begins in Melbourne in the summer of 1923. Georges Elder is an Anglo-French civil engineer who has come to Australia to prepare his Belgian company's tender to build the Sydney Harbour Bridge. He is in Melbourne to consult Richard Stanton, professor of civil engineering at the University of Melbourne and Australia's leading authority on the new steel alloys. He there meets and falls in love with Stanton's daughter Emily, who has just graduated with first class honours in history. Her father had hoped that she would take up a scholarship to read ancient history and classics at Cambridge, but after a hastily arranged marriage, Georges and Emily

---

1 Alex Miller, "Travels with My Green Man", *The Australian*, 31 May 2003, 4.
2 Alex Miller, "The Mask of Fiction: A Memoir", in *The Novels of Alex Miller: An Introduction* ed. Robert Dixon (Sydney: Allen & Unwin, 2012), 33.

return to Paris, where he has an apartment on the Rue Saint-Dominique. Georges' first duty is to present Emily to his mother, Madame Heloise Elder, who has lived in Chartres since the death of her husband from malaria during the construction of the Panama Canal. Back in Paris, Georges is instantly caught up in his work on the bridge tender and abandons Emily to the care of his Tunisian-born friend Antoine Carpeaux, who takes her to Sidi bou-Said and Carthage, where her interest in ancient history is rekindled by the legend of the early Christian martyr Vibia Perpetua.

Although the action of the novel takes place over little more than a year, from January 1923 to June 1924, the larger timeframe of events referred to begins with the construction of the Suez Canal in 1859 and looks forward to the building of Sydney's major urban infrastructure in the 1920s and 1930s: the Harbour Bridge and its approaches, and its integration into the city's underground train network, the City Circle. Other regions and engineering projects referred to include the building of the Panama Canal, and the incursions of European capital into North Africa, especially Tunisia, Morocco and Egypt. Linking these diverse locations is the career of Miller's fictional engineer, Georges Elder, whom he inserts into a series of historical situations. Georges' father, Ross Elder, was the supervising engineer for Couvreux & Hersent, a Belgian company contracted by the French entrepreneur Ferdinand de Lesseps in his construction of both the Suez and Panama canals. Georges works for another Belgian firm, Baume Marpent, which built hundreds of steel bridges in North Africa and the Middle East during the 1910s and 1920s, and was a partner with one of the six firms tendering for the construction of the Sydney Harbour Bridge. The letter from John Bradfield, the Australian engineer charged with oversight of the project, which Georges reads to Emily,[3] is derived from Bradfield's published report on tenders, in which he notes that "the Goninan Bridge Corporation of Newcastle is tendering in conjunction with the firm of Baume Marpent, of Haine St Pierre, Belgium".[4] There is, of course, no reference to the fictional Monsieur Elder.

This set of globalising commercial relations, emanating from Europe but operating in widespread locations – Egypt, Tunisia, Panama, Sydney – accurately reflects the period's complex and dynamic corporate landscape. Like the setting of *The Ancestor Game*, with its Shanghai–Melbourne–Hamburg axes, this structure of relations suggests Susan Stanford Friedman's call for "a new geography of modernism" that would "locate many centres of modernity across the globe", focus on "the cultural traffic linking them", and recognise "the circuits of reciprocal influence and transformation that take place within highly unequal state relations".[5] As Professor Stanton warns, these circuits of commercial exchange are not necessarily identical to the geopolitical interests of the major European empires, and they require a different kind of evidence to come properly into focus. In *Building Beyond the Mediterranean* (2013), Claudine Piaton uses corporate archives to study the forms of agency taken by European capital in building the infrastructure for tourism, high-volume commodity transport, and urbanisation in North Africa and the Middle East in the late nineteenth and early twentieth centuries. European companies like Baume Marpent and Couvreux & Hersent were engaged in the global projection of European-based capital and civil engineering projects that were mobile, modular and opportunistic, and char-

---

3 Alex Miller, *Conditions of Faith* (Sydney: Allen & Unwin, 1992), 352. All subsequent references are to this edition and appear in parentheses in the text.
4 John Bradfield, *Sydney Harbour Bridge: Report on Tenders* (Sydney: Government Printer, 1924), 2.
5 Susan Stanford Friedman, "Periodizing Modernism: Postcolonial Modernities and the Space/Time Borders of Modernist Studies", *Modernism/modernity* 13, no. 3 (September 2006): 429.

acterised by "multifarious networks and exchanges" of personnel, capital and intellectual property. These projects were conducted in specific regional locations – the Middle East, the Maghreb and Latin America (and, we might add, Australasia) yet within "an expanded transnational environment".[6] Miller's interpretation of Australian modernity in *Conditions of Faith* as the local manifestation of these transnational forces, and of networks that are outside the strictly British-imperial context, is a significant achievement of both the historical and novelistic imagination.

The Maghreb, where much of *Conditions of Faith* is set, was gradually annexed to the French colonial Empire from the mid-nineteenth century on, and became the preferred region of activity for French and Belgian companies. Baume Marpent was renowned for its design and construction of steel bridges, supplying more than 150 for Egypt alone between 1894 and 1952, including the Imbaba Bridge in Cairo, whose construction between 1912 and 1924 immediately predates that of the Sydney Harbour Bridge. Other infrastructure built by European firms includes ports, the urban facilities of cosmopolitan cities like Algiers, Sidi bou-Said and Alexandria, which marked the region's increasing attraction as a tourist destination, and the mining towns that housed European company employees. Those built in Tunisia, Morocco and Algeria during the inter-war period had European-style town plans characterised by significant spatial segregation between the "native" and European quarters.[7] Antoine tells Emily that before the war Georges had worked "strengthening bridges . . . in Tunisia and Morocco to take the heavy locomotives from the phosphate mines", and that being half Scots, he "wasn't like the French engineers", and "lived in the camp with his Arab workers" (49).

The great civil engineering projects of the second half of the nineteenth century and the early decades of the twentieth brought vast wealth to entrepreneurial individuals, enhanced the international reputations of major companies, and brought prestige to the nation states in whose names those individuals and companies operated. Yet they were often rocked by scandals that could bring national disgrace, and occasionally ended in bankruptcy and even suicide. The projects that are most significant to understanding Miller's purpose in *Conditions of Faith* are the building of the Suez and Panama canals, for it is in relation to their moral and financial ambiguities that the private lives of Ross and Georges Elder ultimately must be judged.

The opening of the Suez Canal in 1869 literally "made Second Empire France in the eyes of the world". It was seen as "a triumph of finance capitalism and exemplified the power of France to spread western civilization to the Middle East and Asia". Funded by a public float on the Bourse, construction began in 1859 by the principal engineering contractor, Couvreux & Hersent. The project's entrepreneur, Ferdinand de Lesseps, achieved the status of a national hero and was dubbed "The Great Frenchman". The project's successful completion also earned for France a reputation as the world's leading centre of engineering and technology, and conferred international prestige on the *École Polytechnique* in Paris.[8]

---

6 Stuart King, review of Claudine Piaton, Ezio Goldoli and David Peycere, eds, *Building Beyond the Mediterranean: Studying the Archives of European Businesses 1860–1970* (Arles: Honore Clair, 2012), *ABE Journal* 1 (2012), n.p., http://dev.abejournal.eu/index.php?id=551.
7 These details are drawn from the online exhibition and catalogue, *Building Beyond the Mediterranean*, curated by Derya Nuket Ozer for the Turkish Museum of Architecture, http://www.archmuseum.org/Gallery/building-beyond-the-mediterranean_41.html.

It was the success of the Suez Canal that led de Lesseps to form his *Compagnie Universelle du Canal Interocéanqiue de Panama*. Using the same business model as he had for Suez, he retained Couvreux & Hersent as the principal engineering contractor, and the *Compagnie* commenced work in Panama in February 1881. By 1882, however, more than forty percent of the available funds had been spent on hospital facilities to deal with the worsening and as yet misunderstood problem of malaria, and in that year Couvreux & Hersent withdrew from the joint venture.[9] On 4 February 1889, de Lesseps declared himself a bankrupt, exposing some 800,000 French shareholders to financial risk. Three years after the collapse, it was revealed that in 1888, at the height of the financial crisis, the *Compagnie* had bribed government ministers, including Georges Clémenceau, in return for financial and legal concessions, and corruption charges were brought against de Lesseps, his son Charles, and the engineer Gustave Eiffel. Prison sentences were imposed but later annulled on appeal. Baron Jacques Reinach, the *Compagnie*'s chief financial adviser, committed suicide. In the wake of the scandal, a group of private investors later formed the *Compagnie Nouvelle*, with the aim of maintaining the infrastructure in Panama and continuing with the excavations, but in 1903 the building concession was purchased by the United States, which finally brought the project to a successful completion with the opening of the canal on 3 August 1914.[10]

In the publicity associated with these great engineering projects, there is a distinctive combination of national hubris with the celebration of hyper-masculine entrepreneurial personalities like de Lesseps and his American counterpart, Colonel George Washington Goethals, who become personifications of either national glory or national opprobrium. These effects can be seen in the American travel writer Ralph Emmett Avery's two books about America's completion of the Panama Canal. In 1913, Avery published *America's Triumph at Panama*. Its cover image shows a female Atlas supporting the globe (a personification of the United States as Liberty) and flanked by two modern ships surging through the canal, which anticipate the slightly later idea of the liberty ships.[11] A second edition appeared in 1915 with the title, *The Greatest Engineering Feat in the World at Panama*. It is dedicated to "The Men of Brain and Brawn of Our Country, Whose Matchless Skill and Inspiring Courage Made the Dream of Ages a Reality in the Construction of the Panama Canal". Chapters V and VI are titled, respectively, "The French Failure" and "The American Triumph". The frontispiece is a photographic portrait of Colonel Goethals, "The Builder of the Panama Canal", who personifies America's national virtue. The caption describes him as a man "Who might be classed as the most absolute despot on earth, although a benevolent one, and the squarest boss a man ever worked for. He is a thorough engineer, a righteous judge, and a stern executioner rolled into one."[12]

Miller has described this vast and shifting corporate landscape of transnational engineering projects as "the heroic iron world of men" into which Emily Stanton, "with her

---

8   John H. Scott, "Going South: Analysis of an Historic Project Engineering Failure", online conference paper, American Institute of Aeronautics and Astronautics, Space 2009 Conference and Exposition, 14–17 September 2009, Pasadena, California, 2, http://arc.aiaa.org/doi/abs/10.2514/6.2009-6454.
9   Scott, "Going South", 6.
10 Scott, "Going South", 9–10.
11 Ralph Emmett Avery, *America's Triumph at Panama* (Chicago: Regan Printing House, 1913), http://ufdc.ufl.edu/AA00014525/00001.
12 Ralph Emmett Avery, *The Greatest Engineering Feat in the World at Panama* (New York: Leslie-Judge Company, 1915), http://ufdc.ufl.edu/AA00014526/00001.

longing for meaning and her uncertainty", has "blundered".[13] It is the world to which Emily and her mother-in-law Madame Elder are widowed. Although this might seem an inauspicious and even inappropriate framework for what is essentially a *bildungsroman* about a young Australian woman, Miller's point is that it is initially in *this* modern world that his young heroine must make her way. In the first part of the novel, "The Voyage Out", Miller traces Emily's blundering into the iron world, and he engages in a good deal of ironic undercutting of its ethos, particularly the chauvinistic nationalism and masculinity personified in the figure of the engineer.

"The Voyage Out" alludes to the title of Virginia Woolf's 1915 novel about Rachel Vinrace's quest for self-discovery on a voyage from London to South America. At the beginning of *Conditions of Faith*, Emily Stanton's situation also resembles that of Dorothea Brooke in George Eliot's *Middlemarch* (1874). Like Dorothea, Emily is an ardent young woman, eager for emotional and intellectual outlets beyond the relatively narrow scope of her provincial world, yet she lacks worldly experience and self-understanding, and is vulnerable to transferring her ambitions onto an unworthy marriage partner. Dorothea is surrounded by men who are deeply, even obsessively, engaged in their own intellectual projects, but it is Casaubon's scholarship, his *Key to All Mythologies*, that appears to be a window onto the larger world to which she aspires. For Emily, it is Georges' "heroic design" for the new bridge and his association with Paris, which she had visited happily as a child, that provide the unexamined proxies for her aspirations: "it had been a secret pleasure to imagine a mysterious destiny in their meeting; something arcane and concealed from everyone but herself, for which his heroic design for the Sydney Harbour Bridge was to provide them merely with a resemblance of purpose" (7). We might also recall here Teresa Hawkins' infatuation with Jonathan Crow in another Australian novel much influenced by *Middlemarch*, Christina Stead's *For Love Alone* (1945).

In the summer of 1923, Georges is the Stantons' guest on the beach at Port Phillip Bay. Everywhere there are signs of the "iron world" of modernity to which both Professor Stanton and Georges belong: even Georges' skin is covered with "fine coppery hairs" (4), as if the young engineer were made of the very metals with which he works. Two hundred yards offshore is a "partly submerged wreck", while far out on the horizon, "a white-hulled passenger liner was steaming slowly toward the port past anchored cargo vessels; the grey smoke from its twin funnels ... penciled against the white of the sky" (3). While the others swim, Georges sketches in his notebook a vision of Melbourne's future: "The fanciful road of the future escaped into the air from the crosshatched mass of the city and swung out over the distant hills, disdaining the ... natural contours of the landscape" (4). Miller's descriptive prose bristles with irony, and the wrecked ship is a cautionary symbol:

> [Stanton] stood gazing at the rusting hulk of the iron ship that lay scuttled on the rocks two hundred yards offshore. Emily stood on the high side of the sloping deck, a gilded figure silhouetted against the red sun, poised to dive into the deep green water below her. The iron wreck glowed, as if it had been heated in a furnace. (14)

The actual wreck to which Miller alludes here is that of HMVS *Cerberus*, which was decommissioned in 1924, and scuttled off Half Moon Bay on 26 September 1926. *Cerberus* has important connections with Miller's iron world. Built in England for the colony of Vic-

---

13 Alex Miller to Robert Dixon, 22 October 2013.

toria in 1867, she was one of the last surviving examples of the breastwork monitor, a class of warship with a central iron superstructure and iron cladding. Dangerously unstable, she was never to be used in action. On her maiden voyage to Melbourne in 1869, she was also the first ship bound for Australia to pass through the new Suez Canal.[14]

In her discussion of the motif of shipwreck in Australian literature, Brigid Rooney suggests it is central to representations of modernity. Shipwreck is "an allegorical scene repeated across genres", circulating through popular and literary narratives, that can be likened to Mikhail Bakhtin's notion of the chronotope: "a narrative unit that compresses space and time together, thickening scenes and investing them with meaning". Drawing on the work of Michael Titlestad, Rooney argues that "shipwreck is a scene for modernist and postmodernist rehearsals of settler ambivalence and postcolonial identity". Even the spectator experiences "a collapse of epistemological certainties", as if she were "cast adrift in the sea itself, 'living with' and 'building from' shipwreck".[15] Shortly after they meet, Emily shows Georges a photograph taken of her as a child beside a pond in the Luxembourg Gardens, and holding a small sailing ship. He replies enigmatically, "She clings to her little ship of liberty" (7). The image suggests the figure of a young woman as Liberty leading two ocean liners through the Panama Canal that had appeared on the cover of *America's Triumph at Panama* in 1913. But the collocation of women and shipping in modernity is unstable. Does Miller's wreck foreshadow the impending misfortune of his young heroine? Or is it an ill omen for Georges' work on the bridge tender? It is Professor Stanton who first swims out to the wreck – steel, after all, is his business – and he later sounds a note of warning to his young colleague: "We all want big bridges, Georges. But big bridges often destroy the men who build them" (11).

Georges' proposal of marriage is a signal moment in time that demands of Emily a degree of self-knowledge of which she is not yet capable: "She experienced a moment of clarity then, a moment almost out-of-time, as if she stood on her own in the night wind, some way above this scene . . . This man and I are strangers, she told herself calmly" (18). Emily's "moment . . . out-of-time" is what in Ancient Greek is called *kairos*. Ancient Greek distinguishes between *chronos*, chronological or sequential time, and *kairos*, "the propitious moment for the performance of an action or the coming into being of a new state". In the Christian tradition, *kairos* became "the appointed time in the purpose of God", the time when God acts (Mark 1:15). In the period in which *Conditions of Faith* is set, the concept of *kairos* is most directly associated with the work of the German-American philosopher and theologian Paul Tillich. In *The Interpretation of History* (1936), Tillich writes, "We call this fulfilled moment . . . of time approaching us as fate and decision, *Kairos*."[16]

The feasibility of the Suez and Panama canal projects was bound up with calculating the profitability of shipping routes, especially the high-value passenger and cargo traffic circulating between the Americas, Europe and Australasia. In accepting Georges' contract of marriage, Emily surrenders herself to the iron world of men, and in so doing she be-

---

14   State Government of Victoria, "Cerberus", Department of Transport, Planning and Local Infrastructure, http://www.dpcd.vic.gov.au/heritage/maritime/shipwrecks/shipwreck-stories/cerberus.
15   Brigid Rooney, "Time's Abyss: Australian Literary Modernism and the Scene of Ferry Wreck", in *Scenes of Reading: Is Australian Literature a World Literature?* Eds Robert Dixon and Brigid Rooney (Melbourne: Australian Scholarly, 2013), 102–3.
16   Paul Tillich, *The Interpretation of History*, trans N.A. Rasetzski and Elsa L. Talmey (New York and London: Scribners, 1936), 129. This is the first usage in English recorded in the *OED*. I am grateful to Nicholas Birns for this reference.

comes herself a kind of commodity or cargo to be shipped around the world. Georges had originally intended to return to Paris aboard a tourist ship, the Blue Funnel Line's *Demeter* – auspiciously named for the Greek goddess of harvests and fertility, whose loss and subsequent recovery of her daughter, Persephone, foreshadows Emily's story. Instead, with the delay caused by the wedding, they are forced to take passage aboard the ironically named *Kairos*: "The *Kairos* was a merchant ship and Monsieur and Madame Georges Elder were her only passengers ... The holds ... were filled with bales of merino wool for the European spinning mills and there was a smell of sheep in the air" (22). What kind of *kairos* will this voyage be for Emily? Will it bring about her "coming into being" as a fulfilled adult woman? Will her honeymoon be a "propitious moment" or a sacrifice?

The *Kairos* is an iron cargo vessel, the kind for which the Suez and Panama canals were built. In this Conradian world of men, Georges is drawn to the rough friendship of John Anderson, "a Glaswegian like ... himself and the captain of their floating world" (25). Captain Anderson makes available a small, windowless iron chart room adjoining his own cabin, where Georges works obsessively by night on his report to the directors of Baume Marpent on the tender for the bridge. Afterwards, he drinks with Anderson before returning, drunk and exhausted, to his marital bed – it is another version of Ward Rankin's oppressive study in *Watching the Climbers on the Mountain*. While Georges enters more deeply into the obsession of his great project, Emily reads Flaubert's "pitiless narrative of *Madame Bovary*" (27). In the Indian Ocean, the *Kairos* enters the deadly space of a storm. In the ship's mess, in a scene of sadistic inhospitality, Anderson stares malevolently at Emily, challenging her to reveal her womanly fear of shipwreck in the storm at sea: "The propellers raced and the lights dimmed then brightened, and the long, slow stomach-churning dive into the abyss. When the ship began to climb again, Anderson nodded at the raging torrent outside the porthole ... 'There she goes', he said ... 'That's one that's no for us' " (29).

Three weeks out from its destination, the French port of Le Havre, the *Kairos* approaches the Gulf of Aden. This is the shipping route that leads in from the Indian Ocean to the Suez Canal, which Georges' father's firm, Couvreux & Hersent, had excavated sixty years earlier. That night, after Georges has spent "endless hours alone in the confinement of the iron chart room", Anderson opens their second bottle of whisky. When Georges emerges from the Captain's cabin at three in the morning, he looks out on the indifferent ocean and is "dismayed by the desolation" of "a world alien to the civil engineer" (31). As he leans over the rail to vomit, he remembers Stanton's words on the beach that day, "*We all want big bridges, Georges. But big bridges often destroy the men who build them*" (31). Pushing away from the rail as if in fear for his life, he makes his way unsteadily to the cabin where he awakens and makes love to his wife. In an extraordinary descriptive passage, Miller hollows out the heroism of the iron world. As they approach Suez, with Georges unconscious on his bed and Emily lying beside him unsatisfied, she masturbates:

> She lay awake, aroused and unsatisfied beside him, studying his features. His handsome face might have been the face of a dead man ... His manly nakedness was uncompromised by his struggle against the effects of the whisky now and she moved her hand down across his chest and his belly and with her other hand caressed herself. The tension of her pleasure was fraught with the uncertainty that he might wake ... The first strong pulsation of her orgasm drew a gasp from her and she shivered and smiled; the bevelled mirrorglass glinting ... gleams of light in the trembling darkness. (32)

In the shadow of one of the nineteenth-century's most heroic feats of engineering and French national triumph, Georges Elder is emasculated by the rituals of the ship's homosocial world, and by his own inadequacies as a man and a professional engineer. Like Mars with Venus, he is unmanned by the woman who is now his wife, the young woman who "clings to her little ship of liberty". Emily's self-containment, her pleasure in her self-induced orgasm, is expressed through the "glinting" and "gleaming" effects of the light on the mirror in her cabin. An appropriate translation of these words is the French verb, *étinceler*. When we next encounter this word in the novel, it is important to remember that these glimmerings were originally an expression of Emily's own inner need, a projection of her as yet unfulfilled desires.

When Georges and Emily arrive in France aboard the *Kairos* they disembark at Le Havre, so that her first impressions are not of Parisian elegance, but of industrial modernity:

> The great timbers and steam winches of the locks and the rearing bulk of the merchant ships berthed along the quays glistened black and metallic through the smoke and the soft drizzle of rain. On the bridge Captain Anderson stood . . . watching the French pilot ease his ship . . . past the towering transatlantic liners . . . to the Quai Frissard, where she was made fast to the dock in front of the commercial warehouses. (33)

One possible alternative to this world is Chartres, the home of Georges' mother, with its great cathedral and its profound, living connections to the pre-modern world. During their visit to Chartres Cathedral, Madame Elder is especially concerned to impress upon Emily her own appreciation of its architecture and spiritual significance, which she contrasts with the superficial response of the American visitors with their *Baedeckers*.[17] She recommends that Emily read instead Henry Adams' *Chartres*, a copy of which is in the bookcase in her sitting room.

Adams' *Mont Saint-Michel and Chartres: A Study of Thirteenth-Century Unity* was originally published privately in 1904 for his own family circle. In 1912, Ralph Adams Cram of the American Institute of Architects requested Adams' permission to bring out a commercial edition under the institute's imprimatur. Cram recognised that Adams' meditation on these buildings was a way of re-entering the world of the Middle Ages, and that this was in turn an attempt to recover not just its material and aesthetic forms, but also the ways of emotional and imaginative being that had been abandoned by industrial modernity in the second half of the nineteenth century. Adams' medievalism therefore has affinities with the aesthetic theories of William Morris, the Pre-Raphaelite Brotherhood and the British Arts and Crafts movement. Cram wrote in his preface to the 1913 edition:

> And it is well for us to have this experience . . . If it gives new and not always flattering standards for the judgment of contemporary men and things, so does it establish new ideals, new goals for attainment. To live for a day in a world that built Chartres Cathedral, even if it makes the living in a world that creates the "Black Country" of England or an Iron City of America less a thing of joy and gladness than before, equally opens up the

---

17 In his research for the Chartres episodes, Miller consulted *Baedeckers* from the 1920s to ensure historical accuracy.

far prospect of another thirteenth century in times that are to come and argues to ardent action towards its attainment.[18]

It is ironic that Adams' book, with its eloquent challenge to industrial modernity, should sit so incongruously on Madame Elder's bookshelf alongside her husband's copy of Samuel Smiles' *The Lives of the Engineers*. For like his son Georges, Monsieur Elder was one of those "contemporary men" who built the "Black Country" and the "Iron Cities" of the modern world, and whose material achievements stand condemned by Adams' aesthetic and moral vision of the medieval world. *The Lives of the Engineers* was first published in 1874, and Monsieur Elder's copy had been presented to him at Glasgow University in the session of 1877–78 "*in recognition of outstanding achievement*" (65). Monsieur Elder died in Panama in 1900 and Adams' book was not published until 1913. Could it be that *Chartres* was not one of his books after all, but Madame Elder's, and that she bought it after her husband's death as a reflection of her own instinctive aversion to the iron world?

In reading to Emily from Adams' book, Madame Elder is making a kind of confession about her abandonment by her husband which should sound a warning to Emily, if she could only grasp it, about her own abandonment by Georges. This could be another *kairos*, a moment when Emily might attain mature insight and agency in her life. But Madame Elder's confession is made all the more poignant by her oblique and perhaps uncomprehending attitude, and its equally oblique effect on Emily, which Miller so subtly conveys: "Madame Elder's gaze was steady. 'No guide will reveal our cathedral to you as Mr Adams reveals it... Read Henry Adams. You will understand us better'" (87). Miller's irony here is worthy of "Flaubert's pitiless narrative of *Madame Bovary*", for whatever it is that Madame Elder and Emily have experienced together, it is not "understanding".

When Madame Elder describes Chartres as Georges' "spiritual home", she makes the revealing qualification that he has never lived there (87). Georges' actual childhood home was Glasgow, where father and son were trained as engineers. Chartres and Glasgow stand here in opposition, for while Chartres is Adams' great symbol of spiritual and aesthetic values, Glasgow belongs to the "Black Country" of industrial modernity and is therefore, contrary to what Madame Elder would like to believe, the true spiritual home of Ross and Georges Elder. They both belong to that world of "contemporary men and things" that Chartres and all it represents casts in "unflattering" light. Adams' editor, Cram, is quite specific about what this contrast requires of the reader: it requires "judgment".

In speaking about his parents to Emily on the morning of their arrival in Chartres, Georges reveals that his father died penniless, ruining his family and forcing his wife to turn to her sister, Juliette, for charity: "This is Juliette's house, not my mother's. My mother doesn't have a house. What you see here in this room is everything she salvaged from her marriage to my father" (67). This revelation of the intimate details of one family's history provides the moral point of connection to Miller's larger outline of modern history in *Conditions of Faith*, of the late nineteenth-century's heroic projects of venture capitalism, to which men like Ross Elder have mortgaged their families. "Salvage" is what is retrieved from a shipwreck. Georges understands what his father's ambitions have cost his mother, and as a young man he vowed to "Restore the family", to "Restore *her*" (67), but such are the limitations of moral understanding that he seeks to do so by embarking upon the very

---

18 Editor's Note in Henry Adams, *Mont Saint-Michel and Chartres: A Study of Thirteenth-Century Unity*, ed. with a preface by Ralph Adams Cram (Boston and New York: Houghton Mifflin, 1913).

same profession as his father, which now has the potential to bring ruin on his own marriage to Emily.

These intimate details lend authority to Adams' critique of industrial modernity, which Madame Elder bids Emily to "understand". But just as her son has only a partial ability to examine the determining circumstances of his life, so his mother cannot fully express her insights to her daughter-in-law. After reading to Emily from Adams' book, Madame Elder offers her own account of the family history, which she does by showing her photographs of great men. One is a photograph taken during the construction of the Panama Canal. Emily rests it directly on top of Adams' *Chartres*, which she is still holding in her hand. The opposing values could not be made clearer:

> Emily . . . took the photograph from Madame Elder's outstretched hand and she rested it on Henry Adams' book and looked at it. Three men stood side by side on the sloping batter of a huge earthworks. Two of the men were young and tall and faced the camera directly, one with his hands on his hips, the other with his arms folded across his chest. The third man stood between them. He was short, heavily built, and older than they. He had a bushy mustache, thick black eyebrows, and a wild mane of silvery hair. He was holding his hat in his hand and looking away from the camera toward a vast embankment. To the horizon the embankment was crowded with the figures of thousands of men at work among a forest of steam shovels. (89)

At this remarkable point in the novel, Adams' moral vision is brought into immediate contact with the iron world of capitalism, upon which it passes judgement. At the same time, Miller brings history and fiction together by placing Ross Elder in an actual historical situation. The fictional photograph resembles the countless real photographs of the heroic men of engineering, like the portrait of Colonel Goethals used as the frontispiece to *The Greatest Engineering Feat in the World at Panama*. These were the men Georges was brought up to admire: "Our heroes weren't Scott and Amundsen . . . [but] Isambard Kingdom Brunel and John Augustus Roebling. Engineers who'd constructed enormous objects that had changed forever the way cities looked and people lived" (366). Madame Elder goes on to explain to Emily that the three men in the photograph are "the great French engineer Ferdinand de Lesseps", his son Charles, and her husband Ross. They are standing in the failed French excavation of the Panama Canal. She then comes as close as her dignity and self-understanding allow to meeting Adams' moral imperative by passing judgement on the iron world from which she has been forced to salvage her life:

> "The year after that photograph was taken Monsieur de Lesseps and his son were bankrupt and in disgrace. My husband borrowed a great deal of money and formed his own company and in 1900 he returned to Panama and subcontracted the excavations for the Americans. That is where he died. Like thousands of others. From malaria." She reached for the photograph. "Georges' father left us little more than his debts." (90)

What Emily has just witnessed is proof that modernity is like a shipwreck, both in its largest application to an historical epoch and in its more intimate application to the lives of individual families: on the morning of Emily's arrival at her mother-in-law's house, "The rain swept down from the roofs like seaspray over the bows of a ship" (61). This is where the significance of the shipwreck described on the opening page of the novel finally becomes clear: it is evidence of the great debacles caused by the heroic iron world of men and their impact on the private world of women and families.

While Adams' contrast between medieval Catholicism and modernity serves its purpose in the novel, exposing the world-historical forces that have shipwrecked Heloise Elder, Miller's own engagement with these ideas is typically complex and sceptical. His postcolonial perspective on Adams' relation to Europe may even register an implicit critique of America's many appropriations of European culture, in this instance through an imaginative appropriation of Chartres, but also literally through the purchase and reconstruction of Europe's medieval buildings, whose moral ambivalence is explored so memorably in the novels of Henry James. Madame Elder intuits something of significance for her own life in Adams' critique of modernity, but she remains bitter and unreflective, leaving her own situation essentially unexamined and untransformed. When Georges learns that Baume Marpent has accepted his recommendation to tender for the bridge, his mother is triumphant: "Her eyes shone . . . 'You'll do what your father only ever dreamed of doing' " (97). In spite of everything she knows, Madame Elder still worships at the altar of great men. Nor has her own shipwreck made her more compassionate to others. Emily's youthful ardour is a focus for her mother-in-law's bitterness, perhaps even a spur to her vindictiveness – her "steady gaze" resembles Captain Anderson's on the night of the storm at sea. Emily's ardour also leads her into a sexual encounter with a priest in the very foundations of the building that was Adams' great symbol of an alternative moral world – though even here Miller maintains his ambivalence, for Emily is not Father Bertrand Etinceler's unwilling victim.

Emily's interlude at Chartres is not so much a homecoming as a detour. Just as he invokes August Spiess' late-nineteenth-century ideas about the extraterritoriality of art in *The Ancestor Game* only to reveal that they are illusory, Miller invokes Adams' medievalism as a possible alternative to industrial modernity, but he does not share Adams' sentimentality about the past. His historical novel is set in the modern era, in 1923, but it is written from a postmodern and postcolonial perspective. When Emily returns briefly to the cathedral, she finds that Adams' favourite statue of the Virgin has been "defaced by the erosion of weather and the blows of unbelievers" (95), while the nearby Episcopal Palace is as prosaic as an Australian country shire hall (96). Emily's real hope of transformation, her true *kairos*, lies not in Adams' medievalist fantasy, but in her meeting with Georges' friend Antoine Carpeaux. When Emily falls pregnant after her encounter with Father Etinceler, and with Georges busy with the bridge tender, it is decided that she will go with Antoine to recuperate at his home in Sidi bou-Said. This is her true "homecoming" (133). Emily's doctor pronounces that she has chlorosis, a form of anaemia, a lack of iron in the blood (129, 187).

As a Tunisian-born homosexual living in Paris, Antoine, like Emily, is an outsider. He was born in the valley of the Medjerda River and grew up in Sidi bou-Said, even learning Arabic until his father sent him to boarding school in Montpellier, thinking that he would there "be safe from the dangers of Africa and the soulless barbarians" (51). A homosexual *dilettante*, Antoine Carpeaux anticipates Miller's later interest in Arthur Rimbaud, which is more fully developed in *Autumn Laing* (2011). If Emily's first meeting with Georges suggests Dorothea's beginnings in *Middlemarch*, her meeting with Antoine also suggests Isabel Archer's beginnings in Henry James' *The Portrait of a Lady* (1881). Antoine recognises that she is "a woman who's accustomed to her freedom" (52), and like Ralph Touchett in his mentorship of Isabel, he charges Emily to take the test of freedom, encouraging her to remain an outsider rather than becoming just another *Parisienne*. An echo of Ralph's injunction to Isabel, Antoine commands Emily that she "Live a passionate fairy story for us!" (53).

In confirmation of this pledge, Antoine gives to Emily an engraved ivory medallion, an early Christian pyxis from the ruins of the Roman arena at Carthage: "He reached and traced a line across the face of the dark ivory with his fingernail... There were the faint remains of an intaglio figure, robed and holding something under its arm, half turned away, as if on the point of departure" (53). The elusiveness of the figure foreshadows Toni Powlett's image of Marina Golding in his painting *The Other Family* in *Prochownik's Dream* (2005): "her back to the viewer; her figure, surprisingly in the end, draped and evidently in the act of leaving the space of the large central arrangement of the composition".[19] Marina's presence in the painting is enigmatic, the suggestion of her imminent departure from the group indicating her journey of personal freedom away from her husband Robert's powerful influence on her art. Antoine's gift to Emily is the gift of *kairos*, a space of potential becoming in which she might find the conditions of faith, "the problem of a reason for living" (46). In this way, as Ronald A. Sharp observes, Miller establishes an important contrast between the iron masculine world of commodity exchange, which has already turned the young married woman into sacrificial cargo, and the differently ordered world of gift exchange, which is grounded in the more mysterious economy of *kairos*.[20]

Antoine's identification of Emily as a figure of modern freedom who must solve for him "the problem of a reason for living" recalls Miller's earlier use of a passage from Søren Kierkegaard's *Either/Or* (1843) as an epigraph for *The Ancestor Game*: "Our age has lost all the substantial categories of family, state and race. It must leave the individual entirely to himself, so that in a stricter sense he becomes his own creator." In *Either/Or*, Kierkegaard undertakes a highly original reading of Greek tragic drama to ascertain what he believed to be the differences between human agency in the modern and classical worlds, when the individual was subject to what Hegel had called "the substantive determinants" of family and state. In the essay, "The Ancient Tragical Motif as Reflected in the Modern", Kierkegaard offers the figure of the "Danish Antigone" in illustration of the problems of freedom in the modern world.[21] What makes Kierkegaard's Antigone modern, however, is not that she is entirely free of Hegel's "substantive determinants" of family and state, but that she inherits the more complex legacy of both freedom *and* determination: "To the contrary, one must continually contend with the question of whether one's decisions are the results of one's own judgments or whether they are the consequences of the substantive context into which one was born."[22]

As we have seen in his treatment of "the Orient" in *The Ancestor Game*, one of Miller's great achievements in his novels is to explore such seemingly abstract ideas as free will, determinism and "the other" concretely and in specific detail. Emily's voyage to Tunisia aboard the *Gibel Sarsar* is just such a leap from the abstract and the metaphorical to the

---

19   Alex Miller, *Prochownik's Dream* (Sydney: Allen & Unwin, 2005), 293.
20   Ronald A. Sharp, "More Than Just Mates", *The Australian*, 1 July 2009, 11, http://www.news.com.au/news/more-than-just-mates/story-fna7dq6e-1225744152559.
21   For a fuller discussion of these issues, see George Steiner, *Antigones* (Oxford: Clarendon Press, 1984); and Sabina Sestigiani, "A Danish Antigone: The Legacy of Ancient Greek Consciousness in the Fragmentation of Modern Tragedy", *Colloquy: text theory critique* 11 (2006): 60–75.
22   Shoni Rancher, "Suffering Tragedy: Hegel, Kierkegaard, and Butler on the Tragedy of Antigone", *Mosaic: Journal of the Interdisciplinary Study of Literature* 41, no. 3 (September 2008): 78.

historical – specifically, from allusions to Greek myths to the realities of French colonialism in the Maghreb. As Antoine and Emily set off from Marseilles for Tunis, they are sailing the waters of the classical odysseys, again recalling Teresa Hawkins' voyage to Cythera in *For Love Alone*. Antoine points out Sardinia, "the island of giants", and Emily remarks, "You almost expect to hear them bellowing at us" (135). During the voyage, Antoine encourages her in her quest for freedom, but he also lists the "substantive determinates", the "giants" that will stand in her way: "In France the law is the partner of the family, not of friends ... Religion, the law, and the family, they are the three giants in league against friendship's liberties" (141).

Part two, "Perpetua's Medallion", covers the period from the diagnosis of Emily's pregnancy and the summer spent recuperating at Antoine's home at Sidi bou-Said, to the eve of her return to Paris in the final weeks of her pregnancy. During Emily's visit to the ruins of the Roman amphitheatre at Carthage, she meets the Tunisian archaeologist Hakim el-Ouedi, and Drs Olive and Kenneth Kallen from the American Museum of Natural History in New York.[23] The Kallens have come to Tunisia at Antoine's invitation to meet Pere Delattre, a French priest and scholar, and the head of the Catholic Order of the White Fathers. Delattre has led the recent excavations at Carthage, where he has uncovered the cell in which the early Christian martyr Vibia Perpetua was imprisoned, and he is now seeking funds from the United States to continue his work. Both Hakim and Olive Kallen encourage Emily, though for very different reasons, to undertake her own research into the life of Perpetua.

The larger history of French colonialism in Tunisia is condensed in the fictional example of Antoine's house, and his family's history as French landholders. Hakim is the son of the estate manager, and Antoine has been his mentor, paying for his education. Hakim is the only Tunisian to have studied at the Sorbonne and the British School of Archaeology. He has worked at the British Museum and in Athens, and is regarded internationally as a brilliant scholar – Olive Kallen is familiar with his papers in the scholarly journals. But he advocates a politically engaged form of scholarship that contests the evidence from a postcolonial perspective. Antoine explains to Emily, "For Hakim history is a weapon with which he hopes to defeat the French ... He wishes to shape the future of the Arabs in Tunisia with his knowledge of history" (167). The complexities of the colonial legacy are also condensed in the contested provenance of Perpetua's medallion. Antoine gave it to her on the night they met in Paris as if it really were his to give, but when Emily meets Hakim at Carthage he explains that his father found it twenty years ago beside Perpetua's cell and that Antoine appropriated it, as was his right as a French settler (161). In Hakim's view, the talisman is unambiguously Tunisian *patrimoine*.

The meaning of Perpetua's legend is itself subject to conflicting interpretations. For Pere Delattre and the White Fathers, Perpetua was an early Christian martyr. For Hakim, however, who is a descendent of the region's Berber people, Perpetua's story, like her medallion, has been wrongly subsumed into the history of the Christian conquerors. Tertullian's editing of her journal, and his original explanation that she was a Christian martyr, potentially erase the material facts of colonialism in the early Christian era in the same way

---

23 Alex and Stephanie Miller went to Tunisia to do research for *Conditions of Faith* in 1994, and were taken to Carthage by Dr Nejib ben Lazreg, an archaeologist with the *Institut National du Patrimoine* who is also a tour guide for the Archaeological Institute of America, http://www.archaeological.org/tours/leaders/nejibbenlazreg.

that Pere Delattre's proposed restoration of Perpetua's cell is a "whitewash", an expression of contemporary French colonialism (175).

Hakim gifts to Emily her project of reinterpreting the meaning of Perpetua's life, which parallels her own in the same way that the legend of St Theresa of Avila parallels Dorothea's life in *Middlemarch*. He gives her a slim, red clothbound volume titled *Passio Perpetuae*, which he has stolen from the British Museum (174). In Miller's work after Max Blatt's gift of "Comrade Pawel", there is no "origin" to stories: they are always gifted – or stolen. The *Passio* is one of the earliest Christian texts written in Latin, and the first by a woman, the core of which is assumed to be an authentic account of Perpetua's ordeal in the Roman amphitheatre at Carthage during the reign of Septimius Severus, somewhere between 203 and 213 C.E.[24] Perpetua was a twenty-two-year-old woman of "noble birth" with a newborn infant who was imprisoned, together with her pregnant slave Felicitas, for professing the new Christian faith. Her pagan father begged her to renounce her faith, but she refused to do so, even abandoning her baby to the Roman guards. As a punishment, she was forced to fight wild animals in the arena and finally put to death by the sword. The account of Perpetua's ordeal is presented by an editor whom early scholars identified as Tertullian, though the attribution is now less certain.[25] The *Passio* is especially interesting in relation to scholarly understandings of the role of women in early Christian society because Perpetua's adherence to her faith involves the rejection of conventional social roles that were considered natural for women, including the roles of mother, wife and daughter subordinated to paternal authority. The status of women in early Christian society was of great interest to scholars in the 1980s and 1990s, and a number of important feminist interventions were published in those decades, which are foreshadowed by Emily's proposal in 1923 to write a study of *The Secular Perpetua*.[26]

Hakim and his pious colleague, Ahmed, believe that Emily's appearance at Perpetua's cell is auspicious, and that as an outsider, and a young pregnant woman, she is an ideal person to undertake a fresh investigation of the legend that might allow them to wrest it back from the authority of centuries of Christian interpretation. Hakim's belief that Emily's scholarship might advance the cause of Arab nationalism in French-occupied Tunisia anticipates Dougald Gnapun's collaboration with the German historian Max Otto in *Landscape of Farewell* (2007). There is even a suggestion that Hakim and Ahmed see Emily as a reincarnation of Perpetua. In the section of the *Passio* in which the editor recounts Perpetua's ordeal in the arena, her robe is torn when a wild cow mauls her, and she draws down the robe to conceal her thigh from the eyes of the crowd. Herbert Musurillo notes that this erotic motif became a literary topos that was widely imitated in later classical texts.[27] In Miller's account there is a suggestion of this erotic topos when Hakim, who knows the *Passio* well, stares openly at Emily's legs when she appears near the cell (160, 163). In a letter to Emily after her return to Paris, Hakim writes, "Perhaps Ahmed and I are a little influenced by the melancholy and romantic setting . . . He touched my shoulder

---

[24] Miller's source is Herbert Musurillo, ed., *The Acts of the Christian Martyrs: Introduction, Texts and Translations* (Oxford: Clarendon Press, 1972).

[25] Petr Kitzler, "*Passio Perpetuae* and *Acta Perpetuae*: Between Tradition and Innovation", *Listy fiologicke* CXXX, no. 1–2 (2007): 4, http://www.tertullian.org/articles/kitzler_perpetua.pdf.

[26] See, for example, Eva Cantarella, *Pandora's Daughters: The Role and Status of Women in Greek and Roman Antiquity* (Baltimore: Johns Hopkins University Press, 1987); and Gillian Clark, *Women in Late Antiquity: Pagan and Christian Lifestyles* (Oxford: Clarendon Press, 1993).

[27] Musurillo, quoted in Kitzler, "*Passio Perpetuae*", 13.

and said, There she is! . . . We recall then how you appeared to us outside her cell in the arena that day" (242–3). Moved by Perpetua's story and excited by Hakim's contestatory approach to the received history, Emily decides to resume her work as a historian. When Antoine warns her that history can be dangerous, she is inspired by the challenge: " 'I've never thought of history as dangerous', she said. 'I abandoned it because it seemed so very dull and safe' " (170).

Olive Kallen, who is writing a life of Septimius Severus, is another of Emily's "collaborators". She offers Emily another kind of gift: the solidarity of professional women. She warns her that "Motherhood is the greatest test we ambitious women are called upon to meet, and we either meet it boldly and with courage or it defeats us utterly" (259). Olive offers Emily not only her moral support as a successful academic woman, but also more practical assistance, appointing her as her paid research assistant so that she can return to Carthage the following season. This is another form of global finance, but on a much more modest scale than the engineering projects that Georges and his father are involved in, though Olive does speak of the international nature of humanities research funding as "ply[ing] our trade in foreign lands" (258). This reminder of the connections between institutions like the American Museum of Natural History and the Archaeological Institute of America, and the actual sources of the wealth of the great American philanthropists like John D. Rockefeller Jnr., is another instance of the subtlety of Miller's historical understanding, again unsettling any easy oppositions between medievalism and industrialism, the humanities and the sciences, or art and engineering.

In part four, "The Conditions of Faith", Emily returns to Paris in the late stage of her pregnancy and purposefully sets out to resume her vocation as a historian by recovering Perpetua's story from beneath the layers of the early Christian text. Her intervention, we might say, is both feminist and postcolonial. Olive has given her a letter of introduction to a colleague at the Bibliothèque Sainte-Geneviève, and she there calls up volumes three and four of *The Ante-Nicene Fathers*. Originally published between 1867 and 1873, this is a scholarly collection in ten volumes containing English translations of the majority of the early Christian writings, from the beginnings of Christianity to the Council of Nicaea.[28] The volumes Emily orders contain the writings of Tertullian, the founder of Latin Christianity, whom she understands, like many other scholars in the 1920s, to have been the editor of Perpetua's prison diary. Reading ever more widely and deeply in Tertullian's works, she comes to see that his beliefs are informed by a pervasive misogyny, "page after page of it", and that "Hakim was surely right when he cautioned me to distrust everything Tertullian has to say about Perpetua and her motives" (222). She comes to think of Tertullian as "the enemy" (245), and is attuned to "the interminable haranguing tones of [his] writing" about women and the early church, "masking the gentle intimate confidences of Perpetua's journal beneath his rhetoric of power and the law" (249). In Emily's research, Miller suggests the systemic connections that exist between the everyday practices of colonialism, including the spatial practices of occupation, and the practices of scholarly editing and interpretation. Ironically, though, it is in one of Tertullian's own essays, "De Spectaculis", that she locates the Latin phrase that will help her to understand that it is her new vocation as a historian, and not her role as wife or mother, that gives her a reason for living. She writes it into her notebook: "*Qui status fidei* . . . *The conditions of faith*" (265).

---

28   Miller indicates in the front matter of *Conditions of Faith* that he used a 1970 reprint of these volumes.

Miller's principal source on Tertullian was Peter Brown's *The Body and Society: Men, Women and Sexual Renunciation in Early Christianity* (1988). Brown argues that "modern" Christian understandings of clerical celibacy, virginity, continence and renunciation emerged relatively late in the long history of Christian thought, and then depended on the writings of church fathers like Tertullian, whose understanding was theoretical, prescriptive and misogynistic.[29] The meanings of these concepts varied significantly not only at different times throughout the early Christian era, but also in different locations, especially in North Africa. Brown's study of the Mediterranean reveals a spectrum of practices and behaviours that it was Tertullian's achievement to have simplified and reduced to orthodoxy. Perpetua was not a woman vowed to continence, she was a wife and mother, and the head of a household, but Tertullian used the metaphor of the martyr's cell to advocate the repression of sexuality. In his tract, "On the Veiling of Virgins", Tertullian identifies the condition of *Mulieritas*: "the state of a woman aware of her own sexual feelings and capable of inspiring sexual feelings in others".[30] To nullify the dangers of women's sexuality, Tertullian advocated a structure of church leadership that Brown describes as "a spirit-filled gerontocracy", a hierarchy of "elders", widows and widowers who are safely passed the age of sexual activity and child bearing.[31] Written in "clear and compelling Latin", Tertullian's message was not lost on later theologians, including Augustine, the founder of the medieval Catholic Church that for Henry Adams was epitomised in Chartres Cathedral.

In *Conditions of Faith*, Miller reveals that the broad spectrum of beliefs and practices that existed in North African *before* Tertullian ironically continues to exist in Adams' modern church. The widowed Madame Elder is just the kind of pious woman, past her sexually active and child-bearing years, whom Tertullian saw as an ideal authority figure in the church. Yet in her own church, Chartres Cathedral, Father Etinceler is the father of her daughter-in-law's child. *Mulieritas* is precisely what Emily displays in the crypt of Madame Elder's church, and Father Etinceler responds, we might say, with charity. Indeed, Emily's understanding is that she is not the first young woman to have received his comfort. In making these links between the Early Christian Church and the Medieval and modern churches, Miller suggests their underlying continuities. By revealing that a spectrum of meanings and behaviours has always existed around such concepts as virginity, chastity and renunciation, he not only undoes Tertullian's editorial intervention in Perpetua's story; he also questions the teleological history of the modern church that has its origins in Tertullian's writings. In his scholarship, Brown had sought to give back to the men and women of the Early Christian era their "disturbing strangeness".[32] Through his fictional realisation of these ideas, Miller discloses the same "disturbing strangeness" in the idealised church of nineteenth-century medievalists like Henry Adams, in the modern church, and in "The Household of the Elders".

Miller gives a painfully affecting account of Emily's heroic efforts to prosecute her research at the library in late pregnancy, ill with pneumonia and anaemia, her body weakened by bacterial infection: "Sitting there leaning over the desk reading, the distended globe of her belly was pushed down onto her thighs and upward hard against her diaphragm . . . It was a physical effort for her to keep her legs together" (245). When Georges

---

29 Peter Brown, *The Body and Society: Men, Women and Sexual Renunciation in Early Christianity* (New York: Columbia University Press, 1988), xvii.
30 Brown, *The Body and Society*, 81.
31 Brown, *The Body and Society*, 79.
32 Brown, *The Body and Society*, xv.

realises that Emily is going again to the library, he forbids it, speaking "as if he were accusing her of planning a crime" (232), and he calls on his friend Dr Leon Chaussegros for support. Ironically, Leon is not an obstetrician but a paediatrician at the *Hôpital des Enfants Malades* (105), and his diagnoses and advice infantilise her. Georges and Leon see her desire to study as "unnatural", a dereliction of her proper roles as wife and mother, and they advise her that she must surrender herself to the destiny of her biology. Her body is not hers, but an instrument for the birth of the child they assume, wrongly, to be her husband's. Despite his professionalism, Leon's diagnosis is therefore moral rather than scientific: "You've got a local infection . . . It persists only because you . . . insist on dragging yourself out to the library every day in all weather. Intellectual work is depleting . . . there will be nothing medicine can do for you" (253). The attendant at the Bibliothèque Sainte-Geneviève also disapproves of having a heavily pregnant woman in his reading room and decides that she must be expelled by force: "She felt the attendant's hand grip her elbow and his urgent whisper close to her ear: 'Come, madam! . . . You cannot stay here. This is no place for you.' " (265).

In the end, Baume Marpent do not win the tender for the Sydney Harbour Bridge. Professor Stanton had warned Georges of the tensions between corporate and imperial interests driving these large engineering projects, and it is the "imperial connection" that holds: the English firm, Dorman Long, gets the bridge (380). With his reputation as an engineer compromised, as least in Europe, Georges resigns from Baume Marpent and accepts Bradfield's invitation to come to Sydney to work for him on the construction of the bridge approaches. Ironically, with the failure of the tender and his mother's death, Georges finds that he has been liberated from the burden of expectation. His father had been his ideal of an engineer, "out there building the civilized world" (366), and after the debacle of de Lesseps' *Compaigne*, Georges had been driven to restore this ideal both for the sake of his father's memory and for his mother, whose life was ruined by his father's failure. Now, in the midst of his own failure, he speaks of it "as if it were success" (367). Georges understands that "it takes a kind of madness . . . to bring these enormous objects into being", and for him personally "the mad dream" has gone. The release is "like an unexpected gift" (367).

For Emily, the situation is reversed. After the birth of her daughter in "The Household of the Elders", she is liberated to resume her career as a professional historian, but to do so she must renounce the role of motherhood. In exploring the ambivalence of Emily's maternal feelings and the potentially liberating consequences of her renunciation, Miller is releasing in the novel a radical association between Father Etinceler's renunciation of sexuality for God and the modern woman's renunciation of motherhood for the sake of a creative and professional life. Two of the important historical studies of these issues that influenced his thinking use the terms "the myth of motherhood" and "the power of maternal ambivalence".[33] Miller was also aware here of the modern Australian precedent of Joy Hester renouncing motherhood in favour of her art. And yet, as Brown demonstrates in his research on Tertullian, the practice of "permanent sexual renunciation" was itself a myth generated in the early Christian writings and later imposed on the institution of

---

33   See Elizabeth Badinter, *The Myth of Motherhood: An Historical View of the Maternal Instinct* (London: Souvenir Press, 1981); Rozsika Parker, *Torn in Two: The Experience of Maternal Ambivalence* (London: Virago, 1995); and Rozsika Parker, *Mother Love/Mother Hate: The Power of Maternal Ambivalence* (New York: Basic Books, 1995).

the modern church. The reality, then and now, is a "spectrum" of practices; a "disturbing strangeness". By implication, Emily's renunciation of her role as wife and mother for the sake of her scholarship may no more be "permanent" than Father Etinceler's vow of celibacy: at the end of the novel, at the beginning of her return to scholarship, she is, after all, writing to her child in anticipation of their reunion.

At the end of *Conditions of Faith*, Emily experiences the belatedness of knowledge, which is central to the two great nineteenth-century *bildungsromane* it recalls, *Middlemarch* and *The Portrait of a Lady*. Emily realises that both her acceptance of Georges' proposal of marriage and her affair with Bertrand Etinceler had been youthful and imperfect attempts to seize external opportunities as the possible means of fulfilling her own inner need. As George Eliot so wisely puts it, even "great feelings will often take the aspect of error".[34] In retrospect, both events now appear as contingent rather than central to her personal quest. In his previous exchanges with Georges and Emily, Bertrand has seemed impassive and unresponsive, but it is his deep reserve of emotional intelligence that allows Emily finally to understand the belatedness of knowledge. As they separate for the last time, he tells her, "When we met that day in the crypt, you were searching for something." It is not a question but a statement, the gift of a revelation. He then asks, "You've found what you were looking for, haven't you?" and she answers, "Yes" (331). Emily has indeed found her conditions of faith, which means that she must leave Georges and her daughter Marie, allowing them to go to Australia without her, while she returns to Carthage with Olive Kallen. Emily belatedly understands that her acceptance of both Georges' proposal of marriage and Bertrand's offer of passion were attempts to find something that could only be found within herself – and in the fullness of time, in the alternative temporal and ethical order of *kairos*. As her father points out, however, to realise her quest she does need her network of "collaborators".

In a letter supporting Emily's vocation, Professor Stanton describes Dr Kallen as a woman who has "established her authority in her field and possesses an independent intellectual life that is well grounded in the robust and civilized complexities of New York and the American Museum of Natural History" (326). He warns her, "you do not possess the elaborate support women such as Olive Kallen rely on. I know such women. There are several here at the university in Melbourne" (327). The apparent contradictions here go to the heart of Miller's understanding of the relation between individual achievement and the "substantive determinants" of social and historical contexts, between agency and structure. Dr Kallen is an "independent" scholar, but her "authority" is conferred by the disciplinary "field" in which she practises; her "independence" is "well grounded" both in the institution for which she works, the powerful American Museum of Natural History, and in the generosity of her collaborators, her "elaborate support network".

The fulfilment of Emily's quest requires that she negotiate two challenging disjunctions. The first is the supremely inconvenient and even tragic disjunction between opportunities that are externally presented, such as an offer of marriage, or of sex, or employment, and the tragic belatedness of self-knowledge, which means that the consequences of these moments are only ever understood retrospectively. They may be the auspicious moments that the ancient Greeks called *kairos*, or they may be mere contingencies – only time will tell. The second is the paradoxical relationship between free will and determin-

---

34   George Eliot, *Middlemarch*, ed. Bert G. Hornback (1874; New York and London: Norton, 2000), 514.

ism, between "independence" and "collaboration", which Miller returns to again and again in his novels. As Marina Golding says to Toni Powlett, and as Olive Kallen says to Emily, "We do nothing alone" (261). Miller's interest in the belatedness of knowledge, which he shares with George Eliot, Thomas Hardy and Henry James, has also been remarked in the "audacious prolepsis" of Shirley Hazzard's *The Transit of Venus* (1980),[35] whose heroine Caro Bell is also haunted by the imminence of shipwreck. Emily's placement in and progression through a series of architectural spaces (the cathedral, the ironwork of ships and bridges) and her negotiation of temporal moments of knowing or unknowing parallels the reader's own engagement with the elaborate structure of Miller's narrative, with the phenomenology of reading and interpretation as acts embedded in the novel as a temporal structure. This subtle parallel between the temporality of reading and the temporality of self-knowledge is something his novels share with Hazzard's. As Brigitta Olubas observes, "Knowledge for Hazzard's protagonists, as for her readers, is always belated, and understanding is always anachronistic."[36]

In Emily's wrenching separation from her family in the echoing cavern of the Gare Saint-Lazare in 1924 there is perhaps an echo of Miller's own separation from his first family as a young man at Victoria Station in London in 1952, setting out on his own quest for the conditions of faith. And in commencing her journal at Sidi bou-Said on 17 June 1924, Emily realises that although becoming a writer has required a passionate and in certain respects destructive commitment – "We go on, wounded and changed" – she is not, after all, alone: "I have understood that I am not writing to myself" (401).

---

35 Brigitta Olubas, *Shirley Hazzard: Literary Expatriate and Cosmopolitan Humanist* (Amherst, New York: Cambria, 2012), 19.
36 Olubas, *Shirley Hazzard*, 163.

5
The Central Queensland Novels: *Journey to the Stone Country*

Alex Miller had "come out of the bush" when he moved to Melbourne in 1958, but it was not until the late 1980s, when he began *Watching the Climbers on the Mountain*, that he began to draw deeply on that period of his life in writing fiction. Even then, he would again set the Queensland material aside for a number of years while he worked with the very different subject matter of *The Ancestor Game*, *The Sitters* and *Conditions of Faith*. "For more than twenty years", he recalls, "I thought my Queensland days would never be part of my life again."[1] The delay was perhaps more significant than it seemed, revealing a personal disconnection between his present and past lives that corresponded to an equally profound series of disconnections in Australian history and in the contemporary public sphere. Although Miller felt this to be a personal and perhaps unusual experience, in reality it was symptomatic of Australia's dissociation from its frontier history at this time. In 1984, I had myself moved from Sydney via Perth to Far North Queensland, where I first met the historian Henry Reynolds at James Cook University. I well remember the extraordinary impact of the region's climate and landscape, and the palpable presence of its colonial history, and so I understood immediately when Reynolds told me that he would not have begun the research that led to his seminal book, *The Other Side of the Frontier* (1981), had he not moved to Townsville from Hobart some years earlier. Miller's apparently autobiographical sense of disconnection between his regional and metropolitan experiences, the amnesia that seemed to separate these two times and places in his life in Australia, were symptomatic of the era. As a novelist, he was about to commence a major and distinctive new phase of his career, working now in the late 1990s to bring these two parts of the Australian experience together in fiction in a way that would be as significant as the books that Reynolds was writing at this time.[2]

The opportunity for Miller to bridge the two hemispheres of his experience came about once again through a gift of friendship and the sharing of personal stories. Miller had first met Liz Hatte when they were both working at Holmesglen TAFE in 1986. While

---

1   Alex Miller, "The Mask of Fiction: A Memoir", in *The Novels of Alex Miller: An Introduction*, ed. Robert Dixon (Sydney: Allen & Unwin, 2012), 31.
2   Henry Reynold's books include *Aboriginal Sovereignty: Reflections on Race, State and Nation* (Sydney: Allen & Unwin, 1996); *This Whispering in Our Hearts* (Sydney: Allen & Unwin, 1998); *Why Weren't We Told? A Personal Search for the Truth About Our History* (Ringwood, Vic.: Viking, 1999); and *An Indelible Stain? The Question of Genocide in Australia's History* (Ringwood, Vic.: Viking, 2001).

he made the transition to full-time writing, she left teaching to return to archaeology, eventually also returning to her home in Townsville, where she established Northern Archaeological Consultancies, a company that specialises in reports on prior Indigenous occupation for mining companies and government instrumentalities. When Miller visited her in South Townsville in 1997, he met her partner, Col McLennan, a Jangga elder who in his youth had been a ringer in Central Queensland. Miller recalls, "A vital connection was made for me through Col and his story between the two worlds of my early years in North Queensland and my subsequent university and writing life in Melbourne." In 1999, Miller returned to Townsville, and McLennan took him to the country of his people, the Jangga, and to meet his old droving partner, Frank Budby, a Barada elder from Nebo. Liz Hatte, Col McLennan and Frank Budby were the inspiration for Annabelle Beck, Bo Rennie and Dougald Gnapun in Miller's Central Queensland novels, *Journey to the Stone Country* (2002) and *Landscape of Farewell* (2007). Miller says of *Journey to the Stone Country*, which in 2003 won him his second Miles Franklin Literary Award, "It is a reflection of my own realities and the realities of those friends, heightened, simplified and transmuted into the organic whole of story."[3]

Just as Miller's first two novels were initially conceived as a single, larger work, so the Central Queensland novels first emerged in his thinking as a "Reconciliation Trilogy", with a third, projected novel to be called "The Departure".[4] At the dark inner core of both *Journey to the Stone Country* and *Landscape of Farewell* is the persistence of violence in human history, especially the frontier violence of colonial Queensland: in the first novel, a massacre of Aboriginal men, women and children by the first generation of white settlers in Central Queensland, and in the second a massacre of white settlers by Aboriginal people. In "The Mask of Fiction", Miller explains that the distinctive purpose of *Landscape of Farewell* emerged during a visit to Hamburg in 2005, when he began to seek ways of connecting the frontier massacres in Australia with his childhood memories of the Holocaust. As a young schoolboy in London, he had seen the terrible newsreels recording the entry of allied troops into the death camps of Belsen and Buchenwald, and "A sense of guilt-by-association was inescapable."[5] Historian Ian Buruma confirms that in London immediately after the war, "cinema-goers who found they were 'unable to stomach atrocity newsreels' were prevented from leaving by British soldiers".[6] At Springsure in the mid-1950s, Miller had first heard accounts of the massacre at Cullin-la-Ringo Station in 1861, in which a large group of settlers was killed by Aborigines. Inspired by his meeting in Hamburg with Indigenous writer Anita Heiss – the model for Professor Vita McLelland in the novel – he began to sketch "lines of intersection" between these traumatic events. The heroism of Gnapun the Warrior, the leader and strategist of the Cullin-la-Ringo massacre, was also a way of celebrating the contemporary leadership of Frank Budby, whom Miller describes as "a quiet, unassuming and deeply intelligent man", who "rescued his people from the depredations of white culture".[7]

---

3 Miller, "The Mask of Fiction", 35–6.
4 Alex Miller to Robert Dixon, 6 December 2006.
5 Miller, "The Mask of Fiction", 37.
6 Quoted in Joanna Kavenna, review of Ian Buruma, *Year Zero: A History of 1945* (2013), *The Australian*, 30 November – 1 December 2013: 21.
7 Miller, "The Mask of Fiction", 36–7. See also Frank Budby, Elizabeth Hatte and Anita Heiss, "Personal Perspectives on the Central Queensland Novels", in *The Novels of Alex Miller*, 139–55.

Miller's account of the Central Queensland novels in "The Mask of Fiction" also suggests that the lifelong dislocation experienced by his Indigenous friends spoke to his own sense of exile from his home and family in the United Kingdom: "My own displacement from one side of the world to the other, my loss of culture and home, is dealt with silently in my empathy with the displacement and dispossession experienced by the book's principal characters, black and white."[8] The word "silently" carries a great weight, since for Miller these novels are not just about the displacement of their Indigenous characters – they are equally about the sense of personal and cultural displacement of the authorial consciousness that allows the stories of these *other* displaced people to be realised sympathetically in story. As Toni Powlett reminds us in *Prochownik's Dream*, the artist is always visible "at the edge" of his compositions. It is these very different legacies of displacement that make Australia "postmodern": "In Australia . . . we have found ourselves to be the inhabitants of a disestablished world in which the dominant cultural experience is that of displacement."[9]

These are the biographical sources of the Central Queensland novels, but as we have seen, they also have links to broader developments in the public life of Australia at this time. *Journey to the Stone Country* and *Landscape of Farewell* were partly a response, in ways that we are still coming to understand, to the controversial issues associated with race politics in Australia in the 1980s, 1990s and 2000s. Miller first met Liz Hatte on the eve of the Bicentenary of European "settlement" in 1988, which sparked criticism from Indigenous leaders and calls for land rights, sovereignty, and a treaty. It was partly to address these historical injustices and to heal the social divisions exacerbated by the Bicentennial celebrations that the Council for Aboriginal Reconciliation, established by the Hawke government in 1991, advocated the themes of "sharing history" and "walking together" as the means toward national reconciliation: "The reconciliation process seeks to encourage non-indigenous Australians to deepen and enrich their association with this country by identifying with the ancient Aboriginal and Torres Strait Islander presence in Australia."[10] David Malouf, who co-authored the Council's *Declaration Towards Reconciliation* with Jackie Huggins in 1998, argued that there should be "a convergence of indigenous and non-indigenous understanding, a collective spiritual consciousness that will be the true form of reconciliation here".[11] In 1992 the High Court of Australia had delivered its watershed Mabo decision, which gave a basis in law for claims to native title, dispelling the legal fiction of *terra nullius*. In 1997, the year Miller first visited Hatte in Townsville, the Human Rights and Equal Opportunity Commission's report, *Bringing Them Home: Report of the National Inquiry into the Separation of Aboriginal and Torres Strait Islander Children from Their Families*, was tabled in federal parliament, though it was not until 13 February 2008 that Prime Minister Kevin Rudd offered a formal apology in the parliament to members of the Stolen Generations. The intervening years of the Howard–Liberal Coalition government saw what Anna Clarke and Stuart McIntyre called "the History Wars", whose battles ranged from Keith Windschuttle's polemic *The Fabrication of Aboriginal His-*

---

8   Miller, "The Mask of Fiction", 35.
9   Alex Miller, "Modern, European and Novel", *Overland* 128 (Spring 1992): 42.
10 Council for Aboriginal Reconciliation, *Key Issue Paper No 4: Sharing History* (Canberra: AGPS, 1993), 28–9; *Walking Together: The First Steps* (Canberra: AGPS, 1994). See Heather Goodall, "Too Early Yet or Not Soon Enough? Reflections on Sharing Histories as Process", *Australian Historical Studies* 33, no. 118 (2002): 7–24.
11 David Malouf, *A Spirit of Play: The Making of Australian Consciousness* (Sydney: ABC Books, 1998), 39–40.

tory (2002), to historian Inga Clendinnen's 2006 essay "The History Question", in which she criticised Kate Grenville for her depiction of frontier conflict in her novel *The Secret River* (2005), and her apparent claim that fiction could deal with such issues more insightfully than history.[12] Miller's Central Queensland novels were also written in this charged political context, and at a time of "unsettling" debate about the relationships between history and fiction, and fiction and politics.[13] Understanding the novels' complex relation to this intensely contested period in Australian public life is one of the most difficult challenges confronting his readers. In this chapter I discuss *Journey to the Stone Country*, and return to its sequel *Landscape of Farewell* in Chapter 7.

Journey to the Stone Country occupies a place in Miller's body of work similar to that of *Remembering Babylon* (1993) in David Malouf's. In that novel, as Don Randall observes, "the previously established elements of Malouf's vision are now organised around questions of postcoloniality and nationhood".[14] Similarly, Brigid Rooney notices that after the postmodern complexities of *The Ancestor Game, Journey to the Stone Country* signals an "increased accessibility and more explicitly national orientation".[15] When a novelist engages more directly in this way with issues of moment in the public sphere, it is easy for readers to see their work reductively, as if it were simply "about" those social issues or directly reflective of particular opinions held by journalists, politicians, historians or public intellectuals. In using fiction to address debates about colonisation and social justice, Aboriginal dispossession, and the push for and frustration of reconciliation at this time, Malouf and Miller may have attracted a broader readership, but they also drew criticism from some quarters, especially from postcolonial critics, who charged them with complacently reproducing the pieties of official reconciliation policies, including the ideal of a "shared history". One of my principal arguments in this book is that Miller is not a "middlebrow" writer, at least not in the sense that is meant by critics such as Andrew McCann[16] – neither, of course, is Malouf – and that the apparent stylistic transparency of his novels – especially those published after *The Ancestor Game* – in fact requires close literary reading to a degree that we are only now beginning to see.

Reviewers of *Remembering Babylon* noted its relation to the official policies of reconciliation, some of which, as we have seen, Malouf helped to shape. Gia Metherell argued that its acknowledgement of " 'a shared history' coincides with the position adopted by the Council for Aboriginal Reconciliation".[17] Germaine Greer denounced it as a (white) "supremacist fantasy", describing its central character, Gemmy, as a "fake black".[18] Suvendrini Perera accused Malouf of "misappropriating the indigenous body" for "the discourse of happy hybridism", of evacuating the space of the indigenous, and producing "a Prov-

---

12   Stuart Macintyre and Anna Clarke, *The History Wars* (Carlton, Vic.: Melbourne University Press, 2003); Inga Clendinnen, "The History Question: Who Owns the Past?", *Quarterly Essay*, no. 23 (2006): 1–169.
13   Bain Attwood, *Telling the Truth about Aboriginal History* (Sydney: Allen & Unwin, 2005), 29.
14   Don Randall, *David Malouf* (Manchester and New York: Manchester University Press, 2007), 125.
15   Brigid Rooney, "The Ruin of Time and the Temporality of Belonging: *Journey to the Stone Country* and *Landscape of Farewell*", in *The Novels of Alex Miller*, 202.
16   Andrew McCann, "How to Fuck a Tuscan Garden: A Note on Literary Pessimism", *Overland* 177 (2004): 22–24.
17   Gia Metherell, "Babylon Not Always Remembered Fondly, *Canberra Times*, 24 May 1996, quoted in Randall, *David Malouf*, 127.
18   Germaine Greer, "Malouf's Objectionable Whitewash", *The Age*, 3 November 1993, quoted in Randall, *David Malouf*, 126.

identialist narrative of colonization".[19] Reviewers of *Journey to the Stone Country* also understood that it was a response to the national project of reconciliation, Michael Sharkey dubbing it a "parable" of reconciliation, and Paul Genoni again echoing the Council for Aboriginal Reconciliation's official catchphrase, a "shared history", in describing the entwined family histories of the Becks and the Rennies.[20] At its most extreme, this criticism reads Miller's Central Queensland novels as examples of "sorry" literature, arguing that their politics of reconciliation are achieved by invoking "the oldest settler fantasies about otherness: sexuality, land, timelessness". Critics accused Miller of romanticising his Indigenous characters, projecting on to them a register of "new-age wish fulfilment",[21] and corralling "the Aboriginal sacred" as a form of exoticism.[22] While the romantic union of Annabelle Beck and Bo Rennie represents another fantasy of "happy hybridism", and therefore a shared future for settler and Aboriginal Australians, other characters who maintain the old hatreds and demand Aboriginal sovereignty, such as Panya and Les Marra, are rendered unsympathetically and ultimately marginalised. As evidence of this alleged replication of racial stereotypes and New Age wish fulfilment, postcolonial critics Anna Johnston and Alan Lawson cite Annabelle's desire for Bo Rennie's "honey-gold skin . . . [his] gilded, cafe au lait [skin]".[23]

In subsequent and more considered readings of these novels, however, Randall and Rooney, respectively, have convincingly shown that they withstand scrutiny, their literary style and attention to aesthetic form requiring that they be read attentively as "difficult" and "literary" texts that do not simply reproduce middlebrow complacencies, but raise ethical and political issues of considerable complexity, and resist reassuring closure and the uncritical replication of stereotypes. Randall and Rooney demonstrate that the charges of middlebrow complacency were critically naïve in the sense that they read complex, self-reflexive material in a simple, literal way. Prerera, for example, alleges that Malouf presents Gemmy's hybridity as the utopian vision of a reconciled Australia that displaces the authentic Indigenous presence. Yet Randall shows not only that Malouf does *not* do this, but that he uses the resources of literary fiction to offer a critique of precisely that position. It is not Malouf's narrator but the schoolmaster, Mr Frazer, who puts forward Gemmy as a "forerunner" and "exemplum" of the future development of Australian cultural identity.[24] In *Landscape of Farewell*, Miller also raises the possibility of a future hybrid Australian race, but he does so as part of his mid-nineteenth-century missionary–settler's idealistic

---

19 Suvendrini Perera, "Unspeakable Bodies: Representing the Aboriginal in Australian Critical Discourse", *Meridian* 13, no. 1 (1994): 15–26, quoted in Randall, *David Malouf*, 127.
20 Michael Sharkey, "Parable of Roads Taken", review of Alex Miller, *Journey to the Stone Country*, *The Australian*, 28–29 September 2002, 10; Paul Genoni, review of Alex Miller, *Journey to the Stone Country*, *JAS (The Journal of Australian Studies) Review of Books* 16 (June 2003), http://pandora.nla.gov.au/pan/24605/20030715-0000/www.api-network.com/cgi-bin/reviews/jrb.html. See also Lucy Sussex, review of Alex Miller, *Journey to the Stone Country*, *The Age*, 12 October 2003, 9: "*Journey to the Stone Country* is a novel about reconciliation".
21 Anna Johnston and Alan Lawson, "Settler Post-Colonialism and Australian Literary Culture", in *Modern Australian Literary Criticism and Theory*, edited by David Carter and Wang Guanglin, 28–40. Qingdao (China: China Ocean University Press, 2010), 37–8.
22 Bill Ashcroft, Frances Devlin-Glass and Lynn McCredden, *Intimate Horizons: The Post-Colonial Sacred in Australian Literature* (Hindmarsh, SA: ATF Press, 2009), 178.
23 Johnston and Lawson, "Settler Post-Colonialism", 38.
24 Randall, *David Malouf*, 136, 140.

vision of "the new Jerusalem" shortly before he is speared in revenge by the Indigenous leader Gnapun.[25]

In her reading of *Journey to the Stone Country* and *Landscape of Farewell*, Rooney demonstrates that "both texts are more reflexively layered than appears from their surface conformity to verisimilitude", and that Miller is meticulous in his attention to "matters of style and composition".[26] *Journey to the Stone Country* certainly evokes "settler fantasies", including Annabelle's initial romanticising of Bo Rennie, yet Rooney demonstrates that through her "wry modulation" of such tropes, Annabelle is shown to undergo a process of cultural adjustment as she journeys "towards the other": "Cultural stereotypes are registered, but shift, opening the space for other views . . . Attention to style, composition and temporalities, and to the narrative's phenomenological effect on the reader, suggests how *Journey to the Stone Country* does not just describe but simulates the journey towards the other". In a telling criticism of Johnston and Lawson's charge that Miller reproduces racial stereotypes, Rooney shows that Annabelle's awareness of Bo's "honey-gold . . . gilded, café au lait" skin is part of this revision of first impressions, and that these phrases, drawn initially from Annabelle's discovery of her husband's cache of pornography, are "refunctioned here as banalities mockingly unequal to her encounter with Bo".[27] Johnston and Lawson, in other words, have taken Miller's text at face value, failing to grasp its layers of irony. As Ronald A. Sharp rightly observes, in both of the Central Queensland novels, Miller avoids "any facile recourse to half-baked romantic assumptions about the potency of Aboriginal primitivism".[28]

Miller's Central Queensland novels absorb these contemporary debates about reconciliation deeply into their own fabric and processes of self-reflection. They are emphatically not what have been called "sorry novels", but complex ethical meditations that reflect upon both the wish for reconciliation and the series of barriers and recuperations that deny them what Liliana Zavaglia, quoting Dominick LaCapra, calls the "facile uplift" of easy harmonisation, closure or atonement.[29] These issues are incorporated into the novels themselves, and make them ethically challenging, equivocal and unresolved. This is partly achieved by the way Miller opens the novels up to opposing voices – Bo Rennie *and* Les Marra, Grandma Rennie *and* Panya – but also by the way he is always willing, as Sharp observes, "to place at considerable risk the narrative line of the novel and the plotting of events in time and space in order to emphasise the slipperiness of cognition and interpretation".[30] As Rooney puts it, "Miller's prose works to slow down hasty or precipitate reading"; his attention to matters of style and composition "inherent in self-consciously literary works, are deeply constitutive of the fullest range of meanings in play".[31]

Journey to the Stone Country is a contemporary road novel and a love story that purposefully uses the conventions of those forms in what reviewers described as a "parable" of reconciliation and a "national epic". Unlike *The Ancestor Game* and *Conditions of Faith*, it

---

25 Alex Miller, *Landscape of Farewell* (Sydney: Allen & Unwin, 2007), 197.
26 Rooney, "The Ruin of Time", 202, 205.
27 Rooney, "The Ruin of Time", 206–7.
28 Ronald A. Sharp, "More Than Just Mates", *The Australian*, 1 July 2009, 2, http://www.news.com.au/news/more-than-just-mates/story-fna7dq6e-1225744152559.
29 Liliana Zavaglia, "Old Testament Prophets, New Testament Saviours: Reading Retribution and Forgiveness towards Whiteness in *Journey to the Stone Country*", in *The Novels of Alex Miller*, 172.
30 Ronald A. Sharp, "The Presence of Absence in *The Sitters*", in *The Novels of Alex Miller*, 80.
31 Rooney, "The Ruin of Time", 205, 208.

is not a historical novel as such, but a novel about the forms of historical time as they impinge upon the present, in which the motif of the journey spatialises various temporalities: personal, cultural, national and even geological. Despite the seductive clarity of its surface realism, it uses the resources of literary fiction to unsettle the categories of time and space as they had been established in the nation's history prior to what Bain Attwood describes as the rise of Aboriginal history, or the Aboriginal turn in Australian history, in the 1980s and 1990s.

Attwood has described Australian historical narratives as "a means of organizing a sense of time and space" for the settler nation. Until the turn to Aboriginal history in the 1980s, this had meant understanding modernity as "a vision of progress", a "constant movement [forward] that continually breaks with the past".[32] The narrative of Australia as a settler nation begins with the British presence, privileging time over space, and displacing the Aboriginal people in their relationship to country. As this displacement suggests, "forgetting" is fundamental to these strategic deployments of time and space. In his 1968 Boyer lectures, *After the Dreaming*, anthropologist W.E.H. Stanner famously called this foundational act of forgetting "the great Australian silence". History, he argued, is "the story of the things we were unconsciously resolved not to discuss . . . the story, in short, of the unacknowledged relations between two racial groups within a single field of life". In a powerful spatial metaphor, Stanner described this as "a view from a window which has been carefully placed to exclude a whole quadrant of the landscape". It might have begun as a "simple forgetting", but it had turned over time into "something like a cult of forgetfulness practised on a national scale".[33]

Attwood argues that "the turn to the Aboriginal past" in Australian history, beginning with books like Henry Reynolds' *The Other Side of the Frontier* (1981), and continuing through the period of Mabo, Wik, the Stolen Generations and Reconciliation, to the Apology in 2008, "unsettled" many ordinary Australians precisely because it disturbed the apparently settled relations between space and time in the national story, provoking arguments in the public sphere and releasing a powerful spectrum of affects, including "remembering, forgetting, responsibility, guilt, shame, atonement, apology and compensation". The new Australian history "drew into question the moral basis of British colonization in the past and so the Australian nation in the present"; it placed the forebears of contemporary white Australians "in a past in which they were responsible for heinous deeds"; it called for "mourning in respect of another people's historical experience"; it "rejected national unity and told instead of the country's diverse cultures and origins". The prospect of native title, Attwood suggests, "stirred conservative fears, largely because it was informed by a history that overturned *their* . . . nation".[34]

The governing image of *Journey to the Stone Country* is that of Australian colonial history as a vast, unconserved ruin that is slowly collapsing through space and time, like the hourglass-shaped debris suspended over the dining table at Ranna Station: "The brown ceiling sagging in the centre of the room above the table, the grooved ceiling boards split and gaping, straw and grass and leaves and other debris poking through and coned onto the table below, like the dribblings of an hourglass".[35] It is an image that recurs through-

---

32 Attwood, *Telling the Truth*, 14.
33 W.E.H. Stanner, *The 1968 Boyer Lectures: After the Dreaming* (Sydney: ABC, 1969), 24–5, quoted in Attwood, *Telling the Truth*, 17.
34 Attwood, *Telling the Truth*, 29–32.

out the two novels. In the opening pages of *Landscape of Farewell*, Max Otto sees reflected in the mirror the ruins of his younger self, and senses "a further shift in the cataclysm of my last days, a settling of the debris of my life, which had collapsed around me" (10). In the end, Max and Dougald Gnapun stand together at the entrance to the cave in which Dougald's great-grandfather is entombed in the land: "The skeleton was half-buried by an accumulation of debris that had evidently leached from the roof over the years" (265). This image of history as the ruin of time is one that Miller shares with the great Anglo-German novelist, W.G. Sebald. In *The Rings of Saturn* (1995), Sebald uses the debris held in Saturn's gravitational field as a metaphor for the evidence of historical catastrophe, for the stubborn persistence of the past, especially the great caesura of World War II and the Holocaust, its weight bearing down upon the present generations.[36] As Peter Fritzsche puts it, "the far-flung debris of history does not have to be the object of our attention, but it is. As a result, we inhabit a world in which we do see and in which we do draw toward us, like Saturn its rings, the broken stones of history".[37] This link between the Holocaust and the "broken stones" of the Aboriginal genocide, which is implicit in *Journey to the Stone Country*, is made explicit in *Landscape of Farewell*, giving the Central Queensland novels a scope that is at once grounded in a particular time and place, but also transnationally comparative.

With this image of the hourglass of debris, Miller spatialises history as "the ruin of time", although historical time is not thereby "arrested",[38] but remains dynamic. History's ruins are still collapsing, carrying along with them the lives of individual human beings of both the past and present generations. At Ranna homestead, Annabelle explains to Tom Glasson, an engineer representing the company that will build the Ranna Valley Dam, that as a professional historian she does not believe in the conservation of ruins: "It's the decay and the abandonment that move us in the first place, isn't it . . . It's what makes them so poignant for us" (204). The word "move" here has more than one meaning. The ruins of the past "move" in the sense of stimulating emotions, which vary depending on your point of view: where Annabelle, the squatter's daughter, is moved by the ruins of Ranna to feel nostalgia, as a former employee never admitted to the big house, Bo experiences "feelings of injustice", while Les Marra is motivated by hatred and revenge. But the ruins also *move* them all in the sense that they make visible the historical forces that determine their lives. Like the movement of trees, by which we visualise the wind, their unconserved decay is the trace of time's passage. Annabelle comes finally to feel that "her fate was not something she could manage to determine herself but that it would be determined for her by the vast impersonal forces of culture and history" (349–50).

This catastrophic and apparently fatalistic view of history is evoked by the titles of two famous books: Edward Gibbon's *History of the Decline & Fall of the Roman Empire*, which Annabelle finds in the library at Ranna (179), and Oswald Spengler's *The Decline of the West*, which Max Otto's father had kept throughout the war as an emblem of his "private disillusion" (*Landscape of Farewell*, 236). Miller shares with Sebald a sublime and essentially elegiac vision of the entropy of time: for Sebald it finds concrete expression in the haunted and crumbling monuments of prewar Europe; for Miller it is in the failed

---

35   Alex Miller, *Journey to the Stone Country* (Sydney: Allen & Unwin, 2002), 171. All subsequent references are to this edition and appear in parentheses in the text.
36   W.G. Sebald, *The Rings of Saturn* (1995; London: Harvill Press, 1998).
37   Peter Fritzsche, "W.G. Sebald's Twentieth-Century Histories", in *W.G. Sebald: History, Memory, Trauma*, eds Scott Denham and Mark McCulloh (Berlin and New York: de Gruyter, 2006), 291.
38   Rooney, "The Ruin of Time", 208.

project of the pastoral settlement of Australia. *Journey to the Stone Country*, as Shirley Walker observes, "is deeply elegiac, its subtext the passing of all historical eras, including both the Aboriginal and the vast nineteenth-century pastoral appropriation of Central Queensland".[39] Two monuments to these lost civilisations are the abandoned Ranna homestead, once the seat of a great pastoral family, and the stone playgrounds of the Jangga people. Dougald Gnapun's makeshift fibro-cement house, which is literally mobile across the two novels, suggests the unsettlement, dislocation and exile that are endemic in the Queensland postcolony: "The abandoned machinery ... behind the house [in *Landscape of Farewell*] – three huge yellow bulldozers ... looking vaguely like rusting dinosaurs – suggests the relentless cycles of change and decay, for the European settlers as well as the Aborigines."[40] These architectural images of what Chris Healy has called "the ruins of colonialism"[41] are closely related to another of Miller's recurring symbols of grand delusion and failure, the sunken ship, itself a potent reminder of catastrophe in white settler societies, as seen on the opening page of *Conditions of Faith*, and in the empty Picture Palace at Mount Coolon, another of Miller's ghost towns, "the building creaking and groaning" like "the hold of an abandoned ship" (279).

In spatialising Australian history, Miller implies that the nation-making project of settler colonialism, whose founding act was the displacement of the continent's indigenous peoples, has itself manifestly failed. It was at a rally in support of the federation of the Australian colonies in 1897 that Edmund Barton famously declared, "For the first time in history, we have a nation for a continent, and a continent for a nation."[42] Barton's rhetoric was typical of late nineteenth and early twentieth-century cultural nationalisms, which envisaged an isomorphic alignment of land, nation and race. This is an imaginative projection involving what Homi K. Bhabha has called the "recurrent metaphor of landscape as the inscape of national identity".[43] During the Federation era, this impulse found expression in what I have elsewhere called the cartographic imaginary, a term that is meant to focus especially on the role of maps and other visual media in shaping imagined geographies.[44] The most significant expression of the Federation era's cartographic imaginary was *"The Lady Northcotte" Atlas of Australasia* (1908). *The Atlas* includes eighteen maps together with an essay on "The Discovery and Exploration of Australia" that imagines the history of inland discovery as a progressive realisation of the connected and unified nature of both the *continent* as a geographical entity and the *nation* as a social polity. That teleological process is represented in the large map of "Continental Australia", which shows in a tracery of red lines the main public works – the principal railway lines, and the submarine and overland telegraph lines – connecting the six colonies together as the Commonwealth of Australia and connecting the Commonwealth, in turn, to larger politico-geographic entities such as Australasia, Oceania and the British Empire.

---

39   Shirley Walker, "The Frontier Wars: History and Fiction in Journey to the Stone Country and Landscape of Farewell", in Dixon, *The Novels of Alex Miller"*, 161.
40   Shirley Walker, "The Frontier Wars", 164.
41   Chris Healy, *From the Ruins of Colonialism: History as Social Memory* (Cambridge and Melbourne: Cambridge University Press, 1997).
42   Cited in Margaret Rutledge, "Barton, Sir Edmund", *Australian Dictionary of Biography*, http://adb.anu.edu.au/biography/barton-sir-edmund-toby-71.
43   Homi K. Bhabha, *The Location of Culture* (London: Routledge, 1994), 143.
44   Robert Dixon, " 'A Nation for a Continent': Australian Literature and the Cartographic Imaginary of the Federation Era", *Antipodes* 28, no. 1 (June 2014), 161–2.

Miller's spatialisation of Australian history operates at a purposefully regional, even local level that is essentially sub-national, eschewing the larger entity of Barton's continental nation and its capital cities. It even eschews the larger regional centres like the port-cities of Townsville and Mackay, which sit on the outer edges of the map, places to which the older generation of settlers, including the Bigges and the Becks, have retreated after the failure of their pastoral enterprises, or from which their descendants set off on their journeys into the troubled hinterlands of the past. It is as if the entire nation-building project, which flourished throughout Queensland from the mid-nineteenth until the mid-twentieth century, is now well in retreat. The new Australian history of the 1980s and 1990s had "rejected national unity" and told of "multiple origins", and so the space of journeying to the stone country can be entered from any one of a number of points: Burranbah lies "three hundred kilometers inland from Mackay" *or* "a good eight or nine hours" drive down the eastern seaboard from Townsville" (13). Even the standards of measurement are different – space or distance versus speed or time. Susan Bassett's Burranbah Coal Cultural Heritage Study is meant to produce a report and a "location map" (15), but just as there are multiple routes through this country, so there are multiple ways of reading it, including modern maps, photographs, and the Global Positioning System (GPS), but also pre-modern forms such as personal memory, images drawn in sand, and the location of stone artefacts within the larger patterns of country. In Miller's Australia, these different ways of reading the country are not universally understood and the information they yield, which is often contradictory, does not add up to a consensus: there is no agreed national imaginary. The vision of a nation for a continent that Barton had so confidently predicted in 1897 has not been realised.

In his account of Annabelle's first excursion with Bo, to the Burranbah Coal mining lease, Miller brilliantly evokes this failure of the cartographic imaginary. New to the job, Annabelle arms herself with a digital camera, a modern topographical map, and a GPS, but Bo, whose map of the country is stored in his memory, makes fun of her dependence on the new technologies: "his gaze taking in the camera, the GPS on her belt, the mobile phone clipped to the breast pocket of her overalls and the clipboard in her hands" (45). Andrew, the man from the mine, cares nothing for the region's pastoral history, when it was Picardy Station, and its "hieroglyphs" remain unreadable to him (37), but his company is actively conducting seismic mapping beneath the surface. These multiple but incommensurable ways of reading the country are suggested in the comic disagreement between Andrew and Bo over the location of the mine:

> Annabelle reached in to the back seat of the Pajero and fetched out the map... She spread it on the bonnet. The mine man leaned and placed his finger confidently on the word TANK. "We're here." He looked up and pointed. "The mine's through there." He looked down at the map again. "And that's the Isaac."
>
> "Through there", Bo corrected him, gesturing... "The mine's through there, Andrew."
>
> The mine man laughed and looked at Annabelle. "Well roughly", he said. "It's roughly through there."...
>
> "Not roughly. Roughly's no good to you out here. You'll get yourself lost in these scrubs following roughly. The mine's through there!"...

> Annabelle rolled the map and put it on the back seat and she closed the door of the Pajero.
>
> There was a silence. (39)

The cultural survey that Annabelle undertakes with Bo is a lesson in reading the country, but the country is a palimpsest of multiple histories, of multiple, unconnected attempts at place-making, some of which can be read and recovered while others are lost or forgotten. Bo describes this elegiacally as "the sediment of lost histories" (38).

Miller's understanding of history as the ruin of time is spatialised as a journey through a number of "stations", each of which encapsulates a particular era in the histories of either settler or Indigenous culture, or the often lethal intersection of the two. These stations include the Burranbah Coal Mine, Zamia Street in Townsville, Zigzag Station, Ranna Station, Mount Coolon, Haddon Hill and Verbena Station. As Rooney argues, they provide "a clear chronological scaffold" for the novel, but they are also chronotopes in Bakhtin's sense of condensations of time and space, locations that spatialise various forms of temporality and history.[45] John Pizer glosses Bakhtin's definition of the chronotope (literally "time space") as a "dialectic interaction" between "temporal plenitude and concrete localized spatiality", or the concrete "enact[ment of] cultural memory in its spatiotemporal (chronotopic) fullness at the local, regional level".[46] Far from charting a national story that progressively moves forward in time and place from an originary past to a consensual present, these chronotopes form a recursive series, from the Burranbah Coal Mine, in which the past and present implode in the death space of the Anthropocene, through Zamia Street, Zigzag, and Ranna, to the destitution of Panya's house in the ghost town of Mount Coolon and the ruins of Verbena Station. This is neither a linear journey through space nor a temporal narrative of progress, but a recursive spiral of ruin and decay.

The archaic sense of the word "stations" that I am deliberately invoking here as halting places along the *Via Crucis* or *Via Dolorosa* is suggested with Miller's characteristic lightness of touch by a number of allusions to this central topos in Christian art and literature: only implicit in *Journey to the Stone Country*, it is explicit as a structuring device in the more fable-like narrative of *Landscape of Farewell*. At Zigzag Station, the home of the Catholic Ruth Hearn, Annabelle finds herself passing through a door beneath an emblem of the crucified Christ (133). When they return to Zigzag from Ranna Station, Bo Rennie notices the same figure as he passes through the door (218). In the kitchen at Ranna, they find an embroidered motif from Thomas à Kempis' *The Christian's Pattern; or, A Treatise on the Imitation of Jesus*: "Alas thy trials yet are small, nor hast though resisted unto blood, as I and they have done" (156). The "pattern" referred to in the title of this fifteenth-century manual of Christian meditation is a "trial" that takes the physical form of a "journey" or "way". While the idea of "resistance unto blood" has obvious relevance to the history of frontier violence, especially for a family like the Bigges, who carved Ranna Station out of Aboriginal lands in the 1860s, the convention of the "trial" as a journey through a series of stations also has implications for Bo and Annabelle's own journey together in the present and into the future. In so far as the journey involves a personal sacrifice, it will be of

---

45 Rooney, "The Ruin of Time", 210.
46 John Pizer, *The Idea of World Literature: History and Pedagogical Practice* (Baton Rouge: Louisiana State University Press, 2006), 31, 33.

Annabelle's earlier self, her Melbourne and academic self, which she must leave behind like the shed snakeskin Bo finds inside the Ranna homestead. This involves relinquishing the certainties of her old self, and of her academic, Western desire to "know" the other, which she relinquishes in a respect for difference. But Bo is also martyred in the final stages of the journey when he is subject to Panya's curse for refusing to continue the "war" against settler Australia. Humbled, he stands silently in the face of her wrath in a gully outside her shack like the sacrificial figure of Dougald's goat in *Landscape of Farewell*. Bo must find within himself new forms of courage, also shedding like a skin the older codes of violence and vengeance in a journey along the way to forgiveness and atonement.

The recursive rather than teleological nature of Annabelle's journey as a white settler Australian is suggested in a number of ways early in the novel. To begin the journey, Annabelle must renounce any specific point of origin, either in her own past and preconceptions, or from a particular point in space and time. The opening presents a motif familiar from Miller's earlier novels. Annabelle opens the front door of her home and notices her image reflected in the hallstand mirror. Steven Kuen's betrayal unsettles her, precipitating a crisis of self-analysis, a process of becoming and renewal. As she arranges to leave Melbourne and return to her parents' home in Townsville, the image of her reflection in the glass recurs: "the ghostly reflection of herself in the kitchen window, observing her distress from the incurious detachment of a future time" (12). Despite its apparently precise registration – "Melbourne: Winter 1995" – the opening chapter therefore initiates the unsettling of time and place that is a hallmark of the novel. Annabelle is no longer present in her own life, but looks at it from the distant place and time of the future self she is already in the process of becoming. The means of this future becoming will be her journey toward the other in her meeting with Bo Rennie at the third of the novel's "stations", the Burranbah Coal Mine. It will not be a direct journey from one point to another, like Christ's, but a zigzag journey to an unknown destination.

Burranbah Coal represents what is in some respects the novel's most recent and most difficult intersection of time and space to grasp – the Anthropocene. The term for this new geological era was first proposed by the Nobel Prize–winning chemist Paul J. Crutzen in 2000, and elaborated in a short paper in *Nature* in 2002, in which he assigns the term Anthropocene to "the present ... human-dominated, geological epoch, supplementing the Holocene – the warm period of the past 10–12 millennia", suggesting that it "could be said to have started in the latter part of the eighteenth century ... [coinciding] with James Watt's design of the steam engine in 1784".[47] While that date marks the time when human beings switched from wood and other renewable fuels to fossil fuels – first coal and then oil and gas – it also corresponds almost exactly with the founding of the English colony in New South Wales on 26 January 1788, suggesting the close relation between the Enlightenment's instrumental rationality, the Industrial Revolution, colonialism, and postcolonial nationalism.

In an influential discussion of the impact of the Anthropocene on the discipline of history, Dipesh Chakrabarty argues that anthropogenic explanations of climate change now "spell the collapse of the age-old humanist distinction between natural history and human history".[48] Chakrabarty argues that "in unwittingly destroying the artificial but

---

47 Paul J. Crutzen, "Geology of Mankind", *Nature* 415 (3 January 2002): 23.
48 Dipesh Chakrabarty, "The Climate of History: Four Theses", *Critical Inquiry* 35, no. 2 (Winter 2009): 201.

time-honored distinction between natural and human histories, climate scientists posit that the human being has become something much larger than the simple biological agent that he or she always has been. Humans now wield a geological force."[49] The peculiar challenge for historians is how to reconcile the apparent gap between history's traditional concern with human agency, its "finely honed sense of contingency and freedom" as an explanatory mechanism in human affairs, with the more "determinstic" view that follows on from thinking of humans as a species. In species thinking, Chakrabarty asks, "Who is the we?" for there can "be no phenomenology of us as a species".[50] Miller has had an interest in environmental issues since his first novel *The Tivington Nott*, and his characters have always been caught up in the fine distinctions between freedom and determinism, agency and structure – as we will see in chapter 7, this is crucial to Max Otto's calculation of the guilt of his and his father's generations for the Holocaust. But what kinds of agency can there be in accounting for the cultural and ecological devastation caused by climate change, conceived here as the last in a series of events in European modernity that includes the Industrial Revolution and colonial occupation of the new world? What kinds of responsibility arise in the face of such geological forces?

The country into which Annabelle travels with Bo on their journey to Burranbah Coal is a death space, and it is for this reason, and not out of some callous disregard for the lives of animals,[51] that Annabelle registers the road kill on the Bruce Highway – it is part of a pattern of imagery and observations by which Miller's narrative, focalised through Annabelle, registers its comprehension of the past and ongoing violence of the colonial frontier. The mining lease or, more accurately, the country upon which it is merely the latest in a fatal series of cultural impositions, is a palimpsest of multiple times and spaces, of multiple cultures and histories, underpinned by the indisputable facts of frontier violence. One thing is certain in this novel written after Mabo, and that is that the country is not *terra nullius*. Although Annabelle's journey has many possible routes and destinations, and although the full report is yet to be written, at the beginning of the survey Susan Bassett provides her with a singular piece of text that is reproduced in the novel in italics: "*Before the conquest by the white men, all of Australia was land owned under Aboriginal terms by Aboriginal people*" (16). Here at least is a datum from which to start reading the country. The priority of Aboriginal place-making is the report's one indisputable pre-text or starting point.

In his own book about the notorious stretch of the Bruce Highway between Bowen and Mackay, Ross Gibson uses the American term "badlands", traditionally infertile, inhospitable and visually unattractive regions that foil the exploitative gaze of the colonist, to evoke the ongoing legacy of violence on the colonial frontier. In *Seven Versions of an Australian Badland*, he describes this road-safety "black spot" as a place where the frontier is still palpable, where history haunts the present like the heat waves that form mirages on the road, a hypermediated space where the violence of the past is rehearsed in the bizarre crimes that are regularly reported in the popular press, and in the carnage on the roads.[52] Bo points out to Annabelle that even the original vegetation, the brigalow and boxforest,

---

49 Chakrabarty, "The Climate of History", 206.
50 Chakrabarty, "The Climate of History", 214, 220.
51 David Brooks, "Dougald's Goat: Alex Miller and the Species Barrier", in *The Novels of Alex Miller*, 187–200.
52 Ross Gibson, *Seven Versions of an Australian Badland* (St Lucia, Qld: University of Queensland Press, 2002).

has been poisoned and bulldozed, initially by the cattlemen and then by the miners: "the dead forest stood mile upon mile, grey and still. The ranks of lifeless trees like mute sentinels to some past glory, or bleak signposts to an apocalypse yet to come" (34). When they cross a fresh bulldozer scrape along the drill line, Bo pulls up to examine the multiple scars and inscriptions on the land. Annabelle notices that the mining camp, with its lighting towers and security fence, "looked . . . like pictures she had seen of concentration camps" (26). This chronotope is a condensed allusion to the Aboriginal reserves of the assimilation era, to the contemporary use of remote regions by the Australian government to incarcerate asylum seekers, and an implicit comparison of both to the Holocaust, which Miller develops more extensively in *Landscape of Farewell*. The detention of asylum seekers had been controversial in Australia since 1992, and in 2002, the same year as the publication of *Journey to the Stone Country*, Suvendrini Perera would describe the image of the Woomera Detention Centre as it appeared in Annette McGuire's photographs as depicting "the outback as prison . . . a place that is, and yet is not, Australia".[53] In the fictitious Burranbah Coal (apparently based on Moranbah, a mining town in the Carborough Ranges), Miller may also be recalling the history of the South East Queensland town of Barambah, which was itself repressed from public memory when its name was changed to Cherbourg in 1931. Barambah was founded as a settlement for Aborigines and gazetted in 1901 as the Barambah Aboriginal Reserve.

In many of the novel's early intimations of frontier violence there is a slightly oblique quality, as if the full meaning has not been grasped. This includes Annabelle's registration of the road kill, and her sense that the mining compound "looked like" the pictures she had seen of concentration camps. Again, as she and Bo stand together on the banks of the Isaac River: "the far bank fifty metres distant, the riverbed a level stretch of golden sand cutting through sunlit timber like an abandoned highway from some unnamed metropolis of antiquity whose population had been dispersed and murdered long ago" (46). This obliqueness, as if the scene or object literally appearing before Annabelle's eyes has more than one meaning or referent or history, foreshadows a similar doubling in *Landscape of Farewell*. That is because Max Otto's descriptions of Queensland are overlaid with increasingly explicit images of the Holocaust. The obliqueness in *Journey to the Stone Country* is also part of Annabelle's developing understanding, in this case her developing awareness that scenes present to the eye are shadowed by a pre-history of violence that she is only now beginning to comprehend. The scene on the Isaac is "like" the site of a dispersal because it is, although Annabelle is not yet able to "see" this history clearly as it gradually emerges from the space of the great Australian silence. The word "dispersed" has a specific meaning in the history of Queensland's frontier, a resonance within the silence that Annabelle does not quite hear at this early stage of her journey. Her responses to Bo and Trace and Arner are still entangled in webs of as yet unexamined sexism and racism – how could it be otherwise? – although at such moments she is beginning to "see" and to move beyond her own unexamined preconceptions.

For all its apparent realism, then, Miller's Burranbah landscape is constantly threatening to modulate into another register that might be called the postcolonial gothic. Like the landscapes of the Indigenous Queensland painter Gordon Bennett, it is a palimpsest on which the past and the present, and their competing cultural shapings of space and

---

53   Suvendrini Perera, "What is a Camp . . . ?" *borderlands e-journal* 1, no. 1 (2002), http://www.borderlandsejournal.adelaide.edu.au/vol1no1_2002/perera_camp.html.

place, leak into each other through cracks in the surface of the image. These fissures in space and time, which are at once literal and metaphorical, visual and epistemological, can be seen, for example, in Bennett's *Big Romantic Painting: Apotheosis of Captain Cook* (1993), which was used on the cover of Chris Healy's *From the Ruins of Colonialism* in 1997. In *Landscape of Farewell*, the idea of a fissure in the fabric of space and time is vividly realised in the ravine of the Nebo River, where Max Otto undergoes the experience of a *mise-en-abyme*. In *Journey to the Stone Country*, these fissures are less fully developed, but they are beginning to open in the landscape, especially in the death space of Burranbah Coal. In the uncanny time of the Anthropocene, the biblical image of the valley of death is refracted cross-culturally through the lyrics of American rapper 2Pac's "So Many Tears" (1995), which Arner plays on the stereo in his van:

> Bo turned and walked down the hill towards the Pajero. The volume of the music increased, the voice of 2PAC pursuing him along the slope, *I shall not fear no man but God, though I walk through the valley of death* . . . The dry groundcover crackling beneath Bo's boots, releasing the musty odours of dead time . . . Bo seeing the longwall's subsidence cracks meandering through the poisoned timber and thinking of the earth drying out and dying under the treeroots. "The valley of death", he said and spat to one side. (55)

This striking image of "dead time" leaking through cracks into the badlands of the colonial present is repeated when Annabelle finds a stone artefact and Susan advises, "we'd better take it with us or it'll get lost forever down one of the subsidence cracks" (57–8). She also confirms the anachronism of the artefact: it is an object out of its appointed time and place, whose meaning has been lost to Bo and Dougald's generation, "like words from a dead language" (59).

At Annabelle's parents' house at Zamia Street in South Townsville, she also finds that things are leaking through from the realm of lost time. The relations between time and space have been disturbed not only because the interior furnishings remind her of the past, but also because that past has been relocated in space from the pastoral frontier on the Suttor River to the coastal port city of Townsville. Upon entering the home, Annabelle recognises that "time was at a standstill" (93). The heavy Edwardian furniture, originally belonging to her grandparents, had been moved from Haddon Hill when her parents left the land. On the verandah, looking out on an ordinary suburban scene, is her grandfather's squatter's chair, "made for an exhausted man to rest in" to a design that would be inconceivable "in any other culture" than that of Queensland's pastoral frontier. "An enormous heavy black thing" (95), it has a spectral quality that evokes his absent presence. The relocation of these ancestral objects in space signifies the decline of the pastoral era and the retreat to the coastal cities of families like the Becks and the Bigges a mere three generations after the violent founding of their stations on Aboriginal lands in the mid-nineteenth century. But it also means that there can be no retreat from the past: Townsville is as haunted as Burranbah or Haddon Hill.

Annabelle's return to the displaced scene of her childhood prompts a series of questions about the past that parallel those being asked by contemporary historians in their probing of the great Australian silence. Although she feels the abiding spirit of her parents' support for her in their empty home, these spatial and temporal disturbances are unsettling and provocative. In a scene reminiscent of Emily's interview with Madame Elder in *Conditions of Faith*, Annabelle places the stone artefact she has found at Burranbah on her grandparents' Edwardian sideboard immediately beneath a framed sepia photograph of her grandfather: "He was wearing a black three-piece suit and a narrow brimmed hat, just as Bo had remembered him" (96). The juxtaposition is similar to the moment when Emily rests the photograph of the Panama Canal excavations on top of Henry Adams' *Chartres*, contrasting the heroic iron world of the engineers with the spiritual values of the Middle Ages. The silent but accusatory object has returned as if through a rent in the fabric of space and time to confront the reputation of the man who murdered members of Bo's family. Ironically, at the time the photograph was taken, the old cattleman had become senile, and although Bo remembers him, Louis Beck was then incapable himself of remembering the crimes he had committed as a younger man. These disturbances prompt Annabelle and Bo to begin asking questions about their "shared history" that will ultimately break the silence: "How had her own mother and Grandma Rennie been friends enough to share a picnic, and yet their friendship never been spoken of at Haddon Hill?" (107). For Bo, "interrogating his memory", the question is why he and the other Aboriginal children had been warned to keep away from him: "I don't know what it was. It was never explained to us" (111).

While the Zamia Street home is a monument to the now lost past, or at least one version of that past, John and Ruth Hearn's Zigzag Station is a belated version of the pastoral dream that survives precariously into the present. It is also mislocated in space in the rugged and infertile ridge country of the Broken River that was never taken up by early settlers. The comedy of its mislocation is signaled by the angle of the Pajero as Bo pulls up for Annabelle to open the gate: "The Pajero came to a stop, standing on its tail, blue sky and treetops through the windscreen, the washed-out track falling away steeply beside them" (127). A jumble of ramshackled buildings in a clearing scratched out of the rocky mountain top by bulldozer, there is "a raw look of newness and struggle about the settlement, as if it had not yet achieved permanency and might be pulled down and towed away again at any time, leaving the wilderness to heal itself" (128). John Hearn's efforts as an owner-builder and bush furniture maker are a parody of Russel Ward's celebrated Australian type, the bushman who is able to improvise anything with a bit of stringy bark and green hide.[54] The house he has built is grotesquely out of proportion, with a verandah forty feet deep, and the vast dining table that he has fashioned from a felled mango tree is a further image of the failed cartographic imaginary: its shape is modelled, bizarrely, on the island of Madagascar. Knowing that Bo has lived and worked in the district in the past and has knowledge of its original settlement at Ranna, the Hearns regard him as a "traveller who had known their country before their time" (138), but their hopes that he can provide them with information in support of their enterprise in this place are disappointed. He informs them that the Bigges, who settled Ranna in the 1860s, "turned out to be a vanishing race" (141), but they are reluctant to accept their own belatedness: "There was a silence. The Hearns' disappointment. Their unwillingness to accept that they were too late in their dream of pioneering" (144).

The ruins of Ranna Station, with its termite-infested library and its dripping hourglass of debris, are the novel's most telling symbol of the end of that "dream of pioneering". Ranna is a time-capsule that has not been relocated in space, like the contents of Haddon Hill, but in time, washed up in its own future like the set for a post-apocalypse movie. What is out of joint here is the persistence of the colonial era's material culture. The be-

---

54   Russel Ward, *The Australian Legend* (Melbourne: Oxford University Press, 1958).

latedness of the ruin and the entropy of time are symbolised by the noise of the termites eating the books in the library, and the great cone of debris suspended above the cedar table in the dining room, like "an hourglass measuring the decay of the old place" (202). Tom Glasson, the construction engineer from Folson and Harbin, the firm that is to build the proposed Ranna Valley Dam, describes the house as a "museum", a time-capsule like the *Mary Celeste* (202). There are complex ironies here, for the *Marie Celeste* is another wrecked ship, a recurring symbol in Miller's novels of grandiose aspirations, delusion and folly. In Folson and Harbin there is also an echo of Couvreux & Hersent, the company that failed to complete the Panama Canal. Typically, Miller offers multiple perspectives, juxtaposing the Bigges' failed vision of "heroic pioneering effort" (203) with the equally qualified vision of dam building, with its echoes of the iron world in *Conditions of Faith*.

In one sense, the Ranna episode is a pastoral idyll that reanimates the nineteenth-century dream of white settler colonialism: in the kitchen at Ranna, "The five of them sitting up at the table ... the warm light from the trimmed wick a benediction on their faces and hands ... as if they were a working family at their supper" (183). But the idyll is seen from multiple points of view, and each one qualifies it in it its own significantly different way. In Miller's literary fiction, reading and misreading – reading the country, reading each other and reading the signs of the past – are explicitly thematised. The pastoral interlude is compared to a prelapsarian moment in Eden by Annabelle, who is thinking of the romance that has begun there between Trace and Mathew Hearn: "In years to come, Ranna would surely always remain in their memories as the garden of Eden" (187). In the chapter that follows, "A Plague of Dogs", the idea of a fall or expulsion into a less idyllic reality is confirmed for the young couple when they return to Zigzag Station and Ruth Hearn's hysterically racist response to their relationship is exposed.

Ranna is also an Eden for Annabelle. The interlude allows her to return to her own past, reimagining the kind of station life into which she was born as a child. Miller places a great value on his characters' abilities to take on the point of view of another time or culture, and it is the achievement of this chapter to create a range of points of view. Annabelle adopts the perspective of Nellie Beck: "To sit here and write her journal and her letters. Intimate. Private. Solitary. A woman's desk" (208). In adopting the position of that other woman, a woman of the colonial frontier, she rediscovers herself: *Dear Steven, I am not coming back ... I knew him when I was a child. There are connections between us you would not understand. In this place I am becoming myself again*" (208). But there is also the risk that Annabelle will remain the archetypal squatter's daughter, unable to see her own whiteness as a racialised category. Bo is able to inhabit a very different point of view, as we see in his ability, while surveying the Burranbah Coal lease, to recover the perspective of the Aboriginal man who made the stone tools. While Nellie's room provides a vista of the Ranna Creek, allowing her to survey her pastoral domain, the Aboriginal man adopts a strategic perspective on the lookout for invaders of his country, like Nellie's grandfather. Although Johnston and Lawson read *Journey to the Stone Country* as an allegory of reconciliation, these fracture lines between Annabelle's and Bo's perspectives are surprisingly persistent throughout the novel, and they are particularly in evidence in this chapter. The "shared history" of reconciliation is not the same history and it certainly does not mean seeing history in the same way. It recognises differences among points of view that coexist within the same social space and historical time. Annabelle must ask herself, "Were their pasts too similar and yet too different for them to understand each other?" (178).

One of the ways in which the past is still present to Bo is his sense of the legacy of injustice. Bo's view of Ranna is complex. He feels a great affection for the landscape because he associates it with his youth, when he was Mathew Hearn's age. But Bo struggles to contain his emotions of anger, hurt and resentment for the social injustices he has experienced. The chapter is shot through with the tensions this causes between him and Annabelle. Even as they approach the station and gain their first view of the homestead, Bo tells Annabelle, "I was never in there" (153), quietly recalling the system of racial exclusion which meant that as an Aboriginal ringer he was never admitted to the main house, and challenging the invisibility of whiteness as a racial term. He reminds Annabelle that the same regime was maintained by her parents at Haddon Hill. Mathew Hearn is the same age Bo was when he and Dougald worked at Ranna, but Bo is irritated by Mathew's feelings of resentment that his family have to occupy marginal land on the ridges when such fertile country as the Ranna valley is sitting nearby "uninhabited" (168). "Uninhabited" is one of many words in the novel, including "took", "dispersed", and "invasion", that Miller places in unexpected contexts, where they quietly resonate with the new Aboriginal history of the 1980s and 1990s. As Bo reminds him, this country was not "uninhabited" when the Bigges family took it up: it was occupied by "them old Birri people", and in recalling their displacement by pastoralists in the mid-nineteenth century, Bo recalls his own exclusion from the homestead in the 1970s, his love and desire for the land then being just as compelling as Mathew's now, but on the opposite side of a racial divide. Bo's resentment against whiteness and its silent presumptions is frequently on display, though carefully modulated and controlled: "he looked up into the expectant gaze of young Mathew Hearn, and there was a truculence in his eyes that made the young man look away as if he had been challenged" (168–9). Annabelle is herself still learning to "read" this side of Bo's feelings. After the exchange with Mathew, in which Bo reminds him of the fact that the Bigges family is now extinct, she recalls the phrase he had used in talking to the Hearns at Zigzag Station, and she comes retrospectively to grasp the irony and sense of injustice that bubble away beneath his apparently calm surface: "The Bigges of Ranna Station. A vanished race, Bo had said, slipping the irony in among the Hearns like a slim stiletto" (171).

After the sexual consummation of their relationship in the house at Zamia Street, Bo and Annabelle begin the final stages of their journey together, initially to Mount Coolon and then to Verbena Station. Their union takes place under the sign of the cylindrical stone that Annabelle had found at Burranbah, which now sits in the middle of the dining table. She registers that "it was so out of place among her parents' heavy Edwardian furniture" (241). This odd coupling of objects from different cultures parallels the coming together of Bo and Annabelle, but it is also a highly condensed symbol of the novel's overall complexity in its treatment of space and time. Like Bo and Annabelle, these objects come together in a social field whose dimensions are profoundly unsettled. Their movement through space and time charts the long history of the pastoral age, which has now finished. Bo and Annabelle are two individuals caught up in the complex and violently destructive forces of colonial history, and they remain divided by the silent and insidious legacies of whiteness. This unsettlement of the historical field means that their journey together will not be a linear one through either space or time, like Christ's teleological journey through the Stations of the Cross. Rather, it will be a recursive or "zigzag" one. As Annabelle realises when they anticipate returning to Haddon Hill, the return will not be "simple": "She suspected that the symmetry of such an ideal return could no longer be realized in this world" (249). Like the stone artefact placed on the dining table, Bo and Annabelle are joined together as a constellation travelling through space and time, but they are neither stable nor identical objects – their histories and personalities are contingent but different, and both are still actively in development, in the process of becoming, as they journey toward the other. As Miller puts it in an essay about reconciliation published at this time, "It is not a question simply of reconciliation, important as that is, but is the far more difficult question of the acknowledgement of difference."[55]

The great achievement of Miller's novel is that for all its apparent simplicity and realism, it creates this vast unsettlement in the fields of space and time, and then reproduces it in the phenomenology of reading. The novel's ruinous architecture cannot be apprehended from a single point of view, and it cannot be totalised or reduced to a single meaning. It can be entered from multiple locations, traversed by multiple routes, and its destinations are unfathomable. As Bo and Annabelle enter the heartland of the Jangga, space and time cannot be read by the means that Annabelle understands. Unlike European maps or European settlements, Bo's country has no lines, no inscriptions that can fix meaning into singularity: "No signs of habitation . . . An unbroken vista of wattle and bendee, patches of stunted ironbarks, and tall groves of perfumed sandalwood, so close grown it was impossible to step into it" (270). As Bo and Annabelle enter his heartland together, centred on Mount Bulgonunna, he gives her a lesson in the idea of maintaining multiple perspectives, of travelling simultaneously along different vectors, of seeing the past from the present and the present from the future. The mountain, Bo explains, changes its shape "depending on which way you're coming at her". "I'll show you", he tells her, and squats down in the gravel beside the road to draw a map. Unlike all of the other maps that have been described in the novel, this is not a single image fixed in time and space, but an animated sequence of profiles of the mountain as it is approached through a series of journeys in the mind from different directions: "He swept the gravel with the flat of his hand and drew in the dust the shape of the hill before them . . . he drew another shape beside the first . . . he drew a third shape beside the second . . . he drew a fourth contour in the dust" (271). Those critics who have read *Journey to the Stone Country* as a simple parable of reconciliation, or as a parable of reconciliation simply conceived, have not attended to Bo's lesson in reading the country.

At Mount Coolon, Bo and Annabelle find a ghost town, its abandoned houses testifying to the decline of the old pastoral economy. Annabelle is affected by the sadness of the place, the failure of the town to mature, and she realises that her positive memories of it were "the unreliable inventions of nostalgia" (282). May's cottage by the reservoir is another abandoned ruin, but inside, stuffed down a hole in the floorboards, Bo and Annabelle find the sepia photograph that Bo remembers hanging over the fireplace at Verbena Station in his childhood. Miller locates the photograph in the midst of the novel's governing image of the hourglass of debris, the collapsing ruins of history, which now proliferates like a worm-hole between past and present, or like a *mise-en-abyme*. The photograph has been stuffed down a hole in the floorboards with other debris, recalling the "dribbling hourglass" suspended above the dining table at Ranna: "Someone had pushed a collection of rubbish down the hole before leaving . . . Annabelle identified old newspapers and a broken picture frame" (296). Looking at the photograph, Annabelle recognises that it was taken on the verandah at Ranna where she has recently worked. It is if she is able to look into the image and through the French doors, recalling in her memory the image of the falling debris that was not there when the photograph was taken, but is hid-

---

55 Alex Miller, "Sweet Water", *Bulletin* 121, no. 6403, 16 December 2003: 104.

den, as it were, inside the image as a reminder of the passing of time, like death inside a person: "The French doors behind the group opened, Annabelle knew, into the Ranna dining room . . . the ceiling rotted and collapsing, the pile of debris gathering on the table" (304). The photograph, in other words, is not only located inside the collapsing hourglass of time, but that hourglass is also contained within it, though hidden to the people in the photograph and only visible from the perspective of history, from Annabelle's location in the present. Like Walter Benjamin's angel of history, which Miller invokes in *Prochownik's Dream*, those caught up in the ruin of time can only look backwards on to its trail of debris, not forwards into their own future. As Annabelle says to Tom Glasson, "we're observing them from a dimension that's hidden to them. We're their future. But we're scarcely the future they hoped for" (204).

Taken at Ranna by George Bigges, the photograph shows not only Bo's grandparents, but also Annabelle's grandfather, Louis Beck. At first, it seems like the ideal material expression of the Council for Aboriginal Reconciliation's "shared history": "Louis Beck, the son of the founder of Haddon Hill, friend of George Bigges and Iain Rennie. There they were! Together in George Bigge's photograph, the Becks and the Rennies. Her own family and Bo's!" (304). So far, however, is Miller's novel from being a simple endorsement of this contemporary policy, that Annabelle's enthusiastic embrace of this ideal is about to be challenged by Panya's revelation that as children, she and Bo's grandmother witnessed George Bigges and Louis Beck hunting and killing their families, including Panya's brother. Panya's revelation, and her argument that reconciliation is only a salve to white settler guilt, powerfully rehearse criticisms that were made of the Council for Aboriginal Reconciliation's agenda during the late 1990s: "No one ever come here and asked me to forgive 'em . . . All they wanna do is forget. They want us to believe the bad times is over and we all gotta be friends now. Only they got everything for themselves, and they not giving it back. That's what the white man want now. Peace for himself" (344). Panya curses Bo and Annabelle and endorses Les Marra's continuing "war" against white settler society. In a scene that anticipates the sacrifice of Dougald's goat in *Landscape of Farewell*, Bo is shamed and emasculated by her curse: "Dismayed, [Annabelle] watched him walk down into the bed of the stone gully and stand gazing at the ground, head down, as if he were a man waiting to be shot" (346). To survive Bo must change, like Annabelle: he must renegotiate the idea of courage, shedding like skin the older codes of violence and vengeance in a journey along the way of forgiveness and atonement, toward a moral rather than a physical courage.

At the end of their journey at Verbena Station, which is also the beginning of their future, Bo and Annabelle find that the homestead has been demolished: it is "a scene of sudden violent destruction" (355) amidst a landscape that looks like a "deserted battlefield" (353). Verbena is another version of the novel's governing motif of history as an unconserved ruin. The trained historian in Annabelle allows her to distinguish these as postcolonial ruins, the ruins of a white settler society in the new world that mark the failure of the colonial project: there is "Nothing of the European ideal of the picturesque. None of Rose Macaulay's magisterial meditation on the pleasure of ruins . . . She thought how impossible it would be to ever resurrect the grand days of Ranna, when for a brief moment in this country's history such stations had risen as the centres of power in the land" (357–8).[56] The end of the journey is a tentative and cautious one. Bo plans to buy

---

56   The allusion is to British novelist Rose Macaulay's *The Pleasure of Ruins* (1953).

back Verbena and establish it as a working farm that can provide a livelihood for the next generation, for Arner and Trace and Mathew. But that prospect lies in the future, and the novel ends with Annabelle and Bo camping in the ruins. Despite her nostalgia, Annabelle now understands that the ruins of the past are not worth preserving, and that whatever the future is it must be different from the past. In the final lines there is an allusion to the end of Milton's *Paradise Lost*, in which the couple now expelled from Eden walk hand in hand toward an unknown future.

For his part, Bo has had to endure the curse of his elders and renegotiate a new form of moral courage. Although Miller had not read William Faulkner's short story "An Odor of Verbena", there are striking similarities to the ending of the novel.[57] In Faulkner's story, which is set in the ravaged landscape of the post–Civil War American South, the hero, Bayard, defies his caste and breaks with the martial codes of the old South, abjuring killing and revenge in order that a viable civilisation might emerge in a new South.[58] As Maryanne M. Gobble observes, "the mythological symbolism of the flower invokes a complex calculus at the intersection of war and peace, household and battlefield, reflecting Bayard's own conflicted position as he fights his individual battle with the violent Old South code of gentlemanly honor".[59] In Miller's novel, these "intersections" are played out in the competitive tensions between Bo Rennie and Les Marra, who is Panya's "chevalier" of the old order. Verbena Station, with its traditions of hospitality and inclusiveness, represents an alternative past – and therefore future – to Ranna and Haddon Hill, for "Unlike at Ranna, here there had been no attempt to found a landed dynasty according to the old model, a new European aristocracy of the Antipodes" (357).

Annabelle also has to renegotiate her previous ideas and sentiments, relinquishing her Western desire for rational understanding, questioning her nostalgia for the settler past, making the presumptions of whiteness visible, and allowing Bo's difference from her to stand. As they approach the turnoff to Haddon Hill, she instructs him to "Keep going" (353), renouncing her own emotional claim to the land and deferring to Bo's more just claim to Verbena Station: "it was not her country after all" (354). Above all, Annabelle resolves that she will not accompany Bo and Arner to the playgrounds of the Jangga on Mount Bulgonunna. This is part of her acceptance of difference and her renunciation of what Miller has elsewhere described as the European will to know:[60] "It was not necessary to know everything. She realized she had once believed in something called objective inquiry, the right to know everything... Understanding was the least of it... It was their story, not hers. She would wait for them here at the Verbena camp" (363). This is the culmination of Annabelle's deepening understanding of her relationship with Bo as an Indigenous man with whom she shares a past, though from a different perspective. Her willing relinquishment of the will to know is suggested in a telling moment at the Mount

---

57   Verbena Station is based on Glen Eva Station, Col McLennan's grandmother's station, where he grew up. McLennan believes that it should have been named Verbena Station after Verbena Creek, which flows through it, "so that's the name I gave it. To accord with Col's sense of what was right". Alex Miller to Robert Dixon, 17 December 2013.
58   William Faulkner, *The Unvanquished* (1938; New York: Vintage, 1991).
59   Maryanne M. Gobble, "The Significance of Verbena in William Faulkner's 'An Odor of Verbena' ", *Mississippi Quarterly* 53, no. 4 (Fall 2000): 572.
60   In the preface to the exhibition catalogue, "Sanctuary", in Lyndell Brown/Charles Green and Patrick Pound, *Sanctuary – and Other Island Fables* (Herring Island, Vic.: Parks Victoria Gallery), Miller criticised the European will to knowledge and referred in print for the first time to his friendship with Col McLennan.

Coolon Picture Palace, when Bo asks Annabelle to take his portrait with her camera: "Annabelle took the camera out of its case. She put it to her eye and studied him through the viewfinder . . . She pressed the shutter button. Nothing happened. She called, 'We're out of film'" (280). Johnston and Lawson argue that in the end "Annabelle gives in to the inscrutable wisdom of her new Aboriginal 'family'", and that "the ways in which she does are resonant of the oldest settler fantasies about otherness".[61] But there is a difference between a passive "giving in" and an active, principled circumspection and relinquishment in acknowledgement of cultural difference.

Verbena Station, where the journey ends, is not a final destination but a ruin upon which a future might be built. Bo's journey to the stone country is private; it has its own destination elsewhere, and Annabelle will not accompany him there. Verbena may provide a future for Arner and Trace and Mathew Hearn, but Annabelle and Bo will not live there permanently, Annabelle anticipating that her future will be in Townsville, itself a kind of way station en route to and from other spaces and times. Any possible end to the journey in relation to these multiple vectors and locations in time and space remains inconclusive, circumspect, de-centred. What Verbena might represent is not the plenitude of an ending, but a kind of void, a point of emptiness amidst the ruins in which the very absence of certainty at least provides the possibility of a future. It is not so much a defined future as another of Miller's versions of *kairos*, an empty moment out of time, where the content of a traumatic history is mercifully erased, and where future becoming might take on new trajectories. It is, at last, a point in space and time that is *outside* colonial history's "dribbling hourglass" of debris.

Although reviewers described *Journey to the Stone Country* as a "parable" and a "national epic", Miller has progressively exposed in public much more detail about its sources than his other novels. Beginning with the dedication – "to the real Bo and Annabelle, whose story this is" – and the more detailed acknowledgements at the end of *Landscape of Farewell*, Miller has folded around the Central Queensland novels an increasingly powerful epitext grounded in the real-life stories of his friends and collaborators Liz Hatte, Col McLennan and Frank Budby. At Miller's invitation, these collaborators took part in the 2011 symposium at the University of Sydney, further complicating the ontology and politics of the novel as a work of fiction. Miller has included passages from the "Ranna Station" chapter in a published article in support of a campaign against the Queensland Government's proposal to build a dam that would have flooded the Urannah Valley,[62] while Col McLennan presented a copy of the novel to Justice Steven Rares in support of his Native Title Claim on behalf of the Jangga people, which was concluded successfully in the Federal Court of Australia in November 2012.[63] All of this has given the novel an unusually complicated social life as a work of fiction, as a "fable of reconciliation" and a "national epic", but also as a fictional text that openly declares its connection to biography and social history.

---

61 Johnston and Lawson, "Settler Post-Colonialism", 38.
62 Alex Miller, "Sweet Water", *Bulletin* 121, no. 6403, 16 December 2003: 100–104.
63 Trent Dalton, "Written in Stone", *The Australian*, 10 November 2012, http://www.theaustralian.com.au/news/features/written-in-stone/story-e6frg8h6-1226511580106#mm-premium.

6
The Third Hand: *Prochownik's Dream*

In 2002, Alex Miller was invited by Maudie Palmer to open an exhibition at the Parks Victoria Gallery on Herring Island. Palmer was founding director of the Heide Museum of Modern Art, and had been appointed as curator at Herring Island in 1997. She had launched *The Sitters* at the National Gallery of Victoria in 1995. Herring Island is a small artificial island in Melbourne's Yarra River, approximately three kilometres from the city centre, that can be reached either by boat or a punt service from Como Landing. Since 1994 it has been administered by Parks Victoria as a wildlife reserve and sculpture park.[1] *Sanctuary – and Other Island Fables*, a collaborative exhibition by Melbourne artists Lyndell Brown/Charles Green and Patrick Pound, was the inaugural exhibition in the new gallery, and ran from 14 February to 31 March 2002. Miller opened the exhibition and wrote an essay for the catalogue that was later republished in a slightly revised form in *Meanjin*.[2]

The *Sanctuary* exhibition was the inspiration for the meeting between Tony Powlett and Marina Golding on the fictitious Bream Island in *Prochownik's Dream* (2005), which ignites their artistic collaboration and foreshadows their adulterous affair. Miller announced his plans for the new novel at a dinner one night at Brown and Green's home in Richmond shortly after *Sanctuary* had closed:

> I told them I saw a triangle in their relations with Patrick Pound, a potential for betrayal and passion between them that was unlikely ever to be expressed in their real lives . . . I asked if they would mind if I were to write a novel based on their lives and their collaborations . . . Charles and Lyndell were very happy to have been the inspiration for the story, as was Patrick – even though the character of Toni Powlett is not based on him but is an invention.[3]

An extract from the novel in progress, then titled "The Other Man", appeared in 2003, and is set on the island, describing the intense and ambiguous relationship that erupts when

---

1 *Herring Island*, Parks Victoria brochure, http://parkweb.vic.gov.au/explore/parks/herring-island.
2 Alex Miller, "Sanctuary", in Lyndell Brown/Charles Green and Patrick Pound, *Sanctuary – and Other Island Fables* (Herring Island, Vic.: Parks Victoria Gallery), n.p.; and Alex Miller, "The Artist as Magician", *Meanjin* 62, no. 2 (2003): 41–7.
3 Alex Miller to Robert Dixon, 29 May 2013.

the artist, Toni, sketches the sleeping form of Marina Golding, the wife of his former mentor, Michael (later Robert) Schwartz: "It's a beginning... *the problem of Marina Golding taking shape*... The mystery of a work in progress."[4]

Brown and Green began collaborating in 1989, and have since held approximately thirty-five exhibitions, both together and with other artists: the typographical sign of this collaboration is their use of the slash in their joint signature, "Lyndell Brown/Charles Green". As they explain in a position statement associated with the Herring Island exhibition, "We don't think of ourselves as separate artists any more, and we don't have a fixed division of labour... we don't explain who does what because we wouldn't ever want to work separately."[5] To describe this practice they use the term "the third hand", a form of artistic agency that both "compromises [sic] and transcends the two of them" as individuals.[6] Brown and Green's collaborative work is meant to challenge the idea, common to the romantic tradition, that artists and writers work in splendid isolation. In *Prochownik's Dream*, Miller explores the role of collaboration in the creation of art, but also, as Adrian Caesar points out, its potentially destructive effects on friendships and families.[7] After the intimacy of *The Sitters*, which is narrated by the portrait painter in the first person, in *Prochownik's Dream* Miller shifts the narrative point of view to the third person, as if to make visible the social and professional networks in which the painter Toni Powlett is embedded, including curators, agents, fellow artists and mentors, as well as his wife Teresa and his muse Marina Golding. Collaboration is now central to Miller's thinking about artistic practice and yet, as his frequent comparisons of the artist to a hunter, an invader and a parasite suggest, that word also has darker meanings in the sense of betraying one's friends and family, either by destroying something that belongs to them or through complicity with outsiders. These positive and negative meanings are explored in the complex knot of collaborations that join the Schwarz/Golding and Powlett/Prochownik families. Miller has taken Brown and Green's term, "The Third Hand", as the subtitle for part two of the novel, in which the collaboration between Toni and Marina reaches its greatest artistic potential and wreaks its maximum personal damage.

Just before the Herring Island exhibition, Charles Green, who is Reader in Contemporary International and Australian Art at the University of Melbourne, had elaborated on these concepts in his book, *The Third Hand: Artist Collaborations from Conceptualism to Postmodernism*, which includes case studies of leading collaborating artists Gilbert and George, Marina Abramovic and Ulay, and Christo and Jeanne-Claude.[8] Framing the case studies is Green's own "typology of... collaboration", which includes various forms of collective, short-term cooperation; corporate, bureaucratic groups or partnerships; married couples and families; and intensely and publicly bonded couples who create what Green

---

4 Alex Miller, "The Other Man", *new literatures review* 40 (2003): 13.
5 Excerpts from Lyndell Brown and Charles Green, "Statement for *Sanctuary – and Other Island Fables*", Herring Island Environmental Sculpture Park, 2002, http://www.australianphotographers.org/artists/lyndell-brown-and-charles-green.
6 Timothy Morrell, "Lyndell Brown and Charles Green's Islands of Meaning", *Collector's Dossier* 61 (July–September 2012), http://www.artcollector.net.au/CollectorsDossierLyndellBrownandCharlesGreensislandsofmeaning.
7 Adrian Caesar, "An Artist in the Family: Reconfigurations of Romantic Paradigms in *Prochownik's Dream*", in *The Novels of Alex Miller: An Introduction*, ed. Robert Dixon (Sydney: Allen & Unwin, 2012), 101–13.
8 Charles Green, *The Third Hand: Artist Collaborations from Conceptualism to Postmodernism* (Minneapolis: University of Minnesota Press; Sydney: UNSW Press, 2001).

calls "third artists". While Lyndell Brown/Charles Green belong(s) to this final category, Green makes a careful distinction between collaboration, friendship and "sexual partnership". Artistic collaboration, he argues, is not necessarily the same thing as friendship, which is "always fragile since its contract is so unenforceable". Real collaboration, on the other hand, requires "the articulation of contractual relations". Reflecting on the many variables affecting the strength and durability of artist collaborations, Green suggests that couples based on "sexual partnership" – such as Marina and Ulay or Gilbert and George – do not necessarily produce enduring collaborations unless the relationship is also underwritten by "civility", or a sense of obligation modelled on either corporate or family identities.[9]

Brown and Green's studio practice is quite different to Toni Powlett's in the novel, which is grounded in the traditional techniques of portrait painting in oils, and is therefore closer to that of Rick Amor who, as we have seen in Chapter 3, is another important source of Miller's inspiration in writing about art. Brown and Green's collaborative work is more conceptual, involving the appropriation – either directly, or by photography or repainting – of original images from a variety of sources, including books of eighteenth and nineteenth-century travel and exploration, natural history, newspaper and magazine cuttings, famous paintings, photographs, and film stills, which are then arranged by montage within a painted environment before being re-photographed by their assistant, Sandra Barnard, and then printed for exhibition on to transparent Duraclear film.[10] The results are typically playful deconstructions of the follies of instrumental reason and its expression in a series of Western projects, from the reconnaissance and colonisation of the new world since the seventeenth century to the space race and the moon landing in the mid-twentieth century.

In his catalogue essay for *Sanctuary*, Miller elaborates on this critique of what he calls the European "passion to know" and its complicity with colonialism. Unlike science, art deals with the mysterious and the "magical", providing the modern, Western subject with a portal back into the cultural plenitude that is still enjoyed in their everyday lives by the world's first peoples. This general point is supported by one of Miller's earliest public references to the network of Indigenous friends who inspired *Journey to the Stone Country* and *Landscape of Farewell*, including Col McLennan and his Jangga grandmother, whom Miller had met on his trips to Central Queensland in 1997 and 1999. Borrowing a term from Gramsci, he calls this our "lost inventory": "Members of intact indigenous cultures possess this inventory ... The European intellectual, on the other hand, abhors the notion that anything can be placed beyond the right of being challenged and interrogated ... For the European intellectual there is no sanctuary for the other or for the self."[11] This is essentially the same "magical" view of art in its opposition to science that led Freud, in *Totem and Taboo* (1913), *The Future of an Illusion* (1927), and *Civilization and Its Discontents* (1930), to speak of the artist as a magician (*Zauberer*), and of his work as "the magic of art" (*Zauber der Kunst*).[12] Miller gave the title "The Artist as Magician" to an edited version of

---

9 Quoted in Geert Lovink, "The Art of Collaboration: Interview with Charles Green" (6 December 2001), 3, http://geertlovink.org/interviews/interview-with-charles-green/.
10 Excerpts from Lyndell Brown and Charles Green, "Statement for *Sanctuary – and Other Island Fables*".
11 Miller, "Sanctuary", n.p.
12 See the discussion of Freud's influence on the aesthetic theories of Sarah Kofman in Pleshette DeArmitt, "Conjuring Bodies: Kofman's Lesson on Death", *parallax* 17, no. 1 (2011): 6–8.

his catalogue essay that was published in *Meanjin* the following year. As one who deals in the mysterious, the magical and the irrational, it is the role of the artist both to critique the aspirations of instrumental reason and to offer a magical or pharmaceutical escape from the shallow and constricted world it creates: "Art offers us a liberation from the imprisoning treadmill of our culture's passion to know and to possess everything."[13]

Another point of comparison between Green's research and Miller's writing about art at this time is that the collaborations Green takes as his case studies in *The Third Hand* all had their origins in "the defeat of painting" in the 1970s. In an interview with Geert Lovink on "The Art of Collaboration", Green has said:

> The idea of a defeat of painting so close to conceptual artists' hearts – and I started my artistic life as an art student making conceptual art works alongside paintings at the very start of the 1970s . . . is clear in those artists' writings and statements. Painting was a cipher, a metonym, standing in for the 19th century idea of the bohemian artist that artists came to despise.[14]

It is this "defeat of painting" that Amor resisted by his championing of figurative painting during this same period,[15] while in *Prochownik's Dream* Toni Powlett's collaboration with Marina Golding initiates his own productive return to figurative painting after a sterile phase working in conceptual art and installations. Needless to say, in *Prochownik's Dream* Miller explores his own unique spectrum of collaborative relationships, but Green's project of researching the "typology" of collaborations in contemporary art is a suggestive parallel to Miller's concerns in the novel. These shared concerns again confirm that Miller's interest in the relationship between Sidney Nolan and Sunday Reed in the relatively late novel *Autumn Laing* (2011), which Janine Burke convincingly argues was a real artistic collaboration, a "symbiotic working relationship", deeply informed his earlier novels about art and artists.[16]

Like *The Sitters* before it, and like *Autumn Laing*, which in significant respects it foreshadows, *Prochownik's Dream* is a novel about artistic collaboration and inspiration: about the artist and his muse. "We're all collaborators", Marina Golding says to Toni Powlett: "All of us. None of us does this completely on our own".[17] Miller begins with an epigraph from Simone de Beauvoir: "We cannot arbitrarily invent projects for ourselves: they have to be written in our past as requirements." The choice of de Beauvoir immediately suggests a number of subtle connections. By coincidence, Miller's friend Hazel Rowley published her own study of love and collaboration in the same year as *Prochownik's Dream* – *Tête-à-tête: The Lives and Loves of Simone de Beauvoir and Jean-Paul Sartre*.[18] Miller's novel opens with the artist Toni Powlett posing in his studio while his young daughter Nada draws his

---

13 Miller, "Sanctuary", n.p.
14 Quoted in Lovink, "The Art of Collaboration", 2.
15 Linda Short, "A Single Statement of a Single Mind", in *Rick Amor: A Single Mind*, exhibition catalogue, ed. Linda Short (Bulleen, Vic.: Heide Museum of Modern Art, 2008), 66.
16 Janine Burke, *The Heart Garden: Sunday Reed and Heide* (2004; Sydney: Vintage, 2005), 260. Miller did not read *The Heart Garden* until he was doing research for *Autumn Laing* in 2010.
17 Alex Miller, *Prochownik's Dream* (Sydney: Allen & Unwin, 2005), 156. All subsequent references are to this edition and appear in parentheses in the text.
18 Hazel Rowley, *Tête-à-tête: The Lives and Loves of Simone de Beauvoir and Jean-Paul Sartre* (New York: HarperCollins, 2005).

portrait. The location of the studio is significant. Like the gazebo at Coppin Grove, where Victoria Feng writes in *The Ancestor Game*, it is set apart from the house and kitchen, the domain of Toni's wife Teresa. As Toni sits for Nada he is reading *Nausea*, Sartre's novel about a man suffering an existential crisis. It is the Penguin Classics edition, with its instantly recognisable cover reproduction of Salvador Dali's *The Triangular Hour*, and he reads on the cover, "*A novel of the alienation of personality and the mystery of being*" (4). Like the portrait painter in *The Sitters*, Toni is experiencing an artistic paralysis in response to his father Moriek Prochownik's death, and his subsequent abandonment of painting: "his father had died, and he had given up painting and turned to installations" (7). His most recent installation was an assemblage of old men's clothes arranged on timber racks to look like a "crowd of faceless people" (9). Now lying dismantled in his studio, "the smelly pile of old clothes had begun to sicken him" (5).

Like the broken-backed books repaired by the painter's father in *The Sitters*, the clothes are a symbol of failure and despair. And like the book in Rembrandt's *The Anatomy Lesson*, to which Miller refers in the earlier novel, they are an attempt to "conjure" death. Toni's idea for the installation was an immediate response to the news of his father's death four years earlier. It was an attempt both to occlude the fact of death and to represent it in a displaced form: "what had he intended by the gesture? To deny the loss of his father? . . . his dead father became his first installation: the old suit standing out there on its own" (59–60). In these two novels, then, the books and old clothes signify the presence of a series of absences: the death of the father, the abandonment of painting – "He hated and feared the silence in his mind, but he could not pretend to work when there was really nothing there" (5–6) – and the absence of a positive and creative attitude to life. They signify the occultation of that which we are all "in the process of becoming", as Sarah Kofman points out in her analysis of *The Anatomy Lesson*.[19] But like any symptom, the clothes make present the very absences they are meant to conjure away:

> The summer heat was drawing from the old clothes the dispiriting smell of naphthalene. It was a smell that reminded him of the closets of old people and of their preoccupation with the preservation of their things against the inevitability of decay, as if by preserving their most intimate belongings they might thereby contrive the preservation of themselves. (4–5)

The preservation of things against their inevitable decay is also the purpose of painting, and especially portrait painting. According to Alberti, it "not only makes absent men present, as friendship is said to do, but shows the dead to the living".[20]

For the present, Toni Powlett may have abandoned painting, but as he contemplates his own crisis, Nada draws him with remarkable confidence and fluency:

> She had drawn the figure of a man . . . There had been no attempt at a likeness . . . no reference to his pose in the doorway . . . It leaned to one side from the waist up, as if it were being bent by a powerful wind, or was about to execute a difficult leap that would test its

---

19 Sarah Kofman, "Conjuring Death: Remarks on *The Anatomy Lesson of Doctor Nicolas Tulp (1632)*", in *Selected Writings*, eds Thomas Albrecht, Georgia Albert and Elizabeth Rottenberg, trans. Pascale-Anne Brault (Stanford: Stanford University Press, 2007), 238.
20 Leon Battista Alberti, *On Painting*, quoted in Jacques Derrida, *The Work of Mourning*, eds Pascale-Anne Brault and Michael Naas (Chicago and London: University of Chicago Press, 2003), 155.

agility to the limit. Spears of red hair issued from its head like flames – its hair anticipating the violent energies of its intended leap, or perhaps the panic in its mind. (6)

Nada's figure is caught in an ambiguous moment of panic or flight, or of potential transformation – the pose "in the doorway". The image of its bending into a powerful wind recalls Albert Tucker's portrait of Joy Hester, her figure "overwhelmed" by the elemental force of the breaking wave. It also strongly suggests Rick Amor's famous figure of "the running man". This signature motif first appeared in his work in 1983, and it has the same mysterious density of possible meanings as Nada's portrait of her father. In a catalogue essay for a 2005 exhibition, the critic Robert Lindsay noted that "a major recurring motif in Amor's work from the late 1980s to the 1990s is the figure of the running man – poised on one leg, in flight from an unseen, threatened menace".[21] Toni Powlett's panic, his existential and artistic crisis, is therefore richly and ironically signified by the powerful artworks that surround him, as if in confirmation but also in mockery of his own creative impotence: Sartre's *Nausea*, Dali's ticking clock, Amor's running man.

At the end of this opening chapter, Toni Powlett's paralysis is interrupted by a phone call announcing the return to Melbourne of his former mentor, Robert Schwartz, and Robert's wife Marina Golding: "suddenly, Marina's voice on the other end of the telephone, reminding him of those years of hope and excitement that they had shared" (8). Phone calls often cause interruptions in Miller's novels. In *The Ancestor Game*, Lang's call to Steven on the night before Gertrude's exhibition at The Falls Gallery heralds his mysterious absence, while in *The Sitters* Jessica Keal makes her call from the hospital room in London where she is soon to die. News of Moniek Prochownik's death on the production line at the Dunlop plant also comes to Toni in a telephone call. Marina Golding's call is the more desirable interruption of the artist by his muse, but like death, inspiration is also a form of *rapture*, a carrying away of the self by the other. Foreshadowing the manifold and unpredictable consequences of this interruption, the first chapter ends with another version of the running man, the dancer leaning on the wind. Toni is pushing his daughter on a swing, which is itself an act of rapture and collaboration: "He caught her and pushed her higher, the tails of her red jacket flying out behind, the wind of her flight lifting her brown hair . . . His heart contracted in his chest with love for her" (11).

Robert and Marina have moved back to Melbourne after four years in Sydney's Glebe. Prior to their move away, Toni had been an emerging figurative painter and tutored for Robert at art school, but when his father died, Toni lost confidence in himself and turned to installations: "he had attempted to keep on painting . . . but . . . the paintings he did were empty. So, reluctantly, for he loved it, he gave it up" (33). Robert and Marina have invited Toni to their home in Richmond to ask him to collaborate with them in an exhibition. A mutual friend, Oriel Liesker, has been appointed curator of the new Bream Island sculpture park and art space, and she has offered them the inaugural show (28). They plan to exhibit several paintings, but have invited Toni to fill out the space with one of his installations. When Toni confesses that he is in a creative "black space" (34), they press him to accept and it is agreed that he and Marina will visit Bream Island together the next day: "*The Bream Island Inaugural Show – Schwartz, Golding & Powlett*. It *was* seductive" (30).

---

21 Robert Lindsay, *Rick Amor: Standing in the Shadows*, exhibition catalogue (Langwarrin, Vic.: McClelland Gallery, 2005), n.p.

Robert and Marina have always collaborated – "Robert Schwartz and Marina Golding, the brilliant collaborative team" (13) – but during the years in Sydney their working relationship has taken a new form. When Toni examines a canvas-in-progress on an easel, *Man Adrift*, he asks whether it is still "the both of them", and Marina explains the new division of labour: "Robert doesn't paint any more... The ideas are still his, but the brushwork's all mine these days" (22). This is a gendered opposition, Marina and Robert personifying the manual and the intellectual sides of art practice respectively. Robert is an academic art critic and theorist. He has just completed a six month-residency at the University of Minnesota, where he finished his second book: Green's *The Third Hand* was published by the University of Minnesota Press. In *Man Adrift*, Toni recognises "the complicated ideas of Robert, the exemplary theoretician and assiduous practitioner of the contemporary, the *post*-postmodernist" (21). He writes for *Art & Text*, and there is "something of the dean of the faculty" in his manner: even his offer to collaborate is slightly "bullying" (29). Marina, on the other hand, embodies the physical engagement of the painter with her craft and materials: "I love painting", she confesses, and Toni notices the excellence of her technique (22). The fact that Robert and Marina retain their own names in their marriage – Schwartz and Golding – suggests something of the paradox of collaboration – together yet different, black and yellow – that is also captured in the hyphenated Brown/Green partnership.

At the Schwartz/Golding home, Toni notices a "bronze figure of a running man" (17). It is by the successful Sydney artist Geoffrey Haine, who gave it to Robert to thank him for a piece he wrote about him for *Art & Text*. Toni recognises it as the figure that recurs in the artist's "monumental post-industrial landscapes, a solitary fugitive human presence in vast wastelands of rusting machinery and empty office towers aglow with the unearthly light of the end-of-days, visionary scenes" (18). Toni feels the "enormous weight of Geoff Haine's reputation" (18). This is Miller's tribute to Rick Amor, and there are several "Amor" landscapes and settings in the novel, including the scene at Bream Island on the morning that Toni meets Marina at the punt landing:

> Behind him, his old green VK station wagon was parked alongside a concrete pylon under the roadbed of the freeway. Beyond the VK, deep within the darkness under the columns, a slope of rubble. When he'd stepped out of the car he had noticed a dark-stained mattress humped with old clothes, or maybe a recumbent figure slumped in the monochrome of shadows. The scene put him in mind of Geoff Haine's apocalyptic landscapes... Two kilometres to the north, the glass towers of the CBD shone in the midday sun. (36)

The subject matter is an allusion to Amor's urban landscapes, such as *The Gate* (1990), which Miller had admired at the Niagara Galleries in 1991.[22]

What happens between Toni and Marina on Bream Island is another of Miller's signature scenes of friendship, hospitality and gift exchange. The archetype of these scenes is Max Blatt's reading of Miller's manuscript on the kitchen table at Araluen and his gift to him of the story that became "Comrade Pawel", but it is echoed in Ida Rankin's telling Robert Crofts about her trip to Mt Mooloolong in *Watching the Climbers on the Mountain*,

---

22 Gary Catalano, *The Solitary Watcher: Rick Amor and His Art* (Melbourne: Miegunyah Press, 2001), 109.

and in the picnic in the garden at Coppin Grove in *The Ancestor Game*. In a similar scene of outdoor hospitality, Marina and Toni share food and wine, and after lunch they sketch one another while they talk. For his part, Toni gives to Marina the story of his own origins and inspiration as an artist, when he collaborated with his father at night at the kitchen table:

> He'd get up in the middle of the night and sit in the kitchen drawing and painting ... I'd see the light under the door and I'd get up and come out to the kitchen and watch him. To me it was magic. I'd hold my breath. He wouldn't say anything, but he'd slip his arm around me and press me to his side and keep working, and I knew he was glad to have me there with him in the night. (43–4)

Toni is recalling for Marina his own foundational moment as an artist in the act of collaboration with his father in the family kitchen, their site of sharing and hospitality. The child is father to the man both in the sense that Toni is his father's muse, and that the child is learning to become an artist. When Toni asks his father for advice about art, Moniek Prochownik gives him Max Blatt's advice: "*Paint what you love*" (65). The scene in the Prochowniks' kitchen looks back to Miller's relationships with both Max Blatt and his own father, who was an amateur watercolourist: Max Blatt and Miller's father "Jock" were born in the same year, 1907.[23] It also evokes Nolan at Heide. Barrett Reid has described Nolan working on the Kelly paintings at the dining table, often in the presence of Sunday Reed, while Albert Tucker recalled that "the bulk of the time that Nolan [worked] at Heide, Sunday was virtually in his pocket". "Literally", according to Janine Burke, "Sunday stood next to him, watching as he painted. [Reed herself] recalled, 'sometimes he would pick up a brush with his arm around me' ".[24]

While Toni sketches Marina and shares his story with her, she in turn draws the scene of their picnic. It is a chiastic exchange, a scene of friendship and giving that marks a new beginning for Toni as an artist, foreshadowing his return to figurative painting: "he ... [pictured] Marina back in the glade ... doing her drawing: the scene of their own private *déjeuner sur l'herbe*. Sharing with her his memories of his father ... had recaptured something of the intensity of those early years, his passionate hopes for his art" (48). These motifs of friendship, exchange and artistic inspiration are overlaid with another set of images derived from the hunt, and it is part of the novel's sustained ambiguity that they have both artistic and amatory significance. Walking back through the bush to where Marina lies asleep, Toni imagines the island's "hidden glades" as places where "the hunter could ... approach the enemy's camp unseen. A pulsing of bullets through the leaves and the felled bodies lay twitching on the grass ... The *coup de grâce*" (48). It is another scene of rapture. The sylvan setting relates to the subtitle Miller has given to this first part of the novel, "The Mistress of Trees", an allusion not only to the glade in which Toni and Marina share friendship's first exchange, but more literally to the fact that Marina excels at drawing trees. Toni recalls the trees at her parents' home, Plovers, at Mount Macedon, where he has drawn her in the past.

---

23   Alex Miller, "The Story's Not Over Yet", Melbourne Writers' Festival, 23 August 2014. Unpublished speech.
24   Quotations in Burke, *The Heart Garden*, 256.

When Toni finishes drawing Marina there is an exchange between them over the ownership of her image that recalls similar exchanges between Lang and Steven, and the portrait painter and Jessica Keal. In this case, however, the exchange is entered into with mutual professional understanding. Toni has "taken" her image while she slept, an "unobserved voyeur" (50), even using her own pencils and sketching block to do it. When she asks him whether she can keep the drawing, he hesitates, like the portrait painter in *The Sitters*, "his eyes going possessively to the sketching block in her hands" (55). Unlike Jessica, who is an historian, not an artist, Marina understands that the image is his, not hers: "You don't want to let it go. I can see that. You did it for yourself, not me. I'm sorry. I shouldn't have asked" (55). The exchange is completed by Toni taking her image and keeping it: "It was his reference. He needed it" (55).

Toni and Marina's shared investment in his sketch of her asleep on the island arises from the fact, already explored at length in *The Sitters*, that a portrait – and not just the finished painting, but the entire process of its making – is a space of encounter between the artist and his or her subject. Brigitta Olubas makes this point in her essay on *The Sitters* when she describes the portrait as "the point where two stories, or the stories of two lives, grow together . . . in what Miller's narrator calls 'a single image' ".[25] This is why, in contemplating his portrait of Jessica Keal, the painter says, "I'm content, for once, to recognize myself" (2). When Toni returns to his studio with Marina's sketching block, which contains the sketch of her that he has "taken", he finds that the project she has awoken in him to paint a series of portraits has its origin in their shared past. Looking through his Mount Macedon sketchbook, he finds that he has already "taken" a sketch of Marina sleeping at her parents' home, beneath which he has written, "*Marina Golding in the conservatory at Plovers, June 19, 1989*" (66). Like the painter in *The Sitters*, he recognises their mutual entanglement in the image: "The trace of himself off the edge of the drawing, the cast shadow of the voyeur crouched by the sleeping woman taking her likeness" (67). It is here that the epigraph from de Beauvoir acquires its significance. Toni's new project, his return to painting in collaboration with Marina, is not one that he has arbitrarily invented, but something "intended" that emerges as a requirement, a logical outcome, of his past: his desire to realise his father's dream of art, and the fulfilment of his own gift as a painter, which Marina has returned to him. As the allusion to Carson McCullers' *Reflections in a Golden Eye* suggests – "the voyeur crouched by the sleeping woman" – the artist has little choice but to obey the compulsion of desire. Part one of the novel, "The Mistress of Trees", ends with Marina's agreement to take part in the project, which is confirmed by their examination together of his Mount Macedon sketchbook, in which she recognises elements of her own family history entangled with his youthful artistic ambitions: "his old sketchbook linked . . . them and their art to his return to painting" (99).

In the impressive central section of *Prochownik's Dream*, "The Third Hand", Miller offers a remarkably convincing account of how Toni builds up his suite of paintings for the Bream Island exhibition. It is to be called *The Marina Suite*, and comprises four major canvases, *The Schwartz Family*, *The Other Family*, *The Eye of Tiresias* and *The Nymphe*. As the allusion to Green's theories of collaboration implies, "The Third Hand" records the various forms of collaboration in which the apparently solitary figure of the artist is embedded. Miller elaborates his own typology of collaborations. *The Schwartz Family*, which is even-

---

25   Brigitta Olubas, "Like/Unlike: Portraiture, Similitude and the Craft of Words in *The Sitters*", in *The Novels of Alex Miller*, 95.

tually to be painted by both Toni and Marina, tells the story of their entangled lives, and of their mutual journeys both as fellow painters, and as artist and muse, away from earlier mentors and towards artistic independence. As a professional artist, Toni is also supported and inspired by his relationships with rivals like Robert Schwartz and Geoff Haine, his agent Andy Levine, and curators like Oriel Liesker. These professional colleagues are the subjects of *The Other Family*. *The Eye of Tiresias* is an allegorical painting in which Toni's own youthful face is superimposed upon the body of an older man, and is a tribute to his two mentors, his father Moniek Prochownik, and Robert's father, Theo Schwartz, who provide him with contrasting visions of what a life of art might be. *The Nymphe* is his portrait of Marina, his muse, though as we will see, its completion involves a surprising third collaborator.

Painting *The Nymphe* involves Toni in the complex history and politics of the nude, which Miller had already begun to explore in *The Sitters*: "The idea occurred to him then of a naked portrait of her lying on the chaise. A woman . . . looking away from the viewer and thinking her private thoughts, oblivious to the gaze of the onlooker" (93). Toni is caught up in the challenges that Miller has already explored through his juxtaposition in *The Sitters* of the very different approaches to the nude represented by the names Manet, Bonnard and Sickert: "Such a picture could not be the portrait of a child-like odalisque, but must be an intimate picture of a middle-aged artist engaged with her unresolvable erotic tensions . . . Did he have the vision that would remove such an image from the area of the merely prurient?" (93).

As Marina and Toni enter into this difficult entanglement, his very different collaboration with his wife Teresa also reaches a critical phase. Robert and Marina's contract as a couple is based solely on the life of art, and they have made a decision not to have children: "*We decided it is enough that we are artists . . . We realized we couldn't have everything, and we chose art*" (196). Toni and Teresa's contract, on the other hand, is based not on artistic collaboration, but in her practical and emotional support for him as a wife and mother. Acknowledging his vocation as an artist, she is prepared to support him by earning the family income and running the family home. "I don't have that passion for my work that you have", Teresa tells him, but she pledges her support: "We're a team. We're family . . . I wanted to support you in your work." Teresa acknowledges that even this kind of support can be ambiguous, even "bullying", in the same way that any gift can be, including Robert and Marina's gift of artistic collaboration. She asks, "This is not a trap for you, is it? The way I've set things up for you?" (87). Teresa's project, which crystalises for them at precisely the same time as his project to paint Marina, is that she wants them to have a second child. Toni commits to this, too, but retains "a small private guilt" at the thought of his ambivalence (102).

Theo Schwartz, Robert's father, has lived in Germany for the last forty years and has now come home to die. Together with Toni's own father, Moniek Prochownik, he is Toni's mentor in both art and life. An accomplished graphic artist, he works in pen making highly stylised drawings that are not original in style, but modelled on the work of an anonymous German master of the eighteenth century. They are allegorical drawings that feature surprisingly erotic images of himself with his son's wife. Theo gives Toni the book of drawings knowing that he will learn from them in his own efforts to draw Marina and the Schwartz family. Theo, too, understands the ethical ambiguity of such a gift, for he is not only seeking to help the younger man, but also to perpetuate his own artistic knowledge: "It's yours. You'll make use of it, I can see that. A little of my experience may be secured with you for a time, eh? To give a gift can be a selfish act" (128). Toni learns from Theo how to put himself into a painting as its subject – that is to say, as the perspective from which it is seen. He learns from Theo's erotic drawings how to cue the spectator to adopt the hunger of the voyeur, how to desire the content of the paintings:

> Toni was standing in front of *The Other Family*. He was seeing himself in the empty space to the left of the big group; a figure looking on, an onlooker. The voyeur ... The imaginary image of himself in the picture was not so much a likeness as an enigmatic male presence, erotic and naked, a presence bearing a dangerous power to disrupt reality. There was no doubt this self image owed something to the fantastic intensities of Theo's drawings. (219–20)

It was this "something", this "edge", this element of danger in visual desire that had drawn Miller to McCullers' treatment of scopophilia in *Reflections in a Golden Eye*, and which he signifies, in *The Sitters*, by the name of Walter Sickert, and by association with the Camden Town Murder: it was the power of "Theo Schwartz's illicit intimacies that he was drawing upon" (221).

Miller's main achievement in "The Third Hand" is his compelling study of how an artist goes about "building up" his canvases, from the stage of live drawing to painting in oils in the studio. Miller has learned much about the craft of oil painting from the studio practice of his friend and, in a very real sense, his *collaborator*, Rick Amor.[26] In Toni Powlett's return to figurative painting, Miller explores aspects of aesthetic theory and artistic practice that also relate to his own craft as a novelist. As Ronald A. Sharp has said of *The Sitters*, Miller "foregrounds the connections between literary and visual art, between a novelist creating a character and a painter creating a portrait".[27] At the beginning of "The Third Hand", Toni sits on Robert's library steps in the dining room of their Richmond home – that recurring scene in Miller's work of friendship, collaboration and intertextual hospitality – drawing his three sitters, Robert, Marina and Theo. He is "in the zone with his work", and "only vaguely conscious" of the tensions surfacing in their conversation (113). While the artist is in this zone, the sitters are not so much people as the inspiration for his images; they are the source of the essentially formal and aesthetic problems that materialise for the artist in what Miller elsewhere calls the "black mirror" of the imagination.[28] Theo is the origin of one such problem, "*the problem of Theo Schwartz*" (140):

> Toni struggled on for a moment longer with Theo's head. There had been a glimmer, then nothing, the illusion of likeness surfacing then sinking away through the matrix of scumbled charcoal, the ghostly presence of Theo Schwartz a drowned likeness in the depths, elusive and tantalizing, a faint message from a dead man. *Here I am!* Then nothing. (115)

When Toni finishes the session he closes his folder and fastens its ties. The three sitters are watching but he will not show them the images he has taken, since they are not theirs; they

---

26 Miller has said that "when Rick illustrated an excerpt from [*The Ancestor Game*] which [Barrett] Reid published in ... *Overland* it seemed to me that our collusion in the work had become magically real". Alex Miller, "Rick Amor's Show at Castlemaine Gallery June 1 2003", unpublished speech.
27 Ronald A. Sharp, "The Presence of Absence in *The Sitters*", in *The Novels of Alex Miller*, 78.
28 Alex Miller, "Writer's Choice: The Black Mirror", *Art & Australia* 43, no. 3 (2006): 446–7.

are not *them*: they are "his fictions", not "their realities", and he is "impatient, suddenly, to get home to his studio and begin work on the picture" (116).

Toni takes his folder of drawings, his "fictions", back to his studio, where he re-enters the zone of work, this time making the transition from drawing to painting, from working on paper before his sitters to working on canvas in the solitude of the studio at night. Again, he is working with the "black mirror" of the imagination, as the material takes shape on the canvas according to its own inner logic. Toni has been "mining the intimacies of their lives for his art" and his work is their gift to him, "a trust that had been laid upon him, for which he was grateful" (132–3). But the point of a gift is that it is no longer the property of the giver. The images that appear now in the black mirror are not "them", but a set of problems of the artist's own making – not Marina Golding but "*the problem of Marina Golding*",[29] "*the problem of Theo Shwartz*" (140). This is what Teresa does not understand. When she sees images of Marina in Toni's sketching block or on his canvases, she experiences an overwhelming sexual jealousy. But Toni's model, his muse, is no longer there: "Marina left *hours* ago" (136). What appears on the canvas is not "the sitters" but his "figures", which are increasingly detached from the "reality" of their origins: "Some quality of the truth of his drawings had survived the less intimate process of the large painting. But still the background was not right. It was too close to the everyday realities of their Richmond situation" (141). The risk of figurative painting is that its origins may be recognised, or that the figures will be misrecognised as the sitters: "He thought how much simpler it would have been if, instead of hazarding the human likeness, he had become a painter of still lifes like his father" (266). This is revealing of the hazards facing the novelist, of Miller's risk in drawing on his own life in his novels – that is to say, the risks of both misrecognition, the assumption that the novels are merely fictions, and of over-recognition, the assumption that they are merely biographical and autobiographical. The truth of art lies somewhere in between. Miller's understanding of aesthetics here is again similar to Freud's view of "the magic of art". As Pleshette DeArmitt explains, quoting Sarah Kofman, art, like magic, operates "between the realm of reality, which 'frustrates wishes,' and the realm of the . . . imagination, in which wishes are fulfilled". Art, for Freud, "is a conventionally accepted reality in which, thanks to the artistic illusion, symbols and substitutes are able to provoke real effects".[30] Theo warns Toni that it is in this space between reality and imagination, between the "transgressive nature of the imaginative life", and "the daily life of the family", that one is at the greatest risk of confusing "art" with "life" (133).

In its depiction of the relationship between Robert Schwartz and his dying father Theo, *The Schwartz Family* also suggests something of art's "magical" or pharmaceutical properties, its capacity to "conjure" death. The relation between art and death, and the importance of the artist's being-towards-death, are central to Toni's development as a figurative painter. As DeArmitt puts it, "The artistic illusion is . . . a kind of Faustian bargain – it conjures away the threat of death and ironically replaces it with the serenity of a living death."[31] In Miller's account of the work of "the third hand", art's magical capacity to conjure death is proven, as it were, by the red mark beneath Theo Shwartz's eye, that "bright red slash like a wound in the softly weeping tissue of the father's face that was never going to heal" (113).

---

29 Miller, "The Other Man", 13.
30 Freud, *Totem and Taboo*, quoted by Sarah Kofman, *The Childhood of Art: An Interpretation of Freud's Aesthetics*, trans. Winifred Woodhull (New York; Columbia University Press, 1988), 122, in Pleshette DeArmitt, "Conjuring Bodies: Kofman's Lesson on Death", *parallax* 17, no. 1 (2011): 4–17.
31 DeArmitt, "Conjuring Bodies", 9.

Such is the magical power of art that in its black mirror, Theo's wound, the mark of his mortality, is no longer required to heal. Art can conjure death, as Toni understands when he first sees Robert and Marina's painting *Man Adrift*:

> He turned to the large two-metre square unframed canvas. It was an image of a naked man falling upward into a sombre sky of deep lustrous black ... He was not dead, it seemed, but was a man adrift. An ironic *ascent of man*. A suggestion of crucifixion, but without the cross. Below the wrinkled soles of the naked man's feet a *trompe l'oeil* of an open book, the deckled edges of the pages casting a delicate filigree of reflected light onto the black sky, so that it appeared as if an actual book had been artfully attached to the canvas. Toni recognized the complicated ideas of Robert, the exemplary theoretician. (21)

While *Man Adrift* suggests another of Dali's paintings, *Christ of Saint John of the Cross* (1951), it might also be understood as a re-working of Rembrandt's *The Anatomy Lesson*, which Miller had already incorporated into *The Sitters*, where it plays an important role in his meditation on the relationship between art and death. While Dali depicts Christ's crucified body in a state of (surreal) perfection that already anticipates the glorious body of the Resurrection, Rembrandt presents the secular version of the inglorious cadaver, with the distracting image of the open book in the foreground. As we have seen in Chapter 3, in her reading of *The Anatomy Lesson*, Sarah Kofman argues that Rembrandt's modern men of science conjure away death and the religious illusion by diverting the spectator's gaze away from the cadaver to the book. In performing this act of occultation, by drawing a veil over the corpse, they conjure up another illusion, the idealisation of scientific knowledge as a replacement for the older "magical" religion, and a belief in science's capacity to preserve, perhaps even to restore, human life: "a sleight of hand has taken place as the wisdom of man has replaced the word of God and an 'anonymous' cadaver, a common criminal, stands for the body of Christ".[32]

Miller's fictional *Man Adrift* is the work of a "third artist", Robert Schwartz/Marina Golding. Robert has conceived of a postmodern re-interpretation of one or other of these famous paintings that Marina, with her flawless technique, has then realised on canvas. Perhaps Robert, "the exemplary theoretician", had in mind Sarah Kofman's essay on Rembrandt, or Derrida's commentary upon it in his eulogy for Kofman in *The Work of Mourning*.[33] The point is that in the modern world it is no longer the magic of religion or the magic of science that can restore life, but the magic of art – though Robert's intention, as Toni understands it, is ironically to undercut that exorbitant claim for art from a postmodern perspective. As Toni comes to see when he examines the painting again in detail, it is Marina's masterly technique that creates the illusion of secular resurrection and immortality:

> Marina's painting of the naked man adrift in space leans against the pale wall on the mantelpiece behind the silent diners, the wrinkled soles of the man's feet, the anatomical detail photographic and precise, as if his deathless pallor comments on the mortality of the living ... The viewer of this painting is drawn to look closely in order to see how

---

32 DeArmitt, "Conjuring Bodies", 12.
33 Derrida, *The Work of Mourning*, 165.

it has been done, the illusion of flesh in-depth persisting until the eye is close to the paint surface... This is the high craft of the artist's sleight-of-hand and Marina is its master... (109)

What begins for Toni as "*the problem of Theo Schwartz*" therefore becomes a complex meditation on the relationships between art and life, and art and death. In the realm of art, Theo's wound will not heal, but nor will his flesh further decay, unlike in reality, where Robert, who is now fifty years old, is already becoming more like his father, a sign of his death in the process of becoming, as Toni's art inadvertently and ironically reveals. Even as it preserves the dying man, it shows death at work in his son: "[Toni] had begun to see that in his drawing Robert was becoming an effigy of his ailing father" (111).

Yet if oil painting is a "sleight-of-hand", a "*trompe l'oeil*" that can conjure death, there is another irony at work in Miller's novel, another hidden meaning of the book in the foreground of *Man Adrift* that is there in open sight for all to see. It is that *Man Adrift* is itself an illusion conjured into being by words in a novel, Miller's novel, the one that we are reading as we concentrate on Marina's painting – even as we forget that we are reading it – in order to "see" her rendering of the flesh and the light radiating from the book: "a *trompe l'oeil* of an open book... so that it appeared as if an actual book had been artfully attached to the canvas" (21). This is itself a sleight-of-hand. It is not the high craft of painting but the craft of ekphrasis, the art of writing about art, and Alex Miller is its master. Miller's joke is that there *is* an actual book "attached to" Marina's painting, and it is called *Prochownik's Dream*. But there is one more *trompe l'oeil* in this series, and this time it is a real one: that is to say, an actual, visual one rather than one achieved through ekphrastic description. The illustration on the cover of *Prochownik's Dream* is a prepared canvas that makes the book look like a painting: even the staples in the stretcher and the tiny piece of newsprint caught beneath the canvas are "real".

"The Third Hand" culminates with Toni solving the greatest of all his technical problems: the problem of himself, of his own presence in the painting. In working on *The Other Family*, the group portrait of his professional collaborators, he is unable to find a solution to his own presence as a cogent and compelling image. The solution involves the novel's central themes of being-towards-death, and the relation between art and death. Unable to solve the riddle, Toni returns to his father's copy of *Nausea*, which he was reading on the morning Nada sketched his portrait. Drawn to Sartre's imperative, "*I should like to understand myself properly before it is too late*" (223), he buys a cheap full-length mirror at a hardware store and studies himself naked in the studio until he comes to see himself as if he were another person, looking with the dispassionate eye of the artist for "the truth of the visual form of the naked man reflected there" (226). This detail recalls Brian Adams' account, in his 1987 biography of Sidney Nolan, of Nolan's attempt in 1939 to bluff Sir Keith Murdoch into giving him a scholarship to study in Europe. Having no portfolio to support an application, Nolan spent several nights doing a series of brush drawings on blotting and tissue paper: "Nolan stripped off his clothes in front of an old mirrored wardrobe... By the harsh glare of a naked light bulb he used himself as a model and composed a series of abstract figure studies."[34] Toni Powlett's purpose is more serious. To understand himself fully, he must understand his place in the generational succession, which means accepting the state of being-towards-death. This is achieved by placing the head of Theo Schwartz

---

34 Brian Adams, *Sidney Nolan: Such is Life* (1987; Milson's Point, NSW: Vintage, 1992), 33.

on his own body, initially in a separate study titled *The Eye of Tiresias*. As a mentor, Theo is associated with his own dead father, and Toni learns to replace Robert's overly intellectual influence with the wisdom of these two older painters. In this way Toni learns to find his true place in the larger context of generational succession and artistic influence: "There was something beautiful and poignant in the perversity of this image for Toni, the dying man's head on his own youthful torso... [he] knew himself to be in touch at last with that dimension of himself that had always eluded him" (228). All that remains now in the novel's final section, "Prochownik's Dream", is the playing out of his collaborations with Teresa and Marina, his wife and muse.

Marina's and Toni's collaboration on *The Schwartz Family* reaches its artistic culmination when she agrees to complete it by painting over Toni's original background – "the everyday reality" of Marina and Robert's *Man Adrift* on the dining room wall at Richmond – and replacing it with her painting of the trees at Plovers. Toni and Marina are now a "third artist", and Marina compares their work to Picasso's group portrait, *The Soler Family*, for which his friend Junyer Vidal painted a new background (157). In painting a background drawn from her own life, Marina literally paints out the one she had made with Robert, displacing the influence he has had on her art, and allowing her to rediscover her self: "The ghostly remainder of Robert's naked man adrift had gone, sunk too deep under Marina's medium to be visible any longer" (241). Encouraged by Theo, their "secret collaborator", to explore her childhood and the sources of her own art, Marina has recovered herself as an artist: "I'd forgotten how much I'd done on my own before I met Robert... Theo... helped me to see what I had to do... [he] told me not to paint a background for you, but to paint one for myself" (244). This sexual and artistic collaboration is a form of rapture that allows Toni as the "man adrift" to undergo a kind of resurrection or ascension: the events that had "unfolded for him from the moment of Marina's telephone call that day" were not something that he could control; they had "surprised him and lifted him onto a wave of energy and confidence that had made the renewal of his work possible" (249).

Theo Schwartz, as Marina and Toni recognise, has been their "secret collaborator". As the dying man, he represents the importance of being-toward-death, the awareness that life takes place within the ruin of time – that is, in relation to one's own mortality and one's place in the generation cycle. In helping him to his bed after *The Schwartz Family* is finished, Toni has "a glimpse of scarlet ulcers, like sword wounds in his chest and abdomen" (242). These images connect Theo's dying body with the glorious body in Robert and Marina's *Man Adrift*, which flaunts the deceptive magic of art. It also associates him with the inglorious figure of the cadaver in Rembrandt's *The Anatomy Lesson*, and with the surrealistically resurrected body in Dali's Crucifixion. But in *Prochownik's Dream*, the continuing presence of his wound ensures that there will be no sleight-of-hand, no veil drawn over the figure of death.

As soon as the work of collaboration is finished, Theo Schwartz dies. As if completing the pattern of interruption with which the novel begins, the announcement of his death comes again in a telephone call from Robert at the Alfred Hospital, where Theo has been taken after having a stroke. "The sudden grip of death on Theo" makes them all "vulnerable" (254), a recurring word at such moments of rapture and transformation in Miller's work. These are his "doorway" moments, when his characters are on the verge of being carried out of themselves by others, or by death. At the Alfred, Toni finds Robert and Marina in a "curtained cubicle" in the intensive care ward. To enter and leave this space of death, they must all pass through the curtain – the word is used three times in two pages (254–5). In an influential article, the French art historian Georges Didi-Huberman has shown that in European art, from Medieval and Renaissance Depositions and Crucifixions through to spirit photography in the early twentieth century, the fold or veil has been used to invoke the immanence of the spirit world, or the portal between being and non-being.[35] When Toni comes through the curtain, it has a transformative effect on Robert, who is brought out of himself in a moment of rapture: "I don't know why, but seeing you made me cry. I saw you coming through that curtain and it caught me in the throat" (254). In contrast to Jessica's death in *The Sitters*, the artist is now literally present at the scene of death, which he has no need to imagine. He there beholds not the glorious body, falsely created by the techniques of oil painting in Dali's surreal Crucifixion, but the modern, medicalised figure of death shown in *The Anatomy Lesson*. In Miller's lesson on death, as in Sarah Kofman's, there will be no occultation of the corpse, no leading of the eye away from the cadaver to a book or a painting:

> Theo lay on his side with his mouth open, a clear plastic tube going down the black hole of his throat, and oxygen mask clamped over his nose with an obscene pink garter around the back of his head, his wispy hair waving back and forth in the cold stream of the air-conditioning. Theo's eyes were closed and his skin was the colour of stone, one skinny arm out of the covers, a drip insert coming out of the back of his hand. Except for the noise of his breathing he looked dead. (255)

There is no hope here of a religious, a medical or an artistic resurrection, but appropriately for Theo, who recognised death's erotic intensity, the seemingly inappropriate language of sex is invoked in the image of the "obscene pink garter". There is no sleight-of-hand, none of art's "magic", only the banal illusion of life and movement created by stream of sterile air: "Theo died the following night" (257).

Theo has taught Toni and Marina that they are all embedded in that other "cold stream" into which Rick Amor's running man leans. W.G. Sebald had called it "the Rings of Saturn", and Walter Benjamin the "storm" of history.[36] After Theo's death, when Marina has posed naked for him in his studio for the last time, Toni realises that his sitter and muse is also about to be carried away from him by this storm of time:

> He looked at her. In a few minutes she would be gone, and the chair she was sitting in would be the chair she had sat in at this moment – how to capture the strange, beautiful, surprising, dangerous unreality of such a moment? Hold a person preciously within that moment against the rush of time? Hold oneself within the image of the other. (267)

The "rush of time" is another version of the storm that engulfs Klee's "Angelus Novus", and of the "powerful wind" that causes the running man to bend in Nada's portrait of her father (6). It is Miller's central theme of the ruin of time, captured in Ranna Station's "dribbling hourglass" of debris. It is this awareness of being-in-time, of being "within the image of the

---

35   Georges Didi-Huberman and Thomas Repensek, "The Index of the Absent Wound (Monograph on a Stain)", *October* 29 (Summer 1984): 63–81.
36   Walter Benjamin, "On the Concept of History", in *Illuminations: Essays and Reflections* (1968; New York: Schocken, 2007), 257.

other", that Toni captures in his art, and which Miller calls "vulnerability" – vulnerability to the other, to time, to death.

The stunning climax of the novel is Toni's dual confrontation with his wife, Teresa, with her much more prosaic understanding of his art, and his muse, Marina. Toni's relationship with Marina is part of his professional life as an artist, but it is also erotically charged and therefore deeply affects his personal life. As Theo warns shortly before he dies, "We always confuse life and art in the end" (242). Miller's achievement is to leave these ambiguities between art and life in full play. For Teresa, of course, there is no such ambiguity. In a climactic scene, she disturbs Toni and Marina in her own domain, her kitchen, just as they are about to end their relationship after the completion of *The Nymphe*, his painting of Marina naked on the chaise. This painting is Toni's own considered essay in the genre of the nude, and like the Sickerts to which Miller refers in *The Sitters*, it is a distinctively *modern* nude:

> Marina lying naked on her stomach on the cane chaise . . . a woman alone in the privacy of her thoughts. Not a girl. Not a young woman. Not a pale odalisque to tease the eye of the voyeur, but an older woman, naked and alone; an artist, vulnerable and preoccupied with the complexities of her own creativity and anxieties, the uncertainties of her life. (263)

For Toni, this canvas both is and is not Marina. It is in one sense another of his "fictions", the solution to another "problem" in art, but as Theo warns, art's power of representation is always double edged. Teresa responds to the canvas with an act of violence, as if it really were Marina, effectively seeking to murder the woman she sees, not inaccurately, as her husband's lover:

> Teresa gave a strangled cry and snatched the painting from the easel, driving it to the floor and dropping on it with one knee, as if she expected to punch through the canvas . . . There was the delicate aroma of cedar as the stretcher splintered, the sharp crack of the fine-grained wood opening up under Teresa's weight. But the close weave of the linen resisted her. Teresa was panting and letting out moans, wrestling with the canvas as if she had a grip on the flesh-and-blood Marina at last, making contact with her demon. (277)

The crack of the cedar frame is an echo of another act of violence Toni holds in his memory from the day his brother Roy accidentally killed a man who was tormenting their father, the man's head cracking on the concrete like a piece of cedar (284). Teresa's very physical response to the art object, which is in some ways naïve, confuses the representation with its subject, but it is no less valid than Toni's understanding.

In a remarkable scene, Miller now goes on to suggest that even Teresa's apparently naïve investment of passion in the portrait's seemingly "real" subject allows it to be reinterpreted in a valid way. By falling upon it and physically disrupting its finished but uncured surface, Teresa in effect re-paints Toni's portrait of Marina, becoming another of his artistic collaborators. This turns the portrait once more into a site of entanglement where more than one story is inscribed. The canvas is opened up again as a space where three lives converge, as Teresa's sexual jealousy, her self-confessed "hatred" for her rival, is painted into the canvas: "[Toni] wrestled her to the floor, ripping her arm up behind her back and forcing her face into the twisted image of naked Marina, the wet oil paint smearing onto her hair and her suit jacket, the close familiar stench of it in his nostrils" (278).

The newly collaborative artwork now produced by Toni/Marina/Teresa is another intervention in the long history of the nude, which in *The Sitters* and *Prochownik's Dream* Miller traces from Manet through Bonnard and Sickert to its logical conclusion in Francis Bacon:

> The paint was slewed and creamed across Marina's likeness, streaked across her features and twisted into a vivid carmine and yellow candy spiral down her back. The thing she was lying on no longer resembled a genteel chaise longue from leisurely afternoons of tea and toast in the conservatory at Plovers, but appeared to be some kind of shiny metallic contraption, a trolley, its purpose institutional and sinister. The woman on the trolley might have been eviscerated through the back, her organs brutally exposed to a hard clear light without cast shadows. It was an image from the internal narrative. Was she on the butcher's slab? Or in the mortuary? Perhaps interrogators had finished with her? Was that her story? Maybe they had thrown her out of a building, or had torn her apart in a frenzy of senseless cruelty . . . the painting offered no clue. (281–2)

Together, *The Sitters* and *Prochownik's Dream* constitute a remarkable meditation on the historical transformation of figurative painting and the nude from Manet through Sickert to Bacon. The paint "slewed and creamed" across the subject's face by a palette knife, the trolley, the butcher's slab, and the surgical exposure of organs – these are the signature techniques and motifs of Bacon's simultaneous fidelity to and radical interrogation of the great nineteenth-century tradition of figurative painting.[37] The account of Teresa's "collaboration", in which she inscribes her own hatred on to the erotic portrait, is confirmation of Bacon's confronting vision, in which the banality of modern evil and the inglorious body are laid bare in the "hard clear light". When Teresa attacks Toni and his painting, we are reminded, as Adrian Caesar observes, "of all the previous comparisons of . . . the creative process to war, violence and imprisonment . . . We see the capacity for ordinary, decent human beings to be moved to murderous rage . . . we are exposed to the disturbing paradox that love can find expression through violence".[38] In *The Nymphe*, Manet's *chaise* has given way to Sickert's iron bed, which in turn gives way to Bacon's "shiny metallic contraption", his gurneys and butcher's slabs. This is indeed an image of art as "the internal narrative" of modern life, and Toni is correct to recognise its power and the validity of his wife's collaboration. When Marina asks him whether the painting has been damaged he responds, "It's changed. I'm not rejecting the change" (288). This acceptance of her contribution comes not only from Toni, with his artist's eye, but from his brother Roy, a convicted murderer, who knows that the impulse to kill, like art itself, is another form of rapture, of being carried out of the self by one's passion for the other: "You can never tell what people will do when they're hurting badly enough", he tells Toni; "They step out of themselves" (285).

Miller's implicit comparison between "Prochownik", the artist that Toni Powlett has become, and Francis Bacon, whose own art epitomised the violence of the 1930s and 1940s, is again relevant when Toni wonders what his father, who was a Holocaust survivor, might think of what he has become and what he has painted. On the one hand, Toni re-

---

37 Anthony Bond, ed., *Francis Bacon: Five Decades* (Sydney: Art Gallery of New South Wales, 2012).
38 Caesar, "An Artist in the Family", 112.

flects that "He would have been shocked and saddened beyond words and must surely have seen it as a failure in his son to deal with the demands of art in a decent way." But he also realises that "he may even have found in these events an echo of the violence of his own young life. Seeing the violence breaking in upon them again" (293). The problem confronting the person who has been subject to such rapture, whether they be a murderer, an adulterer, or an artist, is whether they can survive that transformation: "He had a growing dread that he had stepped over the line like his brother and there would be no going back to being the person he had been before this. A feeling of having slipped over the edge into something else" (286–7). That is the problem that Toni Prochownik, or, more accurately, Toni Powlett, faces at the end of *Prochownik's Dream*.

Toni's artistic and sexual collaboration with Marina Golding is effectively at an end. Fortunately for him, it is underwritten, as Charles Green suggests is essential for enduring creativity, by another kind of contract: Teresa's everyday commitment to their marriage and family. In the final pages of the novel his own feeling of "slipping over the edge into something else" is arrested by her letter, and by her promise to return to their shared life.

7
The Central Queensland Novels: *Landscape of Farewell*

Reflecting on the origin of the name Zigzag Station in *Journey to the Stone Country*, Alex Miller recalls that like "the zigzag of the whole journey to the stone country", it reminded him of a cartoon he once saw, in which a man is buying petrol: "the servo man filling his car is pointing to a church steeple which can be seen through a complicated crisscross of over-passes and flyways and is saying, 'You can't get there from here' ".[1] This is a deceptively simple account of the intricate structure of *Journey to the Stone Country*, whose characters are carried towards and away from each other in a series of tentative movements along intersecting though utterly different lines of culture and history. In the second of the Central Queensland novels, *Landscape of Farewell*, the relations between time and space are again governed by the rhetorical figure of chiasmus. The narrative present is in Hamburg in 2005, as Max Otto writes the book that we are reading, but the temporal design, as Brigid Rooney observes, "only *seems* linear and conventional". Max immediately goes back to the time of his bereavement in the autumn of 2004, his valedictory lecture, and his meeting with Vita McLelland, which leads to his visit to Mount Nebo in Central Queensland, where the colonial present is haunted not just by the colonial past, but by the modern German past. Max's narrative "takes us through a succession of landscapes in a journey that, once again, provides the novel's chronological scaffold. Yet this linearity is complicated by an extraordinary set of temporal and intersubjective crossings."[2] Miller's distinctive spatialisation of history is represented emblematically by the novel's four parts or "stations", which describe both a linear journey through time and space, and the closing of a circle: "Hamburg, Autumn 2004", "Mount Nebo", "Expedition Range", "Schluterstrasse". The sense of fable and allegory breaking through the apparently realistic surface is gently underlined by Max's ironic allusion when he arrives at Dougald's property to Moses' ascent of Mount Nebo to view the land of Israel (Deuteronomy 34): "despite its name, I could see no mountain from the summit of which I might expect to catch a glimpse of the Promised Land before I died".[3]

---

1 Alex Miller to Robert Dixon, 5 February 2014.
2 Brigid Rooney, "The Ruin of Time and the Temporality of Belonging", in *The Novels of Alex Miller: An Introduction*, ed. Robert Dixon (Sydney: Allen & Unwin, 2012), 210.
3 Alex Miller, *Landscape of Farewell* (Sydney: Allen & Unwin, 2007), 65. All subsequent references are to this edition and appear in parentheses in the text.

The design of the Central Queensland novels might also be compared to that of Daniel Libeskind's Jewish Museum Berlin, which was completed in the late 1990s and opened to the public in 2001. Its famous "zigzag" façade, representing a broken Star of David, spatialises Jewish history. Libeskind has described it as "an irrational and invisible matrix" comprising two principal lines: a straight line that is intersected and broken into fragments or "voids" by a winding or "tortuous" line. Underground, the three tunnels that define the footprint of Libeskind's Museum, intersecting at its centre, represent the three temporal axes of German Jewish history: the "Axis of Continuity", the "Axis of Emigration", and the "Axis of the Holocaust".[4] By analogy, Ranna Station in *Journey to the Stone Country* is a point of intersection between the crossed lines of settler and indigenous histories whose present and future are void, while the ruins of Verbena Station and the playgrounds of the old people are similar points of intersection that might be seen as ambiguous spaces of either termination or becoming.

Landscape of Farewell had its genesis in the period of the *Bringing Them Home* report and the subsequent controversy in Australia over the applicability of the term "genocide". On 28 May 1997, the Human Rights and Equal Opportunity Commission (HREOC) tabled its report on the Stolen Generations, *Bringing Them Home: Report of the National Inquiry into the Separation of Aboriginal and Torres Strait Island Children from Their Families*. The committee of inquiry, chaired by former Australian High Court Justice Ronald Wilson, found that under various United Nations definitions and resolutions, the practice of forcible child removal between 1910 and 1970, in which an estimated 20,000 to 50,000 Aboriginal children were "removed" from their families, constituted "genocide".[5]

A second major contribution to the debate was the opening of the National Museum of Australia for the Centenary of Federation in Canberra in 2001, when it was revealed that Howard Raggatt's design cites the zigzag footprint of Libeskind's Jewish Museum Berlin. Its own "zigzag" section houses displays relating to Indigenous Australia and the colonial frontier. Neil Levi has described this architectural citation as a "massive structural reminder that there is no such thing as an 'exclusively Australian story' ".[6] What seemed especially to incite conservative reaction in the intense debate that erupted in the public sphere was not so much the comparison of child removal to the Nazi genocide *per se*, as the apparent implication that the perpetrators of child removal in Australia were morally equivalent to Nazis.[7] Keith Windschuttle condemned the zigzag design for "signifying that the Aborigines suffered the equivalent of the Holocaust".[8] Christopher Pearson claimed to have been "mortified" by the citation, arguing that "There is no sensible comparison between post-contact Australian history and Hitler's slaughter of 6 million Jews, whose sufferings it demeans".[9] It was Inga Clendinnen's 2001 essay, "First Contact", however, that became "the paradigmatic objection to the term 'genocide' ". This was partly because of the authority of her earlier and well-regarded book *Reading the Holocaust* (1999), and also be-

---

4 Jewish Muesum Berlin, http://www.jmberlin.de/main/EN/homepage-EN.php.
5 Australian Human Rights Commission, "Bringing them Home Report", 1997, http://www.humanrights.gov.au/publications/bringing-them-home-report-1997.
6 Neil Levi, " 'No Sensible Comparison?' The Place of the Holocaust in Australia's History Wars", *History & Memory* 19, no. 1 (Spring/Summer 2007): 131–2.
7 Levi, "No Sensible Comparison?" 137.
8 Keith Windschuttle, "How Not to Run a Museum: People's History at the Postmodern Museum", *Quadrant* 45, no. 9 (September 2001): 11.
9 Christopher Pearson, "Designs on History Derided", *The Australian*, 23 April 2001, 20.

cause of her reputation as a left-liberal author.[10] "When I see the word 'genocide'", she had written, "I still see Gypsies and Jews being herded into trains, into pits, into ravines, and behind them the shadowy figures of Armenian women and children being marched into the desert by armed men."[11] In an astute analysis of this passage, Levi suggests that the first question one might ask in response to it is, "why sixty years of separating children from their families under the influence of eugenic precepts does not conjure up" the term "genocide?"[12]

Surprisingly, perhaps, Miller's initial focus in *Landscape of Farewell* is not on this pressingly familiar Australia context but on Germany, the point of transnational comparison, and on the long shadow cast the by Nazi genocide. Born in 1936 (the year of Miller's own birth), Max Otto is a German professor of history who experiences "guilt-by-association" with the Nazi legacy. Intending to commit suicide immediately after giving a lecture to mark his retirement, he is invited to Australia by Vita McLelland, an Indigenous academic from the University of Sydney. Like Annabelle Beck at the beginning of *Journey to the Stone Country*, Max has recently lost his spouse and contemplates his own image in the mirror at a fixed point in space and time: she in Melbourne in 1995, he in Hamburg in 2004. Seeing there the ruin of his younger self, he offers the same Sebaldian image of time as collapsing debris in which the self is caught up: he anticipates "a further shift in the cataclysm of my last days, a settling of the debris of my life, which had collapsed around me" (10). Like Annabelle, however, Max is no longer identical with that image: he is viewing himself in Hamburg in 2004 from the point of view of a future self he is already in the process of becoming.

Miller locates Max Otto's moral and intellectual crisis in a distinctive and immediately recognisable period of modern German history. Dirk Moses divides it into three phases: Germany's own *Historikerstreit* of the mid to late 1980s; the so-called Goldhagen debate a decade later; and debates surrounding the design of Libeskind's Jewish Museum Berlin.[13] On the night of Winifred's death, Max was reading "a young Harvard professor's *New History of the German People*" (8). This is an allusion to Steven Ozment's *A Mighty Fortress: A New History of the German People* (2005), which was criticised for arguing that modern Germany should allow itself to resume a "normal nationhood" while the book's own narrative remains "in thrall to the mesmerizing power of the Third Reich".[14] Miller is also alluding to the controversy that followed the publication of Daniel J. Goldhagen's *Hitler's Willing Executioners* in 1999. In struggling to understand his father's involvement in the Holocaust, Max is entangled in the same philosophical conundrum of structure versus agency, or functionalism versus intentionalism, that was central to the Goldhagen debate:[15] he is aware that "it is never simply a matter of deciding to do something . . . Certain other forces, complementary to our decision to act, must arise and range themselves along-

---

10 Levi, "No Sensible Comparison?" 140.
11 Inga Clendinnen, "First Contact", *Australian's Review of Books*, May 2001, 7.
12 Levi, "No Sensible Comparison?" 141–2.
13 A. Dirk Moses, "Coming to Terms with Genocidal Pasts in Comparative Perspective: Germany and Australia", *Aboriginal History* 25 (2001): 91–115.
14 Steve Crawshaw, "Trying Not to Mention the Third Reich – But Doing It Constantly", review of Steven Ozment, *A Mighty Fortress: A New History of the German People* (2005), *Independent*, 2 January 2006. See also Thomas A. Brady, "Fortress Under Siege: A New German History", *Central European History* 39, no. 1 (2006): 107–22.
15 A. Dirk Moses, "Structure and Agency in the Holocaust: Daniel J. Goldhagen and his Critics", *History and Theory* 37, no. 2 (1998): 194–219.

side us or, despite our will and determination, we achieve nothing" (16). This is of course a recurring preoccupation for Miller, here serving to explain Max's "paralysing sense of guilt-by-association" with the crimes of his father's generation (12), but also Vita's gift of rapture, for "However great our resolve, we never do anything alone" (16).

Ronald A. Sharp suggests that the relations between Max and Vita, and Max and Dougald, constitute "an elaborate network of gift exchange". The gift is "Miller's central trope ... for the defining act of friendship and the defining act of artistic creation".[16] Following Lewis Hyde's *The Gift* (1983),[17] Sharp distinguishes between "gift exchange" and "commodity exchange", a key feature of the gift being that it must be kept in circulation – in Vita's words, this is what the recipient "owes" to the giver, to keep the gift alive, to keep it moving. The gifts in this network of exchange include Vita's gift of life to Max, and Dougald's gifts of hospitality, the story of Gnapun the warrior, and their final journey to his heartland in the Expedition Range, where they witness together the figure of death in Gnapun's cave. Yet from the beginning, Vita's gift of life is also a difficult challenge to Max.

A well-educated and cultivated German, Max is oppressed by the apparent collapse of European civilisation represented by the Nazi era. He refers to the great German literary scholars Ernst Robert Curtius and Eric Auerbach as "fallen heroes ... whose books in my youth had seemed destined to stand forever as imperishable landmarks in the epic story of a Europe that had, since then, ceased to exist" (21–2). His valedictory lecture on "The Persistence of the Phenomenon of Massacre in Human Society from the Earliest Times to the Present", with its framing quotations from Homer, might be criticised for dehistoricising the Nazi Holocaust. But like the Spiess diaries in *The Ancestor Game*, this is Max's paper, not Miller's novel, and Max has a long journey ahead of him before he returns to this theme in "Massacre", the story he later writes for Dougald at Mount Nebo. It was Max's "guilt-by-association" that prevented him as a young scholar from exploring the historical specificity of the Nazi Holocaust, retreating, instead – like Steven Ozment, who is also a Medieval and Reformation scholar – to the safety of the German Middle Ages. Max admits that his setting aside of the problem of the Holocaust has remained "an unexamined silence throughout my life" (12), an ironic allusion on Miller's part to the source of the novel's epigraph, George Steiner's *Errata: An Examined Life* (1997). Far from Miller approving Max's dehistoricising of "the phenomenon of massacre", the Homeric quotation can be seen to perform precisely that sublimation of historically specific "loss" into the mythical condition of "absence" that, according to Dominick LaCapra, blocks the successful working through of trauma and induces a paralysing melancholia, both for individuals and for nations.[18] In one of the novel's many instances of cultural intersection, there is an echo of Stanner's phrase, "the great Australian silence", which had begun to be broken by the 1980s, in Max's confession to Vita that his generation of Germans "kept the faith of our silence to the end" (48). It is just for this reason that Vita criticises him in public: "How can this man presume to speak of massacre ... and not speak of my people" (15). Her point is that Max deals in abstractions: he has not spoken of his own people either. Her challenge to him is that he must break the "silence" that prevented him as a young German historian from investigating the causes of the Nazi genocide (49).

---

16 Ronald A. Sharp, "More Than Just Mates", *The Australian*, 1 July 2009: 3–4, http://www.news.com.au/news/more-than-just-mates/story-fna7dq6e-1225744152559.
17 Lewis Hyde, *The Gift: Imagination and the Erotic Life of Property* (New York: Random House: 1983).
18 Dominick LaCapra, "Trauma, Absence, Loss", *Critical Inquiry* 25, no. 4 (Summer 1999): 696–727.

It is in this way – and despite the apparent focus on Germany in the opening pages of *Landscape of Farewell* – that Miller so unexpectedly confronts his readers with the very Australian problem of comparing genocides. The novel's first readers, after all, were primarily Australian, so that the subject of the Nazi Holocaust is, for them at least, a cross-cultural refraction of the Aboriginal genocide. As we have seen, Clendinnen's repudiation of the Nazi comparison quickly became canonical. Levi points out, however, that while many American scholars of the Holocaust retained an exceptionalist stance, a number of the most prominent contributors to the debate in Australia, such as Tony Barta, Raimond Gaita, Simone Gigliotti, A. Dirk Moses, Colin Tatz, and Levi himself, defended the value of comparative studies that relate the question of genocide in Australia to the Holocaust.[19] In his own early response to the *Bringing Them Home Report*, Miller's friend, the philosopher Raimond Gaita, conceded that the Nazi Holocaust and the Aboriginal genocide were not equivalent, but insisted that they were comparable. He argued further that the methodology of comparison is important to establishing ethical benchmarks, and to understanding the differences as well as the similarities between any two historical instances of genocide. Gaita, in other words, wanted the Holocaust to be seen not as "one crime amongst other crimes", but as "one which *places* other crimes".[20] This same balance between similarity and difference, he went on to point out, is also necessary for literature to be "great": it must be grounded in the particulars of its own language and historical moment, while also engaging in a significant dialogue with other literatures, other cultures and other epochs. Great literature has "universality", it "speaks to experiences which all human beings share", but it does so "only as translated from one natural language into another". The paradox of great literature is that while its subject matter is "universal", it arises *in medias res*, "in the midst of things".[21] Max Otto's conference paper on the persistence of massacre is not the book that he will later write after he has been to Australia – the book that we are reading now. If we apply to it Gaita's criteria for greatness and ethical insight we can see that it was neither "great" nor insightful because it was not written in "the midst of things", but rather in denial. It was about absence rather than loss and was therefore melancholic. Vita's injunction is essentially comparative: to understand *his* trauma in context, Max must "place" it in relation to hers.

Max's journey to Australia and his friendship with Vita's uncle, Dougald Gnapun, create the means of cross-cultural comparison by which he can begin to work through his own guilt-by-association with the Nazi genocide. It is a friendship that is truly cross-cultural, breaking down the barriers of national exceptionalism. As Sharp observes, despite Dougald's persistent references to Max as his "old mate", the relationship is one of friendship, not mateship, which in Australia has always been "more about national identity".[22] From the perspective of Miller's first readers in Australia in 2007, this must have seemed an outrageous distraction from the national context, the Australian reception of the *Bringing Them Home* report, and the struggle for reconciliation. But as readers of Miller's novels we should now be used to detours: self-understanding is always routed through the other; it is always comparative. It may also appear presumptuous of Miller to assume that Indigenous Australians like Vita McLelland and Dougald Gnapun, while not

---

19   Levi, "No Sensible Comparison?" 129.
20   Raimond Gaita, "Remembering the Holocaust: Absolute Value and the Nature of Evil", *Quadrant* 39, no. 12, December 1995: 8. My italics.
21   Gaita, "Remembering the Holocaust", 9.
22   Sharp, "More Than Just Mates", 1.

yet finished with their own sorry business, should be willing and generous enough to offer the gift of friendship that will allow someone from another culture to heal his own historical trauma. Dougald's hospitality to Max is an extraordinary and moving tribute by Miller to the grace and generosity of his own Indigenous friends and collaborators, Anita Heiss, Frank Budby and Col McLennan.

During the late 1990s and early 2000s in Australia, there was therefore a great deal of anxiety about the ethics of comparing the Aboriginal genocide with the Nazi Holocaust. What is clear now in looking back at the work of those critics and historians who spoke of the value of comparison is how much they felt obliged to defend, explain and qualify their methodology. In initially adopting a German-centred perspective, Miller's novel cuts through these hesitations by grasping the value of comparison not just for Indigenous Australians but also for contemporary German readers, who may have something to learn from the Australian case. While Levi, Moses and other historians argued that Australians have much to learn from the German experience, Miller's novel suggests that the world has much to learn from Australia's colonial history. This is to adopt a transnational, comparative or cosmopolitan perspective on *national* histories. As Graham Huggan argues, such "transnational connections" are valuable because they link "racial discrimination of all kinds to the global modernities within which they are co-implicated – connections that, avoiding the twin temptations of sacralising and banalising the Holocaust, still recognize its authority as a moral source for combating racisms of both the present and the past".[23] Miller's comparative approach avoids these twin temptations, and in granting the roles of host to his Indigenous Australian characters and guest to the German professor, his novel presciently confers "moral authority" on the history of the Stolen Generations as a force for combating racisms of both past and present, both in Australia and elsewhere.

Max Otto suffers from what Miriam Hirsch calls perpetrator trauma and postmemory: that is to say, the transfer of a primary trauma to the second generation.[24] Max provides his own gloss on this concept when he realises that "one lifetime is not long enough to forget" (227). Discussing these ideas in relation to Markus Zusak's novel, *The Book Thief* (2005), which has a number of similarities with *Landscape of Farewell*, Huggan argues that perpetrator trauma blocks the past to which it seeks access, seeking refuge instead in the supplementarity of postmemory, "that surfeit of stories, voices and images that tries – and inevitably fails – to compensate for lack of direct access to the past".[25] Postmemory is a condition of belatedness characterised by the impossibility of access to the original experience. Its characteristic form of expression is the post-Holocaust elegy. Shirley Walker has described the Central Queensland novels as "deeply elegiac", their subtext being "the passing of all historical eras"; Ranna Station and the sacred stone grounds are "two monuments to lost civilizations".[26] By seeking refuge in supplementarity, the post-Holocaust elegy can thus be seen as "a study in *intertextuality* that, while always potentially therapeutic, balances the imaginative refashionings provided by creative writing against an agonized knowledge of the irretrievability of the past. In *The Book Thief*, this intertextu-

---

23 Graham Huggan, "Nazis, the Holocaust, and Australia's History Wars" (2010), 7, http://www.nla.gov.au/openpublish/index.php/australian-studies/article/viewFile/1751/2126.
24 Marianne Hirsch, *Family Frames: Photography, Narrative, Postmemory* (Cambridge, Mass.: Harvard University Press, 1997).
25 Huggan, "Nazis", 9.
26 Shirley Walker, "The Frontier Wars: History and Fiction in *Journey to the Stone Country* and *Landscape of Farewell*", in *The Novels of Alex Miller*, 161.

ality is explicitly thematised in the "benign theft" of stealing and rewriting others' stories about the past".[27] Max also resorts to the supplementarity of other people's stories as a way of filling the void of his own trauma, but he does not have to steal them. In an act of intertextual hospitality that recalls Max Blatt's foundational gift of story to Miller, Dougald gives to Max two texts that have a therapeutic effect: the German explorer Ludwig Leichhardt's journal of exile and the story of Gnapun the warrior.

Postmemory is defined by *temporal* distance, by the insurmountable gap between primary experiences and their secondary recall. But it is also defined by *spatial* distance. In both *Landscape of Farewell* and *The Book Thief*, "the site of storytelling (Australia) is thus irreparably split from the site of remembrance (Germany), though the text still attempts to heal this rift by means of its multiple re-doublings, narrative strategies by which recalled experiences are lived through in 'real time' in the pages of the text".[28] These supplementary re-doublings are also a means of coming to terms with the notorious unrepresentability of the Holocaust as primary scene.[29] In addition, they confirm the value of comparing limit events in so far as they allow us to step outside the national frame, which is fundamental to Miller's project as a novelist. Following Andreas Huyssen, Levi argues that "Holocaust memory can enable a self-critical approach to a nation's history", and that far from always acting as a screen memory, as Bain Attwood suggests[30] – that is, remembering one thing only at the cost of another – it can also "energise some discourses of traumatic memory". Levi argues:

> rejecting Holocaust memory in favour of ... the distinctiveness ... of one's 'own' history can itself indicate a kind of blindness, can mark a form of repression or defense against recognizing the large historical processes, such as colonization and the expulsion or elimination of alien or native populations, involved in the formation of modern nation-states of which one's own history is part.[31]

Similarly, Gigliotti defends comparison as a methodology that can reveal the "barbarism of modernity".[32] As Levi puts it, "One's own history is never entirely one's own."[33]

Max Otto's paralysis arises from the intellectual timidity that becomes possible when a national history is shielded from transnational interrogation. As a young scholar, he had been troubled by the persistence of massacre in human society, but his curiosity as an historian was "paralysed" by "guilt-by-association" with the crimes of his father's generation (12). This is the modern German equivalent of Stanner's "great Australian silence". In his own professional life he has relegated his youthful inquiries to a carton on top of his bookshelves, where they have mouldered for thirty years (6). Even in returning to these "cold ashes" for his final lecture, he begins with the quotation from Homer about the wrath of Agamemnon, a rhetorical convention that de-historicises the Nazi genocide and translates

---

27 Huggan, "Nazis", 10.
28 Huggan, "Nazis", 11.
29 Mark Rothberg, *Traumatic Realism: The Demands of Holocaust Representation* (Minneapolis: University of Minnesota Press, 2000).
30 Bain Attwood, *Telling the Truth about Aboriginal History* (Sydney: Allen & Unwin, 2005), 104.
31 Levi, "No Sensible Comparison?", 127.
32 Simone Gigliotti, "Unspeakable Pasts as Limit Events: The Holocaust, Genocide, and the Stolen Generations", *Australian Journal of Politics and History* 49, no. 2 (2003): 166.
33 Levi, "No Sensible Comparison?", 127.

what might otherwise have been a more searching historical and ethical inquiry into the polite domain of *belles lettres*.

The image of the cardboard carton suggests the psychological mechanism Nicolas Abraham and Mária Török call encryption, in which traumatic memory is locked away rather than dealt with by mourning and working through, which results in paralysing melancholia, and a ghostly leaking through of traumatic memory and affect into the present.[34] Images of encryption recur in Max's efforts to explain the German "silence": "the war had trapped my generation in an iron cage of remorse and silence" (41); Max is caught up in "the awful dragging void of melancholy" (27). Yet from the moment of his meeting with Vita and her challenge that he should investigate the primary scene of the German silence, images begin to leak through, like the music from the neighbouring apartment in Hamburg (47). From this time, his encryption of the Holocaust is generative of postmemory, with its proliferation of doublings and overdeterminations. Max's move in time and space to Queensland sparks a series of supplementary postmemories, dreams and other texts through which he attempts to gain access to the primary scene of the Nazi genocide. This is why it was essential that *Landscape of Farewell* be narrated in the first person by Max Otto, so that his descriptions of scenes in Queensland can be overdetermined by the re-doubling effects of postmemory.

Dougald's fibro-cement house at Mount Nebo is a reminder of the elegiac quality of the novel, the rusting bulldozers in the yard suggesting "the relentless cycles of change and decay"[35] experienced by both settlers and Aboriginal people. The house stands in a landscape of ruins inhabited by misplaced, extinct, exiled and feral species. Yet it is characteristic of Aboriginal generosity that the house is also the primary scene of Dougald's hospitality: Dougald smiles in welcome, picks up Max's suitcase and carries it into the house (66); he sets down a plate of eggs and bacon on the kitchen table, a recurring scene of hospitality in Miller's novels, and Max is "sensitive of my status as a newly arrived guest" (71). Max's descriptions of this primary scene are overdetermined by locations from the German past that are scenes of barbarous inhospitality, specifically of his uncle's farm, but less distinctly of a camp: "the small cell" of his room (67); the toilet in its narrow shed, constructed of timber slabs (68); the wolf-like dogs; the wire perimeter fence between the house and the ravine of the Nebo River. Despite Dougald's welcome, Max "had not felt so abandoned to strangeness" since the day his mother had left him at his uncle's farm" (69). His status as a welcome guest causes him to remember his own inhospitality to the gypsy girl in 1943 who, in a hazel copse at the edge of the farm, had asked him for bread on the very day that her family was murdered by the Nazis (75). Prompted by Dougald's hospitality, he now regrets not having given her food and shelter, and experiences remorse. Vita had said to him in Hamburg, "It's not a sin to have regrets, Max. It's only a sin to deny having them so we don't have to do anything about them" (49). Like Annabelle's oblique intimations of frontier violence at Burranbah, where she senses an affinity with the camp, this is still an early stage in Max's working through of Germany's postwar legacy, and he has not yet become fully conscious of the link between the German and Australian silences. From the outset, however, Miller suggests that there can never be a satisfactory working through. Rather, it is a matter of constant, vigilant attention to the promptings of post-

---

[34] Nicolas Abraham and Mária Török, *The Wolf Man's Magic Word: A Cryptonymy* (Minneapolis: University of Minnesota Press, 1986).
[35] Walker, "The Frontier Wars", 164.

memory and remorse; of attending to the meanings of the silence: "No matter how much we say about these things, no matter how truthful we are, no matter how ruthlessly we expose the terrible detail of those events, there will always remain something we cannot say... something left in the silence" (49).

It is for this reason that Max's first experience of postmemory upon arrival at Mount Nebo is immediately repeated during his visit to the old slab cottage on Dougald's property. The cottage and the objects inside it are obliquely suggestive of the Holocaust. These objects include old tools from Max's uncle's period – "I well understood their utility" (91); "steel-jawed rabbit traps" hanging "by twisted lengths of wire" (91), suggestive of torture; a camp oven, suggestive of the gas chambers; and translucent rabbit skins, which suggest industrially processed human remains, such as the warehouses full of skin and hair photographed at Auschwitz. The smell of the hut causes Max to recall "the smell of human anxiety, rancid and sharp" (93).

These overdetermined images are Max's interpretation of what his father may have seen, but they are located in Queensland rather than in Germany, and in the present rather than the past. Given the logic of postmemory, it is likely that such images would not have come to him without the provocation of temporal and spatial displacement caused by his visit to Australia – that it is to say, the vision is an artefact of transnational memory; it is the potentially therapeutic consequence of Vita and Dougald's gift of hospitality. But in a further re-doubling, the scene is also primary evidence of the colonial frontier itself, and therefore of the "barbarism of modernity". It demonstrates what Tony Barta has called the "linked histories" of Germany and colonial Queensland. Eugenics and colonialism, Barta argues, were the links between nineteenth-century Australia and twentieth-century Germany: "within the modern history in which both countries achieved national unity, Germany proceeded from eugenic preoccupations to radical genocide, while Australia progressed from genocide to eugenics".[36] 1936, the year of both Max Otto's and Alex Miller's births, is the approximate point of intersection between these two histories that moved in opposite directions, confirming Rooney's suggestion that chiasmus is the central rhetorical figure in *Landscape of Farewell*.

But this scene is also evidence of a further displacement of which Max is not yet aware, and it is embedded in the central narrative of one of those crossed national histories. Dougald's slab cottage, which appears to be the spatial point of a temporal intersection between Max's German legacy of genocide and Dougald's legacy as an Indigenous Australian, is not Dougald's country after all, any more than it is Max's. "This is not my country" (117), Dougald explains, "Nothing's ever going to work out up this way" (120). A member of the Stolen Generations, Dougald has been displaced from his own country, which lies in the Expedition Range. Dougald's house sparks Max's postmemory of the Holocaust because Dougald is himself in exile and living in a camp. The colonial frontier is a site of endemic, chronic dislocation, and this is reflected in the presence of the rabbit traps and rabbit skins. Rabbits are not native to Australia, but one of many exotic species brought from Europe in the nineteenth century and acclimatised in the Australian colonies, often for the purpose of blood sports. Like the Jew in Nazi ideology, the rabbit in Australia came to be regarded as vermin, and in the early twentieth century it was subject to a systematic campaign of extermination: the traps are evidence of one phase of that campaign. Gaita

---

36   Tony Barta, "Discourses of Genocide in Germany and Australia: A Linked History", *Aboriginal History* 25 (2001): 50.

observes that "the Jews were murdered as though they were vermin".[37] All of the animals in Dougald's menagerie – rabbits, hens, dogs and the goat – are introduced species, displaced from their countries of origin, like Dougald himself. Far from being inadvertently excluded from Miller's account of modernity, as David Brooks argues in his ecocritical reading of the novel,[38] the sacrifice of animals is therefore central to Miller's comparative methodology, in which the genocidal treatment of animals is given a status equivalent to human suffering and is utterly central to the experience of imaginative sympathy with others.

Max's uncanny experience at the hut inspires him to write in his journal a long recollection of his visit to his uncle's farm during the war, when his uncle told him that his father was not at the front, but "engaged on secret work" (101). That revelation had caused a further series of doublings that remain unresolved: "to this day I possess two unreconciled histories of my father" (103). These doubts about his father's "decency" – an echo of Les Marra's challenge to the Beck family's whiteness in *Journey to the Stone Country* – remain encrypted in silence, leaving a doubled legacy of two fathers and two histories that Max can never reconcile, leading him to imagine the nightmare image of a hole in the wall of his bedroom, where one reality is doubled by another, "a place of death, secrets, war and imprisonment" (103–4). Like the rubbish stuffed down the hole in the floor of Panya's cottage, this is the debris of history that has entrapped and "moved" him since childhood, so that now, as an old man, he still asks, "which of my father's histories would I become?" (107).

For both Max and Dougald, Mount Nebo stimulates comparative or cosmopolitan memory because it is a site of multiple doublings and dislocations that reveal the ubiquitous barbarism of modernity, even as the evidence of that barbarism is relocated in place and time. It is only through the act of comparison, only by imaginatively inhabiting someone else's trauma, that Max is given an oblique glimpse of the originary events to which those at Mount Nebo are supplementary. The therapeutic experience of inhabiting someone else's trauma is precisely what LaCapra means by "empathetic unsettlement", "a kind of virtual experience through which one puts oneself in the other's position while recognizing the difference of that position and hence not taking the other's place".[39] It is also similar to participating in the rituals of sacrifice that lie at the heart of both Jewish and Christian mythologies: its narrative archetypes are, respectively, Abraham's sacrifice of Isaac and the Crucifixion of Christ. It is therefore appropriate that Max's disturbing visit to the slab cottage is closely followed by his accidental killing of Dougald and Vita's goat, a feral species in Australia and an archetypal symbol of sacrifice. In contrast to Max's uncharitable refusal of hospitality to the gypsy girl, and even in the place of his own exile, Dougald has extended his hospitality to Max, who is now himself a kind of gypsy. But one of the laws of hospitality, as we have seen in August Spiess' behaviour in Hangzhou, is that it must be offered despite the guest's potential to bring destruction upon the house into which he is welcomed.[40]

---

37 Raimond Gaita, "Trusting the Words: Reflections on *Landscape of Farewell*", in *The Novels of Alex Miller*, 222.
38 David Brooks, "Dougald's Goat: Alex Miller and the Species Barrier", in *The Novels of Alex Miller*, 187–200.
39 LaCapra, "Trauma, Absence, Loss", 722.
40 Judith Still, *Derrida and Hospitality: Theory and Practice* (Edinburgh: Edinburgh University Press, 2010), 72.

Max's failure to tether the goat leads to her death by hanging above the eroded ravine of the Nebo River. Shirley Walker describes it as a lesson in "unintended guilt, of careless complicity".[41] The scene of the death is another densely overdetermined image: "The ground fell away abruptly at our feet... a dangerous and precipitous place... The exposed tree roots formed the matrix of an elaborate trap. She was hanging by her tether rope... her tongue lolled from the side of her mouth, purple and swollen... her teeth glinting in the rictus of death" (114–5). The word "trap" alone indicates the dense constellation of meanings in this passage: it has already been used in the sense of a trap for animals and, by association, the entrapment and torture of the Jews, but also more generally in relation to the ruin of time, that "iron cage of remorse and silence" (40). Allegorically connected to the Biblical stories of Abraham's sacrifice of his son and the Crucifixion, the body hanging above the ravine also evokes photographic images of Nazi executions directly above burial pits – the "pits" and "ravines" of Clendinnen's nightmare vision – and accounts of "dispersals" on the Queensland frontier. Again, Miller's superficially transparent yet densely allusive style is *khoratic* in Derrida's sense, allowing his description of the dead goat to bear the burden of these multiple meanings, which run out from this point in the text like knotted threads – like Libeskind's "irrational and invisible matrix", or like a *mise-en-abyme* – into many other accounts of trauma, each one different but nonetheless comparable, in the historical experience and narratives of many cultures. As a *mise-en-abyme* – literally, a fall "into the abyss" – the ravine at Mount Nebo is another version of the cracks in the soil at Burranbah and the hole in the wall of Max's bedroom on his uncle's farm. An icon-like image with both mythical and historical resonances, it is a lesson in the methodology of comparative genocide, a surgical opening, as it were, between the time and space of the Queensland frontier and the time and space of other primary scenes in the barbarism of modernity.

It is an inevitable consequence of postmemory that Max's zigzag journey will return him to the scene of the goat's sacrifice. When Max tells Vita on the mobile phone that he has "accidentally caused the death" of her goat – the phrase is as evasive as any German confession of complicity in the Nazi genocide – he apologies at least four times, but Vita insists that he stop merely "saying" he is sorry (130) and give some concrete expression to his complex feelings of guilt, grief and remorse: "What was the point of apologizing if you weren't going to change your ways and make amends?" (132). As a token of this amends, she says, "I hope you gave her a decent burial" (131). Initially, Max tries to write about the day's events in his journal, but writing proves unsatisfactory, and he finds himself compelled to return to the ravine during the night, where the goat's body still hangs, suspended by its tether rope. The setting has a heightened, theatrical quality, making the events a near-mythical performance of abjection and humiliation that now more directly that ever suggests the liturgical implications of the stations of the cross. Walker describes Max's attempt to retrieve the goat as "a ritual act of atonement for the death".[42]

In Max's culture, the supreme ritual of atonement, witnessing the Crucifixion, is expressed in the liturgical form of the Passion, with its formal staging of the stations of the cross: significantly, the music leaking through from the neighbouring apartment in Hamburg was Bach's. I want therefore to approach this complex and deeply affecting scene in the novel through the distinction made by music historian John Butt between the "the-

---

41 Walker, "The Frontier Wars", 164.
42 Walker, "The Frontier Wars", 165.

atricality" of early opera and the "anti-theatricality" of the Passion. Opera encouraged a separation between the world of the audience and the "represented world", between the auditorium and the stage, with its proscenium arch: the purpose of arias in opera is to "fix" the presence of a specific character "within the represented world".[43] The Passion, by contrast, encouraged a radical interplay of identities between characters, performers and audience. This fluidity had a liturgical function in facilitating a complete identification between Biblical and historical times, between the members of the audience and Christ. This radical interchangeability of roles – we might call it a *mise-en-abyme* of subjectivity – is greatly facilitated when the voices of individual performers can be detected in ensemble. The singers "are sharing our reactions, as observers, while also bringing the past to presence", so that "the Passion story becomes real in our own time through the intermediary representation of these . . . singers".[44] In contrast to the "theatricality" of opera, Butt describes the Passion as an "anti-theatrical" form that is more akin to the "realism" of the novel, which encourages exchanges of identity between the real and represented worlds, and a "productive tension between pre-modern and modern elements".[45] Butt calls this "Bach's dialogue with modernity".[46]

In the earlier episode of the death of the goat, Miller had already begun to explore affinities between the form of modern, secular affect that LaCapra calls "empathetic unsettlement", and more traditional forms of affective engagement associated with myth, ritual and liturgy. Since *The Tivington Nott*, Miller's seemingly realistic novels have occasionally pushed the boundaries between realism and ritual or fable. Despite its superficial realism, Max's return to the ravine at night has elements of both the Crucifixion and the Deposition stories, in which Max Otto, in "reality" a modern, secular German, begins as a communicant or spectator only to exchange roles with the ritual's protagonist: the Jew, the Christ, or the sacrificial animal. That this series should also include Aboriginal victims of frontier 'dispersals' seems appropriate in light of Vita's injunction to Max that as an historian of massacres he should always be mindful of the example of her people, and as John Docker points out, animals have often been "a surrogate for the actual historical massacres of Australia's Indigenous peoples".[47] Miller's narrative operates on multiple levels – as myth, parable, and liturgy, but also as psychoanalytic cure. In the beginning, Max is framed by the doorway of Dougald's cottage and about to step out into the backyard, with its stage-like tree, which suggests a crucifix: "The great old tree hung in the frame of the doorway as if it were a theatre backdrop, its limbs black against the luminous sky" (136). Is this a realistic scene or is it theatre? And if it is theatre, is Max part of the audience or is he the protagonist – a pilgrim, perhaps, or a penitent? To adopt Butt's distinction, the episode is suspended, stylistically, between the "theatricality" of opera and the "anti-theatricality" or novel-like "realism" of the Passion. In so far as Max's role is to release the corpse of the sac-

---

43 John Butt, "Bach's *Matthew Passion*", Johann Sebastian Bach, *Matthew Passion* (BWV 244), Dunedin Consort, directed by John Butt (Linn Records, 2008), CKD 313, 9.
44 Butt, "Bach's *Matthew Passion*", 10.
45 John Butt, *Bach's Dialogue with Modernity: Perspectives on the Passions* (Cambridge: Cambridge University Press, 2010), 24, 26.
46 Butt, *Bach's Dialogue with Modernity*, 35.
47 John Docker, "Epistemological Vertigo and Allegory: Thoughts on Massacres, Actual, Surrogate, and Averted – *Beersheba, Wake in Fright, Australia*", in *Passionate Histories: Myths, Memory and Indigenous Australia*, ed. Frances Peters-Little, Ann Curthoys and John Docker (Canberra: ANU E Press, 2010), 57.

rificial goat by disentangling its tether rope from the tree roots, he is playing the role of a disciple in a deposition scene, though the ravine beside which he stands is an abyss rather than a hill, and he plans to use "the lattice of the roots as a ladder" to climb down rather than up to free the carcass (138) – the upward journey will come later, in the Expedition Range. Max finds the moonlit scene estranging, and is aware that he is caught up in events that are regulated by something like "the laws or literature and myth": "Was that it then? An act of contrition?" (140).

A precondition for the spectator's affective engagement in the Passion is that he or she must be prepared imaginatively to exchange roles with the performers and, finally, with the characters they play, to enter fully into the drama of sacrifice and redemption. After the event, Dougald offers an insightful account of the free play of liturgical subjectivities when he suggests that "she [the goat] was the decoy, old mate . . . it was you they were after" (152). Max does not ask him who "they" were, but he assumes that he means "the fates", or some other version of those "blind forces" that determine our lives. As Max climbs down his ladder of roots toward the sacrificial animal, he experiences a splitting of the self: "there were two of us, the I who did the thing and the superior other within who stood aside and commented on the doing of it" (141). In the liturgy, it is of course "the I who did the thing", the I that takes part in the ritual performance, who is most capable of redemption, and as Max finds himself further out along the root of the tree, he feels like "a giant insect that has found a place in which to undergo the transformation of its pupation" (142). In liturgical terms, the mechanism of that transformation is the penitent's identification with the crucified figure, which requires that the spectator become a participant in the sacrifice. At the very moment when Max attempts to free the goat, "the trap" of the tree root gives a "vicious snap" and he finds himself suddenly, involuntarily exchanging roles with the carcass, the perpetrator in effect becoming the victim: "The carcass of the goat plummeted to the river below and the recoil of the root, released from her weight, clamped my foot in a vice-like grip. The pain was fierce. I cried out and involuntarily drew myself downwards towards my trapped foot" (143). The chapter ends with Max at the beginning of his liberation from the "cage" of silence, "crying out with the fierce pain" (144). He has been liberated from the German silence by taking part in a ritual of deposition and burial in which the perpetrator changes roles with the victim and experiences the gift of a new beginning.

The chapter that follows, "Winifred's Naked Shoulders", brings an abrupt shift in time and place that is apparent rather than real. Max has lost consciousness, and while he is literally fixed to the tree in the ravine of the Nebo River, he dreams of his dead wife. In the dream, they are back in their apartment on Schluterstrasse, and he is lying in bed watching Winifred undress. Structurally, this break in the deposition narrative performs the role of an aria in a Passion by allowing the direct expression of Max's grief. Max's lyrical and erotic recollection of his wife's presence culminates in his dramatic return to consciousness in the present, and his direct expression, at last, of his loss, her absence, the shocking ellipsis of death: "The bright light of dawn burst through my closed lids suddenly and drew me up from the depths and I opened my eyes . . . *She was gone!* . . . She is dead, I cried, stricken" (149).

In a final exchange of roles, Max, who began performing the deposition as a supplicant, ends as the sacrificial Jew/Christ/animal and is himself deposed by Dougald. The rhetorical figure that best describes these recurring patterns of exchange and intersection in the novel is *chiasmus*, the shape of the letter "X". The two men end the episode in imitation of the *Pieta*, witnessed by their faithful animals, who act as intermediaries between them: "Pain and grief washed through me and I cried out. He knelt beside me and cradled my head in his arms, holding me to him and murmuring words of comfort. My two brown dogs were licking my hands" (150). The ritual of the "decent burial" – is it of the goat? Of Winifred Otto? Of Max's grief? Of modern German guilt? – has therefore involved Max's passing from the role of spectator to participant, liberating himself from the crypt of silence through empathy, to the direct expression of pain. Yet in this final figure of the *Pieta*, it is Dougald who provides succour to his German friend. In its use of the Christian tropological scheme of atonement, the deposition of the goat draws deeply upon Max's culture as a European, and although Dougald is physically and empathetically involved, there is no suggestion that the ritual appropriates or intrudes upon his own Aboriginal spirituality, which Miller later evokes respectfully in Dougald's disappearance during the night on the summit of the Expedition Range. As an Aboriginal man of the Stolen Generations, Dougald has not yet been given the chance to resolve his own sorry business, and it is to that other business that the two men now turn in the final stations of the novel.

A key point of intersection between the German and Indigenous Australian histories is the destructive events of the fathers' generations: in Max's case associated with Nazism, and in Dougald's the loss of culture in the aftermath of colonial settlement. Max realises that "our inability to memorialize the deeds of our fathers was an affliction he and I possessed in common" (166).[48] Butt's comparison of oratorio's "anti-theatricality" with the free play of identification he associates with the "realism" of the novel is again useful here, as Miller now turns from the ritual aspects of the death of the goat to storytelling and narrative. His interest in the complexity of subjectivity and its fluidity across various modes, including liturgy, myth and literature, is suggested by the chapter titles of the Mount Nebo section, which move from the liturgical and the performative to the literary: "A Decent Burial", "The Storyteller", "The Writer". That is to say, Miller is not only concerned with the ethics and politics of cross-cultural traumatic memory, but also with its aesthetics and phenomenology: with the complex economy of identification and appropriation that take place in a range of media, including myth and liturgy, but especially his own art form, narrative fiction.

In "The Storyteller", Dougald tells Max the story of his father's struggle with the loss of traditional culture, and in "The Writer" he gives Max the oral history of his great-grandfather, Gnapun the warrior, to be translated into a written account that will endure: "he placed his story in my care" (167). Miller is intensely aware here of the complex interchange of subjectivities involved in giving and receiving memories, which must take place textually, through the acts of telling, writing and reading. Dougald's telling of his story, as oral history, and Max's listening to it and subsequent written interpretation of it, are "anti-theatrical" in Butt's sense, in that that they unfix the relations between speaker and listener, between writer and reader, between the "real" and the "represented" worlds, creating a radical instability of identifications. While Max was acutely aware, during his role in the deposition of the goat, of being subject to something like "the laws of literature and myth" (140), so now he is aware of the similarities between writing or listening to a narrative, and being involved in a ritual as a spectator who is compelled to identify with the protagonist of the story, of "giving his story a voice that was intimate to my own voice"

---

48 The German writer Bernhard Schlink also explores "vertical" or intergenerational German guilt in the 2008 Weidenfeld Lectures, published as *Guilt About the Past* (St Lucia, Qld: University of Queensland Press, 2009).

(170). In writing Dougald's story, Max soon finds that "it was not possible to keep myself entirely out of it", so that the spirit of Dougald's story and his own "merged in my imagination and became one" (169).

Max's written version of the story of Gnapun in the chapter titled "Massacre" registers many of the insights of the new Australian history of the 1990s, which Attwood calls the "the turn to Aboriginal history".[49] Miller is aware, for example, of issues of Aboriginal sovereignty, of intricate structures of leadership within Aboriginal society, of the complex border-crossing protocols involved in travelling from one sovereign domain into another, of rituals of hospitality extended by traditional Aboriginal society not only between Aboriginal clans, but even to the white invaders. And he is acutely aware of the historical fact of planned Aboriginal resistance to European invasion and occupation: his novel is a prescient response, in this sense, to Henry Reynold's plea for the inclusion of frontier conflict in Australia's otherwise ubiquitous commemoration of war.[50] Like Bo and Annabelle's visit to Ranna Station, Max's written account of Dougald's story articulates and sets into complex dialogue a number of different cultural perspectives on the colonial project. From the missionary settler's point of view, he is "the instrument of God's plan" in establishing the New Jerusalem (182). From Gnapun's perspective, the disruption to Indigenous culture symbolised by the use of the sacred stones to build walls brings an abrupt end to his ancient civilisation by the imposition of European history into Indigenous space: "Having been taken from their places, Time has been brought to the stones and they are lost to the eternal present of reality" (189). In telling the story, Max also imposes his own, modern German perspective by transposing European phrases and quotations into his account of Gnapun's subjectivity. When Gnapun beholds the destruction of the stone playgrounds, which is not only akin to the allied soldiers' experience in liberating the death camps, but also recalls Miller's experience when he saw the newsreels of the liberation,[51] he reflects that "to sing, after this, would be a blasphemy" (190), an allusion to Theodor Adorno's famous axiom that "To write poetry after Auschwitz is barbaric."[52] The site of the disturbed stones might also be compared to the voids in Libeskind's Jewish Museum Berlin, which represent the destruction at the point of intersection between Jewish and German histories. Gnapun realises that this is "the thing that is greater than death" (190): that is, the death not of an individual but of a culture.

In writing his account of Dougald's story, Max again uses the quotation from Homer with which he had begun his lecture in Hamburg some months earlier. Using the words of Agamemnon, Gnapun tells his followers, "We are not going to leave a single one of them alive ... The whole people must be wiped out of existence, and none be left to think of them and shed a tear" (199). As we have seen, the politics of applying Homeric quotations to the circumstances of the Queensland frontier are unclear. Does this represent a de-historicising of either or both of the Nazi and Australian genocides? It is important that this is the second time Max has used the same quotation. Gaita is one of the few readers of the novel to notice that while Agamemnon's words are used twice, the effect is not to render all massacres equal, but to preserve the balance between transnational comparison and national exceptionalism: he reminds us that "the massacres ... were per-

---

49 Attwood, *Telling the Truth*, 19.
50 Henry Reynolds, *Forgotten War* (Sydney: NewSouth, 2013).
51 Lilian Zavaglia, "From Mabo to the Apology: The Double Movement of Apology and Apologia in the Novels of Reconciliation 2002–2007" (PhD thesis, University of Sydney, 2012), 183.
52 Theodor W. Adorno, "Cultural Criticism and Society" (1949), *Prisms* (London: Spearman, 1967), 34.

petrated for different reasons and in different spirits".[53] We might return here to Gaita's criteria for great literature, which is required to be "universal" while also arising "in the midst of things" – that is to say, from the insights into one's own situation that come from cross-cultural understanding that Max did not experience before receiving Dougald's gifts of hospitality and friendship. Max's first quotation from Homer in his conference paper was offensive because it strove for universality while denying the historical specificity of individual instances of genocide. His second quotation in "Massacre" allows the link to be made between two instances of genocide while respecting their difference, and this is because the gift of Dougald's hospitality has allowed him, through a comparative, transnational approach to traumatic memory, to write from "the midst of things", both in German history and Australian frontier history. The distance travelled between these two positions is suggested by postcolonial theorist Bill Ashcroft's commentary of the gift of the story. Initially, he suggests that "this act of writing . . . appears to be . . . an act of effrontery, an appropriation of cultural story by the white man's writing". Finally, however, he concludes that "the record of Gnapun's story in writing is a powerful gesture of reconciliation because not only does it effect a transformation in Dougald by saving his story . . . it transforms Max by allowing him to enter a different understanding". This is possible, as Ashcroft confirms, because "the gift Dougald gives Max is the gift of a different space from which to write".[54]

But there is one disturbing implication of this fluidity of identification. At one point in "Massacre", in a scene that evokes the Nazi Holocaust, Gnapun becomes aware of the panic of the white victims around him: "A child's sudden wail of fear cuts the eerie silence and its mother cannot comfort it" (202). One of the conundrums that had faced Australian critics in the 1990s was that the charge of genocide forced Australians to compare their forebears with Nazis, and the implication here is that Max has conflated Aborigines with Nazis. If Max is truly to be liberated from the prison house of the German silence, he must identify not just with the victim, as he did in the deposition scene, but with his father's role in the primary scene, as the perpetrator. It therefore comes as a shock to realise that he has only identified with Gnapun: "*So you have identified yourself at last with the perpetrator of a massacre . . .* It was true" (215).

Is the story of "Massacre" a tribute to the leadership of a sovereign Aboriginal leader in the face of colonial invasion, a demonstration in fiction of the arguments Henry Reynolds and others were making about Aboriginal sovereignty and resistance to invasion? Or is Dougald's gift of the story to his friend so generous, so unequivocal, that he surrenders it to the service of many purposes, not only preserving the account of his great-grandfather's leadership for posterity in written form, but also opening it to the unpredictable "realism" of textuality, which allows multiple forms of identification, including identification with the perpetrator? Miller seems to have been interested in the Cullin-la-Ringo massacre partly because of the opportunity it gave him to write about Gnapun's leadership of his people in resistance to European settlement as a 'tribute' to Frank Budby's contemporary leadership of the Barada community, but in focusing on this one, historically atypical example there is the risk of misrepresenting Aboriginal people as perpetrators rather than victims of frontier violence. As Docker argues, 'Massacres of indigenous people are both

---

53 Gaita, "Trusting the Words", 221.
54 Bill Ashcroft, "Australian Transnation", *Southerly* 71, no. 1 (2011): 24–6.

remembered and not remembered, creating in white Australian consciousness a confused energy around the ways Indigenous history is understood."[55]

The final journey together of the two old men to Dougald's heartland in the Expedition Range is a ritual exchange of friendship, a confirmation of their intimacy. At Gnapun's burial cave, Dougald confesses to Max that he could not have returned there alone, while Max has realised that even if they had faced death together, their friendship required his presence and support. In another liturgical exchange, Max imagines them exchanging roles in the *Pieta*: "When the end came I would hold him in my arms while he wept for his loss, just as he had held me in his arms that night at the Nebo river while I wept for my loss" (255). Miller's perfectly formed, cross-shaped sentence enacts friendship's physical exchange through the figure of chiasmus. In so far as *Landscape of Farewell* can be seen as a re-writing of *Journey to the Stone Country*, Dougald and Max also complete together, or now feel able to complete together, the journey to an Aboriginal sacred site that Annabelle Beck felt inappropriate in the earlier novel.

The journey to the Expedition Range begins and ends with allusions to the classical Greek form of the odyssey, confirming modernity's endemic condition of exile. The elderly Greek in the store where Dougald and Max buy their final supplies is a personification of Homeric exile, while at the very end of the novel, back in Hamburg, Max watches a Greek movie he has seen before with Winifred, and of which he only remembers "fragments" (275). In this way, the second of the Central Queensland novels also ends amidst the ruins of modernity, in one of Libeskind's voids, we might say, at the destructive intersection of diverse histories. Yet in so far as the journey to the Expedition Range is a homecoming, a conclusion to the exiles' wandering, there is no symmetry for the two friends. During the night on the mountain, Max encounters "visitors" from his past, Winifred and the gypsy girl, but he realises that as a modern German there is no homeland to which he can return. The Holocaust has erased that past utterly. When Max recalls his mother's "serene, civilised, ancestral Vienna", destroyed, like so much else, during the war, he thinks, "What a fairy tale!" (37, 43). Dougald's return to country, to the cave of Gnapun, is a true pilgrimage "to the spiritual centre of his life" (247). As an Aboriginal man, that "spiritual centre" still has an existing geographical place, at the centre of which his great grandfather is entombed in the land, a material as well as a symbolic presence: "The skeleton was half-buried by an accumulation of debris that had evidently leached from the roof over the years" (265). It is another version of the ruin of time.

With no such homeland surviving, Max envies his friend that the land still entombs his ancestors in material form: "There was, of course, no place such as this that I might return to. Hamburg today is... not the place where I grew up, but is a new construction... and the strange and beautiful countryside... where I encountered the gypsy girl... has been transformed into suburban streets" (233). As Ashcroft observes, this is the essential difference between the superficially similar commitment of the Nazis to blood and soil, and the Aboriginal notion of country. For Dougald, country is "the setting of the dreaming and the connection with the myths that give life and meaning, the site of the connection with the Old People".[56] For Max's uncle, the relation with the earth is finite: "It all ended. Everything. Nothing of him, nothing of his house or ideas, not a thing of it remains" (226). But even at the end, it is the Aboriginal culture that hospitably provides a

---

55 Docker, "Epistemological Vertigo", 62.
56 Ashcroft, "Australian Transnation", 23.

model for Max's way forward. It is through his sojourn in the ruins of the colonial frontier, a gift of hospitality from his friends Dougald and Vita, that he has been able to overcome his impulse to commit suicide and can now find solace in the ruins of modern Europe: "I enjoyed the broken fragment of the film as greatly as I had once enjoyed the whole of it. But there it is, all fragments, and in the midst of it we may know this sense of completion" (275).

Ashcroft sees in the ending of the novel a foreshadowing of Prime Minister Kevin Rudd's apology to the Stolen Generations in 2008, but in a way that transcends nation and confirms the ethical value of the transnational imaginary: "the subtle hope registered by novel is the wider inheritance of Vita's and Dougald's disengagement from nation, the inheritance of a 'transnational' cultural space".[57] For Gaita, however, "nothing ... is resolved in *Landscape of Farewell*". This includes Max's insights at the end of the novel, for even then, according to Gaita, he has not fully understood his relation to the Holocaust, and we do not know whether he will be able to write the book that Vita hopes he might.[58] When Gaita contemplates Vita's injunction to Max to interrogate those we most love and admire about their past ethical behaviour, he suggests that "only someone with no understanding of how terrible the answer might be could do it".[59] Finally, that may be the effect of looking into the abyss.

---

[57] Ashcroft, "Australian Transnation", 26.
[58] Gaita, "Trusting the Words", 221, 224.
[59] Gaita, "Trusting the Words", 229.

8
The Economy of the Gift: *Lovesong*

The relationships between Alex Miller's novels often suggest to me the techniques of relief and intaglio engraving, as if the material that is removed by incising to make the positive image of one novel later provides the substance for another. A more accurate comparison might be the relationship between a photographic negative and the positive print that is developed from it, in which the forms and tones that are dark and recessive in the negative become bright and forward in the print. This is, of course, another version of the rhetorical figure of chiasmus, which is a central organising principle in the Central Queensland novels, shaping the intersections between past and present, between space and time, between one culture and another.

Miller's ninth novel, *Lovesong* (2009), has just this kind of relationship with his fifth, *Conditions of Faith* (2000). In the earlier novel, a young Australian woman, Emily Elder, falls pregnant after a single sexual encounter with a priest, Father Etinceler, and travels from her home in Paris to Sidi bou-Said in Tunisia, where she lives for much of the pregnancy at the home of her Tunisian-born friend Antoine Carpeaux. At the same time, Emily is experiencing a profound reawakening of her intellectual ambitions as a historian and an equally profound desire for independence from her husband Georges. To realise these aspirations, she abandons her newborn child, a daughter whom she names Marie, to return to her archaeological research in the Roman amphitheatre at Carthage. As we have seen, Miller had read widely during his research for *Conditions of Faith* in the contemporary literature on maternal ambivalence, including psychological studies of women's attitudes to maternity and feminist scholarship on the status of women in the early Christian era.

In *Lovesong*, another young married woman, Sabiha,[1] is unable to fall pregnant after fourteen years of marriage to her Australian-born husband, John Patterner. They meet in her aunt Houria's café, Chez Dom, in the Parisian suburb of Vaugirard while John is reading Henry Adams' *Chartres*, and it is in Chartres, where Emily gives birth to Marie, that John proposes marriage to Sabiha. In contrast to Emily, "Sabiha believed herself destined to be a mother"; for her, "the state of motherhood and the state of womanhood composed the same order of being".[2] Desperate to give birth to the daughter whom she has always believed lies waiting in her womb, Sabiha embarks on a brief and opportunistic re-

---

[1] The name acknowledges Miller's friend, the Tunisian-born novelist, illustrator and art historian, Sabiha Al Khemir.

lationship with Bruno Fiorentino, a Italian fruit grower and the father of eleven children, who supplies tomatoes to the Patterners' café. Sabiha's two brief meetings with Bruno in his van at the Paris markets recall Emily's single encounter with Father Etinceler in the crypt of Chartres Cathedral, where he cultivates peaches: both women are left mysteriously smelling of fruit, as if by the visitation of some pagan fertility god. Each of these brief, passionate encounters is quite selfish in the sense that it is motivated entirely by the young woman's personal aspirations and anxieties, and each has the potential to bring ruin upon her home and marriage, and to destroy the reputation of her lover. Knowing that her daughter is now growing safely inside her body, Sabiha returns briefly to visit her dying father, Hakim, in her home-town of El Djem in Tunisia – like Carthage, El Djem is famous for its Roman amphitheatre – before emigrating to Australia with her husband and child, Houria, thereby reversing the direction of Emily's emigration from Australia to Europe.

The chapters of *Lovesong* containing the story of Sabiha's quest for motherhood are framed and repeatedly intersected by another series of chapters in which the novelist, a widower who lives in Carlton with his own daughter, and whom we know only as Ken, describes his meetings with Sabiha and John Patterner, who now live in Melbourne. Ken is fascinated by Sabiha, who runs a patisserie called Figlia Fiorentino. He is drawn to her dignity and exotic beauty, though he suspects some underlying mystery in her life; he has also struck up a friendship with John, who confides in him the story of his marriage to Sabiha. John's autobiographical narrative is to be the source for Ken's latest work of fiction, and Ken has already begun making notes. In a further comparison with engraving, John's story is like the positives in relief engraving, or like the grooves in intaglio engraving, which hold the ink from which the print – Ken's novel – is pulled. These cross-cut chapters reflect, in an often humorous and transparently self-reflexive way, Miller's own long-standing interest in the way fiction is parasitic upon lived experience, and are another version of his central theme of the gift – or is it the benign theft? – of story. Ken is between books, as they say, and has been thinking of retiring. His previous novel had been called *The Farewell*, "a pretty direct hint for reviewers" (12), and also a teasing reference to Miller's own previous novel, *Landscape of Farewell*, in which another widower, Max Otto, delivers what is intended to be his final lecture. John Patterner's oral story is the source of fiction for the novelist, who has begun to make it his own by writing preliminary notes for a novel. This *mise-en-abyme* of borrowings echoes the *khoratic* structure of *The Ancestor Game*, Dougald's gift of story to Max Otto in *Landscape of Farewell*, and Max Blatt's foundational gift to Miller of "Comrade Pawel", though in an amusing twist to this economy of the gift, in the final pages of the novel John Patterner, who is an English teacher and a great reader, surprises Ken by announcing that he has decided to become a writer himself, and that he has begun to write up his own version of the story. Ken cruelly advises him not to give up his day job "just yet" (352), but he conceals from him the fact that he has already begun transforming Ken's story into his own work of fiction.

The intimate relations between truth and fiction, and the ethics of the novelist's plundering of other people's lives – Patrick White famously compared it to vivisection – are suggested in Ken's seemingly innocent comparison early in the novel between himself and "Victor Maskell" (5). Victor Maskell is the central character in John Banville's 1997 novel *The Untouchable*, and is transparently based on Anthony Blunt, whose secret life as a So-

---

2   Alex Miller, *Lovesong* (Sydney: Allen & Unwin, 2007), 41, 96. All subsequent references are to this edition and appear in parentheses in the text.

viet spy was sensationally revealed in the British Parliament by Margaret Thatcher in 1979. The immediate point is that novelists are like spies, and therefore not to be trusted. Banville later offered *The Guardian* a fascinating confession of his struggle with the ethics of basing Victor Maskell's adult life on Blunt's, and his earlier life on that of the poet Louis MacNeice, who had been Blunt's lover. Banville confessed that "Although novelists have robust consciences and think nothing of cannibalizing real lives to feed their fictions, I hesitated." "Would it be wise", he wondered, "to risk infuriating scholars and historians, as well as Blunt's surviving friends and enemies . . . by stealing for my fictive purposes the childhood of one of the finest Anglo-Irish poets?" Banville goes on to explain that this moral dilemma was resolved for him in the late 1980s when he watched on television a press conference given by Blunt immediately before his exposure. Moments before meeting the press, and not knowing that the cameras were already upon him, Blunt had smiled enigmatically to himself, apparently amused, Banville realised in retrospect, by the idea that the journalists hoped to extract a confession from him when the best spy catchers in the land had failed. Banville took it as a sign that he was free to "plunder" the lives of Blunt and MacNeice: "It was one of those moments, rare indeed, when the writer seems to feel the sudden presence of the angel at his back."[3] In a witty reversal of Banville's act of plunder, John Patterner confesses to Ken that it was seeing him speaking on television that had moved him to write and eventually to reclaim his own story: "I saw you on the daytime replay of *The Book Show* and realized you were a writer . . . I decided it was a sign" (343). Ken confesses his plundering of reality in words similar to those that Miller himself has used in interviews: "I have never really liked making it up. My imagination, such as it is, needs the facts to feed off" (107).

The circulation of John and Sabiha's story – in the first instance orally, from John to Ken, and subsequently from Ken, and perhaps from John also, to their readers – suggests Lewis Hyde's distinction between gift exchange and commodity exchange in his book *The Gift* (1983),[4] which Miller had read after seeing it referred to in Ronald A. Sharp's 2009 essay on *Landscape of Farewell*.[5] Hyde argues that unlike a commodity, which is taken out of circulation by becoming private property, a gift must be kept in motion or circulation: "whatever we have been given is supposed to be given away again". It is this perpetual circulation that distinguishes the gift from the commodity, and for Hyde, the qualities of the gift in traditional societies are fatally altered with the fall into the marketplace in modern societies, which transforms it into a commodity. The gift "is a pool or reservoir in which the sentiments of its own exchange accumulate so that the more often it is given away, the more feeling it carries, like an heirloom that has been passed down for generations". The fact that Ken is a professional novelist, and that in the closing pages of *Lovesong* John threatens to take back his gift of story by writing it up for publication himself, and thereby also turning it into a commodity, raises a final doubt about the status of the story from which Ken's novel is derived, placing it ambiguously between the very different economies of the gift and the commodity. The ambiguous cross-contamination

---

3   John Banville, "Omens and Poetic Licence", *The Guardian*, 25 February 2006, http://www.theguardian.com/books/2006/feb/25/johnbanville.
4   Lewis Hyde, *The Gift: Imagination and the Erotic Life of Property* (New York: Random House: 1983). In 2007, Vintage issued the twenty-fifth anniversary edition with a new subtitle: *Creativity and the Artist in the Modern World*.
5   Ronald A. Sharp, "More Than Just Mates", *The Australian*, 1 July 2009, 11, http://www.news.com.au/news/more-than-just-mates/story-fna7dq6e-1225744152559.

of these two apparently separate economies is signalled by Miller's re-location of the exchange of story from its usual place in a private kitchen or dining room to the commercial cafes of inner Melbourne, and by the fact that as restaurateurs John and Sabiha are in the paradoxical "business" of marketing hospitality. Has Ken, in other words, compromised John's gift of story by turning it into a commercial publication? To what extent does this parallel Sabiha's selfish appropriation of the gift of Bruno's love for her, which takes place, significantly, in the market place? Within the framework of *Lovesong*, between John's embedded gift of his story, and Ken and John's potentially conflicting intentions to publish it, there is no way that the reader can resolve the questions Miller has raised about the story's status – that is, about the kind of economy in which it now circulates as "art".

The circulation of stories, whether as gifts or commodities, is suggested by John Patterner's name, a patterner being a person who makes the patterns – not necessarily original – that are used repetitively in the manufacture of commodities such as lace, printed fabrics, and wallpapers. Among the few decorations in Chez Dom are the red and green checked table cloths bought from Arnoul Fort's drapery next door (17, 101). The cover of the first edition of *Lovesong* includes bands of a floral design that resembles printed fabric or wallpaper, in which a repeated floral motif is rhythmically marked out in red against the sepia background of a larger grid. Gail Jones uses a similar image of repetition in *Five Bells* (2011). She describes the French surrealist painter René Magritte "designing repetitions" in a wallpaper factory after the death by drowning of his mother: "it was easy, to repeat. Any loose flourish would appear whole if chained in a repetition. Any single flower became many, any rough abstraction a pattern."[6] In Jones' novel, the repeated patterns evoke the symptoms of traumatic memory, the insistent recall of an image lodged in the memory like a photographic negative located at some mysterious point in the brain. In *Lovesong*, they suggest the economy of the gift, which is kept moving between individuals by re-gifting: specifically, the gift of hospitality, over which Sabiha's aunt Houria and then Sabiha herself preside, but also the gift of motherhood, which is passed on through the line of women in Sabiha's family. Implicitly included are the gift of song, which Sabiha also inherits from her grandmother, and the gift of story, which Ken believes he has inherited from John – though that gift is subject to questions of proprietorship, especially by the possibility of copyright and commercial publication, which would take it out of the economy of the gift and place it in Lynch's economy of the commodity. John's role as a "patterner", that is, as one who facilitates the gift economy, is further suggested by Ken's initial impression of his hands, which are like those of an artisan or a craftsman who makes designs or objects for others to use: "A musical-instrument maker would not have surprised me. I could imagine the harpsichord his hands might lovingly fashion for his beautiful wife" (9). Ken comes to realise, in listening to his "confession", that John does not give himself "a starring role" in his own story; he is "effacing himself" (115). John's relatively passive role is that of the "patterner", the facilitator rather than the originator of the culture transmitted by the line of women, from Sabiha's Berber grandmother and her aunt Houria down to their daughter, also named Houria, the repetition of her name a verbal echo of the floral motif repeated in the design of the book's cover.

The idea of the patterner as a craftsman who replicates unoriginal designs drawn from pre-existing sources, and the implicit comparison with printmaking, also suggests Ken's – and Miller's – craft as a novelist. The word "text" derives from the Latin *textus*, or struc-

---

6   Gail Jones, *Five Bells* (Sydney: Vintage, 2011), 31–2.

ture. The verb *textum* means to weave, or to compose. As Roland Barthes puts it, at once punning on the Latin root and pointing to the positive unoriginality of all narratives, "The text is a tissue of quotations drawn from the innumerable centres of culture."[7] Miller's own corpus of novels, as we are coming to see, is intersected by patterns of repetition, including the names of people and places, snippets of conversation, and journeys through time and space, that are sometimes repeated positively, sometimes negatively, but always suggesting that the novelist's craft involves making variations on a theme. Marie, the name of Emily's daughter in *Conditions of Faith*, is the name of Ken's dead wife in *Lovesong*. As a Tunisian and Australian-born couple, Sabiha and John are a mirror image of another mixed-race couple, Annabelle Beck and Bo Rennie. These intersections between the novels, and between the novels and Miller's own life, suggest again that a series of novels is like a series of prints pulled from the same plate, or photographic prints developed from the same negative or, as Miller once put it, like excavating "a buried city of great complexity".[8] The novelist, like any other artist, is a patterner, a maker of repetitions.

The status of John's autobiographical story is further complicated by Ken's understanding that it is a kind of confession, and that all stories are perhaps meant as confessions: "But isn't that what all stories are? Confessions? Aren't we compelled to tell our stories by our craving for absolution?" (14). The religious context here provides a further twist on the ethics of storytelling, and the obligations it may place upon the listener. It also suggests a further comparison with Emily's liaison with Father Etinceler, which he enters into on the understanding that it is the expression of a personal need or questioning on her part, the answer to which he might passively assist her to discover – again as a male "patterner", for she is not the first young woman whose "confession" he has heard. Is confession a one-way gift to a passive listener, or must it be reciprocated in some way, perhaps by the conferring of absolution or the revelation of the truth about oneself? What obligations does the act of confession entail upon the confessor? Ken tries to convince himself of his "rights" to a story, as its listener or recipient: "My view of this is that when someone tells you a story they give it to you. The story is their gift. It becomes yours. That's the way I look at it" (209). But there are always two parties to this "gift", and their understandings may differ. In deciding to circulate John's story as a published work of "fiction", has Ken breached some implicit understanding that the act of confession is a non-commercial exchange? In a further comparison with the role of the priest in the sacraments, which Miller researched while writing *Conditions of Faith*, is the novelist exempt from ethical obligations because of some "priestly" role as the impersonal conduit of the stories for their tribe? Some such understanding seems implicit in Ken's final reflection: "Sabiha's story had come out of her and been carried to me; now, after I had lived in it jealously myself for a while, I would carry it to others, and in the end would let it go and be done with it, like all the other stories I have carried" (354). Which is to say that the novelist is a "patterner".

Miller appears to be suggesting not only a distinction between a woman's economy of the gift and a male economy of the commodity, but also, following Hyde, a parallel distinction between the gift economy of traditional societies like that of the Berber women from whom Sabiha is descended, and the modern market-based economies of Europe. Yet we

---

7   Roland Barthes, "The Death of the Author", in *Image Music Text*, trans. Stephen Heath (Glasgow: Fontana, 1977), 146.
8   Alex Miller, "This Is How It's Going to Be Then", *Australian Book Review* 127 (December 1990 – January 1991): 30.

know from previous examples, including Henry Adams' medievalism and August Spiess' German romanticism, that Miller rarely takes such complex ideas at their face value. Any such binary opposition – typical of the structuralist and functionalist approaches to anthropology that influenced Lewis Hyde's own work in the United States in the 1970s – is dramatically contradicted by any number of the novel's many twists and turns, including Sabiha's possessive ownership of Bruno's gift – "her" daughter, Marie – and her inhospitality to his son. The hospitality offered at Chez Dom occupies an ambiguous status in between the personal and the commercial. The café was established by a man, Dom Pakos, whose gifts to his partner, Houria, are "happiness" (19) and "faithfulness" (60). After his death, Sabiha is sent there by her father, Hakim, to be a companion to her aunt: "How greatly her own life had been enriched by her brother's generous gift of his favourite daughter!" (59). Through that gift, Sabiha becomes the daughter Houria never had (41). After Houria's death, the café and its obligations of hospitality are passed on to Sabiha and her husband, John Patterner. Sabiha's relationship with Bruno Fiorentino is similarly ambiguous. Although he is in love with her, her objective is utterly to possess rather than to share the child that will be the outcome of their coupling, which takes place, significantly, in Bruno's van in the Paris fruit markets rather than in one of their homes. After Bruno's death, there is an offer of the repetition or at least the continuity of a relationship, whether it be commercial or personal, in the arrival of his son, also named Bruno, who brings another box of tomatoes to the café in honour of his father's memory and his connection with the Patterners: "Please accept this box of tomatoes as a gift from my family" (329). In this act, what was merely a commodity is potentially turned into a gift, but as a gift it is brutally refused by Sabiha, leaving Bruno's son hurt and bewildered: "I can't accept your gift" (329). Her refusal to accept the tomatoes as a gift – or even as a commodity – echoes and confirms her own definition of the relationship with Bruno's father solely as the acquisition of her child.

Clearly, individual objects, like Bruno's tomatoes or the honey-dipped briouats that Sabiha occasionally offers free to her customers, can be either a gift or a commodity depending on the intentions of the giver and the understanding of the recipient. Questions about the status of Bruno's gift of a child to the Patterners remain in the ambiguity of their motivations for naming the new café in Carlton Figlia Fiorentino. When Sabiha is asked by a customer why they gave it an Italian name, she replies that it was named for "a man who gave us something precious for which we can never repay him" (352). She uses the language of the gift and suggests that the gift cannot be repaid, unlike a commodity, and yet she is not entirely transparent or forthcoming, Ken adding, "But of course she never told anyone what this precious thing was that Signor Fiorentino had given them" (352). Ken asks himself the key question: "Whose idea had it been... to call the pastry shop *Figlia Fiorentiono*?" (351). The answer, as it happens, is John, not Sabiha. On the night that she reveals to him that she is "pregnant with Bruno's child" (319) – which is in itself less than the truth, since she has always considered it to be "her" child – it is John who almost immediately tells her, "Don't worry, we won't forget Bruno. We'll think of some way of remembering him" (325). Sabiha's refusal of the gift of tomatoes from Bruno's son shortly thereafter confirms that it is John, not Sabiha, who accepts the child as a gift – for her it is a possession – further confirming his role as a "patterner", a man who selflessly facilitates the female line.

In so far as Sabiha offers hospitality to immigrant workers like Nejib and to travellers like John Patterner, she is a version of the mythological Diana: we might say that Diana is Sabiha's archetype in the same way that Vibia Perpetua is Emily Elder's and St Teresa of Avila is Dorothea Brooke's. In Roman religion, Diana was the goddess of wild animals, woodlands and the hunt, and associated with the Greek goddess Artemis. As a fertility deity, although herself a virgin, she was invoked by women to aid conception and ease of delivery. She was worshipped at the grove of *Diana Nemorensis* on the shores of Lake Nemi at Aricia, near Rome, and in Rome itself at the temple of Diana on the Aventine, established under Servius Tullius in the sixth century BCE. Because the origin of her cult at Aricia was outside the city of Rome, Diana was always regarded as a foreign deity, in the same way that the Tunisian-born Sabiha never feels herself to be truly Parisian. Servius Tullius was born a slave, and in the practice of her cult on the Aventine, Diana was regarded as the protectress of the lower classes (the plebeians) and of slaves, who were permitted to seek asylum in her temple. Her festival on 13 August was a holiday for slaves. She usually appears in art and literature as a huntress with a bow and quiver, and accompanied by a deer or hunting hounds.[9] As always in Miller's novels, allusions of this kind to other texts or to mythical or historical parallels, which give his work an additional dimension, are gently concealed at or just beneath the surface of verisimilitude.

As John Patterner finds, Sabiha's café is not located in the glamorous centre of Paris, but on the *rue des Esclaves* (literally, the Street of Slaves), just across the railway line from the great abattoirs of Vaugirard: "for the locals, the distinctive smell of the slaughterhouse signified work and home" (16). The men from the abattoirs who come to Chez Dom for meals, companionship and even asylum, are for the most part itinerant, Arabic-speaking immigrant workers from the Maghreb (38). They are not only exiles from their homelands, but their status in Paris is uncertain, as confirmed by their sudden and complete disappearance from the district after the murder of Bruno by Nejib's mysterious unnamed brother and the subsequent intervention of the police, which leads to the closure of Chez Dom. By singing for the men the Arabic songs she learned from her Berber grandmother, Sabiha fills them with a sense of "exile", "melancholia", and "nostalgia" (192), but she is also an exile, and has no profound knowledge of her grandmother's culture or of the traditional songs she sings: "Sabiha herself knew only the most faded remnants of her grandmother's ways. Tones of suggestion so weathered, so neglected, so distant they held only shreds of meaning" (196–7). The exile had begun in the previous generation, since by the 1960s Sabiha's aunt Houria had herself lost any deep connection to the "antique past" of the Berber women. Paris is their "city of exile" (26). Bruno Fiorentino is also an exile in Paris, his name literally meaning "Bruno the Florentine". In this condition of exile from her own inherited culture in both time and space, Sabiha is like Dougald Gnapun and Bo Rennie, who are dislocated from their country in the Expedition Range and no longer understand the complex meanings of the stone artefacts found there, which are to them like a dead language. At the same time, like migrants everywhere, Sabiha does not feel a deep connection to her host culture, for "no matter how long she lived in France, she would always be a stranger here; she and John, strangers both of them" (199). As Derrida has shown in his essays on the *sans papiers* in France, such immigrant workers are especially vulnerable to the inhospitality of the French state:[10] "these men all lived without the softening

---

9   "Diana", *Britannica Online Encyclopedia*, http://www.britannica.com/EBchecked/topic/161524/Diana.
10 Judith Still, *Derrida and Hospitality: Theory and Practice* (Edinburgh: Edinburgh University Press, 2010), especially chapters 4 and 5, "Frenchalgeria – (Not) Asking for a Name, Naming, Calling by Name in Tales of Algerians", and "The Dangers of Hospitality: The French State, Cultural Difference and Gods".

influence of their families ... their official standing with the state undecided. They stood on the rim of things, their lives vulnerable and filled with uncertainty, daily reminded by a thousand small things that they did not belong, their presence transient and uncertain" (224–5). Miller has himself been in just this situation as a migrant worker, initially in Exmoor and then in Central Queensland, and as we have seen in his portrait of Bo Rennie, the artist is always visible "on the edge of his compositions". Early in the novel, Ken quotes the English painter Lucian Freud: "*Everything is autobiographical and everything is a portrait*" (12). One of the most poignant reminders of Miller's identification with the exiled status of so many of his characters comes in Sabiha's telephone conversation with her sister Zahira in El Djem, who reports to her the words of their dying father, "*Everything will be all right when Sabiha gets here*" (295). These are the very words spoken by Miller's dying mother, Winifred – "Everything will be all right when Alex gets here" – as reported to him by his sister Kathy (also the name of John Patterner's sister, who lives in Australia) just before their mother's death in England in 1994.[11]

Although she is the patroness of plebeians and slaves, and the goddess of fertility and childbirth, Diana has a very different aspect as the goddess of the hunt, a ritualistic world that Miller had first explored in *The Tivington Nott*. It is in her role as the huntress that Sabiha appears in her essentially selfish relationship with her lover Bruno Fiorentino, and even with her husband John Patterner. Ken makes an implicit connection between the Roman myth of Diana and the pre-Christian mythology of North Africa, having seen "brindle hounds" travelling with Berber women when he was on holidays in Tunisia (106). The association of nubile Muslim women with hunting hounds and their conflation with Diana was something of a convention in nineteenth-century French Orientalist salon painting, such as Gaston Casimir Saint-Pierre's *The Return of the Master* and *Diana the Huntress*.[12] As Brenda Walker has shown, however, this aspect of Sabiha's character is developed most explicitly through a series of allusions to the works of Tolstoy, especially to *Anna Karenina* and *War and Peace*: "The adult Sabiha has become a huntress, reprising an old song she heard from her grandmother about a woman who goes, alone, to kill a lion ... [and she] does not take her husband with her on her hunt for a father for her child."[13]

Tolstoy is the name of the old borzoi owned by Sabiha's neighbours, Andre and Simone, who run the stationers in the *rue des Esclaves*. A "grey ghost of a dog" with "great melancholy eyes" (23), Tolstoy is Sabiha's familiar, appearing instinctively and mysteriously by her side like Diana's hounds, or indicating his nearby presence by his howling at times of crisis or need. The borzoi, as Walker points out, is not a domestic animal but a wolfhound, "deeply foreign" even in Moscow, and evokes the predatory world of ancient ritual, warfare and strategy, "the world of the hunt".[14] Tolstoy may be physically present beside Sabiha on the *rue des Esclaves*, but his "great eyes [are] fixed on the bloody deeds of ancestors who had ripped wolves apart on the wintry steppes of Siberia" (184); his cry at dawn is the cry of "the beast waking from his dreams to find himself alone on the snow-covered steppes of his ancestors" (325). In *War and Peace*, Tolstoy uses the Rostov wolf hunt as an emblem of the elemental self-destruction of Napoleon's forces in retreat from Moscow. The hunt

---

11 Alex Miller, "In the End It Was Teaching Writing", *Australian Literary Review* 3, no. 2 (2008): 17.
12 *La Conchiglia di Venere: The Nude in Art History*, https://conchigliadivenere.wordpress.com/2012/02/03/gaston-casimir-saint-pierre-1833-1916-french/.
13 Brenda Walker, "Alex Miller and Leo Tolstoy: Australian Storytelling in a European Tradition", in *The Novels of Alex Miller: An Introduction*, ed. Robert Dixon (Sydney: Allen & Unwin, 2012), 45.
14 Walker, "Alex Miller and Leo Tolstoy", 44.

is a vast and disciplined operation, involving twenty horsemen and more than a hundred dogs, including forty borzois, but it is also an irrational and elementally destructive force to which Count Nicholai Rostov surrenders himself, as if to a drug or to sexual passion. The comparison between sexuality, battle and the hunt is developed after the sacking of Moscow, when Tolstoy considers that the plight of Napoleon's army was "like the plight of a wounded beast that realizes the end is near, but doesn't know what it's doing".[15] The exhilaration of the hunt and the senseless plight of the army in battle are also emblems of Tolstoy's understanding of history, as Louis Menand observes: history, "the way Tolstoy imagined it", is like "a great, slow-moving weather system in which even tsars and generals are just leaves before the storm".[16] This is another version of W.G. Sebald's vision of history as the debris caught in the Rings of Saturn, or Miller's own image of the ruin of time in the "dribbling hourglass" above the table at Ranna. The helplessness of the individual caught up in such elemental forces, as Sabiha is caught up in her desire for a child, is suggested again by the image of patterns and repetitions across the generations. The patterns suggest not only the immanence of myth within the modern world, but the capacity of modern people to lose themselves and their identities in the universal human experiences expressed in myth. In her role as Diana the huntress, Sabiha is not the first mistress Tolstoy has served: he first appears not as her familiar, but as her aunt Houria's "close and attentive" companion (23), and only appears beside Sabiha after Houria's death. Furthermore, Tolstoy is not even Andre's first borozoi, but "Tolstoy number four – or was it number five?" (145).

In so far as Sabiha's quest for a daughter turns her into a huntress, however, it is not to *War and Peace*, but to *Anna Karenina* that we must turn. Just as the novelist plunders reality for his stories, Sabiha's relationship with John Patterner, an habitual reader who allows himself to enter fully into the fictional world, can be understood as her interpellation of him into her own story, which is paralleled by her interpellation of him into the story of *Anna Karenina*, initially in the role of Karenin and then, by a chiasmatic exchange like that between Max Otto and the sacrificial goat, in the role of Anna. In their first outing together beside a willow tree at Chartres, suggesting Diana's realm of the forest and the hunt, Sabiha compares John's grey eyes to those of Andre's borzoi and John assumes that she is referring to the novelist: "So how do you know what colour Tolstoy's eyes were?" (70). As Walker observes, "to tell any man, but especially a bookish man, that his eyes resemble Tolstoy's, is to anticipate that he may at some point be looking at human complication and historical catastrophe".[17]

Like Anna Karenina, Sabiha enters the world of passionate obsession via the imagery of the train, descending from the daylight world of homes and families into the darkness of the Paris *Métro*:

A street-cleaning machine was crawling along the gutter spraying water, its brooms swishing around, gathering up last night's rubbish.

She waited on the platform. There were few other people waiting with her. She did not look at them and they did not look at her. She would remember later, though

---

15 Leo Tolstoy, *War and Peace*, trans. Anthony Briggs (London: Penguin, 2005), 1120, quoted in Walker, "Alex Miller and Leo Tolstoy", 47.
16 Louis Menand, "Wild Thing: Did the O.S.S. Help Win the War Against Hitler?" *New Yorker*, 14 March 2011, 69–72, quoted in Walker, "Alex Miller and Leo Tolstoy", 46–7.
17 Walker, "Alex Miller and Leo Tolstoy", 44.

imperfectly, the inward-curving advertisement on the wall of the tunnel opposite her proclaiming in gold cursive lettering overlaying a grand old building the words *Stolichnaya Vodka* . . . the train pulled in and she got on and sat by the door . . . She closed her eyes and bent her head.

The train speeding her through the blackness of the tunnels, pursuing a howling fugitive from the underworld. In the screeching of the rails along the curve she heard the screams of the hunted woman. (170–1)

Miller would soon use this imagery again in *Autumn Laing* to evoke the bohemian world of Old Farm, where Pat Donlon begins his adulterous relationship with Autumn, bringing ruin upon his marriage and to his pregnant young wife Edith, who flees by train back to her parents' home in Melbourne. When she emerges on the railway platform from her descent into the underground, Edith finds herself back in the daylight world of children and families. In *Autumn Laing*, it is Eurydice, not Orpheus, who emerges safely from the underworld. As Pat enters the underworld, primed by Arthur's whisky, he experiences a disorientation of the senses. Sabiha's descent is the reverse of Edith's ascent. Her journey away from her home and husband toward Bruno Fiorentino involves a descent into the darkness and a disordering rather than clarifying of the mind, evoked here by the appropriately Russian brand of vodka. As Sabiha makes a final, futile appeal to reason and morality in the face of her headlong rush toward Bruno, "the words that spun in her head, contradicting her meek insistence, were Stolichnaya Vodka" (176). As in *Anna Karenina*, the speeding train is at once the image of Sabiha's passionate obsession and the instrument of her destruction, although in *Lovesong* that destruction is largely displaced on to the sacrificial figures of John and Bruno.

Like Alexei Karenin, John Patterner finds himself initially in the role of a good man, a patient and supportive husband, but "A dread of something terrible touched him; the way she stood there looking at him . . . As if she was not here with him but was in some other place. At the door she turned and lifted her hand to her lips . . . Then she was gone" (169). Sabiha's passionate and irrational compulsion in the hunt transposes John's role in the affair inevitably from that of Karenin to the role of Anna, at least in the sense that it is he who is threatened with destruction by the oncoming train. The hinge between *Lovesong* and *Anna Karenina*, and between John's roles as Karenin and the sacrificial Anna, is John's nightmare in which the sound of Tolstoy's howling at dawn is transformed into the whistle of a train speeding toward him: "He was dreaming Tolstoy's howl was a train hurtling towards him, its trembling light dazzling him. He could not get off the tracks as it flew towards him out of the dark" (326–7). The "death penalty" (190) that Sabiha had anticipated for herself in the *Métro* that morning is anticipated by John, but is ultimately commuted to Bruno. Even before their first encounter at the markets, Bruno senses "the stealthy approach of his enemy" (178) and at the moment of his ejaculation he groans as if "taking a knife in his flesh" (179). At their second encounter, Bruno tells her that he expects to die: "I have seen it . . . I know where it will be." Like Sabiha, however, who is not a Christian, Bruno has stepped outside the bounds of Christianity, lapsing into the realm of paganism, and he can no longer go in good faith to confession (272): "He was like a man on the scaffold who has accepted his fate" (274).

There is some suggestion that Bruno's role as the father of Sabiha's child might be compared to the myth of the *rex Nemorensis*, the priest or king of the grove, that was central to Sir James G. Frazer's seminal study of the Greek and Roman myths, *The Golden Bough*

(1890), whose themes of fertility rites and ritual sacrifice seem often to lie close beneath the surface of Miller's apparently realistic narratives, especially *The Tivington Nott, Conditions of Faith, Lovesong* and *Landscape of Farewell*. Rex Nemorensis was the priest of Diana Nemorensis, Diana of the Wood, at the temple at Aricia, whose succession was determined through trial by combat, in which a challenger must kill the incumbent with a golden bough plucked from one of the trees in the sacred grove. This ritual, which Frazer drew from Ovid, Strabo and other sources, was the basis of his syncretic account of an apparently universal fertility rite in which the sacred king must periodically be slain by a rival. Sabiha already has some connection to the world of the classical myths through her birthplace at El Djem, where the ruined Roman amphitheatre is visible above the wall of her father's courtyard (25). At Chartres, John proposes to her as she sits beneath the shadows of an ancient willow tree, "the great old tree" leaning far out over the river and forming "a canopy of restless shade" (67). When Sabiha later learns that the tree has been cut down, she regards it as an ill omen for their marriage and her fertility (100–1). Bruno's supplanting of John as the father of Sabiha's child and his supplanting, in turn, by combat with Nejib's silent and mysterious brother, has something of the fable-like quality of a fertility rite. At the Paris markets, Sabiha moves towards Bruno through the events in a heightened frame of mind as if she is under the influence of "something *old* in her", some "archaic belief", guided by "her fabled Berber ancestors", and "the realization that she was not the first woman to have ventured this solution to her childlessness"; she ceases to be merely Sabiha and becomes "motherhood itself" (176–7). Sabiha's sense of being taken out of her normal identity and interpellated into an ancient fertility ritual recalls Max Otto's experience during the deposition of the goat of being regulated by "the laws of literature and myth" (*Landscape of Farewell*, 140). Bruno's gift of fertility is given to Sabiha under the sentence of death (179). As a goddess of fertility, Diana is associated with the sky, but also with the moon. Significantly, the exchange between Sabiha and Bruno, conceived by him, at least, as a true gift, is transacted in the marketplace and in darkness: "The light from the crack between the doors of the van behind her was reflected in his eyes, two points of light in the darkness" (267). Bruno's sense that he is surrendering himself to destruction is expressed through his enchantment by Diana's emblem, the moon: "I look at the clouds and at the moon and I speak your name" (267). Bruno's sacrifice – the *ritual* of his sacrifice – is completed by the challenge from Nejib's brother, the holder of the golden bough, who stabs him to death at Chez Dom as if in some practiced ritual, his motives obscure to all, which coincides almost exactly with the death of Sabiha's father.

The ritual-like elements of Sabiha's quest for fertility find expression in the scarcely repressed though often imperfectly understood rivalries between men. From their first meeting in Chez Dom, John senses but does not understand the "veiled rivalries" between Nejib and his brother, and Bruno (154). As she makes her way toward the markets and toward Bruno, Sabiha recalls John's "humiliation" at having to have sperm tests during the early years of their marriage. At the very moment of her coupling with Bruno, she recalls that in testing his semen, "it had been as if they tested him for the quality of his manhood, as if he himself were being brought into question" (174). Sabiha is therefore well aware that the fertility ritual is not just a relation between a man and a woman, but a kind of combat between men, in which one or more will be "humiliated": "She had witnessed the humiliation of it in his eyes" (174). On the night of fatal combat between Bruno and Nejib's brother, John senses that there has been an "old issue" between them, "a matter of masculine pride" (222). On the night of his death, Bruno is "like an animal that has been hunted and does not know where to turn to escape its tormentors" (311). Chez Dom, once a place of asylum for men like Bruno, is also another abattoir, a place where fellow combatants in the fertility ritual gather to be killed, not directly by the huntress but by her champion or proxy – in this case Nejib's brother. After her coupling with Bruno, Sabiha is aware of the presence of "the masked gods" (196), of her ancestors in the form of familiars, domestic animals like Tolstoy and the cat, which confirm the ritual dimensions of the event. Her subjection to "the old beliefs" (231) suggests the immanence in the modern world of the pre-Christian rituals that had survived into the Roman world of the early Christian era at the time of Vibia Perpetua. The suggestion that Hakim views Emily as a reincarnation of Perpetua is repeated in Bruno's vision of Sabiha as Diana.

In one of Ken's contemporary chapters, the combat between men over fertility and paternity is wittily reflected in the combat between writers over the authorship of their material. Just as Bruno has contempt for John Patterner as a husband, expressed by his willingness to usurp that role, Ken tells his daughter Clare that he knows "for certain... that John Patterner was no writer" (207). He boasts that he can always sense when there is another writer about – "Like cats, you mean?" Clare asks, and he agrees, "Yes, just like cats" (204). Ken steals John's story in the same way that Sabiha steals Bruno's seed, keeping secret the fact that he is not just listening to him, but making notes after each meeting, keeping the material to himself in the same way that Sabiha uses a sanitary pad to prevent Bruno's semen from leaking out before it has done its work. John rationalises the theft in the same way that Sabiha does, convincing himself that "the story is their gift... they do that because they *need* to do it. They want their story to go out from them and be somewhere else, with the listener" (209).

Bruno is vulnerable to destruction because unlike John and Father Etinceler, he cannot enter into the affair with Sabiha solely for her sake. Through their association with fruit, darkness and the underworld, Bertrand Etinceler and Bruno Fiorentino have the qualities of modern-day fertility gods, leaving women smelling seductively of peaches and tomatoes. Unlike Bertrand, whom he otherwise resembles physically, Bruno does not have the priest's sense of disengagement as the instrument of another's as yet unformed desires. Bruno lacks the gift – we might call it the priest's and the novelist's gift – of empathetic insight into the other that Bertrand reveals when he tells Emily at their final meeting, "When we met that day in the crypt, you were searching for something", later asking with genuine interest, "You've found what you were looking for, haven't you?" (*Conditions of Faith*, 331). Bruno's attitude to Sabiha is more prosaic and more selfish, and it is left for John to play the priestly role of the patterner, the facilitator of Sabiha's female line of succession. The deaths of Sabiha's father and the murder of Bruno, the biological father of Sabiha's child, which occur in the penultimate stages of the narrative, are also the narrative means that bring about the catastrophic end to Chez Dom, allowing John Patterner to reclaim his roles in the ritual as Sabiha's husband and Houria's father, and to take them away at last to his own home in Australia, as he has long desired to do but until now – until the death of his rivals – has been powerless to achieve.

In my drawing out the mythological underpinnings of Miller's seemingly transparent and realistic contemporary narratives, not only in *Lovesong*, but also in his other novels, especially *The Tivington Nott*, *Conditions of Faith* and *Landscape of Farewell*, there may be a risk of over-reading him. But I want to argue that in this relationship between myth and realism, so delicately evoked that we might easily miss it, we can identify one of Miller's most significant achievements as a novelist, and as an ethically minded observer of the modern world. In an illuminating discussion of the heritage of *The Golden Bough*, whose title Frazer took from J.M.W. Turner's painting, *The Golden Bough* (1834), Jonathan Jones suggests that the real significance of both Turner and Frazer was "to visualize, in a modern, disturbing way, the ancient myths".[18] First published in 1890, *The Golden Bough* begins with a meditation on Turner's painting: "Who does not know Turner's picture of the Golden Bough?", Frazer asks in the first chapter. "The scene, suffused with the golden glow of imagination in which the divine mind of Turner steeped and transfigured even the fairest natural landscape, is a dream-like vision of the little woodland grove of Nemi – 'Diana's Mirror,' as it was called by the ancients." In asking why Frazer begins by invoking Turner's painting, Jones points out that Turner's reputation had changed dramatically during the succeeding period. Spurned by his contemporaries as an eccentric, Turner was recognised by the Late Victorians and by the modernists as a great painter of myths: "Frazer was a Victorian . . . [and] for him, Turner is a painter of stories set in landscapes: a grandiose mythologist":

> Gods and monsters populate Turner's art, and for his first audience, his great achievement was to visualize, in a modern, disturbing way, the ancient myths. In the greatest of all his mythological paintings, *Ulysses Deriding Polyphemus – Homer's Odyssey* (1829) in the National Gallery, the ship representing intelligent, rational human aspiration sails away from the towering, formless mountains where the vague, shapeless giant Polyphemus rages in the clouds. Yet the sea is an unhealthy, fiery colour – the location of this adventure was said to be the Sicilian coast below volcanic Mount Etna – and the sea itself might be about to erupt in fire, anticipating the vicissitudes, the deaths, yet to come.[19]

Jones concludes that in citing Turner at the very beginning of his own book, "Frazer might simply be announcing the kind of book it is".

It is just this sense of the modernity of myth, or better, the *contemporaneity* of myth, of the immanence of Homer's mythic quest in the modern world, that Miller evokes so subtly, as we have seen, in *Conditions of Faith*, and again, though more self-reflexively, in *Lovesong*. As Emily and Antoine embark on their own modern adventure as a homosexual man and a runaway wife, they set sail from Marseille bound for Sidi bou-Said, and as they pass Sardinia, Homer's "island of giants", Emily remarks, "You might almost expect to hear them bellowing at us" (*Conditions of Faith*, 135). This is one way that might we think of Miller's achievement as a novelist – or at least of one aspect of it. As a humble or journeyman "patterner", the novelist's role is to re-animate the ancient myths, the unoriginal stories of the tribe, for the purposes of ethical reflection. To do this effectively, however, they must be introduced "in a modern, disturbing way", just beneath the representational surface of what seems otherwise to be the familiar modern world. When Ken meets John Patterner for a coffee in Carlton, he notices that he has been reading: "I reached for John's book and turned it to see the title. It was an old Penguin Classics edition of Homer's *The Iliad*. The E.V. Rieu translation that my generation had been familiar with . . . There were yellow post-it notes sticking out of it" (114).

---

18 Jonathan Jones, "Modern Myths", *The Guardian*, 10 December 2005, 3, http://www.theguardian.com/artanddesign/2005/dec/10/art.classics/print.
19 Jones, "Modern Myths", 3.

9
Eye of the Storm: *Autumn Laing*

Alex Miller's tenth novel, *Autumn Laing* (2011), was inspired by the relationship between Sidney Nolan and Sunday Reed, who met at Heide in 1938. It was inevitable that Miller would write a novel about Nolan. It was Nolan's photographs of the outback, shown to him in Somerset in the early 1950s, that inspired him to emigrate to Australia as a young man. It was Nolan's friend, Barrett Reid, who first identified the photographs as Nolan's when Miller met him at Heide in 1990. It was also Reid who encouraged him to write a novel about "the life of art Nolan had lived at Heide in his early years as an artist".[1] Reid had made a similar suggestion to Patrick White at a dinner for "the *Overland* crowd" in Melbourne in 1973.[2] Although White dismissed the idea out of hand, *The Vivisector* (1970) was partly inspired by Nolan, who had not yet been excommunicated from White's inner circle.

When *Autumn Laing* was published, the Australian reviewers went straight for Heide and the link between Autumn and Sunday Reed, though some also cautioned against too literal a reading. Morag Fraser notes Miller's debt to Janine Burke's biography of Reed, *The Heart Garden* (2004), but then goes on to ask, "does that mean one should read *Autumn Laing* as a *roman-à-clef*? Absolutely not. *Autumn Laing* is gloriously and fully realized fiction".[3] Diane Stubbings insists that the novel "works best if the 'facts' of history are kept at a distance", and that "any grasping at [the characters'] real-life counterparts can only diminish them".[4] But it is not easy to hold the historical referent at a distance when it is one as fascinating as Heide in the 1940s. Foregrounding the relationship between fiction and the referent is, after all, a defining feature of postmodern fiction. If seeking to read characters in an historical novel in relation to their sources is to "diminish" them, it is equally diminishing *only* to see them as fiction, and to hold their relation to history, and to other texts, at

---

1 Alex Miller, "How I Came to Write *Autumn Laing*", in *Autumn Laing* (Sydney: Allen & Unwin, 2011), 448. All subsequent references are to this edition and appear in parentheses in the text.
2 Reid's suggestion is recorded in an extract from David Marr's then forthcoming *Patrick White: A Life*, published in *Overland* 121 (Summer 1990), the same issue that includes an extract from Miller's own work in progress, *The Ancestor Game*. Miller was not aware of Reid's suggestion until 2012, after the publication of *Autumn Laing*. Alex Miller to Robert Dixon, 28 May 2013.
3 Morag Fraser, "A Space of Its Own Creation: Alex Miller's Indispensable New Novel", *Australian Book Review* 335 (October 2011): 9.
4 Diane Stubbings, "Passion's Hinterland". Review of Alex Miller, *Autumn Laing*. *Canberra Times*, 8 October 2011, 23.

a distance. In his series of novels about art – in *The Sitters* and *Prochownik's Dream* in particular – Miller has long been interested in the creative process, in the way the imagination works upon its source materials, transforming them but also, ultimately, *depending* upon them – that is to say, being *attached* to them. The fictional world as Miller understands it is never its own final cause: "All my major characters in all my novels have been based on real people" (451). While it would be reductive to see *Autumn Laing* only as a *roman-à-clef*, it would be equally reductive to strip that third dimension out of it, leaving at best a two dimensional picture. Miller's historical novels are at their richest and most suggestive when they work with what Geordie Williamson describes as "the clasp between reality and invention".[5]

"Taking" from History

How, then, has Miller "taken" his "fiction", *Autumn Laing*, from history? His two main sources for Nolan's involvement with John and Sunday Reed were Brian Adams' *Sidney Nolan: Such is Life* (1987) and Janine Burke's *The Heart Garden: Sunday Reed and Heide* (2004).[6] His knowledge of Heide was also gained first-hand from frequent visits when Reid lived there in the early 1990s: "Heide was then in its old well-used state, with ash spilling from the fireplace in the library, and the air smelling of cigarette smoke and stale alcohol and books. A magical place."[7] Although it is not essential for reading *Autumn Laing* that readers are completely familiar with the historical events, Miller's exposure of the clasp between fact and fiction is an important dimension of the novel, part of the spectrum of readerly pleasures it has to offer, and having some understanding of its historical sources enhances our appreciation of Miller's brilliant condensation. Although *Autumn Laing* is not just a *roman-à-clef*, as Morag Fraser rightly argues, the novel's many subtle articulations with historical events and people, and with the other texts it incorporates into its own fabric, contribute to its allusive richness as a postmodern re-imagining of the era of high modernism in Australia.

Nolan first went to Heide in 1938, and his affair with Sunday Reed ended in July 1947, when he left to visit Barrett Reid in Queensland. During this period of nearly a decade, the breakdown of his marriage to Elizabeth Paterson and the development of his art unfolded through a series of events that Miller has adapted and compressed with masterly efficiency. At the beginning of 1938, Nolan was a student at Melbourne's National Gallery School and shared a flat with other students above a shop at the corner of Russell and Lonsdale Streets. Elizabeth Paterson, also a student at the school, was then his girlfriend. In a series of interviews with Adams, Nolan has told the story of how he tried to bluff Sir Keith Murdoch, the chairman of the *Herald* and *Weekly Times* and a champion of modern art, into giving him a scholarship to study in Europe, citing the support of William McInnes, the principal of the National Gallery School. Murdoch passed him on to the *Herald's* art critic, Basil Burdett,

---

5   Geordie Williamson, "Autumn's Fading Words Are Pure and Living Art", review of Alex Miller, *Autumn Laing*, *The Weekend Australian*, 1–2 October 2011, 20.
6   Brian Adams, *Sidney Nolan: Such is Life* (1987; Milson's Point, NSW: Vintage, 1992); Janine Burke, *The Heart Garden: Sunday Reed and Heide* (2004; Milson's Point, NSW: Vintage, 2005). See also Barry Pearce, ed., *Sidney Nolan: 1917–1992* (Sydney: AGNSW, 2007). The following account is taken from these sources.
7   Alex Miller to Robert Dixon, 6 December 2013.

who passed him on to George Bell at the Bell-Shore School, who in turn passed him on to the solicitor and art patron John Reed. That night, Reed invited Nolan to dinner at Heide.

Elizabeth Paterson was a talented painter in her own right, and the grand-niece of John Ford Paterson, a significant Melbourne impressionist, a member of the Heidelberg school, and a founding member of the Victorian Artists' Association.[8] Elizabeth was increasingly troubled by Nolan's involvement with the Reeds, and it was probably to secure their relationship that she married him so suddenly on 16 December 1938. The young couple was offered a house rent-free for a year at Ocean Grove near Geelong. From this time the Nolans and the Reeds were regular visitors in each other's homes, though Elizabeth became increasingly disengaged from the friendship, sensing its sexual dimension. In their studio at Ocean Grove, Nolan claimed the well-lit end of the studio and painted his Head of Rimbaud, using Kiwi boot polish, which was shown in the inaugural Contemporary Art Society exhibition at the National Gallery in June 1939.

When Elizabeth became pregnant, in December 1939 the Nolans moved back to Melbourne, where they ran a pie shop in Lonsdale Street. Nolan established himself in a shared studio in a dilapidated building in Russell Street, and was now visiting Heide regularly, though increasingly alone. He held his first one-man exhibition in the Russell Street studio in June 1940 and received a positive review by George Bell. By the time their daughter Amelda was born, on 18 January 1941, Elizabeth had moved back to her parents' home. During Easter 1942, while Nolan was on a cycling holiday in Tasmania, John and Sunday Reed attempted to bring things to a head, Sunday by inviting Elizabeth to move to Heide with Nolan, and John by telling her that Nolan would never become a great painter while he was with her. When Nolan returned from Tasmania, Elizabeth announced that the marriage was at an end and asked for a divorce. Shortly after, Nolan moved to Heide.

On 15 April 1942, Nolan was called up for military service and sent to Dimboola in the Wimmera, where he was stationed until 1944. During this period he returned to Heide whenever he was on leave and Sunday travelled out to visit him when she could. Through their intellectual collaboration, and in response to the Wimmera landscape, Nolan commenced his first major series of paintings, making the transition from abstraction to a fully realised response to the Australian landscape from a modernist perspective. As art historian Richard Haese argues, it was here, between 1942 and 1944, and not later in Queensland and Central Australia, that Nolan ended "the tyranny of the picturesque".[9]

The 1940s was the period of Heide's "Second Circle", when the Reeds were hosts to a circle of poets, painters and intellectuals that included Albert Tucker and Joy Hester, Arthur and Yvonne Boyd, John Percival and Mary Boyd, Max Harris, John Sinclair, Yosl Bergner, Danila Vassilieff and the psychiatrist Reg Ellery. All of them make cameo appearances in *Autumn Laing* under fictional names. This was also the period of the Ern Malley hoax, when the anti-modernist poets James McAuley and Harold Stewart submitted a suite of concocted modernist poems to the avant-garde little magazine *Angry Penguins*.[10] Established in 1940, *Angry Penguins* had been taken over in 1943 by John Reed and Max Harris, and from that time Nolan was closely involved, contributing poetry, essays and illustra-

---

8 Alex and Stephanie Miller own Max Meldrum's portrait of John Ford Paterson's brother alluded to in the novel: "Allan O'Hoy – Lang Tzu – purchased it for me, knowing my interest in Meldrum." Alex Miller to Robert Dixon, 6 December 2013.
9 Richard Haese, *Sydney Nolan: The City and the Plain* (Melbourne: National Gallery of Victoria, 1983), 9.
10 Michael Heyward, *The Ern Malley Affair* (St Lucia, Qld: University of Queensland Press, 1993).

tions. In July 1944, with the Ern Malley obscenity trial running, Nolan deserted from the army and went underground, dividing his time between Heide and a studio that the Reeds had found for him in Parkville.

By the end of the war, in May 1945, Nolan was living full time at Heide, where he made his second major series, the famous Ned Kelly paintings. During the second half of 1946, Nolan lived alone at Heide while the Reeds travelled in Queensland, partly to recover from the strain of the Ern Malley affair, and while in Brisbane they met the poet Barrett Reid. When they returned to Heide in November, Nolan was still working on the Kelly paintings. Although Reid's fictional counterpart, Barnaby Green, is a fixture at Old Farm from the beginning, Reid visited Heide only briefly for the first time late in 1946, and observed the collaboration between Sunday and Nolan. Their work on the Wimmera and Kelly series is compressed in the novel into Autumn and Pat's collaboration on the Hinterland series during their visit to Sofia Station, Barnaby's property in Central Queensland. By the end of 1946, Nolan was exhausted and increasingly troubled by the affair, and his desire to move on was becoming acute. Almost immediately after the Kelly series was finished, on 8 July 1947, the Reeds drove him to Essendon Airport to begin his journey to Brisbane, where he and Reid embarked on a tour of Queensland, taking in Fraser Island, Far North Queensland and the Carnarvon Ranges, where Reid's family had a cattle station. Sunday did not go with him and it was the end of the affair.

Miller's transformation of this source material into the plot and settings of *Autumn Laing* is not only masterly in its efficiency and compression, it is also utterly compelling in its fictional realisation. While much of the material has been liberally re-imagined, Miller clearly takes some of the early episodes, including the dialogue, more or less directly from Adams' 1987 biography, an essential source, since his accounts of these early incidents in Nolan's life were obtained directly from Nolan in interviews. They include the shooting and butchering of the horse for dog food at Ocean Grove, Pat's claiming of the light-filled end of the studio there, his meetings with the newspaper tycoon Sir Malcolm MacFarlane, the art critic Guy Cowper and the solicitor Arthur Laing, in their Melbourne offices, and Pat's arrival at Old Farm. Adams' book was written while Nolan was still alive and is discreet about the affair. He describes the Reeds' visits to Ocean Grove as "raising the emotional temperature" and causing Elizabeth "unease", and in a reference to Nolan's regular presence at Heide during the mid-1940s, he hints that "The French would describe the relationship as a *ménage-à-trois*."[11] In *The Heart Garden*, Burke is more forthcoming, even explaining the sleeping arrangements at Heide.

Miller's condensation of the larger account of events that Adams, Burke and other sources provide might be described as Aristotelian in so far as it strives for a simplicity, if not quite unity, of the essential fictional parameters of time, place and action. It condenses a complex biographical narrative into single events and examples that are at once historically representative and fictionally compelling. There is a quite remarkable sense of temporal compression, as if the entire decade has been condensed into weeks or even days. As Geordie Williamson puts it, "history has been streamlined in the name of literature . . . characters and events have been rearranged, elided or expunged without compunction".[12] The novel's main events are confined to three or four episodes, each corresponding to one of its three parts, and each is confined to the duration of a single day and night. In part one, the details of Nolan's and Elizabeth's moves from Melbourne to Ocean

---

11   Adams, *Sidney Nolan*, 44, 65.

Grove and back are gone. Pat and Edith are already married and living at Ocean Grove, and the two paintings they make in the studio there – her impressionist landscape and his boot-polish abstraction – stand in for the period's complex history of conflict between the conservatives and the moderns. Edith announces that she is pregnant on the morning of Pat's trip to Melbourne from Ocean Grove to meet McFarlane, which culminates in his overnight visit to Old Farm. In part two, the Laings make their one visit to Ocean Grove, where Pat and Autumn begin their affair. Its implications for the two households, and for the history of Australian art, are elaborated during their drive home to Old Farm and the sleepless night that ensues.

Also in part two, in the chapter titled "The Flies", Miller manages to evoke the entire decade-long bohemian interlude at Heide in the course of a single afternoon and night, during which Pat's affair with Autumn is consummated and his marriage to Edith ends. Brief references to the formation of a "new art society" (176) and its proposed exhibition capture the history of the Contemporary Art Society and its series of exhibitions during the 1940s. In the course of a single argument between Pat and the painter Louis de Vries, Miller even brings together at one time and place the entire cast of what Burke calls Heide's First, Second and Third Circles. The alcoholic psychiatrist Freddy Henning, for example, is drawn from the First Circle's Reg Ellery. Barnaby Green, "the beloved poet laureate of our circle" (9), is an established presence at Old Farm before Pat's arrival, foreshadowing Barrett Reid's move to Melbourne in 1951 as part of the Third Circle, and even his much later residency at Heide when Miller knew him in the early 1990s. Barnaby's presence on that day coincides with Edith's definitive break with Pat, enabling him to bear sympathetic witness to the breakdown of her marriage.

While these events are heightened and condensed, others are ellided. The entire Pacific War, Nolan's watershed encounter with the Wimmera landscape, his desertion from the army and the years in hiding, the Ern Malley hoax, and the iconic Kelly series of 1946, are glossed over in the interests of compression and economy. In Part Three, Pat and Autumn's one brief excursion together to Barnaby's property, Sofia Station in Central Queensland, compresses the complicated development of Nolan's art during the 1940s, from abstraction to landscape and figurative painting. The Hinterland series they paint together at Sofia Station stands in for both the Wimmera and Kelly series, and foreshadows those that were to come from the Queensland trip of 1947, including the Eliza Fraser and explorers series. Pat's transformative experience of the landscape of the Expedition Range, especially the view from the air, brings forward in time Nolan's previous experience in the Wimmera, and brings back in time his trips to Fraser Island, and North and Central Queensland in 1947, and his later trip to Central and Northern Australia with his second wife Cynthia Reed, in 1949.

Autumn Laing is the most intricately constructed of Miller's novels since *The Ancestor Game* in 1992. Its eighteen chapters are divided into three parts, each dealing with a different phase of the story, and each illuminated by a network of intertextual allusions that provide a distinctive stylistic register to the individual parts, much like Nolan's suites of paintings. Some of these references might be understood simply as historical detail necessary to provide a convincing fictional realisation of the period, but they also provide

---

12 Geordie Williamson, "Bright Treasures of Perception: Writing Art and Painting Words in *Autumn Laing*", in *The Novels of Alex Miller: An Introduction*, ed. Robert Dixon (Sydney: Allen & Unwin, 2012), 232.

a richly suggestive framework of motifs that illuminate the larger structure of the novel while also enriching Miller's deceptively transparent prose in a way that makes close reading essential. Through this design, Miller suggests something of Nolan's intense awareness of the connections between painting, fiction, poetry, music and the stage, which he shared with his modernist contemporaries, including his friends Patrick White and Benjamin Britten.

Part one comprises eight chapters: the three dated entries of Autumn's memoir for January, March and July 1991, and the five titled chapters: "Edith Black, 1938", "Pat Donlon", "Edith's Announcement", "The Big Picture", and "Arthur". These chapters are the prelude to the affair between Autumn Laing and Pat Donlon, introducing the main characters and bringing the events to the eve of Pat's arrival at Old Farm. The main intertextual presences in part one are Arthur Rimbaud's poem, *Une saison en enfer* (1873) and Guy de Maupassant's novel *Une vie*, or *A Woman's Life* (1883).

Part two comprises three more of the dated entries – one for September and two for November 1991 – and three titled chapters: "Once, If I Remember Well...", "Picnic at Ocean Grove", and "The Flies". This section deals mainly with the central period of the affair and with bohemian life at Old Farm. While there are several intertextual allusions that provide motifs for this section, including *Une vie*, Verdi's opera of bohemian life *La Traviata* (1853), and Patrick White's *The Eye of the Storm* (1973), the dominant intertextual presence is again *Une saison en enfer*, whose opening line is "Once, if I remember well..." In concert with a number of other allusions here and in Part Three, including Dante's *Divine Comedy*, the overarching presence of *Une saison en enfer* subtly shadows the historical events at Heide in the 1940s, suggesting the archetypal myth about sacrifice and the origin of art, the descent of Orpheus and Eurydice into the underworld, as it is represented, for example, in Jacques Offenbach's *Opéra bouffon, Orphée aux enfers* (1858 and 1874).

Part three comprises two dated entries, both for December 1991, and two final titled chapters: "Retribution", also the title of the climactic chapter of *Une vie*, and "Paradise Garden", the title of Nolan's infamous attack on the Reeds in a series of satirical poems and illustrations, published in 1971.[13] The dominant intertextual reference, however, is the *Divine Comedy*, particularly Dante's invocation of his muse, and the poem's overall scheme of an ascent from hell to paradise, which echoes and supports the novel's three-part structure. In this section, Pat Donlon realises his goal of becoming an Australian modernist painter by travelling with his muse, Autumn Laing, to Sofia Station, near the Expedition Range in Central Queensland, where *Landscape of Farewell* is also set.

Into the Fire

Autumn Laing opens with the first entry in the eighty-five-year-old Autumn Laing's memoir, in which she describes the impact of her recent encounters with two women. Edith Black is the first wife of the painter Pat Donlon, with whom Autumn conducted a tumultuous and destructive love affair in the late 1930s. Seeing Edith after so many years inspires Autumn to begin the memoir, in which she intends to ask herself, "whether what

---

13 Sidney Nolan, *Paradise Garden: Paintings, Drawings and Poems*, with an introduction by Robert Melville (London: Alistair McAlpine, 1971). Reprinted in Sidney Nolan, *Nolan on Nolan: Sidney Nolan in His Own Words*, ed. Nancy Underhill (Camberwell, Vic.: Viking, 2007).

we destroyed in the service of his creations was of greater value than what he and I produced" (22). Autumn's second encounter, with her biographer Adeli Heartstone, leads her to burn all of her original diaries and notebooks in a forty-four-gallon drum, the remains of which are still smouldering as she commences the memoir: "I watched the pages curl and catch ... An added delight in watching them burn (knowing there is no return from fire) was that Biographers love nothing more than notebooks" (17–18). It had been Autumn's intention to send her papers to the National Library, but Adeli's arrival at Old Farm provokes this frenzy of self-defensiveness.

Autumn's memoir is to be an act of "confession" and a quest for "absolution" (7). The dated entries, written in the first person, alternate with titled chapters written in the third person that provide a seemingly more objective account of events surrounding the affair fifty years earlier. An "Editor's Note" at the end of the novel, signed by Professor F. Adeli Heartstone of Vassar College, Poughkeepsie, refers to her biography, *Autumn: The New Artists' Group and the Circle of Autumn Laing*, published "to wide acclaim" by the University of California Press in 1998 (441).[14] Adeli reveals that Autumn's papers were not burned after all, and that the account of their destruction is a "fiction": "I had use of all those 'burned' diaries and journals. They are held in the National Library of Australia, where they may be consulted" (443). She explains that Autumn's 1991 memoir was written in "nineteen exercise books" (442), and that in addition to this source, she had full access to all of the records at Old Farm: "The truth ... is that we spent many long hours together going through the immense collection of Laing papers in the dining room" (443).

The reader has to come to terms here with a number of discrepancies. According to Autumn, she burned all of her papers and did not cooperate with her biographer; according to Adeli, the papers were not burned and Autumn cooperated with her research even to the point of collaboration. While the "Editor's Note" refers to nineteen exercise books, the novel contains only eighteen chapters. In a perceptive reading of the novel, Geordie Williamson was the first to ask, "What purpose does it serve the author to include an afterword that muddies the clarity of the novel as a whole?" Such devices are a hallmark of the novels of Vladimir Nabokov, a touchstone author for Miller, whose novel *The Gift* provides an epigraph for *Autumn Laing*: "The most enchanting things in nature and art are based on deception." In *Lolita*, his best-known novel, Nabokov begins with a forward by Humbert Humbert's psychologist, who introduces the narrative as one of his case studies, only to be contradicted at the end by Humbert, who claims it is a work of fiction. As Williamson recognises, "such exercises in deception augment the narrator's legitimacy, not undermine it".[15] In setting up these contradictions between Adeli's and Autumn's accounts, Miller creates a powerful force field in which he is quite free – how could we possibly hold him to account? – to explore the relationships between reality and imagination, life and art, history and fiction.

The burning of Autumn's notebooks is a playful allusion to the widely publicised "rediscovery" of Patrick White's papers in 2006. David Marr, whose biography *Patrick White: A Life* was published in 1991,[16] was aware that White and his partner Manoly Lascaris had destroyed a large cache of letters and manuscripts before moving from Castle Hill to Cen-

---

14   Adeli's affiliation with Vassar College is Miller's playful acknowledgement of two American academic friends, Professors Paul Kane and Ronald A. Sharp. Ironically, on 5 November 2013, Miller himself delivered the annual Gifford Memorial Lecture at Vassar.
15   Geordie Williamson, "Bright Treasures of Perception", 236.
16   David Marr, *Patrick White: A Life* (Milson's Point, NSW: Random House, 1991).

tennial Park in 1963. In 1997, White had written to the director of the National Library, "I can't let you have my papers because I don't keep any. My manuscripts are destroyed as soon as the book is published... and anything unfinished when I die is to be burnt."[17] White died on 30 September 1990. His will was emphatic, but his literary agent and executor Barbara Mobbs demurred, secretly holding on to thirty-two boxes of papers until the death of Lascaris in 2003. On 3 November 2006, the National Library announced, with "immense hoopla", the "rediscovery" of White's papers.[18] Marr recalls, "I was down there in a flash, working quietly with the librarians before the big public announcement, laughing and gnashing my teeth that the old bastard had kept so much from me."[19]

Autumn begins writing her memoirs amidst the smell of burning. Burning one's papers is a way of concealing unwonted personal memories from succeeding generations. At many periods in history it has been an infamous means of censorship and cultural forgetting. It is the way witches were made to tell the truth. As Autumn subjects herself to the traumatic recollection of her passionate sexual and artistic collaboration with Pat Donlon, the burning of her archive foreshadows the imagery of storms, fire storms, waves and whirlwinds that sweep through the novel like leitmotifs in an opera, evoking the ambiguous force of both artistic and sexual passion. The single word that best condenses this powerful combination of erotic and artistic compulsion, as we have seen in Miller's earlier novels, is rapture. Pat Donlon's artistic ambition is "of such rapture its severity frightened even him" (23).

In a reference to both "the furnace of his art" (22) and the force of their sexual attraction, Autumn alludes to the biblical story of the Babylonian King Nebuchadnezzar II, who committed the three Jews, Shadrach, Meshach and Abednego, to execution in a fiery furnace, but lost his sanity when they emerged unscathed from the flames under the protection of the Holy Spirit (Daniel 1–3): "Like heartless Nebuchadnezzar with his three young men, I put Arthur to the fiery test. He survived but he didn't come out unscathed. Burned to the bone, he was. White as ash" (21). The allusive density of Miller's writing here is remarkable. The image of Arthur "trembling" before the flame foreshadows a recurring combination of storm and fire motifs that are braided through the novel, alluding also to Rimbaud's fiery whirlwind, the storms in Robert Burns' "Tam o' Shanter", and Patrick White's *Eye of the Storm*. Autumn's casting of herself in the role of Nebuchadnezzar also suggests Nolan's painting of Eliza Fraser in the pose of William Blake's *Nebuchadnezzar*, and Nolan's own account of Mrs Fraser's abandonment of the convict David Bracefell as an allusion to his treatment by Sunday Reed. Janine Burke describes *Mrs Fraser* (1947) as "an image of woman as beast", and links it to the image of Sunday in Nolan's *Paradise Garden* poems, where she is the seductress Eve who tempted and betrayed Adam.[20] And like Nebuchadnezzar, Autumn has not escaped the power of the flames: "The smell of fire is on me today" (19). Ironically, it is perhaps Edith who is the only one of them to come through unscathed.

Miller has said that the voice of Autumn Laing is that of his friend Barrett Reid, not biographically, but "in the spirit of his energies and determinations and his cussedness,

---

17 Quoted in David Marr, "Patrick White: The Final Chapter", *The Monthly* (April 2008): 30.
18 David Marr, "Patrick White's Return from the Pit", *Sydney Morning Herald*, 3 November 2006, http://www.smh.com.au/news/books/patrick-whites-return-from-the-pit/2006/11/02/1162339990980.html.
19 Marr, "The Final Chapter", 35.
20 Burke, *The Heart Garden*, 272.

and passion for getting the truth out . . . [his] willingness to take the blame, for shriving his soul of guilt before death took him".[21] There are also similarities between the elderly Autumn Laing and Patrick White's Elizabeth Hunter in *The Eye of the Storm*; between Old Farm, and Elizabeth's house on Centennial Park, whose gardens are also lashed by storms. Each woman is surrounded by a comical and grotesque entourage of nurses, doctors and attendants. As Miller was aware, *The Eye of the Storm* had been in the news during 2006 because of the "Wraith Picket" hoax.[22] As an experiment in the vicissitudes of literary reputation, the *Australian* newspaper had sent chapter 3 of White's novel to twelve Australian publishers, changing its title to *The Eye of the Cyclone* and the name of its author to Wraith Picket, an anagram of Patrick White. Ten of them rejected it, and the other two did not respond.[23] The film of the novel, directed by Fred Schepisi, was released on 27 July 2011, the same year as the publication of *Autumn Laing*.

Autumn and Elizabeth are both formerly beautiful women who have been unfaithful to their husbands, and who look back over their lives in an attempt to atone for the damage they have caused to others, the ruin of time providing a release from youthful passion and a potential vantage point for redemptive vision. Autumn's memoir is an act of secular confession, a quest for self-understanding and absolution. It is her "last chance to tell the truth" (11). Elizabeth's nurse, Sister Mary de Santis, sees her as the "ruin of an over-indulged and beautiful youth", but also "a soul about to leave the body it had worn, and already able to emancipate itself so completely from human emotions, it became at times as redemptive as water".[24] Both women seek that "calm in which the self had been stripped, if painfully, of its human imperfections".[25] On Brumby Island, Elizabeth Hunter is literally caught in the eye of a cyclone. In that moment, "she had experienced . . . release from her body and all the contingencies".[26] White's narrator asks, "are regenerative states of mind granted to the very old to ease the passage from their earthly, sensual natures into final peace and forgiveness?"[27]

As part of her quest for absolution, Autumn asks Adeli to present the notebooks to Edith after her death, but Edith declines to read them (442). Unlike the many other people damaged by Autumn and Elizabeth Hunter, Edith is resilient, and a survivor. She has come to terms with her past. Autumn's wish to dedicate her memoirs to Edith, to begin with a portrait of Edith as "a young woman", is also, implicitly, a portrait of the *artist* as a young woman, a portrait of the particular kind of artist that Edith was in the 1930s. It is a belated appreciation of her talent and her art. From a woman like Autumn Laing, who has played such a central role in the emergence of Australian modernist art, this is an act of both personal and historical revisionism. The novel's imagery of destructive flames applies not only to Pat and Autumn's affair, but equally to Pat's artistic ambition, his summoning of the storm of modernist innovation, which has required that Edith's own conventional kind of art be sacrificed: "She was the first to be sacrificed to the violence and the hunger

---

21 "You Could Have Been There (Unmasking the Fictional Voice)". The William Gifford Memorial Lecture, Vassar College, 5 November 2013. *Antipodes* 28, no.1 (June 2014): 222.
22 Alex Miller to Robert Dixon, 25 November 2013.
23 Hilary McPhee, "Publishing White. Or Not?" *The Book Show*, 19 July 2006, http://www.abc.net.au/radionational/programs/bookshow/publishing-white-or-not-transcript-available/3322394.
24 Patrick White, *The Eye of the Storm* (London: Jonathan Cape, 1973), 12.
25 White, *The Eye of the Storm*, 29.
26 White, *The Eye of the Storm*, 429.
27 White, *The Eye of the Storm*, 73.

of his ambition... The first to be fed to the strange dark blessing, the furnace of his art" (21–2). The relegation of Edith's beautiful landscape painting to the loft at Old Farm for more than half a century represents both the Laings' day-to-day repression of Autumn and Pat's affair, about which they cannot speak to each other without pain, and also a cultural forgetting of the kind of art that was sacrificed in order for Pat to make Australian painting "new". In that sense it can be compared to Lang Tzu's youthful rejection of traditional Chinese painting in *The Ancestor Game*, which also takes place in 1937. Sensitive to the judgment of history, Autumn warns, "we would do well not to forget Edith Black and her child. To forget them, as they have been forgotten, written out of our record, written out of Pat's history, is to lie to ourselves about the nature of our culture" (23).

The historical conflict between the conservatives and the moderns in Australia, to which Miller alludes here, was brought to a head by the establishment of the Australian Academy of Art by the Commonwealth Attorney-General, Robert Menzies, on 19 July 1937. Menzies' intention was for the Academy to disseminate funding for the arts and to establish a national gallery in Canberra. He won the support of establishment figures in the art world, including members of the Sydney Society of Artists and the Victorian Artists' Society, by his assurance that modernism would not be supported. In reply there was a surge of resentment among artists and patrons like the Reeds, who supported modern art, which led to the formation of the Contemporary Art Society in Melbourne on 13 July 1938, a breakaway group from the Victorian Artists' Society.[28]

Miller's cast of fictional characters personifies these conflicts of the late 1930s. Autumn Laing, born Gabrielle Louise Ballard in 1906, is one of the Ballards of Elsinore, one of Melbourne's wealthiest and most powerful Protestant establishment families: her real-life model, Lelda Sunday Baillieu, was born in 1905, and her childhood home was Balholmen, in Toorak. Rejecting the Ballards' "cold world of money worship" (13), which has already destroyed her beloved Uncle Mathew, Autumn and her solicitor-husband Arthur Laing buy Old Farm on the Yarra River, where they lead a life dedicated to art and literature, and where they become patrons of a circle of artists and intellectuals committed to modernism. Autumn recognises in the young working class Irish-Catholic artist Pat Donlon the future of an authentically Australian modernism. By contrast, Donlon's wife Edith is the granddaughter of Thomas Anderson, a Scottish-born portrait and landscape painter much favoured by the Ballards' class: "He was not a visionary... His subjects were leisurely pastoral scenes... His was the reassurance of a kindly nature for the drawing rooms of the well-to-do city folk and great country families who were his patrons" (30).[29]

These crosscurrents of the period are focused in the poignantly odd coupling of Edith Black and Pat Donlon in their studio at Ocean Grove. While Edith remains loyal to her grandfather's conservative legacy, Pat rebels against all that Anderson and his brown-toned landscapes represent. The cottage at Ocean Gove trembles from the concussion of the Great Southern Ocean breaking upon the coast, just as it trembles with the force of Pat's artistic ambition and the still-distant storm of international modernism: "Tides in him that swirled and drove against each other. Powerful undertow that dragged him out into the depths and sucked him down" (55). Edith is powerless to resist, and on the day of their

---

28 See Richard Haese, *Rebels and Precursors: The Revolutionary Years of Australian Art* (Ringwood, Vic.: Allen Lane, 1981), 42; and Adams, *Sidney Nolan*, 45.
29 In making Edith Black the granddaughter rather than grandniece of Thomas Anderson, Miller is compounding an error about the relation between John Ford Paterson and Elizabeth Paterson in both Adams' biography of Nolan (40) and Burke's biography of Sunday Reed (192).

arrival Pat claims the sunny end of the room that is to be their studio (37). Edith paints competent landscapes in the manner of her grandfather: she is "obedient to the rules", to "the traditions", but she is sufficiently in touch with the spirit of the times to know that her art will not be favoured by history. Edith has internalised the conventions of the previous generation and is aware that they both enable and constrain her work: "She hates the feeling that she has to get it *right*. For whom? It's not for herself, it's for *them*. Her teachers. Her grandfather. The traditions" (38–9). While Edith works meticulously on a single canvas, Pat (like Nolan) works *en série* and has made five pictures by the end of their first day, including the abstract design using Kiwi boot polish that he will later title *Hommage à Rimbaud* (39, 59). In Miller's compelling descriptions of Pat's manner of painting, he shows him rapt by the force of his native talent, which he fears will be extinguished if he submits to the National Gallery School's training: "he feared [Edith] would plead with him to submit to the discipline of the great tradition" (95). Like Nolan, Pat is inspired in his rebellion against artistic convention by the biographical legend of Arthur Rimbaud, the French poet and scourge of bourgeois values, whose poem *Une saison en enfer* Pat declaims as he works in the studio at Ocean Grove. In his characterisation of Pat Donlon, Miller captures what Kristin Ross calls "Rimbaudian subjectivity".[30]

"Rimbaudian Subjectivity"

Several aspects of *Une saison en enfer* are especially important to Miller's characterisation of Pat Donlon, including Rimbaud's identification with the subaltern, and his exploration of embodied forms of subjectivity that resist instrumental reason and its regime of "work". In her chapter "The Right to Laziness", Ross discusses these themes as an expression of the ideals of the Paris Communards which also anticipate the ideas of the Situationists, Gilles Deleuze and Félix Guattari, and other French theorists of the post-1968 generation. For Rimbaud, the Paris Commune was a unique moment in French history because it sought to dismantle the state apparatus of the Second Empire: literally, it was the moment when "work" stopped.[31] The nineteenth century is imagined in Rimbaud's poetry as the epoch in which instrumental reason triumphed through the institutionalisation of "work" and its inscription on the body of the subaltern: the metropolitan *ouvriers* and the subjected peoples of the French colonies. In part two of *Une saison en enfer*, "Mauvais sang" ("Bad Blood") Rimbaud calls this "the vision of numbers". Ross glosses this phrase as a succinct encapsulation of the Weberian rationalisation of peoples' productive capacities and nature's resources into markets, their rationalisation according to cost accounting, and the breakdown of labour and materials into quantifiable components. The "vision of numbers" is the stage reached when everything in life is calculated. In Rimbaud's poetry this corresponds with the triumph of French colonialism in the Mahgreb, the moment when exotic and distant lands were opened up to European commercial interests.[32]

In London, Rimbaud and his lover Paul Verlaine were involved with the circle of exiled Communards that included Paul Lafargue, whose satirical pamphlet *Le droit á la pareses*

---

30 Kristin Ross, *The Emergence of Social Space: Rimbaud and the Paris Commune* (Minneapolis: University of Minnesota Press, 1988), 66.
31 Ross, *The Emergence of Social Space*, 59.
32 Ross, *The Emergence of Social Space*, 71.

appeared in 1880. It is a parody of the doctrine of the *Droit du travail*. Lafargue exposes the results of overproduction in the advanced capitalist countries, and the necessity of European capital to find new markets in undeveloped lands, and he uses the French verb *lézarder* to describe the freedom of non-colonised space: "Capital abounds like merchandise. The financiers no longer know where to put it; and so they go into happy nations where people lounge [*lézardent*] in the sun smoking cigarettes, to build their railroads, set up factories, and bring in the malediction of work."[33] Although Miller was not to explore Lafargue and Rimbaud's ideas directly until *Autumn Laing* in 2011, they clearly have significance for his earlier interest in the overseas projection of European capital in *Conditions of Faith*, including Ferdinand de Lesseps' construction of the Panama and Suez canals, Georges Elder's work in Morocco and Tunisia before the war, and Hakim el Oudie's sympathy for the anti-French demonstrations at Sidi bou-Said. Arthur Rimbaud's combination of "laziness", decadence and homosexuality, and his identification with France's colonial subjects in the Maghreb, has a particular resonance, in retrospect, for the role Antoine Carpeaux plays in securing Edith's freedom.

Ross argues that Rimbaud's peculiar achievement in *Une saison en enfer* is "to have articulated the strategic position and pathos of the adolescent body approaching and entering what 'the vision of numbers' designates as adulthood".[34] Miller's Pat Donlon is at just this stage in both his personal life and his vocation as an artist, and much of what passes for his ill-bred behaviour might be seen instead as an instinctive resistance to "adulthood" in Rimbaud's sense, a shorthand term for subjection to capital, to the state, to instrumental reason. Rimbaud embraces instead the condition of the abject, investing his desires in those "inferior races" and classes who are marginalised in official French history: "I am well aware that I have always been of an inferior race", he writes in "*Mauvais sang*". It is his primitive ancestors, the Gauls, with whom he identifies, and from whom he takes his "pale blue eyes". For Donlon, it is the Irish and the gypsies: "being called a gipsy did not carry the demeaning force of an insult, implying instead the exotic, a hidden promise of something uncommon" (48–9). Ross argues, however, that the concept of "identification" is inadequate to describe "Rimbaudian subjectivity", which involves a form of *over*-identification in which the Rimbaudian subject in effect *becomes* the subaltern: "There is no I-Rimbaud who suddenly hallucinates an identity with various marginal characters; instead . . . a whole parade of universal history, races, cultures, and populations will be played out on the body of the speaker."[35] In "*Mauvais sang*", the poet *becomes* North African at the precise moment when colonialism and Christianity arrive: "The White men are landing! Cannon!"

Rimbaud's affinity with the subaltern is performative; it is always on the verge of passing over into embodied action. It is also the means of his *dis*-identification with "the vision of numbers" and its regime of work in favour of other modes of subjectivity that Ross, following Deleuze and Guattari, calls *action libre*. While "work" describes the subject's internalisation of the state apparatus, *action libre* is a form of embodied freedom and mobility that has revolutionary potential. In the Commune poem, "*Qu'est que pour nous, mon Coeur*", this is expressed in "the spectacular physics" of the whirlwind, "a word that both literally and figuratively means agitation":

---

33 Paul Lafargue, *Le droit a la pareses* (Paris: Masperio, 1965), quoted in Ross, *The Emergence of Social Space*, 69.
34 Ross, *The Emergence of Social Space*, 71.
35 Ross, *The Emergence of Social Space*, 67.

> Who will stir up whirlwinds of furious fire
> If we do not, and those whom we call brothers?
> Join us, Romantic friends! Forget all others!
> And never will we work, O waves of fire![36]

Rimbaud's distinction between the bourgeois regime of "work" and the "whirlwind" of *action libre* corresponds with Edith and Pat's very different work practices in the studio at Ocean Grove. Edith is subject to what Lafargue had called "the malediction of work". Like Lang Tzu, she has internalised the techniques of her grandfather's tradition, resenting the compulsion to get it "right" by conforming to the rules, yet powerless to resist their control over her hand and eye. The passage Pat recites from *Une saison en enfer* on page sixty-five of *Autumn Laing* is the conclusion of "*Mauvais sang*", where Rimbaud *becomes* the body of the North African at precisely the moment when the *action libre* of the "dance" is subdued by the "march" of the French colonists and their slave caravan. In these lines, Ross argues, "power relations are inscribed on the body as the regulated movement of the march overcomes the whirlwind, the nomadic language of the dance. Space is stratified in a single direction: 'the French way, the path of honour' ".[37] As the house at Ocean Grove trembles with the distant concussion of the Great Southern Ocean, Pat's mode of working is an *action libre* that flows directly from his own internalisation of those "waves of fire", the "tides in him that swirled and drove against each other . . . The dance force in him was never still" (55).

Pat Donlon stands on the verge of "adulthood" both as a man and as an artist. In his art he resists the internationalisation of training and convention. The contrast between this creative freedom and Rimbaud's "vision of numbers", between *action libre* and "work", is expressed in Pat's instinctive preference for his own "childish" handwriting above the copperplate script of Edith's mother, Maude Black, which he glimpses on the envelope of her letter to Edith. Although he is no good at figure drawing, he recalls that as a schoolboy being taught to write he was mesmerised by the expressive power and untutored freedom of the pen:

> he might have been defensive about his own handwriting once upon a time, for it *was* childish . . . When he wrote he stuck the tip of his tongue out the corner of his mouth . . . Having his tongue under control helped him concentrate on the point where the nib was moving across the paper, releasing its lovely mysterious snail trail of dark ink . . . There was . . . no limit to what the ink trail could manage in the way of uncovering and portraying likenesses and even thoughts . . . The day Miss Tasker issued the class with pens and nibs and inkwells Pat was smitten with the power that was handed to him and fell in love with the life of the ink trail. That day, his secret life of words and art began their mysterious dance. (47–8)

Copperplate, which the aptly named Miss Tasker had tried to impose upon him at the behest of the Victorian education department, is a means of enforcing the "conformity of regularity". It is "the enemy" of his burgeoning artistic sensibility, and "he refused with fierce intuition. Seeing the trap at once. To bring the ink trail under their control" (48).

---

36 Quoted in Ross, *The Emergence of Social Space*, 68.
37 Ross, *The Emergence of Social Space*, 69.

Just as Pat's handwriting remains "childish" because he resisted being taught copperplate at school, as an aspiring artist he rejects the training of his eye and hand at the National Gallery School. He recognises Edith's competence as an artist, acknowledging that she is the better draughtsman, but is suspicious of the training she has received, concerned that it will destroy his native abilities: "You've absorbed their training... It's *in* there now. You'll never be free of it. You'll never get it out. I'm not going to pollute my eye with their rubbish" (40–1). In his descriptions of Pat at "work", Miller perfectly captures the embodied freedom, the *action libre* of the Rimbaudian subject, which Rimbaud himself associated with the dance and the whirlwind. Pat imagines himself to be a warrior-artist wielding his brush like a battle axe, and he conflates the dark ink with the blood of the horse he has just butchered:

> He stood at his work table looking at his picture. "Horse's blood", he said aloud, talking to himself without knowing it. He was gripping the edges of the table with his outspread hands, leaning forward and looking down onto his picture... He was drawing quickly on the sheets of butcher's paper. Freely wielding the narrow brush. He loaded the brush from the bowl of rich black ink, carelessly flicking spots and drips of ink about the place. Flicking some of it on purpose. On himself. To join the spots of blood. Scattering his seed. A warrior. (58, 60)

While Pat works in this state of rapture, he chants to himself the final lines of "*Mauvais sang*", in which the dance of the Negro is replaced by the march of the slave caravan: "That's what he was. Being the *voyant* of Rimbaud's youthful intoxications" (60).

Miller's achievement here is to have taken the known facts of Nolan's life and a deep understanding of the significance of Rimbaud's politics and aesthetics, and to have created from these sources a fully realised fictional characterisation that is also an interpretation of "Rimbaudian subjectivity". We have come to see, however, that Miller typically uses texts or concepts to dramatise world-historical forces while retaining his own distance from them. An example is the way he plays Henry Adams' vision of the Middle Ages against Ferdinand de Lesseps' vision of the Panama Canal in *Conditions of Faith*, though without investing in Adams' nostalgic idealism. While Miller provides this vividly realised interpretation of Rimbaudian subjectivity, Pat Donlon's principled "childishness" is revealed, from another perspective, to be a form of adolescent narcissism that has the capacity to destroy others. As he paints, Pat remembers the origin of the nude figures he is drawing, the plump daughter of the local butcher, Mr Creedy, who gave him the paper on which he is working:

> He had tied the paper on the back of his bike and ridden home with his booty. And as he rode he daydreamed that big motherly girl waiting in her father's shop all her life to render this service to him... She was a fitting mistress for a warrior poet... Black ink staining the paper now instead of the carmine blood of the slaughtered sheep and cattle... he might have called her his muse for this enterprise, but muse was a notion he had rejected along with all the other old nonsense form the Gallery School masters. (64)

The irony here is almost Joycean in the way it measures Pat's Rimbaudian vision of himself as a warrior-artist against the provincial banality of the butcher's daughter who inspires him: it suggests, for example, Stephen Dedalus' "epiphany" as he watches the young girl wading on Dollymount Strand in Joyce's *Kunsterlerroman*, *A Portrait of the Artist as a*

Young Man (1916). Is Pat's "childish" attitude to artistic training and convention a principled "laziness" from which will emerge the work of a great artist, or is he also, in another sense of the word, childish – that is to say, immature, self-absorbed, and oblivious to the real value of his wife's art?

Une vie

While the young Pat Donlon identifies with the Rimbaud of *Une saison en enfer*, the main intertextual reference that dominates Autumn's "realistic" portrait of Edith Black is Guy de Maupassant's novel, *Une vie*, or *A Woman's Life* (1883). On the morning that Pat sets off from Ocean Grove for Melbourne and the series of meetings that will lead him to Old Farm, Edith is reading *Une vie*. She is still reading it – though is perhaps further advanced in its revelations – on the stormy day when the Laings visit them for the first time at Ocean Grove. As usual, Miller requires us to linger over the title, challenging his reader's capacity to take part in the experience of reading intertextually: "Her book lying face down on the blanket, the author's name on the cover in small block letters, Guy de Maupassant. The title in the same tone of red that reapers and binders were painted, *Une vie*. A Life. A woman's life, he supposed it was" (98). Pat's comparison of this blood-red book to a reaper and binder – an agricultural machine used to cut and bind grain – is grotesquely inappropriate to Edith's refined artistic sensibility, recalling the young farmhand's near fatal encounter with a threshing machine in *The Tivington Nott* and Tess' deadly encounter with farm machinery in another late-nineteenth-century novel about the fate of women, Thomas Hardy's *Tess of the D'Urbervilles* (1891). When Arthur meets Edith at Ocean Grove she is "like his idea of Hardy's Tess" (252). Pat is uncertain about the gender of the French title, suggesting a lack of understanding of his wife. As in *Autumn Laing*, the action of *Une vie* is accompanied by violent storms, and so it is ironic that it was to relieve "the storm gathering in his head" (98) that Pat had asked Edith to read *Une vie* to him two nights earlier.

Jeannette, the heroine of de Maupassant's novel, is the daughter of the Baron de Vaude, a disciple of Rousseau and a secular aristocrat committed to the ideals of the Enlightenment. Like Autumn Laing, "His great strength and also his great weakness was his kindliness, a kindliness that had not arms enough to caress, to give."[38] Miller has a longstanding interest in the economy of the gift, and Autumn is perhaps his most sustained meditation on the ethically ambivalent motives that underlie the desire to give. It is Autumn's beloved Uncle Mathew, whose "love" for her has ambivalent motivations, who first points out that hers is "the gift of recognition" (15), "an ability to acknowledge the gifts of others" (180). Autumn interprets this to herself in an entirely positive light: "I was gifted to recognize the strengths of others, often before they saw their strengths themselves. I was the one who . . . brought them into their own light" (16). The negative side of giving to others is that it can be a violation of their difference, the creation, in fact of monstrosity, as Mary Shelley demonstrates in *Frankenstein*, and as Dickens shows in *Great Expectations*. In each of these novels, the one whose motives of benevolence or curiosity or ambition

---

38 Guy de Maupassant, *A Life*, translated with an introduction and notes by Roger Pearson (New York: Oxford University Press, 1999), 4.

move them to bring the other "into their own light" also risks violating the integrity of the other, and inevitably incurs their resentment.

The Baron had placed Jeannette in a convent at the age of twelve so that she might be "restored to him pure at seventeen", and he intends now to induct her into an adult life of happiness, benevolence and enlightenment. As they set off for their "Home by the Sea", a chateau called "The Poplars", stormy weather marks the beginning of her downfall. On that day in 1819, Jeannette marks her new beginning on her calendar. Years later, her soul scarred by her husband's infidelities, she will rediscover the calendar in the loft, that repository for "dusty things . . . exiled in a period that is not their own".

At the nearby town of Yport, Jeannette's family meet the Abbe Picot, a worldly priest, who introduces them to Julien le Vicomte de Lamare, who immediately proposes marriage. During their honeymoon on Corsica, Julien first displays his deceitfulness and greed by appropriating Jeannette's purse, a gift from her mother containing two thousand francs that is echoed in Maud Black's gift of money in the letter addressed to Edith in her copperplate hand. After their return to "The Poplars", Julien reveals his ill-temper and a tendency to violence, dominating the family's daily life and assaulting the Baron. In the chapter, "Jeannette's Discovery", Jeannette finds that she is pregnant while her maid, Rosalie, also gives birth to a child. Julien is the father of both children, and he has been sleeping with Rosalie since the first day he came to "The Poplars". When the Baron asks Abbe Picot for advice, the priest makes him confess in front of Jeannette and her mother that he carried on in the same way with his wife's maid. The Baroness merely smiles at the recollection of her husband's escapades, "for she belonged to the sentimental class for whom love adventures are a part of existence". Julien's violence and his selfish disregard for his wife's wellbeing suggest another, more critical perspective on Rimbaudian subjectivity, while his mother-in-law's aristocratic acceptance of infidelity foreshadows the patrician disdain for bourgeois morality that defines the modern *ménage-à-trois* at Old Farm.

De Maupassant is interested in the paradoxical relationship between private and public knowledge, between what people actually know and remember, and what they claim to know; with the way sexual scandals are both "discovered" and concealed. Memoirs and letters, secreted in the drawers of bureaus or in the lofts of homes, condense this paradox of openness and concealment. Jeannette finds her mother crying while reading her old letters: "It is my 'relics' that make me cry", she says, "They stir remembrances that were so delightful and that are now past forever, and one is reminded of persons whom one had forgotten and recalls once more." The Baron, knowing his own secrets and perhaps also suspecting his wife's, gives Jeannette contrary advice: "burn your letters, all of them – your mother's, mine, everyone's. There's nothing more dreadful, when one is growing old, than to look back to one's youth." When her mother dies, Jeannette reads her letters and finds that she had an affair with her father's close friend, Paul d'Ennemare, and to protect her father, and also to protect herself from further unwanted revelations, she collects all of the family's letters and burns them. When Autumn looks through the papers on the dining table of Old Farm and begins writing her memoir, she too is exhausted by the "scourging whip" of memory (71): "The truth, terrifying when you consider it, is that nothing is so forgotten it cannot be brought back to haunt us" (69).

In the beautifully modulated chapter, "Picnic at Ocean Grove", Miller brings the two couples together at the commencement of the affair, Pat and Edith, and Autumn and Arthur, exploring the subtle differences between them as people while never losing sight of the connection between the drama of character and the drama of ideas. The relationship between Autumn, whose wildness as a younger woman has left her infertile, and Edith, who is pregnant and ill with morning sickness, is one of lethal rivalry. Edith's copy of *Une vie*, is prominently in view on her bedside table beside a basin of vomit. Autumn sits beside her on the bed thinking about Pat. In a tableau worthy of de Maupassant or Hardy, Miller describes a fly crawling toward its inevitable entrapment in a spider's web: "A solitary fly dragged its heavy body slowly up the grimy windowpane towards a spider web already damaged and hung about with embalmed corpses of various luckless insects" (241). Miller alludes here not only to Mary Howitt's fable about innocence and experience, "The Spider and the Fly" (1829), but also to Autumn's age and sexual history, echoing Nolan's reference to Sunday Reed's "old plumbing" in *Paradise Garden*: "It seemed to her the web was so old and dusty and so in need of repair that the spider must have died or gone elsewhere long ago, leaving its deadly trap behind – like a sin committed in the past" (242). Edith's emotional intelligence allows her to see Autumn as a threat to her marriage, and she releases her from the obligation to sit with her. In a striking image that recalls Emily's "voyage out" aboard the *Kairos*, Miller confirms the impending sacrifice: "A faint imprint of Autumn's lipstick on Edith's forehead reminded Autumn of the pinkish export stamp on New Zealand legs of lamb" (243).

The climax of *Une vie* is the revelation that Julien is also conducting an affair with the Comtess Gilberte, Jeannette's closest friend and the wife of their neighbour, the Comte de Fourville. In a chapter titled "Retribution", the Comte discovers that Julien and Gilberte have sheltered from a storm in a portable shepherd's hut, which he locks from the outside, wheels to a cliff and pushes over into the sea. The adulterous couple is crushed to death. Jeannette is a witness to the Comte's crime but keeps his secret. The edge of the sea is Maupassant's chosen setting for both passion and "Retribution", as it is for Miller. It is at the cottage by the sea at Ocean Grove where, in the chapter titled "Retribution", Edith's brothers burn Pat's books and paintings, expunging him from the record of their family's history and memory. These scenes of passion and retribution are accompanied by the melodrama of the storm, a motif that resonates through both novels, connecting them intertextually in the same way that Nolan's individual paintings are connected to each other in series, and to other texts.

In *Une vie*, De Maupassant explores the psychic economy of "the loft", that repository of destructive secrets that paradoxically are known to all. Are such secrets best revisited, as Jeannette does, or are they best burned, as the Baron recommends? In *Autumn Laing*, the architectural metaphor for this concealment and recovery of memory is the loft in the coach house at Old Farm. In her entry for November 1991, Autumn recalls the stormy night in 1938 when she and Arthur drove home from Ocean Grove, unable to speak openly about her attraction to Pat Donlon: "The loft was a place where you might stash something you loved but to which painful memories were attached. A thing you wanted to keep, but to keep out of sight" (109).[39] In the narrative present, Autumn has recently recovered Edith's painting from the loft, and the damage caused on that night is expressed again by the violent imagery of the reaper and binder:

---

39 Miller recalls, "I climbed into the loft of the old coach house (now destroyed) for Barrie who was looking for something . . . and found there many rolled up canvasses . . . by some of the Heide artists. And shoeboxes of Nolan's letters. . . . I got them down for Barrie, who was getting a bit frail and didn't feel safe climbing into the loft." Alex Miller to Robert Dixon, 6 December 2013.

> [Edith's painting] remained in the loft for more than fifty years, like a forgotten bale of hay. Tossed.
>
> Once I would have said . . . [it] was forgotten by us. Now I would say we had no wish to remember it. The mind is capable of deep silences on subjects we have no desire to deal with. The loft swallowed it and the problem of Edith's painting conveniently disappeared from our sight for half a century . . . It was enough that it was gone, *like the rainbow's lovely form evanishing amid the storm.* (273)

The line in italics is from another text about a storm, to which Miller also refers in *The Ancestor Game*, Robert Burns' "Tam o' Shanter", in which the ghosts of the past rise up in the coming darkness of a stormy evening. The melting of the snowflake and the "evanishing" of the rainbow of Burns' poem represent not only the sacrifice of Edith's marriage to Pat and Autumn's affair, but also the cultural forgetting of her style of painting, which remains under-appreciated for half a century until Autumn revises her estimation of its worth. In relegating Edith's painting to the loft, the Laings are not only repressing their knowledge of the affair so that the surface of their marriage can be maintained, but also relegating an artistic style to history. Unable to sleep and troubled by the storm, Autumn recalls the "thunder of the waves" on the beach at Ocean Grove that day with Pat:

> Lying there in the dark, strangely awake in the warm intimacy of my bed, it seemed to me that I had danced with Pat Donlon in the eye of life and death; as one might dance in the eye of a storm for an instant before being tossed helplessly to one's death. A *totentanz* of the liberated spirit. (273–4)

Miller brings together here around the literal storm in *Autumn Laing* the melodrama of passion and retribution in *Une vie*, and the destructive force of Elizabeth Hunter's infidelities in *The Eye of the Storm*. When Elizabeth experiences the eye of the cyclone on Brumby Island, the destruction of the summer house and its grounds is said to be "no worse than any she had caused in her life in her relationships with human beings".[40] After Autumn has recovered Edith's painting and examined it again, she experiences remorse not only for stealing Edith's husband and destroying her family, but also for destroying her chance to have become "one of the very few truly gifted Australian women artists of her time" (118). Autumn's return to her repository of lost things is a way of understanding cultural memory and cultural forgetting, and the kind of historical revision and recovery represented by acts of scholarly recuperation like Janine Burke's *Australian Women Artists, 1840–1940* (1980).[41] Just as Autumn is a different person in 1991 to the woman she was in 1938, so her understanding of the changing fashions in art history has been modified: she was not capable of "seeing" Edith's painting in 1938 (118).

The Storm of Modernism

In "The Big Picture", Miller offers a fictional account of Nolan's meeting with Sir Keith Murdoch and the *Herald*'s art critic, Basil Burdett, in 1938. His achievement is to have

---

40 White, *The Eye of the Storm*, 425.
41 Janine Burke, *Australian Women Artists, 1840–1940* (Collingwood, Vic.: Greenhouse, 1980).

taken the bare facts of that meeting, derived from Adams' biography and other sources, and to have expanded them into a richly imagined episode that suggests the broader reception of modernist art in Melbourne in the late 1930s. Murdoch was managing editor of the *Herald* and *Weekly Times*, whose new building on Flinders Street was completed in 1928. His major private interest was in contemporary art. In 1933 he was appointed a trustee of the National Gallery of Victoria, and together with Burdett, he set out to challenge the conservative Melbourne art establishment, whose leading spokesman was the director of the National Gallery of Victoria (NGV), J.S. McDonald. In 1939, Murdoch sponsored an international exhibition that was a watershed moment in the Australian reception of modernism. Organised by Burdett, the *Herald* Exhibition of French and British Contemporary Art opened in the Melbourne Town Hall in June 1939. It was the first direct contact most Australians had with modernist painting and sculpture. Richard Haese describes it as "a major assault on popular and academic taste", exposing Melbourne to "the shock of the new".[42] It was also a personal turning point for Nolan, his first encounter with original works by Picasso, Cézanne, van Gogh and Gauguin. Janine Burke describes Nolan's arrival at the exhibition with a heavily pregnant Elizabeth in October 1939, and wearing gumboots, his only shoes. He was already intimate with the Reeds, who met them there and introduced them for the first time to Joy Hester.[43]

Miller's description of the artworks in the headquarters of his fictional "newspaper tycoon" (144), Sir Malcolm McFarlane, combines, in a single episode, Nolan's meeting with Murdoch in 1938 and the impact upon him of the *Herald* exhibition the following year. Dressed like a "bohemian" and wearing plimsolls, Pat enters a "grand and imposing building" with a domed ceiling, bronze doors and panelled walls hung with original paintings, that at once suggests the NGV, the Melbourne Town Hall, and the *Herald* building. In the foyer, Pat is overwhelmed by Sir Malcolm's latest acquisition, "The Big Picture", which he later learns is by Wyndham Lewis:

> He was in a vast echoing area of shiny marble surfaces under the soaring vault of a high-domed ceiling. An enormous painting in a black metallic frame was hanging on the back wall in the magnificent importance of its own specially mounted spotlights . . . It was obvious what it was. A grand masterwork by one of the great European moderns . . . Pat's heart contracted. A confident arrangement of sweeping geometric forms in tones of carbon blue and sea grey. What seemed to be represented were gigantic human forms, naked and leaping about in some energetic activity, dancing or fucking or fighting . . . The painting was brazenly self-assured . . . Pat had seen nothing like it before outside the pages of glossy art magazines. He felt it like a slap in the face. (125)

Although nothing by Wyndham Lewis was hung in the *Herald* exhibition, he is an appropriate hinge between Miller's fiction and the history of modernism. In *The Modern Movement in Art* (1927), which Arthur Laing is reading on the night he meets Pat (161), R.H. Wilenski describes Lewis as one of the leading figures in British modernism in the period before the Great War.[44] Sir Malcolm later tells Pat that the painting is one of Wyndham Lewis' prewar abstractions that Guy Cowper (Burdett) "winkled out of a private

---

42   Haese, *Rebels and Precursors*, 61–3.
43   Burke, *The Heart Garden*, 193.
44   R.H. Wilenski, *The Modern Movement in Art* (London: Faber, 1927).

collection in London" (146–7). Its blue-grey tones and the subject matter suggest *Kermesse*, one of Wyndham Lewis' most influential works from this period, now lost, that was commissioned for a fashionable London nightclub, Madame Strindberg's Cave of the Golden Calf, and exhibited at the Royal Albert Hall in 1912. The title is a Flemish word for a peasant fair or carnival, and again invokes the Rimbaudian theme of the dance. It was painted on a massive scale intended to overwhelm the viewer, combining Cubist structure with the intensity and violence of Futurist motion: "The central male and female dancer seem to be in a moment of ecstatic unconcernedness, about to tumble headlong into the orgiastic ritual going on around them". Walter Sickert described *Kermesse* as a "revelation of dynamic art".[45] "If it was up to me and Guy", Sir Malcolm boasts, "Wyndham Lewis ... would be hanging in that bloody great mausoleum up the road they call the National Gallery, instead of that brown muck those bloody tonalists call art" (145).

Pat's encounter with "The Big Picture" enacts a confrontation in time and space between international modernism and the belatedness of provincial art. As Pat stands before the painting holding his own shabby folder of experimental drawings of the butcher's daughter, he experiences the "shock of the new", the irresistible storm of modernism. We might recall here the title of Wyndham Lewis' journal, *Blast*. At the same time, Miller suggests the belatedness of provincial culture. The painting forces Pat to realise "that what he had hoped to achieve one day had already been far surpassed by the artist who had painted this picture ... He would never be able to compete with this kind of thing" (126). Even Pat's slight over-estimation of Wyndham Lewis' significance and reputation as "one of the great European modernists" is perfectly calibrated to reflect the extreme reactions the *Herald* exhibition provoked among Melbourne artists and critics. Although conservatives like McDonald famously excoriated the exhibition as the work of "degenerates and perverts", in reality Burdett's selection was confined to British and French paintings, and excluded the avant-garde work of the leading European expressionists and surrealists.[46]

We can use Pascale Casanova's idea of the Greenwich Meridian to understand the cultural geography of modernism implicit in Pat's encounter with "The Big Picture". In *The World Republic of Letters*, Casanova develops a model of international cultural space in which the great centres of Paris, London, and New York represent the precise location of modernity in space and time:

> what might be called the Greenwich Meridian of literature makes it possible to estimate the relative aesthetic distance from the center of the world of letters of all those who belong to it. This aesthetic distance is also measured in temporal terms, since the prime meridian determines the present of literary creation, which is to say modernity ... At stake in the competition ... is mastery of just this measure of time (and space), which is to say the power to claim for oneself the legitimate present of literature and to canonize its great writers ... or, to the contrary, to dismiss a work as an anachronism or to label it "provincial".[47]

---

45 "Exuberant and Orgiastic: Wyndham Lewis and his *Kermesse*", http://renaissanceutterances.blogspot.com.au/2012/03/exuberant-and-orgiastic-wyndham-lewis.html. The title and subject of another of Wyndham Lewis' paintings, *Inferno* (1937), are appropriate to the novel's historical period, and its themes of conflagration and descent into the underworld. It was acquired by the NGV in 1964.
46 Eileen Chanin and Steven Miller, *Degenerates and Perverts: The Herald Exhibition of French and British Contemporary Art* (Carlton, Vic.: Miegunyah Press, 2005).

To be far from the centre, as Pat is in Melbourne, is to be relegated to the cultural province and not to be of the current moment. This is the "diffusionist" account of modernism that has been disputed by advocates of "the new modernist studies", such as Susan Stanford Friedman, who replace it with a geography of multiple modernities and multiple centres of innovation. As we have seen, it is this de-centred model that Miller develops in his earlier historical novels set in the modern era: Hamburg, Shanghai and Melbourne in *The Ancestor Game*; Sydney, Paris and Sidi bou-Said in *Conditions of Faith*. In *Autumn Laing*, Miller will also go on, in part three, to present Pat's invention of an Australian modernism in Central Queensland. But in part one, which is set in the late 1930s, prior to that moment, he presents the perception of colonial belatedness that the imported works in the 1939 *Herald* Exhibition caused in Melbourne, even for people like Nolan and the Reeds. The experience is repeated when Pat enters Sir Malcolm's panelled office, whose walls are hung with other works by "British and European modernists": "In their presence [Pat] was aware of his provincialism and the vastness of his ignorance" (143).

Yet Miller is not content to allow the impact of "Wyndham Lewis' masterpiece" (152) to render Australian art irredeemably provincial. When Pat returns to the foyer from Sir Malcolm's office on the fourth floor, he has the opportunity to re-view the big picture, just as Autumn is given the opportunity, fifty years later, to revise her opinion of Edith's Ocean Grove landscape. Pat now sees "it is not enough for a work of art to follow the fashions imported from elsewhere: it must also spring from the sources of its own culture; it must be authentic". While Sir Malcolm had insisted on the importance of following what people are doing in Europe, Pat aspires to do "the things that no one else is doing" (149). Later, in his argument with Louis de Vries at Old Farm, when his understanding of his own mission as an artist has become clearer to him, he will put this more succinctly. Pat's challenge is not simply to make it new in the way that the Europeans already have: it is also to make it Australian. Louis advocates Pound's injunction to "make it new", but he associates the new with the Greenwich Meridian of Europe, unwittingly condemning modernism in Australia to be belated and reactive – and, in a word, provincial: "It takes enormous skill and heroic persistence to make something new in art. Either we follow Europe in this, or we Australians will fall by the wayside and remain a pointless backwater forever" (302). Pat, however, refuses to locate modernism solely in Europe, and counters that "making it new is Europe's problem". When Louis asks, "what *is* our problem, Patrick?" Pat replies, "Our problem is to make it Australian" (303–4). In the progression from Pat's initial deference to imported British modernism, to his sense of its inappropriateness in another context, to his more refined arguments at Old Farm, and their final realisation in the practice of an Australian modernism at Sofia Station, Miller describes the arc of Pat's aesthetic and intellectual development as the hero of his *Kunstlerroman*.

The Underworld

Pat's arrival at Old Farm is described in the chapter "Once, if I remember well . . .", which is the opening line of Rimbaud's *Un saison en enfer*. The bare facts of that night, as told by Nolan to Adams, are that while Sunday went into the kitchen to prepare the meal, "the

---

47 Pascale Casanova, *The World Republic of Letters* (1999; Cambridge, Mass.: Harvard University Press, 2004), 87–8, 90.

two men sat down in the library in easy chairs before the empty fireplace with large glasses of whisky".[48] It was the first time Nolan had drunk whisky, and not having eaten all day he soon became light headed. Miller's style, however, is far from realistic. We are in the register now of another Nolan-like suite of paintings or stage settings whose leitmotifs suggest the modernist aesthetic of intertextuality and the fusion of different art forms. Miller's allusion to Rimbaud suggests that Pat's meeting with the Laings is a descent into the underworld that will at once be creative and destructive, especially for Edith Black. As usual, he foregrounds the intertextuality, so that we have to read the episode through the texts that are woven into the fabric of the dialogue and description. Before leaving the library to go into the kitchen, Autumn leaves the English translation, *A Season in Hell*, open on the arm of the couch (194). Pat reads aloud the opening lines: "Once, if I remember well, my life was a feast where all hearts opened and all wines flowed" (195). In Rimbaud's poem, these lines are bitterly ironic, evoking an idyllic past that may or may not have existed, but to which there will certainly be no return in the present. As the speaker descends into hell, he embraces self-destruction through a deliberate derangement of the senses by drug taking and identification with abjection that repudiates "the French way, the path of honor".

A gentle and urbane man, Arthur Laing often communicates enigmatically by citation, leaving his listeners to supply the missing lines, or to clarify the meaning of his quotation for themselves. He now repeats the lines that Pat has already read, "My life was a feast . . . ", teasing out their possible meanings: "He gave a small satisfied laugh with the warmth of the whisky and the fire in it . . . 'It gets rather gloomy after that lovely opening if I remember' " (198). As Arthur well knows, no word in English could be less appropriate to describe Rimbaud's poem than the anodyne "lovely". Does Arthur really believe this or is he being ironic, fully aware of what these lines presage? As Pat drinks Arthur's whisky, he unwittingly echoes the opening lines of the third section of *Une saison en enfer*, "Night in Hell": "I have just swallowed a terrific mouthful of poison . . . My guts are on fire". When he drinks the first glass, he holds it at arm's length and looks at it "as if it had contained acid" (195). While Arthur stokes the fire, Pat is overwhelmed and disoriented, the heat in the closed room interacting with the alcohol to disorder his senses: "Pat looked at the piece of wood in the fire and drank from his glass. The whisky burned its way down his throat and lay in the void of his stomach like a pool of mercury, an eye of unease" (198–9). There is an echo, too, of Sabiha's encounter with Stolichnaya Vodka in her own descent into the underworld in *Lovesong*. Pat's thoughts, as they are represented in Miller's focalised narration, are disordered and fragmented, in imitation of Rimbaud's style. Arthur describes the abstract painting by Roy de Maistre over the fireplace as "strong", but for Pat "the word had no meaning . . . Everything was strong, wasn't it? Water. Fire. Hate. Envy. All of it. Love. The smell of shit . . . He wondered if the day would ever come when he would murder someone. The thought came into his head unbidden like a silent dream" (201–2). Staring at the showers of sparks racing up the chimney, Pat hallucinates "a flight of children and mothers crying out in dismay, a whole town of innocents raped and murdered" (195). Lines from *Un saison en enfer* rise up involuntarily in his memory like the sparks or like whisky fumes. This is another, altogether more dangerous aspect of "Rimbaudian subjectivity": "His head was going places on him. He stood up, then abruptly sat down again. *I contrived to purge my mind of all human hope*. Rimbaud's poem was on the loose in him" (202).

---

48   Adams, *Sidney Nolan*, 39.

While the opening lines of *Une saison en enfer* hold out the tantalising prospect of a pastoral idyll only to withdraw it, Pat thinks about his beautiful young wife Edith, alone in their cottage at Ocean Grove with her book, "*Une vie*, a woman's life". He asks himself a question that he has not yet been able to answer: "What sort of a woman's life was it?" (203). The layers of intertextuality here are complex, *Une saison en enfer* and *Une vie* facing each other like two mirrors that create a *mise-en-abyme* of tragic irony. Just as Rimbaud's poem begins by withdrawing its hollow promise of an idyll, the domestic idyll that Pat imagines as he descends into hell is also denied to Maupassant's heroine, Jeannette, by her husband's infidelities. Pat imagines that he can hear "Edith's lovely soft voice reading the French to him" (203), but the text she reads is an accusation of the crime against her that he is soon to commit. In so far as this episode recalls another descent into the underworld by Orpheus, the archetypal artist, Pat's inward glance at Edith through the "eye of unease" seals her fate as his Eurydice.

In Bohemia

The chapters "Once, If I Remember Well . . . " and "The Flies" are like two of Nolan's panels that belong to the same suite or series by virtue of their common leitmotifs, variations on the theme of the artist's descent into the underworld. "The Flies" is the core chapter of part two, dealing in the course of a single afternoon and night with Pat and Edith's first visit to Old Farm, evoking the bohemian life of Heide's first, second and third circles, and culminating in both the sexual initiation of Pat and Sunday's affair and the definitive breakdown of Pat's marriage to Edith. It is a bravura performance. Miller's characters converse in a web of quotations from poetry and opera. A young painter tries to seduce Alice Meadows by reading Yeats, while Louis de Vries sums up his impression of Pat Donlon by citing a couplet from T.S. Eliot's "Choruses from the Rock": "*The heathen are come into thine inheritance, And thy temple have they defiled*" (298). Barnaby's singing of the famous chorus from Verdi's *La Traviata*, "Ah! Godiamo, la tazza" (303), allows the episode to move easily between the registers of realism and metafiction, lending a self-reflexive quality to Miller's evocation of *la vie Bohème*, while also suggesting its tragic and destructive possibilities in the fates of Alfredo and Violetta. The characters' visual imaginations are also captured through ekphrastic description. The drunken painter George Lane, for example, leers at Alice Meadows as she walks past and he turns her into an Albert Tucker painting in his imagination: "he had a tight smile in his eyes, visualizing a series of Alice in gipsy dresses with bloodstained fangs, her thighs gaping, revealing some kind of dark evisceration . . . Was it a fairground in hell?" (300).

Our understanding that these well-educated people of the 1930s, with their modernist tastes, should be familiar with the poetry of Yeats and Eliot is fundamental to the craft of the historical novelist in building a convincing sense of the period. Yet in Miller's hands, intertextual allusions are also part of the way he brings his characters to life on the page. Fearing that he will lose his wife to Pat Donlon, Arthur speaks to Autumn the first two lines of W.B. Yeats' poem, "Maid Quiet": "Arthur spoke into the silence, his voice tempered to the rhythm of the poem, 'Where has Maid Quiet gone to, nodding her russet hood? The winds that awakened the stars are blowing through my blood.' He looked at Autumn" (318). When Autumn asks, "And the rest?" Arthur makes an impatient gesture and replies, "It's gone from me for the moment" (318). Miller also expects his readers to be actively engaged in this intertextuality: we are required to know and to supply the missing lines: "O how could I be so calm/ When she rose up to depart?"

During the afternoon, as Autumn and Pat drift toward their affair, Autumn enters the garden through a rose arch on which the climbing rose is "*Félicité et Perpétue*", an echo of *Conditions of Faith* and its theme of female martyrdom, while Pat observes a praying mantis lying in wait on a leaf for its prey (309). At night, when Pat and Autumn go down to the river while Arthur keeps his vigil in the library and Edith sleeps, they are all aware of a vixen prowling in the garden, which Edith thinks of as a place of evil (328), a "garden of death" (331). After Pat has sex with Autumn on the river bank he experiences hallucinations like those on the first night at Old Farm, this time imagining that he is being tormented by flies: "His brain was infested with small back figures leaping and running about in the eerie darkness, climbing over each other. An insane directionless panic of small black flies with grey markings on their backs" (321). For Edith, the imagery of flies epitomises her sense of the evil of Old Farm and its bohemian visitors: "the people who gathered here were trapped in an invisible web of disdain for the rest of humankind . . . They were like . . . flies with their legs caught in . . . sticky paper" (328–9). The motif develops from the earlier allusion to Mary Howitt's poem, "The Spider and the Fly". It may also allude to the hilarious blowfly aria in Jacques Offenbach's *Orphée aux enfers*, his satirical operetta about the decadence of the Second Empire, in which Eurydice, during her entrapment in the underworld, is serenaded by the lecherous Jupiter in the guise of a giant golden blowfly. During the night, as Pat goes with Autumn, Edith recalls George Lane leering at her that afternoon: "When George's drunken gaze had settled on her breasts a shiver had passed through her. It was as if he had touched her insides. His eyes frightened her" (329). The earliest indication of the motif is during Pat's mendicant visit to Sir Malcolm's office, dressed in his faux-bohemian clothes: "He noticed that a fly had got into the office and was buzzing around the back of Sir Malcolm's head . . . Sir Malcolm moved his head and the fly took off, then landed on the shoulder of his suit and began cleaning its legs" (144). While this first reference to the flies seems inconsequential, in retrospect we can see that it is part of a subtle critique of the ethics of bohemia and bohemians, who prey upon the hospitality of people like Arthur and Edith: "Arthur's impulse was ever to be generous" (344). Again, critics have yet to come to terms with the textures of Miller's style. It is reductive to suggest that in this chapter "each figure's more expansive meaning is suggested through strictly realist means".[49] The allusions to Verdi's and Offenbach's satires on the worldliness, decadence and bohemianism of the Second Empire perfectly balance Rimbaud's suicidal embrace of abjection and his excoriation of the French bourgeoisie in *Une saison en enfer*.

As if Miller wished briefly to register the existence of an alternative intertextual and moral realm, at the end of this harrowing chapter, Edith is rescued from the bohemian underworld of Old Farm by her brother Phillip, whom she calls her Phillip of Macedon. As a young girl she had written into his school textbook, Grote's *History of Greece*, "You are my hero, oh noble son of Amyntas" (333). The name of Amyntas' wife was Eurydice. At the railway station, away from the childless Laings and their frenzied commitment to art – though without her husband – the pregnant Edith emerges "courageously" into the daylight world of ordinary families: "mothers with prams, their older children at their heels . . . Fathers striking ahead, gripping a boy or girl's hand, and calling to their families

---

49 Williamson, "Bright Treasures of Perception", 237.

to hurry up or they would miss the train... She had been buried alive beneath the cold earth" (334). Edith's triumphal ascent is the mirror image of Sabiha's descent into the underworld of the Paris *Métro* in her quest to become pregnant in *Lovesong*.

After the breakup of his marriage to Edith, Pat lives at Old Farm and Miller evokes the period of Heide's notorious *ménage-à-trois*: "We were three, not two and one" (354). Edith's return to the world of children and families suggests Miller's detailed sense of what we might call the sociology of bohemia. This is something he has already examined in *Prochownik's Dream*, in the relations between the studio and the house, between the muse and the wife, and in Emily's decision in *Conditions of Faith* to abandon her role as wife and mother to pursue her vocation as a historian. Like Robert Schwartz and Marina Golding, Autumn and Arthur Laing are childless and, in a sense, married to art – though as patrons rather than practising artists. Autumn reflects that in her youthful fervour she had "put the idea of happy families a poor last on our list of choices?" (349). As art patrons from Melbourne's wealthiest social class, they have a sense of *noblesse oblige*: "There was no place where we felt ourselves to be free from the need to contribute. It had been bred in us" (358). Pat, on the other hand, has "no sense of social obligation. He felt no need to make a contribution." This is more than a legacy of his working class, Irish origins: it is his Rimbaudian status as an artist and outsider. His qualities are a kind of amoral "freedom" and "detachment" from obligation (358). But Pat is also burned by his season in the underworld. When Autumn asks him whether he has seen Edith and he confesses that he has lost her, Autumn sees that Pat's development as an artist has come at the cost of sacrificing his wife and child: "I saw there were tears in his eyes and I suddenly realized how much he was suffering" (369). The relationship between creativity and loss – even sacrifice – was explored in *Prochownik's Dream*, when Toni realises that in pursuing his collaboration with Marina he has been slipping "over the edge" into a place from which there may be no return. At the end of that novel, Toni is rescued by Teresa's promise to return to her marriage and the family home, but there will be no such reconciliation between Edith and Pat. Autumn sees that they have reached this furthest stage: "we're two of a kind. We're the destroyers, aren't we? But are we also the creators?" (370–1). Pat misses the life that he and Edith had created together at Ocean Grove; he grieves for its destruction, for the pain he has given her, and for his lost child. Like Joy Hester, who also abandoned her child, Sweeney, for her art, Pat has slipped over the edge into the space of destruction – and creativity. Autumn recalls this period at Old Farm as "the eye of the storm" (353).

An Australian Modernism

To introduce the final chapter, "Paradise Garden", Autumn consciously adopts the scheme of Dante's journey in the *Divine Comedy*: "Dante begins his journey at the portals of hell, and through long endeavour climbs slowly upward until he at last reaches the portals of paradise, but not without help" (385). This puts in place the final section of the book's mythic and intertextual underpinning, in the artist's descent into the underworld, the sacrifice of Edith/Eurydice, and the final emergence of his true art, in this case the Australian modernism that he has been imagining since his first encounter with Wyndham Lewis' British version of international modernism. But as Autumn says, we do nothing alone, and Miller's artist is to go into this final phase of discovering his creativity only through collaboration, which is also a form of inspiration. Miller invokes Dante's own invocation of the epic muse: "Dante appealed to Apollo to fire his imagination for his last labour . . . In what is surely the most perfect invocation to inspiration in the poetic world, Dante quietly pleads, 'Come into my breast and breathe there' "(385).

The title "Paradise Garden" is taken from Nolan's excoriating recollection of his affair with Sunday Reed, published in 1971. Miller's use of this title has complex implications. Janine Burke describes *Paradise Garden* as "an act of revenge administered as a public violation", which Nolan dedicated to his second wife, Cynthia. By contrast, Autumn's memoir is an act of private confession and atonement, dedicated, in effect, to the woman she has most damaged, Edith Black. Burke notes that while Nolan's title refers to the enclosed gardens of ancient Persia, "it can also refer to the Garden of Eden, a place of beauty, temptation and banishment, an archetypal symbol of loss".[50] Miller therefore subsumes much of the irony and bitterness of Nolan's title into the Dantesque scheme of the ascent from the underworld, the schema further reinforced by the implications of "Sofia Station", the last station in the journey, and the attainment of wisdom. As in the Central Queensland novels, Miller invokes the archaic meaning of "station" as a stage, in this case the final stage, in a *Via Dolorosa*. In a dense series of associations, the site of this artistic consummation has rich biographical and autobiographical significance for Nolan, for Barrett Reid, and for Miller himself, for whom the Expedition Range in Central Queensland is the location of his youthful first experience with Australia and of his later encounter with Indigenous Australia through his friends Col McLennan and Frank Budby. Like the location of the final scenes of *Landscape of Farewell*, the Hinterland series is a memorial to those friendships.

Pat and Autumn's journey to Sofia Station with Barnaby therefore has complex, overlapping historical, biographical, autobiographical and intertextual references. In her journal, Autumn writes about the extraordinary impact of the place and people after coming from Melbourne, the apparent clash of two completely different places and cultures within the single Australia, which Miller himself experienced for more than twenty years, and was finally able to put back together again in his Central Queensland novels, which were inspired by and are set in the same country. Their flight from Bundaberg in the historically authentic Beechcraft Staggerwing condenses into a single journey of autobiographical significance for Miller the historical sources of Nolan's watershed journeys to Queensland in 1947 and to central Queensland in 1949, when he and his second wife, Cynthia Reed, flew over the desert in a mail plane. In her journal, Autumn captures the transformative effect of aerial vision that reveals Australia to Nolan: "I was twisted around in my seat . . . Mesmerised by the scene below me I soon forgot my fears and became lost in the unfolding revelation of my country (389). In writing up her journal, a manifesto of Australian modernism, and then presenting it to Pat, Autumn repeats the foundational act for Miller of the gift, especially the intertextual gift of story or vision. This act of giving is the confirmation of their collaboration: "She would do as Uncle Mathew had predicted and acknowledge another's gift: encourage this man, Pat Donlon, to the vision and confidence that would help him to make a reality of his dream; an art of his country untutored by the traditions of Europe" (393). The novel concludes with a compelling account of the realisation of Pat Donlon's vision of an authentically Australian modernist art as he paints his fictional Hinterland series, working with Autumn at his side as Nolan did with Sunday Reed when he painted the Kelly series: "He came over and stood close beside her, his bare shoulder touching her upper arm . . . They stood like that, neither of them breaking the contact" (403).

---

50 Burke, *The Heart Garden*, 402.

10
Reading Lessons: *Coal Creek*

In *Coal Creek* (2013), which he has said will be his last novel, Alex Miller returns to the period and setting of his first published novel, *Watching the Climbers on the Mountain*: remote rural Queensland in the late 1940s. Reviewers have compared it to Marcus Clarke's *For the Term of His Natural Life* (serialised 1870–72),[1] Rolf Boldrewood's *Robbery Under Arms* (serialised 1882–83),[2] and Herman Melville's *Billy Budd, Sailor* (written 1886–91).[3] That is, they have compared it to a number of classic late-nineteenth-century novels about individuals in conflict with the power and authority of judicial, carceral or military institutions: innocent convicts, working-class lads, or young subalterns persecuted by corrupt systems and pathological individuals. Miller confirms, *Coal Creek* is "a parable ... to do with innocence and wisdom and the cruelty of systems".[4] The comparison with *Robbery Under Arms* is especially relevant, since Boldrewood was liberated to achieve some of his freshest and most original writing by using the voice of his currency lad hero, Dick Marston, who like Bobby Blue, narrates his tale from prison and is rewarded by the love of Gracey Storefield, who waits for him as Irie Collins does for Bobby. Bobby's proleptic references to the tragic events to which his account inevitably leads, and his tone of regret and remorse, resemble Dick Marston's narrative: "It was ... Irie, that taught me to read and write properly, or I would not be writing this account of the trouble that come on us now."[5] The central paradox of this deceptively simple novel is that Miller's semi-literate narrator provides a true and ethically reliable account of events that are otherwise persistently misinterpreted by those with more authoritative claims to truth, including the police, the judiciary and the press. Learning how to read, and learning to distinguish between what is true and what is not true, are the central themes of the novel. This makes *Coal Creek* itself

---

1 Anthony Lynch, "Real Men Roll Their Own", review of Alex Miller, *Coal Creek*, *Sydney Review of Books*, 14 March 2014, http://sydneyreviewofbooks.com/real-men-roll-their-own/.
2 Peter Pierce, "The Tragedy of People in the Wrong Place", review of Alex Miller, *Coal Creek*, *The Australian*, 21 September 2013, http://www.theaustralian.com.au/arts/review/the-tragedy-of-people-in-the-wrong-place/story-fn9n8gph-1226723001604.
3 Geordie Williamson, review of Alex Miller, *Coal Creek*, *The Monthly* (September 2013), http://www.themonthly.com.au/issue/2013/september/1377957600/geordie-williamson/alex-millers-coal-creek.
4 Alex Miller to Robert Dixon, 3 April 2014.
5 Alex Miller, *Coal Creek* (Sydney: Allen & Unwin, 2013), 16. All subsequent references are to this edition and appear in parentheses in the text.

a lesson in reading: it challenges the reader to make the right interpretation of people and events, and not to contribute further to the moral panic in which Bobby is engulfed.

Among the other parables of injustice to which it has been compared, *Billy Budd, Sailor* is particularly suggestive. Like *Coal Creek* in Miller's *oeuvre*, *Billy Budd* is one of Melville's late works. He began it in 1886 while in his late sixties, at a time when he was increasingly preoccupied with memories of his early life at sea, "in the time before steamships",[6] which has a similar role in his biographical legend to Central Queensland in Miller's. There are many parallels. Billy Budd, Bobby Blue and Ben Tobin are all twenty – just short of manhood – illiterate and without families, though Bobby's parents are still with him in spirit. Billy and Bobby are silent young men who find it difficult to anticipate trouble, partly because they do not like to think ill of others. Like the newly appointed Police Sergeant Daniel Collins, who is an outsider in Mount Hay, Melville's Captain Vere is a bookish and pedantic man who never sets out on a voyage without a freshly stocked library. Although Collins knows nothing about the country, he has brought with him some books on "the local people and history", and is proposing to "do some reading" and "become an expert" (13). On a ship of the line like the *Bellipotent*, the role of the master-at-arms John Claggart was "a sort of chief of police charged among other matters with the duty of preserving order on the populous lower gun decks".[7] The false accusation of inciting mutiny brought against Billy by Claggart is paralleled in *Coal Creek* by Rosie Gnapun's accusation against Ben Tobin that he has abducted her under-aged niece Deeds, and by Daniel and Esme Collins' belief that Ben and Bobby have engaged in a conspiracy to abduct their daughters Irie and Miriam. In each story, a moral panic develops within a small, isolated community controlled by a single institution, and a crime, real or imagined, is met with a pedantic and unjust interpretation of the law under pressure of exceptional circumstances: striking a superior officer in time of war, and the alleged abduction of minors. Melville rightly observes that during such "emergencies involving considerations both practical and moral", it is difficult to judge right from wrong when one is in "the fog" of the action. At such times, institutions and isolated communities require both a "sacrifice", and the performance of "proper usage". Billy, Bobby and Ben are "martyr[s] to martial discipline".[8] Melville and Miller dramatise the ambiguities of these situations through the "suggestive juxtaposition" of a series of contrasts: "the conflict of military duty with human feeling", shaped through a series of "congruent dichotomies": "nature versus society, feeling versus reason, rights-of-man versus ordered forms, Christian morality versus war, and so on".[9] When Billy strikes Claggart, Captain Vere sums up the moral and legal conundrum in his announcement, "Struck dead by an angel of God! Yet the angel must hang!"[10] Melville's condemned sailor is associated with the crucified Christ, and for years afterwards, pieces of the spar from which he is hanged are regarded by other bluejackets as "piece[s] of the Cross".[11] Bobby's mother, who sees the world in Manichean terms, warns him on the opening page of *Coal Creek*, "We all hang on the cross, Bobby Blue" (3), and later in the novel, Bobby glosses his mother's expression as meaning, to "suffer . . . injustice" (64).

---

6 Herman Melville, *Billy Budd, Sailor (An Inside Narrative)*, eds Harrison Hayford and Merton M. Sealts Jr. (Chicago and London: University of Chicago Press, 1962), 43.
7 Melville, *Billy Budd*, 64.
8 Melville, *Billy Budd*, 114–15, 117–18, 121.
9 Hayford and Sealts, Editors' Introduction, Melville, *Billy Budd*, 36.
10 Melville, *Billy Budd*, 101.
11 Melville, *Billy Budd*, 127, 131.

Coal Creek also has strong structural and thematic affinities with Miller's own, earlier Central Queensland novels, *Watching the Climbers on the Mountain*, *Journey to the Stone Country* and *Landscape of Farewell*. The relations between the principal characters have clear affinities with those in Miller's earlier essays in what I have called his Northern Gothic mode. Like John Hearn, who in Bo Rennie's view is brow-beaten by his wife, Ruth, Daniel Collins allows his professional judgement to be unduly influenced by his wife Esme. The tensions that develop between Robert Crofts, Ward and Ida Rankin and their daughter Janet are echoed, though in less sexualised forms, in the relations between Bobby Blue, Irie Collins and her parents – Janet and Irie are the same age, and both are eventually sent away to boarding school on the coast. The topography of the Rankins' homestead, with its separate men's quarters, is repeated in the police house at Mount Hay, while the violent climax of Collins' torture of Bobby Blue and the shootings of Daniel and Miriam Collins have their parallels in Ward Rankin's bullying of Crofts. One reviewer has even suggested that *Coal Creek* completes a Central Queensland "trilogy".[12] In one sense it does – but its origins go deeper, having none of the immediate engagement of *Journey to the Stone Country* and *Landscape of Farewell* with the political issues of the day. It is significant that *Coal Creek* goes back not to the mid-1950s, when Miller arrived and first worked in Australia, but to the immediate postwar years, to "1946 or 47" (9), when he was a boy in London. This is to suggest that *Coal Creek* might best not be read, after all, through comparisons with the works of other writers, but by driving our response to it right back as deeply as possible into Miller's body of work and its personal origins – at least in so far as they are accessible to us. The return to rural Queensland in "1946 or 47" is symptomatic: this is a highly distilled, introspective, "late" work that returns again and again to themes already familiar to readers who have begun to excavate Miller's "buried city of great complexity".

The location of *Coal Creek* is far north-west Queensland in the fictional town of Mount Hay, somewhere in the area of Mount Isa and "the Wheel" (9, 11), apparently a reference to the border town of Camooweal. Like Burke and Hungerford in Henry Lawson's stories of the 1880s, Mount Hay is "the end of the line" (9), "played-out mining and poor scrub country", but for Bobby it is "My country. I have no other" (49). Bobby has been out in the bush working as a stockman with his dad since he was ten, and is illiterate and innumerate: "I know the facts but I am not reliable around dates and numbers" (9). The narrative begins with his dad's death just after the war, when old George Wilson, the local policeman, also retires. Bobby's mother has died a decade earlier. The story has a pared-back, minimalist quality that is echoed in the blankness of the landscape. Like the stories Lawson wrote after his trip to the border towns of Burke and Hungerford, there is a sense that the land is blank, and that this visual failure to realise a landscape represents the failure of civil society. The funeral of the mother suggests archetypal images of the 1890s such as Frederick McCubbin's *A Bush Burial* (1890). Like Mount Coolon in *Journey to the Stone Country*, Mount Hay is a ghost town. There is a police station, a milk bar, a burned-out picture theatre, "a couple of unoccupied shops", a disused tennis court, and a public hall whose timbers are eaten by white ants (13). Many of the timber and fibro-cement homes are left empty as people die or move away. As in his description of Mount Coolon, Miller coveys the failure or retreat of pastoral settlement in Australia, a settler society in decline, though the echoes of Lawson suggest that it was ever thus, that these towns at the end of the state railway lines and roads have always been marginal, never quite reaching the point

---

12 Lynch, "Real Men Roll Their Own", 7.

of social and economic viability: "There was no real centre to Mount Hay like there had once been" (15). This is a failure of what I have called the cartographic imaginary, the failure of settler Australia to fulfil Edmund Barton's prophecy of "a nation for a continent":[13] "I do not know why they put a school so far away, but maybe they thought the town would grow out to meet it. But it never did" (14).

Daniel Collins' arrival at Mount Hay as the new police constable is the classic initiation of a Western plot, the arrival of a "stranger" in a small town. The old ways, the local ways, have been based on silence and toleration. Bobby's dad "never did have much to say", and if he did, "he raised his whip hand and indicated". He was "a silent man" (5). George Wilson "always give [trouble] a bit of clearance to sort itself out before stepping in" (10). Collins and his wife Esme are "coastal people". He makes it clear that he will do things "by the book" (12).

The events of the novel are generated by the pivotal relationship between the intuitive, deeply thoughtful and in some respects otherworldly narrator, Bobby Blue, and his damaged, dangerous, unpredictable friend, Ben Tobin. Bobby has many of the qualities that Miller admires in his Aboriginal friends, Col McLennan and Frank Budby. He has said that although Bobby is not an Aboriginal man, he has learned a great deal from being around Aboriginal people all his life.[14] The character of Ben Tobin, who is the catalyst of the trouble, was partly based on a school friend from the Downham public housing estate in south London, where Miller grew up, who had been sent to "Borstal": "He would've done very well in the Wild West, where there was no law . . . being with him led you into situations where if you'd been on your own you would never go."[15] These and other biographical sources that shadow the central pairing of Bobby and Ben provide a remarkably powerful set of contrasts, suggesting that in the two young men Miller is drawing together the crossed lines of the wisdom and maturity of old age with the volatility of youth.

Unlike the orphaned Billy Budd, Bobby comes from a loving family who bequeath to their son a legacy of love and support that he continues to draw upon many years after their deaths. Although he is uneducated and given to silence, Bobby has both a strong emotional intelligence and an active, inquiring ethical mind, which operates a constant dialogue between people, places, and events in the present, and his internalised memories of his parents. To this is added his sensitivity to the animal and natural worlds: "I take notice of the signs animals give us. They can save our lives" (56). There is a moment right at the centre of the novel, when Bobby is camping at night at the stone playgrounds of the district's Aboriginal people, when his affinities with Aboriginal spirituality are manifest. As he lays awake in his swag looking at the night sky, it seems as if the stars are rotating around him, and as he thinks about his troubles, he takes consolation in the peace that arises from this ancient and sacred place. At that moment his dead mother lays her hand on him and gives him a smile of benediction (145). He will be guided by her values until he is himself taken up the hill to the cemetery, that ruin of time, where his parents lie buried, as the Keal women lie buried beneath a tree on the farm at Araluen in *The Sitters*.

Bobby still weeps for his mother and cherishes his father's dying words of love for him, "hearing him say them often in my mind when I have struck a patch of trouble". These

---

13 Quoted in Robert Dixon, " 'A Nation for a Continent': The Cartographic Imaginary of the Federation Era", *Antipodes* 28, no. 1 (June 2014), 161.
14 Alex Miller, eulogy for Frank Budby, 14 April 2014, Holy Trinity, Mackay, unpublished.
15 Quoted in Jane Sullivan, "Interview with Alex Miller", *Sydney Morning Herald*, Spectrum, 5–6 October 2013, 28.

words were the simple statement, "I love you, son" (7). Bobby wishes that his father were still present to guide him, that "he had the chance to step in and redirect us with one of those indicating signs of his" (6). When Bobby meets new people, the spectral presence of the dead allows him to assess them according to his parents' values. He can see, for example, that Irie Collins will be "the kind of woman my mother and father would have had a high opinion of", and he wishes they could have known her (17). This is an active, not merely passive process of ethical inquiry, a real dialogue with his parents. Bobby may be silent for much of the time, but he is deeply thoughtful, especially on ethical matters and issues of justice. There is very little speaking in the novel, but Bobby's first-person narrative reveals his active inner life of ethical discrimination. When he first realises the weight of his "feelings" for Irie, he engages in a silent conversation with his mother: "I lay on my bunk at night ... and in my thoughts I told my mother of my feelings for that girl and my mother understood my feelings, as I always knew she would" (34–5). When Bobby realises that Daniel is over-eager to be liked, he thinks of him as someone whom his dad would have left to himself. Knowing how his father would react helps him to see and to understand Daniel's weaknesses, but it registers as "the flicker of what you might call contempt in myself for Daniel" (18). Bobby goes beyond this, not wanting to see the worst in people, and monitoring his own negative reactions: "it was something I rebuked myself for as I only knew him to be a good man and never deserving of anyone's harsh judgement" (18).

The generative core of the "trouble" that erupts in the novel is acknowledged to be inter-generational male violence. Bobby offers a subtle and insightful account of the origins of Ben Tobin's volatility. He knows that Ben has "a well of cruelty his old man put in him with the beatings he give him as a child" (33), and from Bobby's perspective, this accounts for his acts of aggression and bravado. As a young man, Ben displays the telltale cruelty to animals that is often a sign of parental abuse, deliberately breaking a dog's leg with his horse's hoof to show off to the other men (33), and beating a stockman who speaks to Bobby in the pub. At school, "he enjoyed taunting [the other boys] to show them how weak they was" (32). Ben's unpredictability and violence are a legacy of humiliation. Bobby understands that these actions do not express his friend's essential character, but are symptoms of his upbringing, a negative gift from his father: "it was like Ben had to keep proving for himself how weak other men were beside him and how they would take it from him, like he always had to take it from his old man" (38). But Bobby is precise in distinguishing between inner character and learned behaviour, between rational explanation and human feelings. He allows his relationships to be governed by "the heart", and believes "it is not a matter of forgiving or understanding but of just loving": "It is the heart that knows the truth in us" (38–9). The importance of feeling in Miller's ethical thinking is close to George Eliot's search for a humanist ethics that might replace the formal statement of ethical principles by institutions such as the church and the law, which informs her evocation of community in *Middlemarch*. In her 1858 essay on Edward Young, for example, Eliot argues that "dependency upon a rule or theory only is necessary when moral emotion is weak".[16] Miller has said that like Eliot, "I would myself assert that morality is not a matter of rules and principles but is a matter of feeling and behaving."[17]

---

16 Quoted in Rebecca Mead, *The Road to Middlemarch: My Life with George Eliot* (Melbourne: Text, 2014), 238.
17 Alex Miller to Robert Dixon, 12 April 2014.

Ben has previously given Rosie Gnapun's son Orlando a beating, and under Aboriginal law Orlando is not able to return home unless Ben apologises to the family. Rosie falsely reports to Collins that Ben has beaten her niece, Deeds, who now lives with Ben in his hut at Coal Creek. Without inquiring properly into the truth of the accusation, Daniel arrests him. Again out of bravado, Ben pleads guilty and is sentenced to a month in Townsville's Stuart Prison. The event is clearly presented as a matter of "injustice", or of differing ideas about "justice". Bobby is careful to explain how the outcome, which appears to be clear to the police, is actually a messy event arising from the collision of Rosie's resentment, Ben's bravado, Collins' inexperience and lack of understanding or even curiosity about the local people, and Bobby's own failure to explain and interpret the event to Collins: "I did not say nothing about my thoughts on this to Daniel or to Esme" (33). The challenge is to understand the events in all their complexity, not as they appear to be on the surface, or from only one of the several points of view involved, least of all from the powerful and privileged point of view of the law.

As Miller develops the crisis of "justice", he challenges his reader to see it not just as Daniel and Esme Collins see it – as modern, "coastal" people see it – according to the law, but as Bobby narrates it from his point of view, contributing his subtle insights into the tangled and often impure motives of the participants. This is something that Miller's fable of injustice has in common not only with *Billy Budd, Sailor*, in which we must set aside the naval panic about mutiny to grasp the underlying moral issues, but which it also has in common with *Billy Budd*, the opera that Benjamin Britten adapted from Melville's novella, and with Britten's other great opera about moral panic, *Peter Grimes*. Grimes is an outsider, a misanthrope and almost certainly much worse, but it is precisely because of his faults that we are challenged to overcome the prejudices that sweep through the community – our prejudices – and to see the underlying moral complexity. That is to say that any parable of injustice and moral panic will have at its core an ambivalent figure like Ben Tobin, whose shortcomings challenge us to set our prejudices aside – to see deeper than the people caught up in "the fog" of the moral panic can see. Despite his central role in the novel, Ben does not often appear directly, except for the night Bobby spends with him and Deeds at Coal Creek. Rather, he is present to the reader in the opinions of others. But when Bobby does offer a description of him on that night, he is like Lang Tzu, having a dual or divided face: "He looked handsome in the soft yellow light of the kerosene lamp. Being handsome is in a man's eyes. And being ugly is in his eyes too. Ben could look both" (132).

The remarkable thing about the first arrest is how incurious Collins is about the motivations of those involved, and how little concern he shows for the rules of evidence. Later that day, lying on his bunk, Bobby thinks about "the way things had gone that morning" (31). Bobby knows that Rosie Gnapun holds a grudge against Ben for beating her son, but Collins does not make any inquiries about her motives. When Daniel arrests Ben without questioning him, Bobby notices not only that Ben and Deeds have a loving relationship, and that "she did not look to me like a girl who was beaten" (30), but that Collins does *not* notice or make any evidential inquiries: "Daniel did not ask her nothing, which I remember as it surprised me" (30). Bobby is a noticing witness, concerned with truth and evidence. When Ben is sentenced, he comments, "it was the first time in Mount Hay we ever knew a whitefeller go to gaol for giving a black woman a hiding" (32). The remark is Bobby's considered expression of his cynicism and lack of faith in the justice system, which has not worked to secure real justice for Aboriginal people in the past. Bobby realises that the truth has to be arrived at by careful thought and feeling: "there was some things I did not understand about that day and I was troubled thinking about them" (39). He grasps intuitively that these insights cannot always be captured by reading and writing. Miller's use of Bobby's voice and his ungrammatical locutions allows him brilliantly to demonstrate his central ethical point: that Bobby's speech and writing are inaccurate and uneducated, but he is absolutely accurate in his thinking and feeling, and in his moral insights into people and events.

Miller challenges his readers to overcome their own prejudices against other ways of thinking. Issues of race, gender and underage sex will be as difficult for contemporary readers to prevent from clouding their judgments of the "justice" of the matter as military discipline in time of war was for Melville's readers or homosexuality for Britten's audiences in postwar Britain. This would seem to be the case when the "trouble" resumes for the second time, and Rosie Gnapun returns to the Mount Hay police house to bring another charge against Ben Tobin, this time for killing her niece. Miller seems to suggest here the idea that in the bush, women play the role that Anne Summers famously described as "God's police".[18] Reflecting on Esme Collins' complicity in and support for the first arrest, and moments before Rosie's arrival at the police house to instigate the second pursuit of Ben, Bobby speculates:

> It was her young age, I believe, that they sent him to Stuart for, for that and for Esme insisting to Daniel that it was his duty to protect the women of Mount Hay from brutal men. Esme had some ideas about it. She had a strong hold over Daniel in her opinions. I heard him call her The Reformer, like she was a horse that would buck him off if he didn't set the saddle on her just right. Daniel might have eased back and taken a bit of a look around if he had been left to himself to do his policing his own way, but you could see Esme was not going to leave him alone to do his policing his own way. (43)

In his reading of this passage, Anthony Lynch comes close to asserting that Miller is reinvoking the bush legend, with its stereotype of women as God's police:

> What is Miller saying? That good strong men know their own minds and weak men let manipulative women disrupt the natural order. Certainly Miller's inland is a very muscular, male world, despite or assuaged by the tenderness of certain female figures.[19]

I want to suggest, however, that Bobby's use of the phrase "brutal men" is part of a more complex revisiting of historical debates about the bush legend.

Miller has set for his modern reader the ethical task of listening to the voice of an uneducated bushman of an earlier era, and to do this we have to overcome our own prejudices against that voice and to grasp that it is capable of speaking truth. The idea of reading and misreading, even of taking lessons in reading, is thematised within the novel in Irie's lessons to Bobby in reading and writing. In seeming to reinvoke the stereotypes of brutal bushmen and women as God's police, Miller re-visits the bush legend of the 1890s, not only as it was created by writers like Vance Palmer and Russel Ward in the 1950s, but also as it was reinterpreted by feminist critics and historians of the 1970s and 1980s, such as

---

18   Anne Summers, *Damned Whores and God's Police: The Colonization of Women in Australia* (Ringwood, Vic.: Penguin, 1975).
19   Lynch, "Real Men Roll Their Own", 6.

Anne Summers and Marilyn Lake. A leading and highly influential example of that feminist critique was Marilyn Lake's article "The Politics of Respectability", in which she argues that there was a distinctive and systemic "masculinist" culture during the 1890s, a backlash against the first wave of the women's movement and other attempts to constrain male behaviour, such as the temperance movement.[20] Lake specifically repudiates the gender dichotomies of the period, including the opposition between "damned whores" and "God's police", and the opposing styles of masculinity represented by the misogynistic bushman and the "respectable", domesticated man. The adoption of such conceptual frameworks, she argues, "has [only] served to obscure . . . the contest between men and women at the end of the nineteenth-century for control of the national culture".[21]

Bobby's first-person narration and the setting of Mount Hay recall the short stories of Henry Lawson, including the early stories from the trek to Burke and Hungerford, and the later Joe Wilson series. Lawson's presentation of gender in those stories lies at the heart of the 1980s feminist critique of the bush legend. "Joe Wilson's Courtship", to which Bobby's first-person narrative has some similarities, is a good example:

> I wasn't a healthy-minded, average boy: I reckon I was born for a poet by mistake, and grew up to be a Bushman, and didn't know what was the matter with me – or the world – but that's got nothing to do with it.
>
> . . . I think that the happiest time in a man's life is when he's courting a girl and finds out for sure that she loves him and hasn't a thought for any one else. Make the most of your courting days, you young chaps, and keep them clean, for they're about the only days when there's a chance of poetry and beauty coming into this life. Make the best of them and you'll never regret it the longest day you live. They're the days that the wife will look back to, anyway, in the brightest of times as well as in the blackest, and there shouldn't be anything in those days that might hurt her when she looks back. Make the most of your courting days, you young chaps, for they will never come again.[22]

Lawson's sensitive, morally upright narrator bears no relation to the "brutal men" of the bushman stereotype. Joe Wilson is no more a "brutal bushman" than Bobby or Ben Tobin. Terms like "The Reformer" and "brutal men" appear superficially to arise directly out of this debate. But "The Reformer" is Daniel's nickname for his wife, and as we have seen, he is a professionally negligent and even incompetent judge of character. The term "brutal men" is Bobby's ironic repudiation of that stereotype. As Paul Eggert argues, Lawson "often reacted against, as he simultaneously explored, an existing set of assumptions about contemporary male behaviours. Tonally subtle and emotionally complex . . . his stories . . . resist historical and ideological categorizing. Their testimony is more complex."[23] The same can be said of Miller's novel.

---

20 Marilyn Lake, "The Politics of Respectability: Identifying the Masculinist Context", *Historical Studies* 22, no. 86 (1986): 116–31.
21 Lake, "The Politics of Respectability", reprinted in *Debutante Nation: Feminism Contests the 1890s*, eds Susan Magarey, Sue Rowley and Susan Sheridan (Sydney: Allen & Unwin, 1993), 2.
22 Henry Lawson, *Short Stories and Sketches 1888–1922*, ed. Colin Roderick (Sydney: Angus & Robertson, 1972), 537.
23 Paul Eggert, *Biography of a Book: Henry Lawson's* While the Billy Boils (Sydney: Sydney University Press, 2013), 290.

A modern, "coastal" woman, Esme Collins has a prejudiced perception that the bush is inhabited by "brutal men", which is not borne out by Bobby's recollections of life in Mount Hay and is revealed to be an unfair and inaccurate generalisation. This is not to say that there is no brutality at Mount Hay. Miller and his narrator squarely place intergenerational male violence at the centre of the troubles, but even Ben Tobin is a complex man, not a stereotype: "Things could go either way with Ben, sweet and gentle or cruel. It was not easy to predict" (33). The loving relationship Bobby recalls between his mother and father, and his own internal conversations with his mother in evaluating people and events further belie the stereotypes. Miller's point is not just that Esme and Daniel use these stereotypes, which Lynch rightly identifies, but that they are not accurate.

When Rosie Gnapun brings her second accusation against Ben, Daniel again exhibits a lack of professional curiosity. Bobby has some understanding of Aboriginal people, and his intense observations allow him to notice that Daniel cannot understand what she is saying: "I could see that he was not understanding half of what Rosie was saying to him" (54). Daniel has trouble with the protocols of Aboriginal communication, which involve speaking and looking away out of respect. It is ironic that Daniel acts against Ben on the basis of Rosie's accusation but cannot actually understand what she is saying to him. Bobby sees this clearly. As Daniel struggles with his decision about how to respond to Rosie's accusation, Bobby assesses his weakness astutely: "People like the Collins knew the city and the coast and they had another way of seeing things that was not our way of seeing things" (66). He sees that Daniel is driven by a desire for moral clarity in a world where things and people are more complex: "Esme and Daniel wanted things clear cut. But there wasn't no clear cut with Ben" (70). Bobby's persistent thoughtfulness is based on astute observation of the evidence and retrospectively "worrying" over it. Bobby knows that Ben is a "mixture of things in himself" (69) and hopes not to "misjudge" him (70). He does not like to hear Esme "judging on Ben" because she is insensitive to his complexity. Like Bobby, though for different reasons, Esme needs lessons in reading.

Miller's thinking here has certain affinities with the ideas of the French sociologist Bruno Latour, who has contested the supposed objectivity of a range of disciplines, including science, religion and the law, arguing that their truth-making processes involve an artificial separation of nature and society, subject and object, and that these disciplines and their objects of inquiry are, alike, "messy", "hybrid", and "entangled". From his earliest books, Latour has consistently rejected what he describes as the "modern settlement". This involved the obsessive "purification" of knowledge production, in which the world is categorised according to rigorous binary distinctions between the scientific and the social, the human and the non-human, subjects and objects, the modern and the non-modern: "Modernisation consists in continually exiting from an obscure age that mingled the needs of society with scientific truth in order to enter into a new age that will finally distinguish clearly what belongs to atemporal nature and what comes from human."[24] It is from this modern settlement about knowledge, as Roger Luckhurst argues, that a modern politics emerges: "nature is to be dominated; other cultures, refusing to accept the disciplining of the progressive, linear time of modernity, are regarded as objects, sunk in nature".[25]

---

24 Bruno Latour, *We Have Never Been Modern*, trans. Catherine Porter (1991; Cambridge, Mass.: Harvard University Press, 1993), 71.
25 Roger Luckhurst, "Bruno Latour's Scientifiction: Networks, Assemblages, and Tangled Objects", in *Science Fiction Studies* 33, no. 1 (March 2006): 6, http://www.depauw.edu/sfs/backissues/98/luckhurst98.html.

Latour's project has been to expose the imperfections of the modern settlement across a range of knowledge-producing regimes, including science, philosophy, religion and, most recently, the law. As Luckhurst puts it, "the fury of purification is driven by a secret history of miscegenation, of the intermixing of categories. *We have never been modern.*"[26]

Latour sets out to reveal this "fury of purification" not through theoretical intervention – he is also critical of post-structuralism and postmodernism for their theoreticism, their lack of pragmatism – but through ethnographic observation. In a series of books, he has used a "fly-on-the-wall" approach to reveal how a succession of disciplines form their own truth-regimes through the everyday exclusion of their others – of nature, of emotion, of everyday lived experience, of the nonhuman world. His project has been "to visit successively and to document the different truth production sites that make up our civilization".[27] The object of this ethnography, in turn, was "to resituate science and technology [and other disciplines, including law] in their perceived relations to the social world".[28] In *Laboratory Life* (1979)[29] and *Science in Action* (1987),[30] Latour used participant-observation in American scientific laboratories to reveal that the laboratory is not, after all, a sterile, inhuman place, but a "leaky" object "saturated with the social and political", and that "the technical cannot be artificially divorced from these concerns".[31] *The Making of Law* is an ethnography of the French *Conceil d'État*,[32] revealing that "Law, seen as networks of practice, must also be seen as operating within environments of experience and understanding permeated by social forces that originate beyond those networks."[33] In *Politics of Nature*, Latour extends his critique of the modern settlement, arguing that humans and nonhumans must be networked together, "in order to add a series of new voices to the discussion... The voices of nonhumans".[34] This aspect of his work has been taken up in Donna Haraway's recent attempts to connect "companion species" into the network of voices contributing to the wider critique of the modern settlement.[35]

In referring to Latour's critique of the modern settlement, I do not mean to imply that *Coal Creek* is influenced in any systematic way by such theoretical ideas, any more than that Miller's writing about friendship and mourning in *The Ancestor Game* was influenced directly by late Derrida. My point is that from their own philosophical and sociological perspectives, Derrida and Latour elaborate on concepts that Miller also explores as a novelist, and that they do so in ways that make them illuminating interlocutors in our reading. *Coal Creek* is centrally about the impurity of the "modern settlement". Miller's fa-

---

26 Luckhurst, "Bruno Latour's Scientifiction", 6. My italics.
27 Robert Crease, "Interview with Bruno Latour", in *Chasing Technoscience: Matrix for Materiality*, eds Don Ihde and Evan Selinger (Bloomington: Indiana University Press, 2003), 18.
28 Luckhurst, "Bruno Latour's Scientifiction", 1.
29 Bruno Latour (with Steven Woolgar), *Laboratory Life: The Construction of Scientific Facts* (Beverley Hills: Sage, 1979).
30 Bruno Latour, *Science in Action: How to Follow Scientists and Engineers through Society* (Cambridge, Mass.: Harvard University Press, 1987).
31 Luckhurst, "Bruno Latour's Scientifiction", 2.
32 Bruno Latour, *The Making of Law: An Ethnography of the Conseil d'État*, trans. Marina Brilman and Alain Pottage (2002; Cambridge: Polity, 2010).
33 Roger Cotterrell, "ANT's Eye-View of Law: Bruno Latour at the Conseil D'État", *Journal of Classical Sociology* 11 (2011): 1, http://papers.ssrn.com/sol3/papers.cfm?abstract_id=2315963.
34 Bruno Latour, *Politics of Nature: How to Bring the Sciences into Democracy*, trans. Catherine Porter (Cambridge, Mass.: Harvard University Press, 2004), 69.
35 Donna J. Haraway, "Cyborgs to Companion Species: Reconfiguring Kinship in Technoscience", in *Chasing Technoscience*, 58–82.

ble of injustice reveals, from the fly-on-the-wall participant observations of Bobby Blue, that Collins' decisions about the administration of justice are not abstract and rational, but subject to "leakage" between his professional and private lives, between reason and emotion, and that the two arrests and convictions of Ben Tobin are "messy" objects in the sense that they are produced by a range of diverse participants with conflicting motivations. The traditional ways of life conducted by Rosie Gnapun's ancestors, and by Bobby and Ben's fathers and grandfathers, may have been displaced in the postwar era by people from the coast like the Collinses, but their non-modern lifeways and forms of knowledge are still to be reckoned with. Miller's contrast between the people of Mount Hay and the people from the coast opens the possibility of questioning "the modern settlement" by respecting the knowledge of people and communities excluded from that settlement, even by listening to the voices of the nonhuman, including companion and "wild" animals.

As Collins and Bobby drive through the scrub together in pursuit of Ben Tobin, in pursuit of "justice", Miller offers a lesson in reading and misreading that recalls Bo Rennie and Annabelle Beck's drive into the scrub around Mount Bulgonunna. Like Bo and Annabelle's journey, this search for justice is not a linear or teleological journey, but a zig-zag one: "It was not one track out to Coal Creek but many tracks" (73). It is significant for Miller's larger critique of modernity that they cannot get there in the Jeep, having to return it to the police station and try again on horseback. The journey of these two men is an allegory about knowledge. Travelling together in the wrong mode of transport, they are indeed an odd couple: the "boss" and his subordinate, the coastal man and the bushman, the bookish man and the illiterate man, the driver and the expert horseman. Bobby comments, "It made me feel like a dumb idiot sitting up there next to that man" (74). Again, Miller brilliantly exploits the disjunction between Bobby's semi-literate account of events and the absolute precision and care with which he navigates the track through the scrub. Bobby can read the signs of people and events but Daniel cannot: "Daniel was not reading the signs that was there, and was too busy looking for the signs that was not there ... He was a foreigner in our country and was not comfortable knowing he might make a mistake anytime" (75). This is another important difference between them. Daniel does not know when he does not understand something, and will not ask for help. The contrast with Bobby is clear: "I could have told him the way of things in the scrubs, just as Irie told me the way of reading and writing and I was happy to learn from her" (76). The negative example of Daniel and Esme Collins' "judging on Ben" is offered as a challenge for the reader of Bobby's story to interpret things correctly: "Daniel was to die a stranger in that country that had not formed him but had bewitched him like a story bewitches a child" (77). This meditation on knowledge and alternative ways of knowing – coastal and rural, rational and intuitive, modern and non-modern – is underpinned by the novel's great conceptual paradox, which is the disjunction between words and truth: "Words is not good for much when it comes to ... feelings" (108). The sublime irony of the novel is that Bobby's entirely reliable insights into the truth of people and things are couched in the deliberately distracting envelope of his semi-literate speech. When Collins gets lost, unable to see the route through the scrub, he stops the Jeep: he has become lost in his quest for justice in the same way that he has become lost in the bush.

At this impasse in their journey together, Bobby's attention is caught by the presence of eagles in the sky. The incident is foreshadowed by the return of his mother's voice: "My mother always come near me when I was in trouble. In her death too she was my mother" (78). The words she speaks to him are: "God's eagles. The eagles of Christ" (78).

This suggests that the natural world for Bobby is a kind of parable, a reminder of Christ's use of parables in the New Testament to speak of truths that evade more complex language and narrative forms. In the Christian tradition, the book of nature is an alternative to God's other form of revelation, the Bible, but Daniel is blind to it. Daniel requires a lesson in reading nature in the same way that Bobby takes lessons from Irie in reading books, including the Bible. Bobby's response to this ethical conundrum is unspoken, but he intuitively knows that Daniel has failed to see beyond his own prejudices. Instead of speaking out his understanding, he silently and intuitively turns to a metaphor from the natural world, at once seeing an eagle in the sky and imagining himself to be seen by it: "In my eye then gone then back again in my eye as if they could make themselves disappear and appear again, mesmerizing their prey with the magic of themselves a thousand feet above the country. Was I no more than a black speck in the eye of the eagle?" (83). This is of course a version of William Blake's aphorism from *The Book of Thel*:

> Does the Eagle know what is in the pit,
> Or wilt thou go ask the Mole?
> Can Wisdom be put in a silver rod,
> Or Love in a golden bowl?

Blake's motto is recalled in Roger Cotterrell's review of Latour's *The Making of Law*, which he punningly titles, "ANT's Eye-View of Law". "ANT" is the acronym of "actor–network theory", which has been derived from Latour's theories, in demonstration of the fact that scientific and legal interpretations are not a product of the sovereign reason of individuals, but of the messy constellations or networks of many actors. Cotterrell's title has the same effect as Blake's aphorism, suggesting that Latour's fly-on-the-wall (or ant-on-the-ground) ethnographic perspective on legal process gives a different perspective to that of legal practitioners in the same way that Blake's eagle and mole have incommensurable perspectives on the world. Being a "coastal" person, Collins has "forgotten" that there are other perspectives. To understand the men of the bush, like Ben Tobin, he needs to seek out their point of view, not project his own on to them. Blake also undermines the kind of thinking that would associate wisdom with institutional authority, like that of the justice system Collins represents, like "wisdom" put in a "silver rod". The symbols of that invalid authority are Collins' old sidearm and his defective shotgun. Bobby is able to sum up this complexity of points of view by turning to the voices of the animal world: "An eagle is an eagle. We are not that. We are only men . . . there is the sky and the eagles and the scrubs going on forever into them great stone escarpments. No man knows himself to be the boss of that" (83–4).

This constellation of the non-modern – Bobby, Indigenous knowledge, and the lives of animals – is celebrated in the important episode close to the centre of *Coal Creek* to which I have already referred, when Bobby is returning at night on his horse, Mother, to Mount Hay after apparently proving Ben's innocence to Daniel Collins. While Collins navigates with difficulty, unable to control his mount and fearing the scrub at night, Bobby chooses to camp overnight at the stone playgrounds of the old people, satisfied that he has demonstrated his friend's innocence, and in communion with the spirit of his mother, with nature, and with the animal world: "There was an animal rattling among the dry ground litter off behind me toward the red wall. Mother raised her head and looked over that way. I always felt calm on my own in the scrub and I was in no hurry to get back to the police house" (145). On his way back, he finds, with Mother's help, that Collins and Finisher have got "bushed" on the way back to Mount Hay. Bobby's night with Mother amid the stone artefacts of Rosie's ancestors is one of the final moments of calm in the novel before the moral panic and its "fury of purification" commence. The episode has intimations of the sacred and the ecological sublime: the shining stones in the moonlight, "the stars rotating around me", and the spectral presence of his mother, which seems to become more manifest as the story progresses: "My mother laid her hand on me and give me that sad little smile of hers", and the companionship of animals, both companion and wild (145). Again, this otherwordly element in Bobby, which establishes his fundamental innocence, has the qualities of Aboriginal knowledge. In his eulogy for Frank Budby, who passed away on 6 April 2014, Miller writes, "I gave some of that noble pride to my main character in my last book."[36]

The crisis of the novel is precipitated by Irie Collins' revelation to her parents that she loves Bobby Blue. Irie runs to the men's quarters and embraces Bobby in full view of her father, asking him to take her away to live together in the scrub. For his part, Collins does not confront Bobby that night, giving Irie a chance to speak with him. The following morning Daniel and Esme interview Bobby in the police office, accusing him of betraying their trust and asking him to leave, but giving him a chance to explain himself. Like Billy Budd in the Captain's cabin, he says nothing in his own defence: "It put me down from the word go and I sat there knowing myself to be a judged man, and found guilty" (207). He goes on to say, "I did not believe I had done nothing criminal and was not expecting Daniel to charge me ... Their judging of me made me angry" (208).

It is the irresolvable complexity of these circumstances, the "messy" constellation of actors and motivations, that now gives rise to the events that form the climax of Bobby's account. Collins wakes Bobby in the night, announcing, "the girls are gone", and threatens, "If anything has happened to my girls I will kill you" (212–13). The ensuing events constitute what can be described as a moral panic. The term is defined by British sociologist Stanley Cohen as occurring when "A condition, episode, person or group of persons emerges to become defined as a threat to societal values and interests; its nature is presented in a stylised and stereotypical fashion by the mass media; the moral barricades are manned by editors, bishops, politicians and other right-thinking people."[37] Those who start the moral panic are known as "moral entrepreneurs", while those seen as a threat to the social order are "folk devils", "visible reminders of what we should not be".[38] The capacity for a moral panic to be generated is increased when the issue at its centre is a "taboo" subject, which prevents evidential and judicial consideration, and allows the mythologisation and displacement of issues onto the "folk devil". Such taboo issues include homosexuality, miscegenation, and under-aged sexuality.

While it would be possible to read aspects of Bobby's thoughts and behaviour in relation to Irie as problematic, the crucial issue of the moral panic is that the reader risks being drawn into the same misreading of Bobby and Ben's motivations as the Collinses, the courts and the media. There are several references to the fact that Irie is legally a minor, so that the issue is voiced in the novel by Bobby, but Miller is scrupulous to show that he is

---

36 Alex Miller, eulogy for Frank Budby.
37 Stanley Cohen, *Folk Devils and Moral Panics: The Creation of the Mods and Rockers* (London: MacGibbon and Kee, 1972), 1.
38 Cohen, *Folk Devils*, 2.

innocent, and the reader is challenged to "judge" this matter carefully and not to make the same reductive judgements as the Collinses. When Irie shows signs of moving their relationship on to a more mature footing, Bobby is firm to resist: "The way I seen it Irie Collins was still a child at that time and that is how I wished things to go on between us. I give Irie a hard look, like I was her teacher" (156). Again, when they sit on the verandah talking at night, Bobby stresses, "And that's all it was. Talking was enough for me and Irie" (191). He is an innocent, ethically rigorous, somewhat otherwordly young man. It is also important that, at twenty, Bobby is just short of the legal majority in the 1940s: like Irie, he is not yet an adult. The challenge Miller has created is for the reader to interpret correctly on the eve of the crisis both Bobby's innocence and Ben's complexity, and not misread them as the Collinses do: "For Esme I was always to be the villain who had betrayed her and her family. She never shifted on that once it was fixed in her mind" (172). Reading, Bobby warns, cannot take place if things are fixed in our minds. Daniel and Esme, as we have seen many times, are bad readers. Not only do they not know how to read the people and places of the bush, but unlike Annabelle Beck they do not know that they are bad readers, and they get lost without asking for help.

During the crisis, Bobby is handcuffed and repeatedly beaten as he helps Daniel and Esme to track the girls in the scrub. The presence of both the husband and wife confirms that their actions are the result of leakage between the legal and moral domains, between reason and emotion. Bobby can see that they are driven by panic, fear and ignorance: "I seen there was a kind of panic and fear had got hold of them in their need to see their girls safe ... Them two had a fear of the scrubs. A fear of their own ignorance" (216). The panic is sensed and echoed by the animals and it is contagious: "I did not wish to be affected by that fierce panic that was in Daniel and Esme but I felt it around me, just as the horses felt it. It was like a sickness without a cure and I knew I could not stay clean of it" (218). Like all moral panics, there is a lack of moral clarity. Daniel is a police officer who has arrested Bobby on suspicion of conspiracy to abduct two under-aged girls, and Bobby has admitted to his "feelings" for Irie, but Daniel and Esme's understanding of the situation is a misrepresentation of Bobby and Ben's actions. In such circumstances, there can be the appearance and performance of justice, but it will not be purely judicial: it will be tainted by emotions of fear and panic. Collins' arrest and beating of Bobby is in excess of the law. The incommensurability of their perspectives is reflected in their encounter in the scrub: "I said, I have committed no crime. You have no right to hold me in these cuffs. Daniel stepped back and said, How about conspiracy to kidnap my children?" (243).

In these climactic events, Miller draws on but also critically examines several narrative conventions associated with colonial fiction: the conflict between bushrangers and the police, culminating in the apotheosis of the convict hero; the motif of the lost child, and the captivity narrative. All three of these narratives can be seen as invested in the moral confusion and anxiety about the legitimacy of whiteness and modernity that trouble settler colonies. In his book *The Country of Lost Children*, Peter Pierce argues that the motif of the lost child expresses fundamental uncertainties of settler identity and belonging, and that it is one of the recurring motifs of Australian art, literature and cinema.[39] The figure of the lost child, especially lost in the bush, is epitomised by Frederick McCubbin's painting *Lost* (1886), while the media event associated with the Azaria Chamberlain case, the in-

---

39   Peter Pierce, *The Country of Lost Children: An Australian Anxiety* (Cambridge: Cambridge University Press, 1999).

fant taken by a dingo at Ayer's Rock in the 1980s, is a late-twentieth-century version of this motif, illustrating its continuing power to cause moral panics and to cloud issues of justice. One of the leading examples in Australian literature is the death of Mary O'Halloran in Joseph Furphy's *Such Is Life* (1903), who dies because her immigrant father cannot read the signs of the scrub, and whose body is eventually found by an Aboriginal woman who is blind in one eye.[40] These issues of competing forms of knowledge and the desire for authentic settler belonging, displaced onto the figure of the lost child, are repeated in Miller's novel. Bobby dismisses Daniel Collins as a "coastal" man, able to read books but unable to read the scrub, and he has already been lost in the bush twice before: once while returning from Coal Creek on Finisher, and again when driving there with Bobby in the Jeep. During the search for the missing girls, Bobby is aware that the Collins' alienation from the bush is contributing to their panic, and that without him they would themselves perish: "I stood and waited for them again. In some stupid way they seemed to me like children. I had never seen two people more in the wrong place than them two. I hoped they would be going back down the coast once they got their girls back" (244).

The captivity narrative is another archetypal myth of white settler anxiety, in which feelings of estrangement and non-belonging are displaced on to the Indigenous population, while the pursuit and freeing of the captive white woman becomes a myth of what the American critic Richard Slotkin calls "regeneration through violence".[41] Important Australian examples of such legends that have been built around the supposed captivity of white women by Aborigines include the legend of the so-called White Woman of Gippsland and the Eliza Fraser story.[42] In her study of the Eliza Fraser story, Kay Schaffer argues that captivity narratives function as a "foundational fiction" for the settler nation.[43] Bobby can see that Esme's moral panic is motivated by thoughts of her daughters' captivity: "From being a young and friendly woman, Esme had taken on the look of an old deranged woman with nothing in her mind but a picture of her daughters in captivity to the violent and cruel man she believed Ben Tobin to be" (248). In the classic pattern of captivity narratives, it is the innocence of the captive and the perceived depravity of the captor that motivates and justifies the otherwise illegal actions committed by the "moral entrepreneurs" in what the city newspapers call "the Coal Creek Massacre" (259). This distortion of events is the classic role of the media in creating moral panics: "Once the people had that story from the newspapers there was no going back to the truth ... the newspapers lied and twisted the truth around to make people get excited" (259). The community of the nation is regenerated by the moral and actual violence directed at its "folk devils", its martyrs to discipline.

Miller sustains the incommensurability of these different perspectives until the very moment of Ben's hanging in Stuart Prison. On the morning of his hanging, the other inmates make a hero of him, inducting him into the very bush and convict legends that reviewers had invoked by their original comparisons of *Coal Creek* with *Robbery Under*

---

40   Joseph Furphy, *Such Is Life*, ed. Frances Devlin Glass et al. (1903; Sydney: Halstead, 1999).
41   Richard Slotkin, *Regeneration through Violence: The Mythology of the American Frontier, 1600–1860* (Middletown, Conn.: Wesleyan University Press, 1973).
42   See Kate Darian-Smith, Roslyn Poignant and Kay Schaffer, *Captured Lives: Australian Captivity Narratives* (London: Menzies Centre for Australian studies, 1993) and Robert Dixon, *Writing the Colonial Adventure: Race, Gender and Nation in Anglo-Australian Popular Fiction, 1875–1914* (Cambridge: Cambridge University Press, 1995).
43   Kay Schaffer, *In the Wake of First Contact: The Eliza Fraser Stories* (Cambridge: Cambridge University Press, 1995).

Arms and *For the Term of His Natural Life*: remarkably, the Governor of Stuart Prison, who eventually secures Bobby's parole, is named Dawes – an echo, perhaps, of Clarke's "good Mr Dawes". After Ben is taken down to be hanged, Bobby can hear the other inmates singing the convict ballad, *The Wild Colonial Boy*: "Gradually all the men joined in, until they was all singing like a loud challenging chant of the song, as if it was the war cry of a crazy horde of warriors. *There was a wild colonial boy, Ben Tobin was his name*... And I seen how they was making a legend and a hero for themselves out of Ben" (275). Yet to the very end, Bobby Blue, the "fly-on-the-wall", "ant-on-the-ground" observer of the justice system, refuses either to take part in this hero-making or to accede to the findings of the court, holding on to his own conviction of the moral complexity of people and events: "We was neither of us wild colonial boys... Ben Tobin was not a saint, but he was not an evil man neither" (274). Twenty-five years later, Bobby's determination to resist the common view on these issues echoes the boy's decision, in *The Tivington Nott*, not to report the location of the deer's soiling pit to the villagers.

At their trial, Ben is charged with murder, and both Ben and Bobby are charged with conspiracy to kidnap minors. The sentence of the court is echoed in the distortions of the press, which accuse them of "indecency", of "luring their daughters into the bush and leading them to where Ben Tobin could capture them and take them to his hideout in the wild scrubs for his own indecent purposes" (266). The moral panic aligns the judgement of the court, the reports of the press, and the interpretation of Bobby and Ben made by Daniel and Esme Collins with the novel's governing metaphor of reading, and the slippery relationship between language and truth. Bobby is an illiterate bushman, but he has always been an accurate witness to events, an intuitive reader of peoples' motivations, and a reliable, honourable and ethical man. The irony is that he is a semi-literate bushman whose accurate testimony is given in the grammatically inaccurate form of his first-person narrative. The Collinses on the other hand, are educated coastal people, but they do not know how to read the people of the bush, and they reduce them to the stereotypes of "brutal men" and "God's police". Unlike Bobby, Daniel does not know that he needs a lesson in reading, and he repeatedly gets lost both in his journeys through the scrub and his search for justice. The challenge Miller places before the reader of Bobby's account is whether they will read it as Esme does, and as the courts and the newspapers do, or whether they will see that Bobby has committed no crime, and that his friendship with Irie has been made to look like something it was not. Are we prepared to listen to Bobby's voice, to read carefully and deeply his reliable and accurate account of events? Or are we to adopt the shrill, moralising voice of the newspapers, which speak of "the kidnap and molesting of the two innocent young Collins girls" (258), leading people to believe that "the country was lawless and filled with brutal types of men"? (259) Buried away in the final pages of *Coal Creek*, which are filled with the misreadings of the court and the press, is Bobby's quiet explanation of what might have happened instead: "If Ben had had the chance to do it his way, it would have been an opportunity for him and the Collins to reach some kind of trust and even a friendship. Them people might have learned something about themselves and the people of the ranges" (255).

Afterword

In looking back over my study of the novels of Alex Miller, there is perhaps a handful of key words or phrases that best sums up his methods and preoccupations as a writer: among them are friendship, intertextual hospitality, generosity, collaboration, migrancy, being-in-time, being-toward the other and being-toward death. These terms also describe the experience of reading, which is also, I have come to see, an intensely collaborative experience. In my reading, re-reading and writing about Miller's eleven novels, he and I have become collaborators of a kind. In the course of that collaboration there have been some special moments of intertextual hospitality. I want to end this book not with a formal conclusion, but by sharing one of these textual gifts. It can be seen as an epitome of Miller's work.

On Sunday 6 April 2014, Miller's friend, the Barada elder Frank Budby, died. As we have seen, Frank was the inspiration for Dougald Gnapun in *Journey to the Stone Country* and *Landscape of Farewell* and, in part, for Bobby Blue in *Coal Creek*. Miller spoke at the funeral on Monday 14 April, at Holy Trinity, Mackay, as Central Queensland was buffeted by Severe Tropical Cyclone Ita. He wrote to me on the following day:

> I got home around midnight last night, tired but very happy that I was there to see Frank go over to his Old People. The family and huge congregation were very happy with the eulogy... The most moving moment for me was at the graveside when they lowered the coffin into the ground and a young fellow played the didgeridoo and Frank's son and daughter stepped forward and set Frank's old stockman's hat and his whips on to the coffin, they then set about shovelling in the soil. We'd had many inches of rain on Sunday evening and through the night as a spillover from the big storm...
>
> While flying up and back I read Nikos Papastergiadis' *Modernity as Exile*, and was greatly struck by the discussion of the relations of the stranger to the literature of a country. I also saw that I opened my novel-writing period with a book about the power of the stranger who is without formal authority but who nevertheless unsettles the social balance in a closed and static society, and that I closed my novel-writing period with a book about the power of a stranger – or two – endowed with formal authority in a small and closed society to bring about tragic consequences. *The Ancestor Game*, which sits between these books and was my most serious attempt to write the subject, is most deeply concerned with the liberating force of migration away from restricted social

norms ... Migration for me, in other words becoming the stranger, was an act of empowerment. To be so at home up there with the Barada Barna people around the grave of Frank on Sunday, one of their most respected elders, was a deeply moving experience for me.[1]

This apparently simple account of a personal event encapsulates many of the themes of my book about the novels of Alex Miller. As with so much of his prose, there is a sense of the symbolic and the mythical breaking through the lucid and apparently realistic surface. The novelist, who emigrated to Australia from London as a young man, has just attended the funeral of an Indigenous friend whose life inspired his fiction. At the funeral, the novelist has spoken of and for the other in an act of friendship and mourning, just as Max Otto speaks of and for Dougald Gnapun in *Landscape of Farewell*. The funeral is a poignantly familiar ritual, though in this case it is a cultural hybrid, drawing upon both European and Indigenous burial practices. At the visual centre of the event he describes is an open grave. It is a version of the ruin of time that recurs throughout the novels: the dribbling hourglass of debris at Ranna, the objects stuffed into a hole in the floor of Panya's cottage, the burial cave of Gnapun the warrior at the summit of the Expedition Range, the grave of the Keal women, "there", beneath the tree on the farm at Araluen. As the friend's body descends into the earth, we might imagine him gazing backwards toward the living like Klee's *Angelus Novus*, drawing along with him the symbols of his life on earth, and even the earth itself. The hat and stockwhips are the tokens of one of those lost worlds that Miller records so elegiacally in his novels, like the stone tools slipping into the cracks in the soil at Burranbah Coal. The remains of the big storm suggest the catastrophic, even eschatological vision of history that Miller shares with his friend, the painter Rick Amor, whose autumnal landscapes are so often dominated by storms, betokening the imminence of death.

Miller's return flight from Melbourne to Mackay describes the figure of chiasmus that is so familiar to readers of his novels, linking him to his friend as Max Otto and Dougald Gnapun are linked together in grief and mourning, but also linking together the two worlds of Miller's own life: his youth in the bush of Central Queensland and his adult life in Melbourne and Castlemaine. Like Steven Muir in the final pages of *The Ancestor Game*, he is "attempting a crossing" toward his friend, but his friend is not there, he is elsewhere. The novelist is in transit, dwelling in travel, dwelling in time, but he is not like Kierkegaard's subject of modernity, cut loose from "the substantive categories of family, state and race", an individual "entirely to himself". He is in transit but his journey is a purposeful one, precisely located in space between his own and his family's home in Castlemaine, and the homeland of his friend in Central Queensland. During the return flight, each of these spatial coordinates is a point of departure and destination in turn.

While travelling, the novelist is also a reader, ingesting the work of another writer that will help him to formulate the account of his own life that he has recently begun to write. It will be called "Horizons". By coincidence, I began the work of re-reading and writing about Miller's novels at the same time that he had ended what he here calls his novel-writing period. The two of us have been engaged in parallel, though very different, exercises in assessment and evaluation; my role as a critic has been both enabled and constrained by his role as autobiographer. We have surveyed together, at much the same time, the same body of work, book-ended, as he describes it here, by two very different novels about the power

---

1 Alex Miller to Robert Dixon, 15 April 2014.

of the stranger to transform a community. Modern air travel is conducive to such moments of introspection and retrospective summation. It is also an ideal perspective from which to contemplate the distant horizon.

Works Cited

Abraham, Nicolas and Mária Török. *The Wolf Man's Magic Word: A Cryptonymy*. Minneapolis: University of Minnesota Press, 1986.
Adams, Brian. *Sidney Nolan: Such Is Life*. (1987) Milson's Point, NSW: Vintage, 1992.
Adams, Henry. *Mont Saint-Michel and Chartres: A Study of Thirteenth-Century Unity*. Edited with a preface by Ralph Adams Cram. Boston and New York: Houghton Mifflin, 1913.
Adorno, Theodor W. "Cultural Criticism and Society". In *Prisms*, 19–34. London: Spearman, 1967.
Amor, Rick. *Rick Amor Recent Paintings 30 July – 7 September 2013: 30 Years with Niagara*. Richmond, Melbourne: Niagara Galleries, 2013.
Ashcroft, Bill. "Australian Transnation". *Southerly* 71, no. 1 (2011): 18–40.
Ashcroft, Bill, Frances Devlin-Glass and Lynn McCredden. *Intimate Horizons: The Post-Colonial Sacred in Australian Literature*. Hindmarsh, SA: ATF Press, 2009.
Attwood, Bain. *Telling the Truth About Aboriginal History*. Sydney: Allen & Unwin, 2005.
Australian Human Rights Commission, "Bringing them Home Report", 1997. http://www.humanrights.gov.au/publications/bringing-them-home-report-1997.
Avery, Ralph Emmett. *The Greatest Engineering Feat in the World at Panama*. New York: Leslie-Judge Company, 1915. http://ufdc.ufl.edu/AA00014526/00001.
——. *America's Triumph at Panama*. Chicago: Regan Printing House, 1913. http://ufdc.ufl.edu/AA00014525/00001.
Badinter, Elizabeth. *The Myth of Motherhood: An Historical View of the Maternal Instinct*. London: Souvenir Press, 1981.
Banville, John. "Omens and Poetic Licence". *The Guardian*, 25 February 2006. http://www.theguardian.com/books/2006/feb/25/johnbanville.
Barta, Tony. "Discourses of Genocide in Germany and Australia: A Linked History". *Aboriginal History* 25 (2001): 37–56.
Baron, Wendy and Richard Shone, eds. *Sickert: Paintings*. London: Royal Academy, 1992.
Barthes, Roland. *Camera Lucida: Reflections on Photography*. Translated by Richard Howard. New York: Hill and Wang, 1981.
——. "The Death of the Author". In *Image Music Text*, 142–8. Translated by Stephen Heath (Glasgow: Fontana, 1977).
Bhabha, Homi K. *The Location of Culture*. London: Routledge, 1994.
Benjamin, Walter. "On the Concept of History". In *Illuminations: Essays and Reflections*, 253–64. (1968) New York: Schocken, 2007.
Berger, John. *About Looking*. (1980) London: Vintage, 1991.
Berman, Marshall. *All That Is Solid Melts into Air: The Experience of Modernity*. London: Verso, 1983.

Works Cited

Blanchot, Maurice. "Literature and the Right to Death". In *The Station Hill Blanchot Reader*, edited by George Quasha, translated by Lydia Davis, Paul Auster and Robert Lamberton, 359–99. New York: Station Hill, 1999.

Bond, Anthony, ed. *Francis Bacon: Five Decades*. Sydney: Art Gallery of New South Wales, 2012.

Bradfield, John. *Sydney Harbour Bridge: Report on Tenders*. Sydney: Government Printer, 1924.

Brady, Veronica. "A Portrait of Absence and Silence". *Australian Book Review* 170 (May 1995): 43.

Brennan, Bernadette. "Literature and the Intimate Space of Death". *Antipodes* 22, no. 2 (December 2008): 103–9.

Brooks, David. "Dougald's Goat: Alex Miller and the Species Barrier". In Dixon, *The Novels of Alex Miller*, 187–200.

Brown, Lyndell and Charles Green. "Statement for *Sanctuary – and Other Island Fables*". Herring Island Environmental Sculpture Park, 2002. http://www.australianphotographers.org/artists/lyndell-brown-and-charles-green.

Brown, Lyndell, Charles Green and Patrick Pound. *Sanctuary – and Other Island Fables*. Herring Island, Vic.: Parks Victoria Gallery, 2002.

Brown, Peter. *The Body and Society: Men, Women and Sexual Renunciation in Early Christianity*. New York: Columbia University Press, 1988.

Buckridge, Patrick. "The Age of Appreciation: Reading and Teaching Classic Literature in Australia in the Early Twentieth Century". *Australian Literary Studies* 22, no. 3 (2006): 342–56.

Buell, Lawrence. *The Environmental Imagination: Thoreau, Nature Writing, and the Formation of American Culture*. Cambridge, Mass.: Harvard University Press, 1995.

Burke, Janine. *The Heart Garden: Sunday Reed and Heide*. (2004) Sydney: Vintage, 2005.

——. *Australian Women Artists, 1840–1940*. Collingwood, Vic.: Greenhouse, 1980.

——. "Hester, Joy St Clair (1920–1960)". *Australian Dictionary of Biography*, Australian National University. http://adb.anu.edu.au/biography/hester-joy-st-clair-10493.

Butt, John. *Bach's Dialogue with Modernity: Perspectives on the Passions*. Cambridge: Cambridge University Press, 2010.

——. "Bach's *Matthew Passion*". Johann Sebastian Bach, *Matthew Passion* (BWV 244). Dunedin Consort, directed by John Butt. Linn Records, 2008, CKD 313. CD.

Caesar, Adrian. "An Artist in the Family: Reconfigurations of Romantic Paradigms in *Prochownik's Dream*". In Dixon, *The Novels of Alex Miller*, 101–13.

Cantarella, Eva. *Pandora's Daughters: The Role and Status of Women in Greek and Roman Antiquity*. Baltimore: Johns Hopkins University Press, 1987.

Capet, Antoine. "Walter Sickert: The Camden Town Nudes". Courtauld Gallery exhibition, 25 October – 20 January 2008. http://www.thearttribune.com/Walter-Sickert-The-Camden-Town.html.

Caputo, John D., ed. *Deconstruction in a Nutshell: A Conversation with Jacques Derrida*. New York: Fordham University Press, 1997.

Carbines, Louise. "A Book of Freedom and Belonging". Review of Alex Miller, *The Ancestor Game*. *The Age*, 15 August 1992, 9.

Casanova, Pascale. *The World Republic of Letters*. Translated by M.B. DeBevoise. (1999) Cambridge, Mass.: Harvard University Press, 2004.

Catalano, Gary. *The Solitary Watcher: Rick Amor and His Art*. Melbourne: Miegunyah Press, 2001.

Chakrabarty, Dipesh. "The Climate of History: Four Theses". *Critical Inquiry* 35, no. 2 (Winter 2009): 197–222.

Chanin, Eileen and Steven Miller. *Degenerates and Perverts: The Herald Exhibition of French and British Contemporary Art*. Carlton, Vic.: Miegunyah Press, 2005.

Clark, Gillian. *Women in Late Antiquity: Pagan and Christian Lifestyles*. Oxford: Clarendon Press, 1993.

Clendinnen, Inga. "The History Question: Who Owns the Past?" *Quarterly Essay* 23 (2006): 1–72.

——. "First Contact". *Australian's Review of Books*, May 2001, 7.

Cohen, Stanley. *Folk Devils and Moral Panics: The Creation of the Mods and Rockers*. London: MacGibbon and Kee, 1972.

Works Cited

Cooppan, Vilashini. *Worlds Within: National Narratives and Global Connections in Postcolonial Writing*. Stanford: Stanford University Press, 2009.
Council for Aboriginal Reconciliation. *Walking Together: The First Steps*. Canberra: AGPS, 1994.
——. *Sharing History*. Canberra: AGPS, 1993.
Corrigan, Peter. "A Civil Society". In Short, *A Single Mind*, 127–9.
Cornwell, Patricia. *Portrait of a Killer: Jack the Ripper – Case Closed*. London: Little Brown, 2002.
Cotterrell, Roger. "ANT's Eye-View of Law: Bruno Latour at the Conseil D'Etat". *Journal of Classical Sociology* 11 (2011): 506–10. http://papers.ssrn.com/sol3/papers.cfm?abstract_id=2315963.
Crane, Susan. "Ritual Aspects of the Hunt *a Force*". In *Engaging with Nature: Essays on the Natural World in Medieval and Early Modern Europe*, edited by Barbara A. Hanawalt and Lisa J. Kiser, 63–84. Notre Dame, Indiana: University of Notre Dame Press, 2008.
Crawshaw, Steve. "Trying Not to Mention the Third Reich – But Doing It Constantly". Review of Steven Ozment, *A Mighty Fortress: A New History of the German People*. *Independent*, 2 January 2006.
Crease, Robert. "Interview with Bruno Latour". In *Chasing Technoscience: Matrix for Materiality*, edited by Don Ihde and Evan Selinger, 15–26. Bloomington, Indiana University Press, 2003.
Critchley, Simon. "*Il y a* – Holding Levinas's Hand to Blanchot's Fire". In *Maurice Blanchot: The Demand of Writing*, edited by Carolyn Bailey Gill, 108–22. London: Routledge, 1996.
Cronon, William. "The Trouble with Wilderness; Or, Getting Back to the Wrong Nature". In *Uncommon Ground: Rethinking the Human Place in Nature*, edited by William Cronon, 69–90. New York: Norton, 1995.
Crutzen, Paul J. "Geology of Mankind". *Nature* 415 (3 January 2002): 23.
Dalton, Trent. "Written in Stone". *The Australian*, 10 November 2012. http://www.theaustralian.com.au/news/features/written-in-stone/story-e6frg8h6-1226511580106#mm-premium.
Dalziell, Tanya. "An Ethics of Mourning: Gail Jones's *Black Mirror*". *JASAL: Journal of the Association for the Study of Australian Literature* 4 (2005): 49–61.
Darian-Smith, Kate, Roslyn Poignant and Kay Schaffer. *Captured Lives: Australian Captivity Narratives*. London: Menzies Centre for Australian Studies, 1993.
Davis, Peter. "New Book Like Chess Played on Mirrors in Three Dimensions". Review of Alex Miller, *The Ancestor Game*. *Canberra Times*, 2 August 1992, 22.
DeArmitt, Pleshette. "Conjuring Bodies: Kofman's Lesson on Death". *parallax* 17, no. 1 (2011): 4–17.
Derrida, Jacques. *The Work of Mourning*. Translated by Pascale-Anne Brault and Michael Naas. Chicago and London: University of Chicago Press, 2001.
——. *Adieu to Emmanuel Levinas*. Translated by Pascale-Anne Brault and Michael Nass. Stanford: Stanford University Press, 1999.
——. *The Politics of Friendship*. Translated by George Collins. London and New York: Verso, 1997.
Didi-Huberman, Georges and Thomas Repensek. "The Index of the Absent Wound (Monograph on a Stain)". *October* 29 (Summer 1984): 63–81.
Dirk Moses, A. "Coming to Terms with Genocidal Pasts in Comparative Perspective: Germany and Australia". *Aboriginal History* 25 (2001): 91–115.
——. "Structure and Agency in the Holocaust: Daniel J. Goldhagen and his Critics". *History and Theory* 37, no. 2 (1998): 194–219.
Dixon, Robert. " 'A Nation for a Continent': Australian Literature and the Cartographic Imaginary of the Federation Era". *Antipodes* 28, no. 1 (June 2014): 161–74.
——. *Writing the Colonial Adventure: Race, Gender and Nation in Anglo-Australian Popular Fiction, 1875–1914*. Cambridge: Cambridge University Press, 1995.
Dixon, Robert, ed. *The Novels of Alex Miller: An Introduction*. Sydney: Allen & Unwin, 2012.
Docker, John. "Epistemological Vertigo and Allegory: Thoughts on Massacres, Actual, Surrogate, and Averted – *Beersheba, Wake in Fright, Australia*". In *Passionate Histories: Myths, Memory and Indigenous Australia*, edited by Frances Peters-Little, Ann Curthoys and John Docker, (Canberra: ANU E Press, 2010), 57–72.
Doyle, Laura. "The Racial Sublime". In *Romanticism, Race and Imperial Culture, 1780–1834*, edited by Sonia Hofkosh and Alan Richardson, 15–39. Bloomington: Indiana University Press, 1996.

Edward, Second Duke of York. *The Master of Game*, edited by W.A. and F. Baillie-Grohman. London: Chatto and Windus, 1909.

Eggert, Paul. *Biography of a Book: Henry Lawson's* While the Billy Boils. Sydney: Sydney University Press, 2013.

Eliot George. *Middlemarch*, edited by Bert G. Hornback. (1874) New York and London: Norton, 2000.

Esau, Erika. *Images of the Pacific Rim: Australia and California, 1850–1935*. Sydney: Power Publications, 2011.

Faulkner, William. *The Unvanquished*. (1938) New York: Vintage, 1991.

Flynn, Greg. "Mills and Boon Meets the Colonial Potboiler". Review of Alex Miller, *Watching the Climbers on the Mountain*. *The Weekend Australian*, 19–20 November 1988, 9.

Forsyth, William H. "The Medieval Stag Hunt". *Bulletin of The Metropolitan Museum of Art*. http://www.metmuseum.org/pubs/bulletins/1/pdf/3258066.pdf.bannered.pdf.

Fraser, Morag. "A Space of Its Own Creation: Alex Miller's Indispensable New Novel". *Australian Book Review* 335 (October 2011): 9–10.

Friedman, Susan Stanford. "Periodizing Modernism: Postcolonial Modernities and the Space/Time Borders of Modernist Studies". *Modernism/modernity* 13, no. 3 (September 2006): 425–43.

Fritzsche, Peter. "W.G. Sebald's Twentieth-Century Histories". In *W.G. Sebald: History, Memory, Trauma*, edited by Scott Denham and Mark McCulloh, 291–9. Berlin and New York: de Gruyter, 2006.

Furphy, Joseph. *Such Is Life*, edited by Frances Devlin Glass et al. (1903) Sydney: Halstead Press, 1999.

Gaita, Raimond. "Trusting the Words: Reflections on *Landscape of Farewell*". In Dixon, *The Novels of Alex Miller*, 217–230.

———. "Remembering the Holocaust: Absolute Value and the Nature of Evil". *Quadrant*, 39, no. 12 (December 1995): 7–15.

Geason, Susan. "Imagining China". Review of Brian Castro, *After China*, and Alex Miller, *The Ancestor Game*. *Sun-Herald*, 6 September 1992, 118.

Genoni, Paul. Review of Alex Miller, *Journey to the Stone Country*. *JAS (The Journal of Australian Studies) Review of Books* 16 (June 2003). http://pandora.nla.gov.au/pan/24605/20030715-0000/www.api-network.com/cgi-bin/reviews/jrb.html.

Gibson, Ross. *Seven Versions of an Australian Badland*. St Lucia, Qld: University of Queensland Press, 2002.

Giese, Diana. "Two-Way Asian Mirror". Review of Alex Miller, *The Ancestor Game*. *The Weekend Australian*, 6–7 November 1993, 7.

Gigliotti, Simone. "Unspeakable Pasts as Limit Events: The Holocaust, Genocide, and the Stolen Generations". *Australian Journal of Politics and History* 49, no. 2 (2003): 164–81.

Gobble, Maryanne M. "The Significance of Verbena in William Faulkner's 'An Odor of Verbena' ". *Mississippi Quarterly* 53, no. 4 (Fall 2000): 569–82.

Goodall, Heather. "Too Early Yet or Not Soon Enough? Reflections on Sharing Histories as Process". *Australian Historical Studies* 33, no. 118 (2002): 7–24.

Goss, Fred. *Memories of a Stag Harbourer: A Record of Twenty-Eight Years with the Devon and Somerset Stag Hounds 1894–1921*. London: Witherby, 1931.

Green, Charles. *The Third Hand: Artist Collaborations from Conceptualism to Postmodernism*. Minneapolis: University of Minnesota Press; Sydney: UNSW Press, 2001.

Haese, Richard. *Sydney Nolan: The City and the Plain*. Melbourne: National Gallery of Victoria, 1983.

———. *Rebels and Precursors: The Revolutionary Years of Australian Art*. Ringwood, Vic.: Allen Lane, 1981.

Hansen, David. "Vacant Possession". In Short, *A Single Mind*, 95–109.

Healy, Chris. *From the Ruins of Colonialism: History as Social Memory*. Cambridge and Melbourne: Cambridge University Press, 1997.

Heyward, Michael. *The Ern Malley Affair*. St Lucia, Qld: University of Queensland Press, 1993.

Hewett, H.P. *The Fairest Hunting: Hunting and Watching Exmoor Deer*. London: J.A. Allen, 1963.

Hillis Miller, J. "The Critic as Host". *Critical Inquiry* 3, no. 3 (Spring, 1977): 439–47.

Hirsch, Marianne. *Family Frames: Photography, Narrative, Postmemory*. Cambridge, Mass.: Harvard University Press, 1997.

Works Cited

Hitt, Christopher. "Toward an Ecological Sublime". *New Literary History* 30, no. 3 Ecocriticism (Summer, 1999): 603–23.

Huggan, Graham. "Nazis, the Holocaust, and Australia's History Wars". (2010). http://www.nla.gov.au/openpublish/index.php/australian-studies/article/viewFile/1751/2126.

Hyde, Lewis. *The Gift: Imagination and the Erotic Life of Property*. New York: Random House, 1983.

Jewish Museum Berlin. http://www.jmberlin.de/main/EN/homepage-EN.php.

Johnston, Anna and Alan Lawson. "Settler Post-Colonialism and Australian Literary Culture". In *Modern Australian Literary Criticism and Theory*, edited by David Carter and Wang Guanglin, 28–40. Qingdao, China: China Ocean University Press, 2010.

Jones, Gail. *Five Bells*. Sydney: Vintage, 2011.

Jones, Jonathan. "Modern Myths". *The Guardian*, 10 December 2005. http://www.theguardian.com/artanddesign/2005/dec/10/art.classics/print.

Judkins, Ryan R. "The Game of the Courtly Hunt: Chasing and Breaking Deer in Late Medieval English Literature". *Journal of English and Germanic Philology* 112, no. 1 (January 2013): 70–92.

Kavenna, Joanna. Review of Ian Buruma, *Year Zero: A History of 1945*. *The Australian*, 30 November – 1 December 2013, 20–21.

King, Stuart. Review of Claudine Piaton, Ezio Goldoli and David Peycere, eds, *Building Beyond the Mediterranean: Studying the Archives of European Businesses 1860–1970*. Arles: Honore Clair, 2012. *ABE Journal* 1 (2012): n.p. http://dev.abejournal.eu/index.php?id=551.

Kitzler, Petr. "*Passio Perpetuae* and *Acta Perpetuae*: Between Tradition and Innovation". *Listy filologicke* CXXX 1–2 (2007): 1–19. http://www.tertullian.org/articles/kitzler_perpetua.pdf.

Kofman, Sarah, "Conjuring Death: Remarks on *The Anatomy Lesson of Doctor Nicolas Tulp* (1632)". *Selected Writings*, edited by Thomas Albrecht, Georgia Albert and Elizabeth Rottenberg, translated by Pascale-Anne Brault, 237–41. Stanford: Stanford University Press, 2007.

Knight, Stephen. *Jack The Ripper: The Final Solution*. London: Collins, 1977.

LaCapra, Dominick. "Trauma, Absence, Loss". *Critical Inquiry* 25, no. 4 (Summer 1999): 696–727.

Lake, Marilyn. "The Politics of Respectability: Identifying the Masculinist Context". *Historical Studies* 22, no. 86 (1986): 116–31.

Latour, Bruno. *The Making of Law: An Ethnography of the Conseil d'État*. Translated by Marina Brilman and Alain Pottage. (2002) Cambridge: Polity, 2010.

———. *We Have Never Been Modern*. Translated by Catherine Porter. (1991) Cambridge, Mass.: Harvard University Press, 1993.

Lawson, Henry. *Short Stories and Sketches 1888–1922*, edited by Colin Roderick. Sydney: Angus & Robertson, 1972.

Levi, Neil. " 'No Sensible Comparison?' The Place of the Holocaust in Australia's History Wars". *History & Memory* 19, no. 1 (Spring/Summer 2007): 124–56.

Lilly, Marjorie. *Sickert: The Painter and His Circle*. London: Elek, 1971.

Lindsay, Robert. *Rick Amor: Standing in the Shadows*. Langwarrin, Vic.: McClelland Gallery, 2005.

Lovink, Geert. "The Art of Collaboration: Interview with Charles Green", 6 December 2001. http://geertlovink.org/interviews/interview-with-charles-green/.

Luckhurst, Roger. "Bruno Latour's Scientifiction: Networks, Assemblages, and Tangled Objects". *Science Fiction Studies* 33, no. 1 (March 2006): 4–17. http://www.depauw.edu/sfs/backissues/98/luckhurst98.html.

Lukács, Georg. *The Historical Novel*. Translated by Hannah and Stanley Mitchell. (1962) Harmondsworth: Penguin, 1981.

Lynch, Anthony. "Real Men Roll Their Own". Review of Alex Miller, *Coal Creek*. *Sydney Review of Books*, 14 March 2014. http://sydneyreviewofbooks.com/real-men-roll-their-own/.

Macintyre, Stuart and Anna Clarke. *The History Wars*. Carlton, Vic.: Melbourne University Press, 2003.

Magarey, Susan, Sue Rowley and Susan Sheridan, eds. *Debutante Nation: Feminism Contests the 1890s*. Sydney: Allen & Unwin, 1993.

Malouf, David. *A Spirit of Play: The Making of Australian Consciousness*. Sydney: ABC Books, 1998.

———. *Remembering Babylon*. Milson's Point, NSW: Chatto and Windus, 1993.

Works Cited

Mann, Bonnie. *Women's Liberation and the Sublime: Feminism, Postmodernism, Environment*. Oxford: Oxford University Press, 2006.
Marr, David. "Patrick White: The Final Chapter". *The Monthly* (April 2008): 28–42.
———. "Patrick White's Return from the Pit". *Sydney Morning Herald*, 3 November 2006. http://www.smh.com.au/news/books/patrick-whites-return-from-the-pit/2006/11/02/1162339990980.html.
———. *Patrick White: A Life*. Milson's Point, NSW: Random House, 1991.
———. "From: *Patrick White*". *Overland* 121 (Summer 1990): 6–7.
Masson, Sophie. "Where Are You from Really?" Review of Alex Miller, *The Ancestor Game*. *Australian Book Review*, 143 (August 1992): 4–5.
Maupassant, Guy de. *A Life*. Translated by Roger Pearson. New York: Oxford University Press, 1999.
McCann, Andrew. "How to Fuck a Tuscan Garden: A Note on Literary Pessimism". *Overland* 177 (2004): 22–24.
McCullers, Carson. *Reflections in a Golden Eye*. (1941) London: Cresset, 1942.
McMahon. Elizabeth. "Continental Heartlands and Alex Miller's Geosophical Imaginary". In Dixon, *The Novels of Alex Miller*, 125–38.
McPhee, Hilary. "Publishing White. Or Not?" *The Book Show*, 19 July 2006. http://www.abc.net.au/radionational/programs/bookshow/publishing-white-or-not-transcript-available/3322394.
Mead, Rebecca. *The Road to Middlemarch: My Life with George Eliot*. Melbourne: Text, 2014.
Melville, Herman. *Billy Budd, Sailor (An Inside Narrative)*, edited by Harrison Hayford and Merton M. Sealts Jr. Chicago and London: University of Chicago Press, 1962.
Miller, Alex. "The Story's Not Over Yet". Melbourne Writers' Festival, 23 August 2014. Unpublished speech.
———. Eulogy for Frank Budby, 14 April 2014, Holy Trinity, Mackay. Unpublished.
———. "You Could Have Been There (Unmasking the Fictional Voice)". The William Gifford Memorial Lecture, Vassar College, 5 November 2013. *Antipodes* 28, no.1 (June 2014): 215–26.
———. *Coal Creek*. Sydney: Allen & Unwin, 2013.
———. "Rick Amor: The Poetry of What Is Seen". In Amor, *Rick Amor Recent Paintings*, n.p.
———. "The Mask of Fiction: A Memoir". In Dixon, *The Novels of Alex Miller*, 29–41.
———. *Autumn Laing*. Sydney: Allen & Unwin, 2011.
———. "Once Upon a Life". *The Observer Magazine*, 26 September 2010, 12–13.
———. *Lovesong*. Sydney: Allen & Unwin, 2009.
———. "Waxing Wiser than Oneself". *The Australian*, 7 October 2009, 24–5.
———. "In the End It Was Teaching Writing". *Australian Literary Review* 3, no. 2 (2008): 17.
———. *Landscape of Farewell*. Sydney: Allen & Unwin, 2007.
———. "Writer's Choice: The Black Mirror". *Art & Australia* 43, no. 3 (2006): 446–7.
———. *Prochownik's Dream*. Sydney: Allen & Unwin, 2005.
———. "The Artist as Magician". *Meanjin* 62, no. 2 (2003): 41–7.
———. "Rick Amor's Show at Castlemaine Gallery, 1 June 2003". Unpublished speech.
———. "Sweet Water". *Bulletin*, 16 December 2003, 100–4.
———. "The Other Man". *new literatures review* 40 (2003): 6–16.
———. "Travels with My Green Man". *The Australian*, 31 May 2003, 4.
———. *Journey to the Stone Country*. Sydney: Allen & Unwin, 2002.
———. "Sanctuary". In Lyndell Brown/Charles Green and Patrick Pound, *Sanctuary – and Other Island Fables*. Herring Island, Vic.: Parks Victoria Gallery, 2002.
———. *Conditions of Faith*. Sydney: Allen & Unwin, 2000.
———. "Impressions of China". *Meridian* 15, no. 1 (1996): 85–9.
———. "My First Love". *The Age*, Sunday Extra, 18 March 1995, 3.
———. "Inside Buckingham Palace". *Brick: A Journal of Reviews* 48 (1994): 35–8.
———. "Playing the Ancestor Game: Alex Miller Interviewed by Simon Caterson". *Journal of Commonwealth Literature* 29, no. 5 (1994): 5–11.
———. "In Touch with the Displaced". *Sydney Morning Herald*, 20 November 1993, 13.

———. *The Tivington Nott.* (1989) Ringwood, Vic.: Penguin, 1993.
———. "Modern, European and Novel". *Overland* 128 (Spring 1992): 38–43.
———. *The Ancestor Game.* Ringwood, Vic.: Penguin, 1992.
———. "This Is How It's Going to Be Then". *Australian Book Review* 127 (December 1990 – January 1991): 30.
———. "From: *The Ancestor Game*". *Overland* 121 (Summer 1990): 8–11.
———. *Watching the Climbers on the Mountain.* Sydney: Pan, 1988.
———. "Comrade Pawel". *Meanjin Quarterly* 34, no. 1 (1975): 74–85.
Morrell, Timothy. "Lyndell Brown and Charles Green's Islands of Meaning". *Collector's Dossier* 61 (July–September 2012). http://www.artcollector.net.au/CollectorsDossierLyndellBrownandCharles-Greensislandsofmeaning.
Musurillo, Herbert, ed. *The Acts of The Christian Martyrs: Introduction, Texts and Translations.* Oxford: Clarendon Press, 1972.
Nolan, Sidney. *Nolan on Nolan: Sidney Nolan in His Own Words*, edited by Nancy Underhill. Camberwell, Vic.: Viking, 2007.
Olubas, Brigitta. "Like/Unlike: Portraiture, Similitude and the Craft of Words in *The Sitters*". In Dixon, *The Novels of Alex Miller*, 89–100.
———. *Shirley Hazzard: Literary Expatriate and Cosmopolitan Humanist.* Amherst, New York: Cambria, 2012.
Ouyang Yu. "Out of the Orient". *Modern Times*, September 1992, 30–31.
Ozer, Derya Nuket, ed. *Building Beyond the Mediterranean.* Turkish Museum of Architecture. http://www.archmuseum.org/Gallery/building-beyond-the-mediterranean_41.html.
Parker, Rozsika. *Mother Love/Mother Hate: The Power of Maternal Ambivalence.* New York: Basic Books, 1995.
———. *Torn in Two: The Experience of Maternal Ambivalence.* London: Virago, 1995.
Parks Victoria. *Herring Island*, brochure. http://parkweb.vic.gov.au/explore/parks/herring-island.
Pearce, Barry, ed. *Sidney Nolan: 1917–1992.* Sydney: AGNSW, 2007.
Pearson, Christopher. "Designs on History Derided". *The Australian*, 23 April 2001, 20.
Perera, Suvendrini. "What Is a Camp . . . ?" *borderlands e-journal* 1, no. 1 (2002). http://www.borderlandsejournal.adelaide.edu.au/vol1no1_2002/perera_camp.html.
Pierce, Peter. "The Tragedy of People in the Wrong Place". Review of Alex Miller, *Coal Creek*. *The Australian*, 21 September 2013. http://www.theaustralian.com.au/arts/review/the-tragedy-of-people-in-the-wrong-place/story-fn9n8gph-1226723001604.
———. "My Memory Has a Mind of Its Own: *Watching the Climbers on the Mountain* and *The Tivington Nott*". In Dixon, *The Novels of Alex Miller*, 55–65.
———. *The Country of Lost Children: An Australian Anxiety.* Cambridge: Cambridge University Press, 1999.
———. Review of Alex Miller, *The Ancestor Game*. *Bulletin*, 15 September 1992, 100–1.
Pizer, John. *The Idea of World Literature: History and Pedagogical Practice.* Baton Rouge: Louisiana State University Press, 2006.
Rancher, Shoni. "Suffering Tragedy: Hegel, Kierkegaard, and Butler on the Tragedy of Antigone". *Mosaic: Journal of the Interdisciplinary Study of Literature* 41, no. 3 (September 2008): 63–78.
Randall, Don. *David Malouf.* Manchester and New York: Manchester University Press, 2007.
Reynolds, Henry. *Forgotten War.* Sydney: NewSouth, 2013.
———. *An Indelible Stain? The Question of Genocide in Australia's History.* Ringwood, Vic.: Viking, 2001.
———. *Why Weren't We Told?: A Personal Search for the Truth About Our History.* Ringwood, Vic.: Viking, 1999.
———. *This Whispering in Our Hearts.* Sydney: Allen & Unwin, 1998.
———. *Aboriginal Sovereignty: Reflections on Race, State and Nation.* Sydney: Allen & Unwin, 1996.
———. *The Other Side of the Frontier.* Ringwood, Vic.: Penguin, 1981.

Works Cited

Rooney, Brigid. "Time's Abyss: Australian Literary Modernism and the Scene of Ferry Wreck". In *Scenes of Reading: Is Australian Literature a World Literature?* Edited by Robert Dixon and Brigid Rooney, 101–14. Melbourne: Australian Scholarly Publishing, 2013.
———. "Pathological Geomorphology and the Ecological Sublime: Andrew McGahan's *Wonders of a Godless World*". *Southerly* 72, no. 3 (2012): 55–77.
———. "The Ruin of Time and the Temporality of Belonging". In Dixon, *The Novels of Alex Miller*, 201–16.
Rosello, Mireille. *Postcolonial Hospitality: The Immigrant as Guest*. Stanford: Stanford University Press, 2001.
Ross, Kristin. *The Emergence of Social Space: Rimbaud and the Paris Commune*. Minneapolis: University of Minnesota Press, 1988.
Rothberg, Mark. *Traumatic Realism: The Demands of Holocaust Representation*. Minneapolis: University of Minnesota Press, 2000.
Rowley, Hazel. *Tête-à-tête: The Lives and Loves of Simone de Beauvoir and Jean-Paul Sartre*. New York: HarperCollins, 2005.
Rutledge, Margaret. "Barton, Sir Edmund". *Australian Dictionary of Biography*. http://adb.anu.edu.au/biography/barton-sir-edmund-toby-71.
Sanderson, Sara. "Artful Game Twice Played Reflects yet Another Mirror". Review of Alex Miller, *The Ancestor Game*. *Indianapolis News*, 30 July 1994.
Schlink, Bernhard. *Guilt about the Past*. St Lucia, Qld: University of Queensland Press, 2009.
Scott, John H. "Going South: Analysis of an Historic Project Engineering Failure". American Institute of Aeronautics and Astronautics, Space 2009 Conference and Exposition, 14–17 September 2009, Pasadena California. http://arc.aiaa.org/doi/abs/10.2514/6.2009-6454.
Sebald, W.G. *The Rings of Saturn*. (1995) London: Harvill, 1998.
Schaffer, Kay. *In the Wake of First Contact: The Eliza Fraser Stories*. Cambridge: Cambridge University Press, 1995.
Shapcott, Tom. "There Is Another World and It Is Here". Review of Alex Miller, *The Ancestor Game*. *Overland* 128 (Spring 1992): 79–81.
Sharkey, Michael, "Parable of Roads Taken". Review of Alex Miller, *Journey to the Stone Country*. *The Australian*, 28–29 September 2002, 10.
Sharp, Ronald A. "The Presence of Absence in *The Sitters*". In Dixon, *The Novels of Alex Miller*, 78–88.
———. "More Than Just Mates". *Australian Literary Review* 4, no. 6 (July 2009): 18–20.
———. *Friendship and Literature: Spirit and Form*. Durham: Duke University Press, 1986.
Short, Linda, ed. *A Single Mind: Rick Amor*. Bulleen, Vic.: Heide, 2008.
Sestigiani, Sabina. "A Danish Antigone: The Legacy of Ancient Greek Consciousness in the Fragmentation of Modern Tragedy". *Colloquy: Text Theory Critique* 11 (2006): 60–75.
Slotkin, Richard. *Regeneration Through Violence: The Mythology of the American Frontier, 1600–1860*. Middletown, Conn.: Wesleyan University Press, 1973.
State Government of Victoria, "Cerberus", Department of Transport, Planning and Local Infrastructure. http://www.dpcd.vic.gov.au/heritage/maritime/shipwrecks/shipwreck-stories/cerberus.
Steiner, George. *Antigones*. Oxford: Clarendon Press, 1984.
———. *Extraterritorial: Papers on Literature and the Language of Revolution*. New York: Macmillan, 1971.
Still, Judith. *Derrida and Hospitality: Theory and Practice*. Edinburgh: Edinburgh University Press, 2010.
Stubbings, Diane. "Passion's Hinterland". Review of Alex Miller, *Autumn Laing*. *Canberra Times*, 8 October 2011, 23.
Suleri, Sara. *The Rhetoric of English India*. Chicago: Chicago University Press, 1992.
Sullivan, Jane. "Interview with Alex Miller". *Sydney Morning Herald*, Spectrum, 5–6 October 2013, 28–9.
Sullivan, Michael. *A Short History of Chinese Art*. London: Faber, 1967.
Summers, Anne. *Damned Whores and God's Police: The Colonization of Women in Australia*. Ringwood, Vic.: Penguin, 1975.
Tickner, Lisa. "Walter Sickert: *The Camden Town Murder* and Tabloid Crime". In *The Camden Town Group in Context*, edited by Helena Bonett, Ysanne Holt, Jennifer Mundy, 2012.

http://www.tate.org.uk/art/research-publications/camden-town-group/lisa-tickner-walter-sickert-the-camden-town-murder-and-tabloid-crime-r1104355.

Tillich, Paul. *The Interpretation of History*. Translated by N.A Rasetzski and Elsa L. Talmey. New York and London: Scribners, 1936.

Tucker, Albert. *Faces I Have Met*. Melbourne: Hutchinson, 1986.

Walker, Brenda. "Alex Miller and Leo Tolstoy: Australian Storytelling in a European Tradition". In Dixon, *The Novels of Alex Miller*, 42–54.

Walker, Shirley. "The Frontier Wars: History and Fiction in *Journey to the Stone Country* and *Landscape of Farewell*". In Dixon, *The Novels of Alex Miller*, 156–69.

Walker, Trent. "Rick Amor: Artist Profile". *Australian Art Review*, 5 July 2012. http://artreview.com.au/contents/8518968-rick-amor.

Walkowitz, Rebecca L. and Douglas Mao. "The New Modernist Studies". *PMLA (Publications of the Modern Language Association of America)* 123, no. 3 (2008): 737–48.

Ward, Russel. *The Australian Legend*. Melbourne: Oxford University Press, 1958.

White, Patrick. *The Eye of the Storm*. London: Jonathan Cape, 1973.

Wilde, Oscar. *The Critic as Artist: With Some Remarks Upon the Importance of Doing Nothing*. In *Intentions*. London: Methuen, 1913.

Wilenski, R.H. *The Modern Movement in Art*. London: Faber, 1927.

Williamson, Geordie. Review of Alex Miller, *Coal Creek*. *The Monthly* (September 2013). http://www.themonthly.com.au/issue/2013/september/1377957600/geordie-williamson/alex-millers-coal-creek.

——. "Bright Treasures of Perception: Writing Art and Painting Words in *Autumn Laing*". In Dixon, *The Novels of Alex Miller*, 231–44.

——. "Autumn's Fading Words Are Pure and Living Art". Review of Alex Miller, *Autumn Laing*. *The Weekend Australian*, 1–2 October 2011, 20.

Windschuttle, Keith. "How Not to Run a Museum: People's History at the Postmodern Museum". *Quadrant* 45, no. 9 (September 2001): 11–19.

Windsor, Gerard. "Fruitful Mating of Cultures". Review of Alex Miller, *The Ancestor Game*. *The Weekend Australian*, 15–16 August 1992, 4.

Zavaglia, Liliana. "From Mabo to the Apology: The Double Movement of Apology and Apologia in the Novels of Reconciliation 2002–2007". PhD thesis, University of Sydney, 2012.

——. "Old Testament Prophets, New Testament Saviours: Reading Retribution and Forgiveness Towards Whiteness in *Journey to the Stone Country*". In Dixon, *The Novels of Alex Miller*, 170–86.

Index

2Pac 109

Aboriginal dispossession 98; *see also* Stolen Generations
Aboriginal genocide 102, 138, 141
Aboriginal history 97, 101, 112, 151
Aboriginal sovereignty 152
Abraham, Nicolas 144
actor–network theory 206
Adams, Brian 130, 170, 172, 189
Adams, Henry xvi, 82, 110, 155, 160
Adorno, Theodor 151
Age (Melbourne) 21
Al Khemir, Sabiha 155
Alberti, Leone Battista 34, 121
Amor, Rick xi, xii, 25–27, 53, 123, 127
   The Beach 27
   Celestial Lane (Three Trees) 26
   Celestial Lane 26–27
   "Contemporary Authors Series" 53
   The Gate 26, 123
   The Room (Memory) 60–61
   The Window 61
The Ancestor Game ix, xi, xii, xiii, xvii, 16, 19–21, 23–52, 95, 100, 122, 124, 140, 178, 189, 212
Angry Penguins 171
Anthropocene 105, 106
Aristotle 33
"The Artist as Magician" (by Miller) 119
artistic collaboration 118–120, 122–124, 126, 131, 134–135
Ashcroft, Bill 152
Attwood, Bain 101, 143
Auerbach, Eric 140
Australian Academy of Art 178

Australian settler narratives 100, 101, 103, 107, 109–110, 113, 115, 208
Autumn Laing xii, xii, xvi, 85, 169–194
Avery, Ralph Emmett 78

Bach, Johann Sebastian 147
Bacon, Francis 68, 134
Bakhtin, Mikhail 80, 105
Banville, John 156
Bao Chien-hsing 24
Barta, Tony 141, 145
Barthes, Roland xi, 58
Barton, Edmund 103, 198
Baume Marpent 76, 81, 85, 91
Bell, George 171
Benjamin, Walter xiv, 114
Bennett, Gordon 109
Berger, John 16
Bergner, Yosl 171
Bhabha, Homi K. 103
bildungsroman xvi, 79, 92
biography of Miller xii, xiv–xiv, 1, 2, 16, 17, 23, 75, 95, 117, 119, 155, 169, 172, 182, 198, 207, 211
Blake, William 176
Blanchot, Maurice 58, 62
Blatt, Max x, xi, 31, 123, 156
Blatt, Ruth 24
Bloom, Harold 42
Blunt, Anthony 156
bohemia 164, 173–174, 187, 191, 193
Boldrewood, Rolfe xvi, 195, 209
Bonnard, Pierre xvi, 57, 58, 70
Borges, Jorge Luis 29
Boyd, Arthur 171
Boyd, Mary 171

Index

Boyd, Yvonne 171
Brady, Veronica 54
Brault, Pascale-Anne xi, 31
Brennan, Bernadette 62
Bringing Them Home report 97, 138, 141
Britten, Benjamin 174, 200
Broinowski, Alison 24
Brooks, David 24, 146
Brown, Lyndell xi, 117–119
Brown, Peter 90
Buckridge, Patrick x
Budby, Frank xi, xii, 96, 116, 142, 194, 198
   eulogy for Frank Budby (by Miller) 207, 211
Buell, Lawrence 12
Burdett, Basil 170, 186
Burke, Edmund 10–11
Burke, Janine 120, 176, 187, 194
   Australian Women Artists 186
   The Heart Garden 25, 169–170, 172
Burns, Robert 176, 186
Buruma, Ian 96
Butt, John 147, 150

Caesar, Adrian 118, 134
Camden Town Murder 67–73, 127
Capet, Antoine 71
Carbines, Louise 51
Carter, Paul 25
cartographic imaginary 103–104, 198
Casanova, Pascale 188
Castro, Brian 24, 24
Catalano, Gary 60
Caterson, Simon xvii
Central Australia 173
Central Queensland novels (by Miller) 96, 97, 98–100, 102, 116, 137, 142, 153, 155, 162, 194, 196, 212
Cézanne, Paul 187
Chakrabarty, Dipesh 106
Chamberlain, Azaria 208
Chartres 155, 165
chiasmus 137, 149, 155, 212
China 23, 26–27, 42, 59
Christie murders, 1950s 68
Christo and Jeanne-Claude 118
chronos 80
chronotope 80, 105
Cicero 33, 34
Clarke, Anna 97
Clarke, Marcus 195, 210
Claudel, Paul 5
Clémenceau, Georges 78

Clendinnen, Inga 98, 138
climate change 106–107
Coal Creek xii, 195–210
Cohen, Stanley 207
colonialism xvi, 98, 106–109, 109, 119, 137, 145
"Comrade Pawel" (by Miller) xi, 156
Conditions of Faith xii, xiii, xvi, 75–93, 95, 100, 109, 155, 159, 166–167, 180, 189, 192–193
Contemporary Art Society 171
Corrigan, Peter 61
Cotterrell, Roger 206
Council for Aboriginal Reconciliation 97, 98, 99, 114
Couvreux & Hersent 76–77, 81
Cram, Ralph Adams 82–83
Crane, Susan 5
Cronon, William 11
Crutzen, Paul J. 106
Cullin-la-Ringo massacre 96
Curtius, Ernst Robert 140

Dali, Salvador xvi
   The Triangular Hour 121
   Christ of Saint John of the Cross 129, 131, 132
D'Alpuget, Blanche 25
Dante, Alighieri 174, 193–194
de Beauvoir, Simone 120
de Lesseps, Ferdinand 76
de Maupassant, Guy xvi, 174, 183–186
DeArmitt, Pleshette 63, 128
Deleuze, Gilles 179
Derrida, Jacques xi, 32, 59, 161, 204
   Adieu to Emmanuel Levinas 42, 66
   The Gift of Death 42
   khora 30–31, 147, 156
   Of Hospitality 42
   on friendship 42
   on hospitality 35, 37, 42
   on mourning 31, 39, 42
   The Politics of Friendship 59
   The Work of Mourning 63
Diana Nemorensis 160–163, 166
Dickens, Charles 183
Didi-Huberman, Georges 132
Dixon, Robert ix
Docker, John 148, 152
Doyle, Laura 11
Drewe, Robert 25

ecological sublime 11–16, 207
Edward, Duke of York xvi, 5–6, 8–9
Eggert, Paul 202

Index

Eiffel, Gustave 78
ekphrasis xii, 53, 54, 57–59, 74, 191
Eliot, George 79, 92–93, 199
Eliot, T.S. 191
Ellery, Reg 171
Elliot, Helen 26
Ern Malley hoax 171–173
eugenics 139, 145
Eurydice 164, 174, 191
Exmoor 1, 10, 11, 19, 21
extraterritoriality or exile of the artist 23, 42–46, 51, 85, 97

Faulkner, William 115
feminism 89, 155
Flaubert, Gustave 81
Forsyth, William H. 8
Fraser, Morag 170
Frazer, Sir James G. 164, 167
Freud, Lucian 68, 162
Freud, Sigmund 68, 119, 128
Friedman, Susan Stanford 48, 52
friendship 31, 33–37, 38, 152
Fritzsche, Peter 102
Furphy, Joseph 209

Gaita, Raimond 31, 141, 152
Garner, Helen 25
Gauguin, Paul 187
Geason, Susan 24
Geertz, Clifford 5
Genoni, Paul 99
Germany and German history 126, 139, 145, 153
Gibbon, Edward 102
Gibson, Ross 107
The Gifford Memorial Lecture (by Miller) xi
Gigliotti, Simone 141, 143
Gilbert and George 118, 119
Gobble, Maryanne M. 115
Goethals, Colonel George Washington 78, 84
Goldhagen, Daniel J. 139
Golding, Marina 193
Goss, Fred 3
great Australian silence 101, 109, 143
Green, Charles xi, 117, 118, 119
  The Third Hand 118, 120
Greer, Germaine 98
Grenville, Kate 98
Guattari, Félix 179

Haese, Richard 58, 171, 187
Hamburg 46, 48, 51, 76, 96, 137, 139, 144, 151, 153, 189
Hangzhou 24
Hansen, David 53
Haraway, Donna 204
Hardy, Thomas 93, 183
Harris, Max 171
Hatte, Liz xi, xii, 95, 97, 116
Hawke government 97
Hazzard, Shirley 93
Healy, Chris 109
Heide 25–26, 53, 57, 124, 169–171, 173–174, 193
Heidegger, Martin 62
Heidelberg school 171
Heiss, Anita xi, 96, 142
Herald (Melbourne) 170, 186
Herald Exhibition of French and British Contemporary Art 187, 189
Hester, Joy 57–59, 91, 171, 193
Hewett, H.P. 3
Hillis Miller, J. 42
history and fiction 98, 175
the History Wars 97
Hitt, Christopher 11
Hobart 95
Holocaust 96, 102, 107–108, 138–143, 141, 153–154, 154; *see also* World War II
Homer 140, 151, 153, 167
homosexuality 85, 167, 180, 201, 207
"Horizons" (forthcoming, by Miller) xviii
hospitality 33, 37, 45–47, 152, 158, 160
Howard government 97
Howe, James 5
Howitt, Mary 185, 192
Huang Yuanshen 24, 46, 50
Hueston, Penny 17
Huggan, Graham 142
Huggins, Jackie 97
hunt, ritual of the 1–16, 162–164
Huyssen, Andreas 143
Hyde, Lewis 140, 157, 160

impressionism xiii, 43, 171
"Impressions of China" (by Miller) 23–24
"In the End It Was Teaching Writing" (by Miller) xiii, 162
Industrial Revolution 106
intertextual hospitality 40–43, 143
intertextuality xi, xv, 42, 142, 173–174, 183, 190, 191–193

Jack the Ripper and the Ripper Murders 68–69
James Cook University 95
James, Henry 85, 92–93
Jewish Museum Berlin 138–139
Johnston, Anna 99
Jones, Gail 158
Jones, Jonathan 167
Jones, Rod 24
Jose, Nicholas 24
Journey to the Stone Country xii, xvii, 20–21, 33, 95–116, 138, 197, 208
Joyce, James 182
Judkins, Ryan R. 5

kairos 80, 92
Kant, Immanuel 10, 11
Kempis, Thomas à 105
Kierkegaard, Søren xvii, 51
Klee, Paul 132, 212
Koch, Christopher 25
Kofman, Sarah 63, 66, 121, 128, 129, 132
kunstlerroman xvi

LaCapra, Dominick 100, 140, 146, 148
Lafargue, Paul 179
Lake, Marilyn 202
Landscape of Farewell xi, xii, xviii, 20, 21, 102, 106, 108, 137–154, 157, 174, 194, 197
Lascaris, Manoly 175
Latour, Bruno 203–204, 206
Lawson, Alan 99
Lawson, Henry 202
Levi, Neil 139, 141–143
Levinas, Emmanuel 58–59, 66
Lewis, C.S. 29
Li Yao, 24
Libeskind, Daniel 138, 147
Lilly, Marjorie 68
Lindsay, Robert 122
literary awards received by Miller xviii, 23, 25
London 48, 51, 96
Lovesong xi, xiii, 155–167, 193
Lovink, Geert 120
Luckhurst, Roger 203
Lukács, Georg xvi, 16
Lurie, Caroline 17
Lynch, Anthony 201
Lyndell Brown/Charles Green 119; *see also* Brown, Lyndell, Green, Charles

Mabo decision 97, 101, 107
Mackay xvii, 33, 104, 107, 211

the Maghreb 77, 161, 180
Magritte, René 158
Malouf, David 97–98
Manet, Édouard 134
Marin, Louis 34, 39
Marina Abramovic and Ulay 118–119
Marr, David 175
masculinity 165–166, 201–203
"The Mask of Fiction" (by Miller) 0–97, 1, 54
Masson, Sophie 51
McAuley, James 171
McCann, Andrew 98
McCubbin, Frederick 197, 208
McCullers, Carson xvi, 17–18, 125, 127
McGuire, Annette 108
McInnes, William 170
McIntyre, Stuart 97
McLennan, Col xi, xii, 96, 116, 119, 142, 194, 198
McMahon, Elizabeth 33
McPhee, Hilary 17
Meanjin 117, 120
medievalism xvii, 160
Melbourne xiii, xvi, 17, 21, 24, 25, 28, 29, 33, 36, 48, 57, 75, 76, 79, 80, 96, 106, 122, 139, 156, 183
  art scene in xii, 26, 38, 44, 53, 169, 171, 187, 189, 193
Melville, Herman xvi, 195–196, 200
Menand, Louis 163
Menzies, Robert 178
metafiction xv, 191
Metherell, Gia 98
Millar (née Croft), Winifred xiii
Millar, Alexander 'Jock' McPhee xiii, 124
Miller, Stephanie 24
Milton, John 115
miscegenation 207
mise-en-abyme 29–40, 109, 113, 147, 156, 191
modern art 43, 57, 69, 170, 177, 187
  Australian modernism 178, 193–194
  British modernism 187
modernism and modernity xvi, 47–48, 75, 76, 79–80, 82, 83–84, 146–147
Moffitt, Ian 25
moral panic 207–210
Morris, William 82
Moses, A. Dirk 139, 141–142
motherhood 155, 156, 165
mourning 31, 38–39, 144, 204
Murdoch, Sir Keith 130, 170, 186
Murray-Smith, Stephen 25
Musurillo, Herbert 88
"My First Love" (by Miller) 21

Index

Naas, Michael xi, 31
Nabokov, Vladimir 175
National Gallery of Victoria 117, 171, 187
National Library of Australia 176
National Museum of Australia 138
National Portrait Gallery 57
nationalism 103, 106
native title 116; *see also* Mabo decision, Wik decision
Nebuchadnezzar II 176
Neil, Anne 53, 57
Niagara Galleries 123
Nolan, Sidney 16, 21, 57, 120, 124, 130, 170, 186, 189
   Head of Rimbaud 171
   Hommage à Rimbaud 179
   Ned Kelly series 172–173, 194
   Paradise Garden 176, 194
   relationship with Sunday Reed 169–170, 194
Northern Australia 173
Northern Gothic 16–22, 197
nostalgia 102, 113–116, 161

Offenbach, Jacques 174
O'Hoy, Allan xi, xii–xiii, 23, 29, 31, 35, 38, 53, 68
Olubas, Brigitta 54, 58, 125
Opium Wars 27, 45, 49
Orpheus 164, 174
"The Other Man" (by Miller) 117
Ouyang Yu 24, 25
Overland 25, 26, 53, 169
Ozment, Steven 139

Palmer, Maudie 117
Palmer, Vance 201
Papastergiadis, Nikos 211
Paris xiii, 23, 75, 77, 79, 81, 85, 87, 88, 189
Parks Victoria Gallery 117
Paterson, Elizabeth 170–171, 187
Paterson, John Ford 171
Pearson, Christopher 138
Percival, John 171
Perera, Suvendrini 98
Perth 95
Piaton, Claudine 76
Picasso, Pablo 187
Pierce, Peter 25, 208
Pizer, John 105
Plato 30
"Playing the Ancestor Game" (by Miller) 45, 52
portraiture 125, 134
post-structuralism 204

postcolonialism xviii, 89, 98, 99, 106, 152
postmemory 142–143, 145, 147
postmodernism 45, 98, 170, 204
Pound, Patrick xi, 117
Poussin, Nicolas 60
Prochownik's Dream xi, xii, 68, 114, 117–135, 170, 193
Proust, Marcel 31
provincialism 182, 188–189

Queensland 95, 96, 108, 119, 170, 174

Raggatt, Howard 138
Randall, Don 98, 99
Rares, Steven 116
rationalism 106
realism xv, 101, 108, 113, 148, 152, 165, 190–191
Reconciliation 97–101, 113, 141
   shared history 99, 110
Reed, Cynthia 173
Reed, John 25, 57, 170–171, 190
Reed, Sunday 25, 57, 58, 120, 171, 176, 189
   relationship with Sidney Nolan 169–170, 194
Reid, Barrett xi, xii, 25, 31, 57, 124, 169–170, 172, 194
Reinach, Baron Jacques 78
Rembrandt xvi, 63–64, 121, 129, 131
Reynolds, Henry 95, 101, 151–152
Rimbaud, Arthur xvi, 85, 174, 179, 189
   Rimbaudian subjectivity 179–183, 190
Rolls, Eric 24
roman-à-clef 169, 170
romanticism 160
Rooney, Brigid 80, 98–100, 105, 137, 145
Rosello, Mireille 46
Ross, Kristin 179
Rowley, Hazel 120
Rudd government 97, 154

Saint-Pierre, Gaston Casimir 162
Sanctuary (exhibition) 117, 119
Sartre, Jean-Paul 130
Schaffer, Kay 209
Schepisi, Fred 177
Sebald, W.G. x, xiv, 102, 139, 163
Severus, Septimius 88, 89
Shanghai 24, 46, 48, 49, 51, 76, 189
Sharkey, Michael 99
Sharp, Ronald A. x, 33, 54, 127, 140, 157
Shelley, Mary 183
Sickert, Walter xvi, 57, 59, 67–74, 127, 134
Sidi bou-Said 76–77, 85, 87, 93, 180, 189

Sinclair, John 171
The Sitters xii, 53–74, 95, 121–122, 127, 133, 170, 198
Sitwell, Osbert 68
Slotkin, Richard 209
Smiles, Samuel xvi, 83
Smith, Gray 57
Southern Gothic 18–19
Spengler, Oswald 102
Spiess, August xviii, 160
Stanner, W.E.H. 101, 143
Stead, Christina 79
Steiner, George xvii, 140
Still, Judith 42, 45
Stolen Generations 97, 101, 138, 145, 150, 154
Stubbings, Diane 169
Suleri, Sara 11
Sullivan, Michael 24
Summers, Anne 201, 202
"Sweet Water" (by Miller) 112
Sydney Society of Artists 178
Sydney 51, 91, 95, 122, 189

Tatz, Colin 141
Tertullian 87, 89–90
Thatcher, Margaret 157
The Tivington Nott xi, xvi, 1–22, 19, 148, 183, 210
"This Is How It's Going to Be Then" (by Miller) 27, 159
Tiananmen Square protests 24
Tickner, Lisa 68
Tillich, Paul 80
Titlestad, Michael 80
Tolstoy, Leo 162–164
Török, Mária 144
Townsville 95, 104, 106, 109
trauma 140, 142–144, 146–147
Tucker, Albert 171
Tunisia 76, 85–86, 88, 156, 161, 162
Turner, J.M.W. 167

University of Melbourne 4, 118
University of Sydney 116, 139

van Gogh, Vincent 187
Vassilieff, Danila 171
Verdi, Giuseppe 174, 191
Victorian Artists' Association 171
Victorian Artists' Society 178

Walker, Brenda 162
Walker, Shirley 103, 142
Ward, Russel 201
Watching the Climbers on the Mountain xii, xvi, 1–22, 25, 81, 95, 123, 195, 197
Weekly Times 170, 187
White, Patrick 25, 156, 169, 174–176, 177
Whiteley, Brett 68
Wik decision 101
Wilde, Oscar xv
Wilenski, R.H. 187
Williams, Meg 60
Williamson, Geordie 170, 172, 175
Wilson, Ronald 138
Windschuttle, Keith 97
Windsor, Gerard 26
Woolf, Virginia 79
World War II 62, 102; *see also* Holocaust
"Wraith Picket" hoax 177
Wright, Judith xvii, 52
"Writer's Choice: The Black Mirror" (by Miller) 54
writing style and process of Miller xv, 17, 53
Wyndham Lewis, Percy 187, 193

Yeats, W.B. xii, 191
Yeh Ching 24
Young, Edward 199

Zavaglia, Liliana 100
Zusak, Markus 142

www.ingramcontent.com/pod-product-compliance
Lightning Source LLC
Chambersburg PA
CBHW081825230426
43668CB00017B/2382